Journal

Journal

Passages in a Turbulent Life

Lois Henderson Bayliss

DRAWBRIDGE PRESS
2018

Library of Congress Control Number: 2018932869
ISBN 978-0-9974641-3-9

Contents

Introduction

Lois Henderson Bayliss (1903–1989) left behind thousands of manuscript pages of her writings—poems, novels, short stories, letters, and journal notebooks.

This journal—written in spurts from the time she was raising three children during the Great Depression to her early seventies living alone in Boston's South End—provide a look into her troubled, passionate, creative, and sometimes witty soul, as well as glimpses into the society around her from the early years of the twentieth century.

Lois was the middle child of Arthur Richard Henderson, born in Ireland, and his second wife, Isabel Jacobs, who grew up in Cambridge, Massachusetts, daughter of a lawyer and granddaughter of Bela Jacobs, minister of the First Baptist Church in Central Square, Cambridge. (Isabel was raised as a parishioner of St. Peter's, the Episcopal church a few blocks away, where she was married in 1898 and where her children received their religious upbringing.) Arthur Henderson was assistant postmaster of Boston, a Cambridge alderman, and owner of a real estate and insurance business. For many years, the family spent time at a summer house at Pigeon Cove on Cape Ann, which was, according to the journal, a happy place for Lois as a child.

At the age of fifteen or sixteen, Lois contracted encephalitis lethargica ("sleeping sickness"), a neurological epidemic that spread across the world beginning in 1916. Her family suspected that the effect of the disease on her brain was what caused her to create endless difficulties for herself, her family, friends, and any organization she became part of. She herself, in her journal pages, alludes to being called crazy from her teenage years.

Lois and Henry Balos married in 1925. Three children—Jonathan, Sandra, and Peter—quickly followed, and then separation and divorce.

Among the vivid descriptions in the journal are memories of Cambridge in the days that horses pulled fire-trucks and of childhood summers by the seashore at the northern tip of Cape Ann, attempts at suicide, struggles raising children alone and in poverty during the Great Depression, literary ambitions, love affairs, religious passions, time spent in the Paraguayan jungle in the 1950s with a Bruderhof religious community, and life in the slums of Boston in the 1960s.

A reminiscence by Laura, the youngest Henderson child, is included at the end of this volume and provides another view of Henderson family life and Lois's history—corroborating some of Lois's stories and casting doubt on others.

Lois died in Boston at the age of 86 after suffering dementia for about a decade and is buried in her family's plot at Mt. Auburn Cemetery, Cambridge.

Her life was rich in experiences: the variety of jobs held (publicist, cook, governess, rooming-house manager, ship stewardess, and pantry-maid are just a few), her hundreds of residences in North and South America, the types of men she became involved with. Not many women have had such a diverse life and written about it in so much (mostly contemporaneous) detail.

The sentiments that she expresses in any one part of her journal must not be taken as her final word. Her opinions about particular men and women, for example, vary often in these pages. And it is impossible to know how much to take as pure fact, since these are the memories and insights of a gifted story-teller who also suffered some sort of neurological disorder.

In the journal Lois Henderson Bayliss reiterates her fervent desire to see her writings in print; she is deeply disappointed when manuscripts are rejected by publishers. She also indicates a willingness for her diary to be read by others. Here it is.

Catherine Bayliss
March 2018

"I am able to see, although blows between the
eyes have numbed me plentifully, that all my
exigencies have been due to this groping, groping
for a way out of loneliness." —LHB (1933)

LHB at Cambridge High and Latin School, January 16, 1920.

Journal 1931–1953

April 29ᵗʰ 1931

Is a journal of any kind worth keeping? Why do people write diaries, anyway? Always *to the gallery!* And supposing one's husband is *really* a little sentimental as he says he is, the diary I might keep would never be really read. Henry wouldn't read it. He'd *believe* he didn't *want* to. Shove the old corpse into the crematorium and fly off to beloved Paris to join the women he's always dreamed of. He wouldn't waste any time shedding tears (in spite of himself) over a dead-and-gone fatty who had been physically a 'mess' (the words are his first real lover's) and mentally 'half-cocked.'

No, any jottings done for him would be unavailing in that case. And the funny part—tragic (my dear, I wish I were a *great character)* part is that any journal I ever write or start writing will be written for you.

I used to think my words were facile—that I *could* really express myself. But in loving you, Henry, I can't do it. Much verbosity means (darling, you're (ALMOST) always right!)—much verbosity means much self-conviction. The lady protesteth too much, etc.

I'll die without any fame. People will say 'poor thing' when they read of my demise. She did so many, energetic, unavailing things. And her husband was much to be pitied.

Poor dear. I guess he was. But if he only knew how his Loly loved him, in spite of everything including him and her, he'd have been a mite happy about it. He always said the admiration of fools was worth having.

Philip, now—he's an IDEA. Not a man at all. If he does honestly live and drag one foot after the other, and get emotional about "Russia's noble experiment," then it's in another existence. He never was really real to me. I made a most convincing picture of his precise little psyche all for myself. All in pastels, Heliotrope cerebrum. Green dreams. Lavender feelings—all pastels except the old libido. That had to be vermillion, like his actual passion. What went on in his mind during MY sublimity may have been almost anything. I was (as you've said) the stronger of us, and I got a perfectly grand feeling of self-supremacy out of it. I had a right to it. If he ever could in any way appreciate it, he'd feel *less,* not more conceited.

Now—with the vermillion erased, his pastel shades look like dust-covered wood that doesn't show its bright colors.

When—if—I am honest enough, Henry, I admit I hope it'll happen again—no vermillion is here with me, maybe he'll be a little tin god again.

Oh, God, thinking of the moon and the hillside makes me crazy! But I don't, didn't, and can't love him.

~

You, I love. When we are in embrace (Ha-ha!)—(it sounds so dignified)–'in embrace' when we are having each other, dear, I know YOU are the stronger. Don't deny it. You know I know it. I *give* myself to you … I *took* him. All the difference in the world.

Yes, it's K.M.'s journal that's actually encouraged me. Theodora almost managed to. I have a hunch Theo's going to get farther than I. No side-trades divert her, poor girl.

Did it strike you that K.M.'s journal was empty? Un-full. She knew she missed something essential. In two or three places, she confessed she wished she had a baby.

Her writing is lovely, more minutely thought than any of mine— perhaps. But do you really believe it was any *better? Really* better? I wonder.

Style doesn't exist now, does it? except in simplicity?

~

The Baptists don't treat me well. They don't know about Bela. As 'The Rag' I am beyond the redemption of Jesus C., who died to save all men! Poor RAG!

April 30ᵗʰ 1931

What are we going to do—we two and our three?—We are always poor.

It would be infinitely bad if I didn't have you. With you alive and loving me, I can grin (almost) about (almost) anything.

You were right—I forgot to take my books back to the library.

Lois with Jon and Sandy, June 1929, at 3959 Bliss St., Sunnyside, NY. "Peter was being prepared for." [LHB]

Lois, her Three, and dog Algy, Rowayton, Connecticut, summer 1930.

Sandy and Peter, Boston Public Garden, 1931.

Sandy and Jon, 1931. "We lived at Garden St., Beacon Hill, Boston, winter (Oct to May) 1931-'32." [LHB]

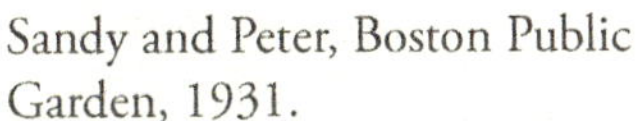

Your being right is such an institution I'd feel lost if you fell down. Please be right all the time. One thing you must admit (albeit silently) I'm a pretty cheerful loser. I take my being in the wrong rather well, don't I? But I don't mind telling you (in this way) that I hate it.

I hope we keep Elma. She's the proper handmaid. And self-respecting as well.

I've suffered awfully today. I often do, darling—and you'd never understand. I've suffered because I've been told at long length that I'm a 'funny child.' My mother used to say it in the same way, when suddenly in a burst of repentant generosity I'd kiss her and forgive her because (even as a tiny child) I saw she knew no better. And for all my generosity I'd be told in a dull tone I was a 'funny child.' How many hours I've cried for that. And it still hurts—in spite of my 'hardness'—

It appears that the "RAG" is wholly misunderstood—by the "400" women. It also appears that my women-friends here are not confidential with their husbands. They're lady-spiders, I guess. (You know what I mean: you always do.) Anyway that lack of understanding explains a lot—immorality, I mean. Why support one woman in preference to another? if you get *no SOUL'S COMFORT out of either!* Darling, do I give you soul's COMFORT:—I mean to. You do give it to me.

These little cats have such a swell time scrapping together. So do Jon and Sandy. And we 'adults' have courts of law and miss all the lovely best of battle—for civilization's sake. (Oh yea (?) I guess it's to keep our limbs intact, rather!) All civilization's selfishness—a protective mechanism for the human hide. Otherwise people wouldn't get away with being so thin-skinned.

Now I'm going to write some articles for the Rag.

Peter's a much lovelier child than the RAG. They all are. It's their salvation and mine that I can get 'het up' about the RAG. She's my brat. Begotten in the sin of vanity. Anything it gets me & our three used to mutual independence. Nay?

After a long, drugging sleep, my being hurt by the woman who called me a 'funny child' is all over. Probably my subconscious goes to the laundry while I snore.

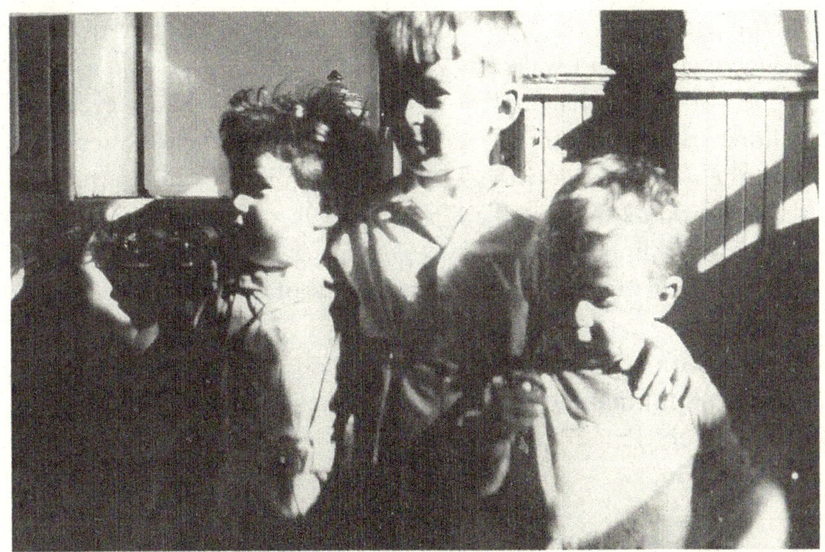

Sandy, Jon, and Peter, in the kitchen on Garden St., Beacon Hill, Boston, 1931 or 1932.

Jon, Sandy, Peter, and cats, summer 1932, Abington, Massachusetts. "We lived away from Henry." [LHB]

Too bad you don't dream, or can't believe you do. I'm always a new woman when I wake up.

Do you know that I'm more in love with you than—even the children? I know I could live with you without them better than with them without you. That, of course, provided I had never *had* them. Now all four of you are *sine qua non*.

I earnestly hope you & I aren't going to get financially lost again. This law-suit (Star Mk't) horrifies me. Your car will be attached. Beloved!

Most women are terribly unfortunate. I consider myself (since the Fine-Kauffmann episode's over) the most blessed of all. To hell with money.

I love you.

May 5th '31

The tumult and shouting temporarily suspended. The 'Rag in bed.' I have talked myself deaf & blind.

Much excitement broils within. Shall I go to Dogtown to meet Garry? Why should I? Much better, of course, for him to come here. But it piques my curiosity. I don't know WHAT I'll do. He wants sex, I think. And if I allow Spring, Dogtown, etc to influence, he'll probably get it. Wish-wash, my nature. Why on earth have I never been able to take an even stand?

I know why I weaken in thinking of it—I want *you*, H. To steady myself, I'll have you. G. can find another woman, darn him.

May 6th '31

Sent Laura a birthday-card, which expressed as much goodwill as my mailing Mrs H a RAG a few days ago.

Didn't keep 1 o'clock appointment. Didn't want to—honestly. (Garry Paul—of the gray drawers—prancing about of Father McK's business—spreading damnation against my rag.

They called me the RAG-woman (I suspect maybe even the RAG-bag (ugh!)) but a new name is now coined—the RAG doll. Oooh, Mamma, buy me that!

I love you, Henry, in spite of $165 (cold cash), owing.

May seventh

Honeykin, are we ever going to get up on our financial peak? Why are we always so hell-poor!

This "Hokker" failure of mine undermines me completely. Why can't I ever succeed? You said when I had written something really sincere—. I aimed at that in "Hokker." It is sincere, because it has 2 aims—(1) to sing my own (inside) beauty and (2) the perfections of Cape Ann. Again I reiterate that Philip and Jonny were not one. Philip's looks, and my SELF (if I'd been a boy) made up Jonny. And it was also truly sincere because not a whit of my own experiences of joy or dismay intruded. Please dear, if it ever is successful, don't resent Jonny.

I'd never be able to write about you. You're a *principal,* you know. *Do* you know it?

~

There are times when I KNOW that you are worth 0, Henry! When I SEE very clearly through the sham you work beneath. When I know that besides being profoundly a gyp financially, your whole life is a cheat. You aren't ANYONE. You are low.

It is just—(this belief I have that you understand me)—that you have learned my 'patter.' With cleverness you have contrived to convince me.

You cheat in every way.

You have intimacies with women, your strange periods of money-lessness are due to that. You hold me very cheaply.

You do not deserve to hold me.

I would die, easily, happily, gratefully—but *I* alone am able to make my children fine.

(I shall by tomorrow be ashamed of this.)

~

I *was* ashamed—a while, and then something happened that made me sure of it again.

May 10ᵗʰ

I'm logey.

Lydia Pinkham's visit.

I have what I suppose your much-despised female mystic-novelists would call a 'certain knowledge' that I'm not going to live much longer. The worst part of it is I don't seem to care. Laziness. I have no outlook. I know I'll have no more children.

And if I have an operation I know that horrible abdominal scar will disaffect you from me, and when I see it, far from being hurt, I'll just be cold.

I'm cold enough now, Heaven knows. I have no Desire. There's no picture or memory or hope or anything that piques my sexual feelings.

I hate living. I don't mind dying.

This, of course, is very unreasonable, especially in the face of my having so much nervous energy. I never wear out. I get tired with the RAG but still I write, write, in dreams all night. I know no book of mine will ever see the light of publication. I know the RAG is stuff and nonsense.

I don't really hate or feel resentful towards a living-being. I am nervous and horrid.

At times the only thing I love is Tinkie.

At other times I love only Sandra.

Sometimes it is Peter I love.

But all in all my feelings seem to be dulled. I am weary, & want only to live the life of a well-fed spayed female dog, who's not required to think, has no future, and no eternity.

I am dull as an old rusty knife.

Alas, I can't weep for this!

If an operation will make me a better wife and mother, I'll have it. Today, I don't care what I am—all I want is oblivion.

May 22

I love you … There's always that prevailing condition. I love you, and I hate to see you oppressed and harassed for want of money. — Darling!

Today, I did a very foolish thing. Mr. Brown, the Assistant Postmaster, is so sweet, so pathetically striving for beauty, and being

Rockport-bred, takes so hard the disillusionments about 2" x 4" characters in this town.

He asked me for an "opinion" of him. As I told you, I think he and I have a temporary, lurking, feeling for each other. Certainly, he is just such a man as I admire—or rather, feel warm about. He is clean-minded, -hearted, -physically—every way. He's young in spirit, too. And he's so pathetic! His eyes are the color of the water. And his face is sweet, with worried lines.—

No doubt, however, what I did was very foolish. —Will either deprive me of his friendship (because of a 'feeling of guilt') or will make him moon around. (The latter, I know, is what I am angling for … At times like this, I can't restrain myself. I want all sorts of kisses now. But in another week I shall be cold again. I am getting old: more and more I am old, for long times together.) It would be unjust for him to moon around. And depending on myself, it might be effective. I should—at this very moment—like his arms about me. —The last thing that would have entered my mind a week ago. A thing that will not, in another week, be a happy thought.

You understand, dear, what I mean. *You* know I am always *your* love, in spite of these exaggerated emotional (and, alas! physical) CURVES of mine. By the time you read this, you'll know, anyway. And perhaps you'll see how much I discount 'em, myself.

I wrote Brown an article:

"Editor Topples for Assistant Postmaster"
"Spring Weather Said to Have Caused Fall"

with a humorous court-trial, in journalistic style, of Editor, tried by jury of old maids, with conscience as judge. Editor ends up by appealing for trial in Highest Court—(God's) etc. I hope he'll see the fun in it, and not overrate the compliments.

He *is* a dear. But one never knows—! And in my "public life" it was a very ill-advised departure from impersonalities.

Fool that I am!

And, especially, with my love for you the biggest thing in life!

March 1933

I've gone beyond—at last—making statements, declarations. At 30, I simply have to sit back and watch everyone, including myself.

What am I going to do next? I'll certainly cherish myself more later if I eliminate forever those 'exquisitive,' 'natural,' 'beautiful,' passions completely. If it's not too impossible I will. Perhaps, if I have my troublesome gall-bladder dug out, I'll get over imagining the insistence of the body. The poor soul has so vastly learned the inevitable reaction that sets in after the libido has been appeased.

I shall have my cherished and as yet unstifle-able dream of publishing a book. I continue to pass my free hours with writing.

These three children are blessings. Looked at any way. The Big Bad Wolf's my chiefest enemy. But I have conquered panic. And found Leslie Glenn and a way to exercise my unkilled Faith in God.

September 1933

September—two years later—the week of Jonathan's seventh birthday. Under the bridge, plenty of tumultuous water has rolled, making me quite an old woman.

Thank God! —Yes, God, in whom I most sincerely believe—we have got together again—those of us who really matter—Jonathan, Sandra, Peter—and I, their thrice-blessed mother.

Henry is elsewhere, has been for some time. He will weave his tissue of lies about others; never again about us, who trusted him as long as even the most fatuous human belief could last.

About myself I am not exactly alarmed. I am lonely, but very busy. This past 13 months has been Hell on earth, with the children away, and a series of "tough breaks." I am able to see, although blows between the eyes have numbed me plentifully, that all my exigencies have been due to this groping, groping for a way out of loneliness.

Now for a bare twenty years, I shall gather my children in and warm my heart against their youth.

If other blessings accrue, then God be praised! —That's all; I certainly *expect* no blessings!

This year's mishaps seem to have proved the rule of "Right is Right"—and vice versa. That awful result of 517 was such a reminder of divine intervention as I will never forget!

I'd like to find love—the very real thing. But I'm not looking for it now: it must find me.

Spring 1934

Finding Love at thirty after 12 years of wasting expressions of tenderness on unworthy unreciprocators is all very well. Even though C.L.G. is utterly unattainable and always will be so, resignation to this knowledge doesn't deter the deepest love I've ever felt, because I've always known that since Tuck's time I'd never have the answer to those dreams I've always cherished.

Never mind, Lois, you know deep in your inmost heart how little you could ever deserve so tremendous a felicity. (Your daring to love Leslie Glenn is proof positive you're an overweening fool, full of bold rashness.) And though each of that blessed man's tiny pearls of encouragement to your benighted soul is a perfect gem of beauty to your starved spirit, you know, a fool! that to polish those pearls and gloat upon them is abject folly. Mountains made of molehills will never survive the traffic of reality, which drives straight over hill and valley, mercilessly.

May 12 '34

I wonder if I will ever grow up? These impossible fulfillments of my dearest hopes continue to make the dreams of my sleep my sweetest refuge, my most happy hours. And when I go so far as I went Friday morning at dawn, and actually believe I have been 'visited' by the spirit of that *beautiful man* during my sleep, I see either infancy or dotage in my psychic condition. Easy enough to say "You deserve at least *that* much consolation, you poor unloved child!"—But that's not 'adjusting,' is it? —Nor bravery, nor courage! And if this tremendous love I have for that *beautiful man* had grown gradually, and almost imperceptibly out of the gratitude my wounded, scarred, weatherbeaten soul is vibrating with, it would be certain and sure that I had just deliberately gone in for a hopeless love because of that 'defeatist' attitude I have.

However, I continue to solace myself with mumbling over the quotations my thankful memory records—words that feel from *that beautiful man's* own sweet lips, between his two rows of white teeth, over that delightful dimple near his chin. (When he's terribly earnest, the *dear man* stutters and 'snocks' as Jon used to do in early babyhood.)

[Oh, Lord, thanks for him, your own servant. And continue to give me a lady's grace to keep from letting my own inner disturbance embarrass him. —Georgie's really rather sweet, you know. And I always did like tactless people for their sincerity, so I have no kick coming. Jonathan says Georgie looks 'motherly,' which is true, but took a child's perspicacity to point it out in her girlishness.]

May 15

I see rather clearly that what old, scorching Christians used to call 'temptations of the Devil' are the simple animal desires we can conquer only by what powers we may have over our bodies. Whereas I was accustomed (even *after* hearing that *beautiful man!*) to give way to temptations in what I consider a philosophy of rationalism, I have waked up enough now to see those easy defeats as the causes for my profound unhappiness and perpetual feeling of inferiority. I was complacent about that sin—prolonging adolescence unbecomingly. I hope my awakened state will continue. I hope my hopelessness about financial matters won't weaken my better spirit. I hope when the 'Devil' tempts me in that form again, I may summon to me my memory of that beautiful man clearly. In his presence or in the presence merely of his memory, it is impossible to allow oneself defeat: he sets a dazzling standard.

God give me Faith enough to wait for his counterpart before I feel male flesh beneath my sensuous hands again.

Oh, beautiful man, you have saved me from unutterable depths of loneliness. Those Sunday treats are feasts for soul and eye. May our Father [who makes us all kin] bless you eternally.

May 17, 1934

(After several futile attempts to write it, I finally composed this letter and sent it, praying for its auspicious reception.)

> You dear, beautiful man: —
> —First of all, please don't put on that frown of disapproval because I begin my letter so. Don't deny me the pleasure of loving you for your dearness and beauty. It would be distinctly evil-minded of you to impute an ulterior motive to my taking

pleasure in loving you in gratitude and admiration. Ask Mrs. Magoun, if you don't believe me: my tremendous feeling about you is quite decent and pleasant. Nor will your kindly-meant ignoring of me for MY sake make the slightest difference. I saw you misunderstood the ditty on the Western Union blank. That was silly of you. Do you think I'm a youngster with a 'crush'? Don't be an ass (though you'd make a lovely ass, even!). I'm as old as your great-grandmother, and quite resigned to never having Love as I visualized it in my girlhood.

Your being a factor in my life these last ten months has been of such tremendous and vital importance to my shattered soul that it would be a lie, if I said with smug respectability that I DIDN'T love you! Mrs. Magoun knows all about it, and says it's good and healthy. Therefore, please, Leslie Glenn, don't give way to the sin of vanity and imagine me a moon-*cow.* I'm a millennium older than you in my heart. But watching your sweet spirit expand itself every Sunday has given me a grasp I had almost lost. So consider me a professional disciple. And of course you are beautiful, which makes everything you say even sweeter and more valuable.

If you will promise both myself and you not to be evil-minded, I can be so much happier! I have to have an outlet when I'm stirred. And you've stirred me tremendously. I want to be able to tell you how each time I see your face with its light, I am happier for long hours. Even your short letters are like cold showers after tennis. And if that's love, why I'm not ashamed of it. Just let my fountain gush—as long as it doesn't do so conspicuously—for my sake. Even *you* should find a surplus of love acceptable: you talk of it on Sundays. I refuse to be confounded with a bunch of disappointed spinsters, a covey of sentimental widows, or a flock of giggling adolescent females!

Without sacrilege I love you for God's sake, because you are so graciously generous with inspiration for me. Mrs. Magoun tells me the horrid news that *some* people don't get anything at all from hearing you, and merely sit there gawking politely till the doxology.

Not I! —There's never been a movie, play, concert, lecture, dance, ball-game, swimming-meet nor what have you that I look forward to as I do to service at 11, when you preach. (Preserve me from Bishop Babcock!)

If you continue to be evil-minded and smug and in your pious heart mouth prim phrases about ethical ecclesiastical attitudes towards over-emotional females—then *I'm* a fool, because you are and I was sure you weren't!

Thank you for your check. I apologize for needing it. One day, rich and beneficent, I shall put a window into Christ Church—just a beautiful plain blue window, through which the light may shine as it shines through your eyes. That will be only a token: nothing could pay a debt such as mine to you.

Why, you beautiful thing, I was abject, desolate, unutterably hopeless until I first heard you preach—and now I'm happy! And not because of any 5 & 10 ¢ emotionalism.

So much do I mean that I love you perfectly, that I have trained my children to think of you as a good, wise model—told them if, when I die, they feel forlorn, to look for you.

And please show this letter to your Georgie, or she might misinterpret it as one of those lonely-widow affairs. I'll tell her straight to her face how I love you, if it would interest her. And she couldn't be hurt. —Proud, rather, to have another occasion for rejoicing in her house-mate.

—And I shall be honored frightfully when you to come to 'dinner'—supper, we have to have—and I can look at both of you!

May 26, 1934

I still love you, dear, beautiful man! And more, because I understand now how foolishly, rashly wicked my attitude was when I sent the letter (previous page) in which I declared my love's purity! Sweet man, I paid you no compliment. I underrated your earnestness in modeling your life after Christ's. And I should be ashamed to play however unconsciously the part of temptress. Your sweetness is too profound for my blind eyes to see. Your last Sunday's sermon taught me so gently, but forcefully, why you are 'priggish'—Darling, saintly soul!

For everyone's sake who believes in me may "Hokker" have found its niche at last! (Lothrop, Lee & Shepard)—

May 27, 1934

It was a cruel punishment—but a deserved one—for me to have to miss yesterday's service—or, rather, the sermon I'd have heard if the Beautiful One were to have preached today. I lay in bed, sleeping after a sad night of neuralgia of the jaw. And the children, careful not to wake me, turned the nursery inside out and had half the neighborhood in the house when I woke. I had half-intended to go to church to see what crumbs some inferior man would scatter. But then it was too late. I wrote all day, passing page 320 in "Closed Chapters." Perhaps I shall call it "Look Not for Love."

June 2, 1934

At the Sunday School Picnic today—the first such picnic of my life—I was exquisitely happy. In the hot, wind-swept meadow we sat all together—grown-ups and some children—and we talked. It was lovely seeing how sweet Leslie Glenn is, in spite of my ill-expressed effusions; I can almost believe he *knew* what sincerity of honest love they meant.

Sandra won three ribbons, racing.

June 3, 1934

The children's commencement service came first today. Jonathan had an honors certificate. Leslie Glenn wins the children with his sincerity (I saw how tenderly he loves his little Tertia yesterday at the picnic) just as he charms grown-ups. I have called him "Poet of the Pulpit." He spoke today at the later service—in a sort of half-farewell way, which may mean that he is to be gone all the greater part of the summer—of the reply of Abraham to the sinful rich man who asked that one should rise from the dead to prove to those of weak faith that there was after-life. "If Moses and the prophets could not convince ye,"—said Abraham.

I thought of Henry, who had learned of Moses & the prophets, & couldn't accept God; and of Henry again when Leslie Glenn spoke of how much we talk—so glibly—of religion we have never *felt* or practiced; Henry had regaled him last spring with 2 hours of his "religious knowledge." The answer of the angel might have applied to me, if I hadn't *always* believed in God. But how sinfully I forget Him!

June 18, 1934

I have been silly about that Beautiful Man. *Dear* Mrs. Magoun says my effusions are "insulting junk that any decent man would resent." Oh, my dear inspirer, I apologize (as secretly as I love you) because I could never care to insult *you*.

So it is well that no Sunday School services are going on and I can't get to church to hear you say goodbye. The rest of my real devotion to your ideals will be my strength while you are in Europe.

~

I need another husband. I am lonely and desirous. But where can one ever be found for me—a sage-and-sinner is not in demand. Self-righteousness and success combine to make attractive men insufferable to me. Maybe—some day—soon—

June 19

I am in a dangerously acute state of need for love and companionship. Stranded here among my darlings I find so little to solace that part of me which is so anciently mature. And I must not, with that part of me, make my children too old for their years.

Oh, man—if you are alive—come to me now, while I need you so desperately. While I am still hot for love and beautiful enough to please you. What do you look like? —It is futile to search the faces I meet in Cambridge, where no free souls can live? —Never was there such a sterile atmosphere. It *hurts* me.

But I am determined to wait. No more of the experimental search. My love is too great to give away freely. It is as full of integrity as Chinese jade. When will you come? And where?

I miss Church vitally.

July 4

The beautiful man sailed for Europe—or left here—today to sail for Europe on the 9th. He came July 2 for farewell encouragement.

He said he couldn't sleep. He said he loved my effusive letters. And oh! to look at his dear face is to love exquisitely the strong clean soul behind it.

~

I *proposed* to J.R.W. today, and was (as expected) courteously— oh, very, very gallantly!—rejected. It was rather a relief. I cannot foresee very great good fortune. But since last August I have learned to love only one soul truly.

God care for him; and bring him back restored. I shall always love him exquisitely. What a privilege!

I've been singing in the choir. I thought J.R.W. was a sign from Heaven. He won't be a party to my mysticism.

July 5

I can't say that loving CLG is folly. It's joy made more beautiful by pain. And I thank God there is no covetousness in me ... Shall I have strength to live to love him without smirching the beauty of it? (The spirit is so willing. The flesh—well, definitely, it is less weak than it was as I grow happier in the thought of that Beautiful Man!)

July 7

Hark, how the Wolf howls!
Since CLG *can't* be had, is it wrong to love S.R.—or anyone else—physically—and save all the real beauty for that unfulfillable? I get so rotten-tempered and morose if I do not have physical expression. Hell's bells (as CLG would say), all science and logic goes to point out the advisability of an unsentimental feeling about sex *per se*. But it's this question I shall be all my life learning an answer to.—

Down with DIVORCE!

July 8

Church. Choir. 11 o'clock service—CLG *away!* There is no preacher with CLG's magnetism. It made me feel sorry for his successors in Christ Church pulpit. I love to hear his liquid syllables, so vibrant with his own beautiful faith. Today's service failed to give inspiration!

I wonder why my soul and body must be continuously at war.

~

Hark—the Wolf! Louder than ever before!

July 10

SJR at 9:30 tonight—?

July 20

These are days of self-conquest. I have battled it out with my neighbor "The Mayor." —By laying down my foolish paranoid notions I have discovered her to be rather nice. She teases, in a friendly way: the whole group of chair-sitters on the front lawn are tittering about S-R and his 'beautiful horse' "Nelly." There is something natively nice and sweet about S.R. … But I have no intention of making any great mistake. We move soon to a good-sized house.

Tom Coward has both "Hokker" and "Look Not for Love" (to read *himself,* at his holiday in Peace Dale)! I can think of no person in whose hands I would rather have my brain-children. Oh, God! May I have a happy answer from him. High status! Tom Coward is N.Y.'s best editor, one hears. Henry thought so: he's a good judge. Henry's checks continue. Once (by mistake, I think) he remitted $3 extra. He is so little in my thoughts now—causes me no pain. This is easier; but somehow I regret that love was less than I thought. However, Henry was the whole world more to me than anyone else. I can never regret him. He fathered the children 'Enid' *had to have!*

September 8, 1934

Jonathan was eight years old yesterday. He had a birthday. My current (and rather superior in the run) lover was there presenting the most valued present (knife). Because he was there, I was quite distrait. He tries to "wrastle" with the Devil the way I have done so futilely. I begin to believe God doesn't object to my sojourns in Elysium. I can now go to church without any feeling of inferiority, thanks to Mrs. Magoun, for whom thanks to C.L.G., whom I still do love with utter purity and delight. But there's absolutely no sense to holding out against sex, because it can't (with sanity) be managed. I love it. Now I am both free of regret and happy in my naturalness—but I'm a little afraid of this tormenting, fomenting feeling I have for D.G. … He's really terribly exhilarating. Rich, deep. More like Henry than anyone I ever met. Schizo-phrenic—says his brother was. Dangerous, too. Probably more *available* (since I worked successfully (up to a point) upon Henry, & know the technique).

Having busted down the barriers on these two pages, I foresee the rest of this book will read pretty much like the scarlet truth. Oh, but I love the bodily delights. Mrs. Magoun has cleaned up the old Psyche more than I knew. I want a husband: could I dwell in a slaughter-house? Or do I mistake E.P.'s overtures? I may be more of a fool than even *I* believe myself!

No work yet! It's a wonder we live. For this we can thank Henry for his checks, me for my prudence, & my mother & creditors.

September 10

D.E.G.

—And if, in this peculiarly *enormous* mood of agitation, I were to go on, doggedly to attain it (which I want so desperately) would the attainment be sufficient for all time?

I am, as Mrs. Magoun points out (without accusation, dear soul!), not monogamistic.

(Dan pointed out he was being substituted for Henry. After that, I recoiled wholly, and feel rather surprised at the whole episode.)

September 12

Mr. Glenn in Church *makes* Church God's dwelling-house. The man is beautiful and radiant, full of love and cleanliness. His soul animates that big, big organization he himself created by the magic power of faith. If ever I have loved with divine inspiration, I have learned it from the Light upon his face.

Oh, Henry, listen to Leslie Glenn, and be freed of ALL your agonies!

Sept 29 '34

I am growing up—by quick degrees. (I don't even need to worry about my crazy behavior—it's forgotten, owing to my insignificance!)(Henry is coming to supper. I feel certain that he is more eager to be with us than he can recognize. He thinks himself in love with someone (?). I hand him this letter tonight after the meal. Will it work? —God knows the answer. I can only pray!)

Dear Henry:

I am *such* a poor tactician that I must not try to speak the words in which I would surely garble and fail to convey the tremendous message my heart has been carrying for you for so long.

Tonight, my dear husband, cast adolescent 'loyalties' to one side: instead of imposing an artificial standard (that so surely will only increase complications in your life) look deeply into yourself. Your children have bound you to me, willy-nilly. Look past the thick veil of my follies and failings that obscure the essence of me. The enormity of your decision in this matter cannot be gauged. Little 'involvements' are nothing to this great bond between us. Needless to say you yourself are well-enveloped in a veil—a *caul* (so infantile!)—of folly and failing. There are three spirits whose lives have 25 years' longer span than ours. Can't we *both* lay aside our selfish aims to do "a better job on them than our parents did for us"? (I quote your injunction in a recent letter, urging me to do this job—a*lone!*) I can carry big loads. I have proved it. But I am *not* twins.

Symbolic of your real surrender to the CHILDREN, please, from the moment of receding, live here with us. As time goes on, concessions must be made cheerfully on both sides. But while you flounder between youthful selfishness and adult sacrifice, these three little lives are growing more and more away from you. It is alarming (to me) that when I said, individually, to Sandy & to Peter, "Who's to be our guest tonight," they *both* said, first, and with delighted hope, "Mr Glenn?"

It's not his own charm that radiates so from him, for he has so devoted himself that his life is almost impersonal. But the Grace on his shining face brings crowds of eager people—cynics, "Harvard agnostics" disappointed, hard-boiled people—to his church.

Symbolic of your laying down SELF, of abrogation, of better living, dear, come now upstairs. Let me put you into your clean little bed. If you love your Lillian of the streaky hair, I won't defile your lips with my impure mouth. But after sleep, there is family breakfast. (The morning struggle is lovely after the loneliness of a hall room.) And, cereal-stuffed, come with us to hear Leslie Glenn.

You know my two stipulations are: (1) I ask you to come every Sunday to the aesthetic treat of hearing the Poet of the Pulpit, (2) I ask you to hand me over $20 weekly & leave all the worry to me. You shall see no bill-collectors. I want to make *home* for *you* because you're ours. Only *you* can be!

Alas, Lillian wants you for that same thing. A man to a woman is merely a vehicle. (The less *auto*motive the better!) But poor Lillian will have to face all the disappointments I did, and have recovered from, before she finds her man. Because, however long and obstinately you may struggle against the Only Right way, your soul will not be at peace until you take this way with Lois, Jonathan, Sandra, Peter, who are Yours to live for *forever.*

~

Having copied it out (and taken note of its eloquence & sincerity) I wonder—*what* will it avail? Q.E.D.:—?

Answer: Henry prefers to maintain his policy of "living for himself." He must express himself—*run?*

Thus: *finit!*

After the answers he gave, I rushed for CLG, who, because he, too, was eager for happiness for us all, had drilled me for the event. He came at once. His attitude now is that Henry must be not forgiven but forgotten. I am too befuddled to know what *I* think, except that Henry in his stench of evil is really fascinating only as a force of negative flow. Quite the reverse of That Beautiful Man.

Oct. 5

"Hokker"'s gone to Tom Coward again—half of it, in much better style than formerly.

Oct 6

What is Mrs. Magoun's purpose in pointing again and again to my devotion to That Beautiful Man? —I don't know. I'm eager to discover. He wants to see "Look Not for Love." I can't bring myself to show it to him—unless Mrs. Magoun advises it.

~

Reading back over this, in point of time, there have been only Tuck, Henry, Phil—and—not in the same breath, C.L.G. … The other things & maybe all of these except for CLG have been physical fumbling only. What a mess I've made of 'love.' Leslie Glenn *is*—Thos. Jefferson Jones III.

Oct. 7

Leslie Glenn is the Creator's masterpiece!

Oct 8

—I wrote and asked her. Tomorrow she should have replied. Leslie Glenn sends me a lawyer. Divine wrath.

Oct 22

Much eventfulness: I had Henry here to supper, after he had taken the children to ride and asked them "How would you like a step-mother?" During the evening, he could not contain himself, but hinted (after getting his birth certificate from me) that he was going to N.Y. to meet "my girl" (just returning from Europe & a singing scholarship)—and get married. When I asked what made him suppose her to be willing to marry *him,* out of a worldful of men, he said I must not "Impugn the honor of the woman I love." It takes a considerable amount of objective sense of humor for a woman in *my* position to have her delinquent ex-husband run to her, like a child to Mama, to boast about his triumphs with "another fat blonde." When I look back over the spiritual and mental progress I have made since I stood shivering beside him through the marriage service on that dreary Dec. afternoon in 1925, I realized that Henry represents all that is the exact antithesis of what That Beautiful Man stands for. And I was so sorry for the poor ambitious little 22-yr-old singer that I tried, by writing the NYC license bureau & the Dean at the Conservatory, to have her made aware of the facts. I was no doubt confounded with all jealous women. (And of course I was a little put out. "Impugn the honor of the woman I love—" was so ironic, in the face of his history of 'loving' me!) I don't want Henry. There is no one I want—*really!* If I can do it financially, I will like best to stand alone. The only man whom I *wholly,* unreservedly admire and revere is C.L.G. Mrs. Magoun saw me briefly, and says it is well I have disposed of Henry. Alas, I shall not see her till Christmastime. She is ill, and must rest. C.L.G.—That beautiful man—bawled me out in this wise [after reading a paper on "An Intelligent Pauper Accused (by him) of Socialistic Attitudes" (in which I bewailed the ways of social agencies). He had misinterpreted my meaning, but the scolding is a *classic.* And I love him more for it. [N.B. Mrs. Magoun points out that I use such words as 'love' extravagantly. It was she who said I had never loved anyone (but the children) in my whole life—making me thoughtful, & not sure.]

Here is the divine wrath:—

"You have a swell lawyer. Don't bother him. Remember you have neglected this for a long time, & you can't expect the US Judicial Department to work nights at the last minute. I told the E.R.A. to take you, too. Remember the head lady belongs to this church. I expect free tickets to all the shows. The Lord help you if you let Henry slip out of your fingers this time, job or no job.

"About these social agencies, don't get off this guff! They are doing the best they can. There is absolutely no reason why you should be taken care-of by nickels and dimes collected by Fam. Welf. Soc'y or Christ Church Communion Alms ($2.35 a Sunday, average) when your Uncle & Mother are still eating in Duxbury. You ought to see the letter I wrote him today because he failed to answer my first letter! It is illogical for you to say you like Mrs. Magoun & me but not the Fam. Welf. Soc'y and Mrs. Paine. After all the F.W.S. is simply 1,500 Mrs. Magouns, each of whom gave $15 (all they could afford); and Mrs. Paine is an extension of my right arm. Maybe she's terrible, but she doesn't get paid much & if she did not do it, *nobody* would. You don't mind my telling you where to get off once in a while, do you, now that things are going well. And while we are on this subject, next Dec. you are going to make a subscription to Christ Church & next June you are going to give me the deuce for not coming to see you "a regular parishioner & member of the Church." And there are 2 doz such people I have not been near this year because of the time (gladly spent) on you & your barristers. Next year I'll be roaring around with more people in dutch—on *your* money. I just mention this because now that you are a member of the Frat you ought to see how the wheels go round. Not being loyal to this church this summer was bad, wasn't it? After all, is this a show here, or is it a band of people who try to help each other and who carry on, no matter what? Having got this off my chest I will now write a sermon on the fleecy cloudlets or autumn nostalgia."   "CLG."

—And may God bless *me*, Lois Bayliss, if I ever met a more righteous and delightful soul than This Beautiful Man! —I deserve practically all the foregoing. Points well taken.

I really ought not to go on feeling poetic thoughts about him, but he *is* poetic, & I can't help it. I love him. [I don't mind being extravagant!]

One thing: The "head lady" Lydia Walker is member of the parish, which means I must behave circumspectly all through this— Dan Goodhue notwithstanding. And it's to be a good test of Old Lois vs New Lois—of Henry's Lois: vs: Leslie's Lois.

Currently, Henry is to come to court Nov. 5 to speak up & tell Daddy Judge what makes him such a selfish boy. A good test for him. Can his dissembling art avail him then? —It won't, if CLG is there. [Lately I have tried to feel so good inside that I may be a light in the world, too.]

Again: O, God, I love your Leslie Glenn!

Oct 23

CLG called *twice* while I was away today. I retire *in stitches!* — Just suppose—! (P. S. —it was only *Ware!*)

Oct. 26

Discovered: that H has lied about *poverty* all along! Has had $35 weekly while I *sweated*. Dan Goodhue isn't at ERA Drama project.

I am to be mere "walk-on" (apparently) plus publicity. I love Leslie Glenn as always. *God's principle,* after all, is the only law of justice. Helen Moakley to have a 4th child! God bless her for her lovely soul.)

Oct 30

Saw CLG twice today. Once in his beautiful dark blue suit—with his crinkly lovely smile. Refreshed me tremendously. (Oh, I *love* him!) And again at the kids' Hallowe'en party, dressed as a lovely Sea Scout. He is dear, delightful. Certain things make me cherish crazy hopes that he— But that's too silly.

Nov. 1

Drama project opens today.

Nov 3

Darling Beautiful Man! He writes me a positively saintly letter—sending back his reply to my fool question "Are you a showman?" on the margin of my scrawl. "I am an engineer, who believes in God." And he kept (or destroyed) 3 pages of the letter in which I told him how, why, etc. I love him. So tactful. Not a word of protest against the love, or silly hinting, or scolding. Only just sweet, Brotherly reply.

I love him. *His* father was a carpenter!

Nov 5th

Well! What a day! It opened, as it were, in court, with Henry & McNulty vs. me, Lin Ware, Mrs. H., Uncle, CLG, and Myra Mitchell. Our side fell through, owing to my temporary job (FERA Drama). And we all, after a couple of hours, heard Judge Leggatt snap out that H. mustn't *ever* fall behind on his $8, which was good for H to hear. Although I put everything into my cause, the whole thing was lighted by that beautiful man's dear face. My mother fell for him, too. And when C.L.G. brought me home (he declared he didn't know what I *meant* by 'misbehavior,' quite as if he didn't object to the poetry of the love my grateful heart feels for him) we talked only about the case. (But *he* is so *adorable!*)

It was a very *sane,* normal day. My first such day since late childhood. I had lunch as new member of the Church's Junior Guild.

To hear those gay, sporty girls babble—and serious purpose is behind it, T. G.!—made me feel *alive* again. [Just more of dear Leslie's vicarious blessings. Praise him, God!] Georgie sang out, rudely, but with intelligence on her fellow-members' part; one can't help but *like* her!

And then home. A walk. Met Claire Howe, who gave me a dress and *grand* shoes. (Needed so sorely!) Then saw Nan Montgomery. (Heaven bless her, too!) She joins the Project tomorrow. I am to attend a dinner, maybe with Cush. Toppan. And a Ball (no less) mayhap with Dan Goodhue! And tonight the Geroulds & Nan for rarebit. Normalcy despite poverty!

Nov. 7

J.M. Curley, against my hopes, was elected to govern a Commonwealth whose foundations were laid upon stern integrity. O, bitter decline of New England! when such a thing could come to pass in Massachusetts.

I told Collacci (juvenile in the ERA play) that I had threatened to move if Curley won, but that I had no moving money. "I should think anyone would be willing to provide you with it!" he cried quickly, chalking one up in our friendly battle.

Nan Montgomery has joined the Project. It is good for her. Poor Tom is in N.H. mending shattered health. I'm having a great time doing news-publicity.

But there is no Light in the City: CLG went to Buffalo on Monday, & will not return for a week.

Love is a silly word to use in this connection. But it's the best available at present.

Nov 18

Dear Leslie-soul. I love you too much for any expression. The love accumulates, expands. It colors all the world. It came from God, as my life's greatest gift after the children. It offends nothing in me, not even the vanity of my pen which would like to express everything my soul feels. Dear Leslie! The shadow of Death will come to me before I can ever, as I so long to do, touch your sweet face with my all-loving hands—lay my fingers on the lids of your beautiful eyes, feel the hard roughness of your big head against my breast. I can't rebel against God for making you so perfect that it would be *unthinkable* for me even to touch you. You are human treasure. O, my love! I deserve this. My wantonness—so casual, so unthinking—is thus paid fully. For these eyes are far from blind, nor is my soul dulled. As I write I feel the fever of my soul burning on my cheeks, which may never know the infinite blessing of your cooling touch. O, love, love, Leslie! I have found love—and it came from Heaven to show me all the folly of the world's passions. Adored one!

Nov. 18

I sent this to CLG. I sent a letter full of love. Will he reply to it?

I love him *so exquisitely.* I want him to be always perfect. O, Lord bless him!

I seem to have scored a triumph over Lydia. Q.E.D.!

Still no news of "Hokker." I pray nightly.

Nov. 19

Seriously, is this love healthy? In its very fact I see no flaw. But still it consumes me while it heals. Dear soul!

Nov. 20 (AM)

This may be worse than mere foolishness, simple 'insulting junk.' It may be perverse. My motives, deeply, are perhaps that simply because of the "List" and all that it signifies, I am planning to topple over the whole new Kingdom of Heaven just to see if I can get a response from CLG. Oh, Lord! preserve me from such folly. Even the brief bliss of touching that dear face with my fingers would be unavailing—would be dust and ashes!—if I ever came to it. It would *overthrow him.* And so my dreams of it are all evil. "There is no health" in me. I am a perverse and wicked soul, adulterous-minded.

I go to church and pray. May I be given the beauty of *God!* I cannot defile the church with my maunderings. It is a sorry state when Evil in my heart, disguised as Good, should plot for such a cataclysmic catastrophe. H always said I was self-destructive; and surely if I ever perpetrated such a thing [how immense my evil would have to be to master his good] I would be destroyed; and all of Earth and Heaven, too.

Dynamite, my soul! Steer toward the stars, which have no flesh and blood!

PS. Yet, Angel Magoun advises me to go on with loving you.

~

Music—organ—Biggs—at Appleton. I simply said to my soul "These fugues and things are the soul of Leslie Glenn—Listen!" Oh, what a message!

To bed.

Nov. 22, 1934

I have been, at Angel Magoun's suggestion, reviewing the kind of things I have said about CLG. I must watch my step—*learn,* once & for all time, that one is *always* misunderstood—for if any breath of scandal should ever result from the praise I sing for that beautiful, untouchable soul, I could only live long enough thereafter to dig myself a shallow grave.

—And still not *one word* from "Hokker" in New York. I don't know *what to think.* Probably only that he is still ill—Tom Coward—or that the MS is lost or forgotten. But I have written twice, and there has been no answer! O, God Almighty! —You know the message!

Ditto! Ditto! Ditto!

(Perhaps God considers I need further discipline before I find success.)

Nov. 26

Heard Sherrill. Saw CLG. (Oh, God, thank you.)

Christianity is the only aristocracy.

"God so loved the world that he gave His only Begotten Son, Jesus Christ—"

I've thought of that endlessly this past year. And now, at last, I am a Christian.

As for CLG, he is unbelievable.

His prayer for purity of thought—was it made for me?

Nov. 27

A perfect housemaid at last! T. G.

Nov. 29 Thanksgiving Day

A Perfect Day.

First, an absolutely delectable sermon! Including a tip that "when temptation appears, one acknowledges it, and then laughs it off."

Billie Hill came for dinner, as last year; and promised us next year, too. We enjoyed him.

Dec 9

My progress fluctuates horribly. CLG is out of the city: as usual, I have felt the absence of Light. Heard John Grainger preach today. Not bad.

Dec. 15

Sandra has had her sixth birthday today. At ten tonight it will be exactly 6 years since I produced my little daughter, *quite alone!* — (Henry having gone to "New York for the week-end"). That was a profound shock. Queerly enough, to celebrate the anniversary, Henry is *here* tonight, *showing off* for the children at all speed—working hard, with cheap gifts, to cement a "friendship" with those whose birthright he has abrogated … He says (8:55 PM, Dec. 15, 1934) that my attitude in saying that Jonathan "likes to show off just as much as he does" is filthy.

Ho-hum! To him, I have always been filthy—or less. The love-letters he used to write he now pronounces the result of his "abject delusion."

O—have I been loved!

But last night, my little daughter and I—alone, together—heard the English Boy Choristers at Ch. Ch. Hearing the wonderful pure harmony of their innocent voices lifted me so far above sphere of the suffering that Henry—poor child!—still lives in.

Nan Montgomery is very ill with pneumonia at the Beth Israel.

And poor little Leslie Gerould at the Children's Hospital—she was due at Sandy's party—with peritonitis. Poor souls! —If my prayers are heard …!

I was ousted from the Theatre project as a "temperamental disturbance" … I will now begin to put up, shut up, say nought, see nought—So help me God. And I need no one's counsel except my own to teach me, or re-teach me.

"The Goose Hangs High" was a great success. I distinguished myself as press-agent. We had capacity audiences. I received no applause.

Lydia Walker is riding for a fall. I'll stand by and watch. I won't be sorry—the old battle axe!

My feelings for CLG are all sorted out and properly pigeon-holed now. How could I have been so strangely psychopathic?

God bless Angel Magoun!—

Dec. 17

Transferred from Drama Project for antagonizing … Oh, death! Oh, death where is thy sting!

Dec 19

Nan died!

Dec 25

A very lovely Christmas, even though Dec 24th I antagonized a large sector of Christ Church. Alas! And resisted the Devil himself in the early evening, thank God!

Dec. 30

Dinner at Stoughton Bell's—and I suggested a newspaper for Cambridge.

Dec 31—my wedding day!

And I wrote to tell the gov't not to admit Henry as a citizen! O, dear, dear, dear! It was all my fault. I had pictured Henry as something he was not. And that's what Les Glenn and I quarreled about. It was brutal of me to expect him to live up to a crazy ideal!

New Year's Day—1935

Yesterday, the last day of an otherwise up-and-up year, I was quarreling with Leslie Glenn! O, my soul! And the awful thoughts that tortured me while the whistles blew the year in will be vivid for the rest of my life. I called him up today, from Liggett's in the Square. And wept and was hysterical. Tomorrow, I'll have a chance to set him right, to show him *why* I was so awful. O, my dear man! —Of course, it's because you are always so busy!

January 2—1935

Both by Leslie Glenn & by God Himself I have been instructed to hold my tongue. Mrs. Magoun adds wise advice to behave like an adult. Something (God) tells me to go up high somewhere—the attic?—and stay quiet, waiting for further instruction. Something great is About to Happen to Me. God knows— —?

I continue hoping for "Hokker."

There is Stoughton Bell's introduction to Murray.

There is need for a typewriter.

There is need for paper. For coal. Money. Time. Quiet. Leisure. A friend (besides God & CLG and Angel).

Lord, make Jeanne B Magoun well. I have never loved a better woman better!

Jan. 11

I progress. I actually become conscious of a little sedateness, and a desire for more. The Lord has it in His wise hands now whether or not I shall be made a Cambridge editor—and whether *Hokker* will be published. I continue to love Leslie Glenn—and the love grows wide enough and peaceful enough to include Georgie. My besetting sin is conquered forever, I am confident. I tremble in indecision regarding the Oxford Group. All of it is good, if well-handled. But I see a real dignity in Leslie's and Georgie's attitude.

N.B. I must remember dear Sarah Lewis's injunction "Don't talk

yourself out of your job." I've heard that before. I don't want to behave so that I need to hear it again.

Jan 13

HOKKER made the home port again yesterday … I submit my
luck as a published author to the will of God—remembering that
He helps the self-helpful.

I was *bad* all day yesterday. Despairing and rotten. Mrs. Butler
came to the rescue. And her dear, gentle but intellectually fiery old
ex-minister husband, helped, too … He hits the nail astutely on the
head.

—Today—Leslie Glenn and a good sermon on the pillow and
the pillar.

Tomorrow: —Nawsty ERA clerking.

A snow storm outside. I love Mary Walters for her rough goodness.

Jan 30

Another housemaid. The roughness overcame the better instincts
of poor Mary Walters. The present incumbent, Mildred Roy, is
MEEK as well as vigorously hard-working. Oh, Lord, what do You
will for *this* situation?

Feb 3

Indeed, when I try to deny my love for you, Pie Face, I am utterly
dismayed; when I confuse it with other, unworthy, impulses, I am
deluded. I love you. I love you. What a dear man you are to be
near—to listen to—to live for, and by. God give you all His Grace.

~

How ironic it is that I, who I am assured have no friends (except
my innocent children) should write down any of my lovely
thoughts. What a wonder it would be to others who find me "offen-
sive," "antagonistic" etc. to know that in this world, where there has
been (except for God's wonderful fulfillment of the children) nothing, materially of wealth or security, I loved all that is beautiful, all

that is good. My sympathy and affection for the world's people (who declare frankly that they do not like me, and are uncomfortable in my company) have been unnecessarily indulged: what I touch "turns ashes—and anon, lighting a little hour or two—is gone," because I have not Leslie Glenn's lovely gift of winning.

Today I learned the secret of his winning. He is dedicated—*truly* dedicated—to the Father Son and Holy Ghost. My failure—all my heart-breaking failures—are due to my willful placing of myself before God's will. I have obstructed all my own success—spiritually, mentally, financially.

I feel ill. Every day more lifeless and weak. My temper is wholly unreliable; and in spasms of uncontrollable rage I have "taken out" on innocent little Peter furies of wrathful indignation I feel for his worthless father.

Henry must not—Law or no Law—have my children if God pleases to remove my nuisance from this earth. They are my children and God's. Henry himself never wanted them—asked, entreated, bullied me to destroy them unborn. In our married life he neglected and shirked his obligations to them. Now that he has turned into the strange perverted half-alive monster he is today, he must NEVER be allowed to mould their lives.

Death—if God wills it—would be a release, from a selfish point of view. Knowing now so indisputably that no matter what I may do or feel in relation to others, I displease my compatriots, I would be happier if they might forget me. A wildness and spasm comes over me—it shook me terribly in church today—a sort of "seizure" (though I can bring it on willfully, I can no longer shake it* off quickly)—that comes when I am most intense, or most dismal. It comes often now, and leaves me weak and dizzy, lasting longer.

All through my life, I have never met two more extreme embodiments than Henry's of utter egomaniacal madness and Leslie Glenn's perfect selfless Life!

Lord, what was I to do in this world? Oh, give me some answer! Guide me to understanding, if I am to stay …

* I do it in hatred, or anger, or impatience, or utter joy (as in church) or in self-disgust. I begin by tensing every muscle, holding my breath. My whole body quivers: it is a very ecstatic feeling, but

consumes immense energy. My brain as well as my physique is exhausted after it. What is it? I am morally certain it is not automatic ever: I do it willfully; and it acts like a mental and physical catharsis … [Henry would say, of course, that I did it in religious hysteria. The first time it ever happened I did it in a fit of hating him for his vileness.] I am terrified for fear a big attack—or an abandonment to this spasmodic ecstasy will leave me dead some day. I wonder—oh, the 100,000,000 times I have wondered it!—if I am mad? —Yet, I understand madness and if I am mad, I'll guard the children against knowing it and suffering for it!

~

I can safely say that as proved by complete denial since 5 months ago, I have conquered the word Folly.

Feb. 6

To two letters—one a none-too-gentle harangue, with *love* in it—and the second an apology for the harangue—a declaration of my love for him, and my resolution, inspired by his sermon, to lay aside certain faults of selfish vanity, my dear Beautiful Man wrote: "If you need a cook, let me know. Thanks for your letters" (Feb 4).

I expected no more. But I hoped and longed for more acknowledgment. I know, dear soul, that he is perfect as a man can be, and would compromise no one thru fair, insincere words.

Then—today—what a joy that he sent me this (mailed from Boston! —He thought of me on his busy rounds, as he thought of me enough to send a card from Switzerland last summer):—

> Thanks & thanks! I got a terrible qualm for fear you would think my typewritten snatches written when I'm trying to find jobs for forlorn cooks, were meant to be answers, or something.
>
> I can't answer. You are too nice sending encouraging letters about terrible sermons. I wish you *could* see what I always mean to say in the pulpit—that would be all right—but the reality is another thing.
>
> C.L.G.

Oh, the angel! The comfort of my life in its present days. Only

to know that such a soul as his lives and drinks the air we breathe—
we common, fallible brutes! —Oh, Lord, God, Jesus, thank you for
this lovely gift of hope and inspiration in my faulty life.

To see his dear, dear shoulders, and his modest, gentle beauty
every Sunday—that radiant, gentle, laughing face—that gentle fun
in his so-blue! eyes—and oh, his voice! —Just to hear his voice, even
though it is not addressed to me.

"You know very well," he said almost indignantly, about a month
ago, "that I put in lots of things (in his sermons) just for you!" Oh,
Lord, what a lovely, kind gift to give me.

I was so surprised, I was not even gracious. "We are never
alone—" he said last year—meaning that God and His Son are with
us always. But God, dear God, I have my lovely friend your golden
ministrant, too—always, forever.

Now that I have known him, and basked (unworthily) in his
beautiful light, I need never fear human* loneliness in life or death.

God grant me my dearest dream of Heaven—that there, with
perpetual peace, my poor soul may talk with his dear soul undisturbed by interruption, uncluttered by my noxious faults and vanities—during eternity ... Oh, Father in Heaven, for only 10
minutes of eternity.

Bless him, God. Oh, bless him!

My reply to him:

(No—It shouldn't be written. I am a hussy.)

* He is surely the epitome of human realization.

~

What are the results of love?

Should love result?

Should love like this be checked, stifled, crushed to earth?

It's *not* an earthly love. I love him imperishably with my eternal
soul. Damaged by my finite being as my infinite being is, there
seems nothing that can mar this glorious exultation ... Oh, Lord
of ours, he is no common man. I believe (credo) that he understands. That in the precise spirit of my giving, he accepts: I dare to
believe he returns my love in part. O, Lord, is this evil?

> Why, be this Juice the growth of God, who dare
> Blaspheme its twisted tendril as a snare
>   A blessing we should use it (and I do!)
> But if a Curse, why then who put it there?

If it is mere vernal seasonality that invades me now, still there is blessing in that. The rumba-rumba-heat of the animal & vegetable world, the rhythm of all life & love, are God-made, and God intended.

But with all this, I ask our God that I may have Strength in this love, by very reason of its strength.

Feb. 8

Martin Luther threw a classic inkwell at the Devil.

And I can't sleep.

Once he told me he couldn't sleep. That was last spring. (Mrs. Magoun says my imagination will make me believe almost anything. And I boldly proceed to gather up stray remarks of his to weave a story of solace to my love, which asks requite (although I've denied it), although it is enough and enough just to be able to see him and to hear his voice. He said "You know very well I put a lot of things into my sermons *just for you!*" (And I didn't *know* that. I dared not believe it. Oh, Beautiful Man, *thank you!)* Was it for me that he urged people to *recognize* temptation, and laugh at it? (Oh, what laughter!) Why did Mrs. Magoun repeatedly advise me to go on loving him? It was *one* sentence: "Go on with any sexual affair you like as long as it doesn't interfere with your knowledge that Leslie Glenn is the most beautiful man on earth"—that one sentence definitely stopped my interest in any man—any sort of interest at all—except … I can't put him in the same category with other male creatures.

I want to be godly. It is good. It is happiness. But I am weak enough to want to know that those letters of mine have disturbed him. That is not sacrificial love, because I want him tranquil. Oh, my dear, my Beautiful man, I am a selfish sinner.

And I can't sleep. It should be enough just to live from glimpse to glimpse, from sermon to sermon.

"Thou shalt not covet—"

"Thou shalt not commit—(even in thought—the merest, approaching thought)"—

"Lord have mercy upon us, and incline our hearts to keep this law."

I can't say "Do you love me?" I never did, in so many words. But he *knows*—for he is alive & sensitive & kind.

"I can't answer," he says.

He can't! Of course he can't. And Lord please remove the Devil. He is just as active and tormenting as he was for poor good Luther.

Rest, rest, my soul, until that longed-for Paradise when our two souls may commune in the Heavenly air.

Feb. 9, 1935

I'm awfully glad Katharine Sturgis came back again to see me today! I hope this will be a *real,* satisfying friendship—that will endure! Nan's dying was such a real deprivation for me, because I valued her.

C.L.G. preaches at St. "S{?}" tomorrow. But Mr. Shoemaker, who first sent CLG into the ministry, a la O.G.M. ... and K. Sturgis says C.L.G. is too O.G.M. ... *I don't care!* CLG is never anything but perfect in his preaching. [And oh how I love him—so wholly!] Anyway, I am awfully eager to hear Mr. Shoemaker. I feel as if Something Enormous were about to happen to me. Oh, Lord ... May it, please?

—I feel awfully detached, somehow, from my growing children. They are growing into personalities. It is so fine for them that I am not going to be dependent upon them. And what jewels they are! What adorables!

Feb. 10

I heard Shoemaker. I was convinced there can be no compromise. And my dear Beautiful Man IS—he can't be anything else—on the fence! Oh, Leslie. Beautiful and good you are, your whole *personal* life surrendered to Jesus Christ, your "prophet, priest & king." My dear, my beautiful, old love of all my dreams—you are *too* tolerant.

You cannot bear to wrench the Complacent from their Comfort. You could do it. If anyone could ever do it, dear, you could. And I know why you don't. I know the secret of your fear. My dear, my love. It makes my heart melt with love for your sweet, gentle indulgent soul. But here—here—! Lord, in order to do Thy will must I depart from him? May I never know the same trust in him again? —Must I be aware, always, that that great, lovely soul has its weak spot based on the least of the created factors in his being. Lord, I love him. And I love him. And I love him. But I see very clearly.

Morning dreams must stop. I, like all your people, must be about my father's business. And never, never, never will I cease to love Leslie Glenn. The temptations resulting from my discovery of his secret failing have been Enormous. Oh, Enormous!

Feb. 17

On Feb. 12 (Lincoln's Day) I confessed to Anita Ritter of the Oxford Group Movement that I wished to live the life advocated by Jesus Christ, based on the four principles of absolute honesty, absolute unselfishness, absolute purity & absolute love. I went that night to hear the "International Team" of O.G.M. people at the Hotel Continental, with Robert Hornsby. There I saw people with whom I had grown up at St. Peter's. Miss Ritter's guidance was that I resume long talks with Ann Harding. I find friendship—real informal, heart-to-heart friendship among the Group people. More than that, after severe—severe!—fight with my old self, I feel the singing sensation of conquest in my heart. What a triumph that in talking with Henry last night before he set off for 6 months in Florida, I touched his "stony" heart enough by talking—with the 4 "absolutes" in my heart—so that he cried. And now I set off to hear Leslie Glenn preach, to listen for the first time with the ears of proper understanding. God bless my children & our home.

Mar 9

A long period of thought & progress & loss. And always struggling to be better. (I *am* better, thank God) and always loving that

Beautiful Man. I *went to sleep* Wednesday p.m. instead of hearing him preach! (I can't understand that.)

Now I am thinking of so many strange things I have been unable to write.

A six of clubs is always unlucky for me. On Mar 6, Friday—(any connection with 6?) I applied for the H-M Fellowship award. Oh, the thing is with God. God told me (in Guidance) that there was much need of further patience.

I left ERA for a week. *Very* likely I'll go back on Monday. It was a mistake.

I am very lonely. But resigned—perhaps too much resigned.

The Wolf? Yes! And his whole horde of brethren!

March 16, 1935

Tomorrow it will be a year since I wrote "The Savant & the Cynic" & "Ch. Ch. Service." I have learned and lived a lot in 365 days. I am happy, confident, calm, & kind. I owe it all—*every* particle—to God's gift of Leslie Glenn. Tomorrow evening at church I present "The Lesser Lights"—"when my heart tunes its lute" & an annual pot of shamrock.

~

My leaving the ERA for "private industry" proved abortive. I rejoined the regiment thankfully. Uncle Sam is a good employer, though frugal with salaries. I am incalculably happy these days.

~

"Hokker" is at H.M.'s for the "Fellowship Award" I pray; and have asked the prayers of C.L.G., Angel M., Theodora, Katharine Sturgis, Tom Coward, Bill McFee.

~

Will renting the attic to Ted Hersey be wise? I know I can be *strong!* (Thanks, God; thanks, Leslie!)

~

Shall I actually go cycling with Stan R tonight?

A second spring—revification.

I need less & less to write this diary as I grow more and more happy & secure. O, what a joy is in life.

The chickens have measles. They are developing very needy. What ever is in store for me now that I have begun to live a life of happiness?

Blessed, blessed, blessed—C.L.G!

Hokker again rejected.

May 29

These weeks full of work & emptiness—and another household moving. I reached a very low pitch of emptiness. —What saved me from it? C. Leslie Glenn, of course. Always, always my dear resurrector! It was such a thing—his sermon on the REALITY of religious experience. I never heard him preach like that! He has promised, too, to read "Hokker"—offers a typing machine. The church school picnic again Saturday! Was ever a woman my age in such a condition of yearning for a S.S. Picnic? Never—but there was never a minister like him. We are to have a long talk soon.

My love for him one very lovely morning released tears I haven't been able to shed for so long—so long.

July 3 35

Jonathan is exultantly happy in his Camp life. He has learned much. I love my boy.

July 20

For months I had been praying for a perfect lover—someone to really waken my furies. And then Joe—July 3, 1935—began an assault—a positive assault—upon me. —Wicked? Yes.

I am to marry again!

Mother would surely disapprove of the 'low caste' of Jo. But what does that mean—'low caste'? He will be good and steady, and true and kind. Good to my babies. He has been lonely; I have been lonely. He is so full of *verve* and enthusiastic plans for our future.

God answers my prayer!

Joe is as beautiful as a prince. Small, dark, vivacious—a "typical Frenchman" (though he's Portuguese).

He'll go with me on my Rockport adventure. And we'll get on swimmingly.

He says he had designs on me *even before I even saw him! Somebody* loves me for *myself.*

Thank God.

I am writing that Beautiful Man now.

Sunday, July 28

My brilliant mind has had little or no thought to occupy it since Jojo was gone. But *plans, plans,* and hopes. And last night, frightful nightmares. Mrs. M (Jojo's mother) is a hellion combining all the awfulness of amalgamated provinces. She will roar through our lives, unless we either elude her, or are invincible. She haunted my dreams last night. Oh, Jojo, when you come home tonight don't fail to keep your promise. "I will not change my mind!" you declared again and again. You, whose temperament is so satisfyingly like mine. When your Ma looses her tongue upon me, will you be influenced? Oh, praise God, you will take me to be what I am, in God's sight. — The nightmares were awful.

Jojo, I will love & make you happy. God's grace! God's grace!

Aug 10

Down goes the ship of proposed matrimony. Jojo's Ma did her stint; and she began it long before I was aware.

A NEW LEAF, Lolo.

Henry is marrying in Europe.

I am jobless and penniless.

Jo-jo is lying and laughing and sneering.

Of all the humans whom I trust, *Mrs. Magoun* and *Leslie Glenn* and *Katharine Sturgis* and Rose Cutter and Laura and Mother and Dottie (these three mean much more to me now) and Margaret Sutton and Anna Duffy and Elizabeth Small and Ralph Scheibe and Mollie Zang and Helen West …

But most of all

Jonathan
Sandra
Peter.
Thank God for these children!

Aug 10, 1935

When romance enters the feminine heart, all reason, all ramparts are powerless.

May the Lord punish me severely if I ever lose my head again!

Oh, for the "passionlessness" of the 'frigid woman.' All this dreaming and suffering were due to the starved *libido*. Women, unless they can have lovers who can be trusted without agonizing tests, should all be married. *Penis in vagina* should be the rule. But even then—there is much to be said for unfulfillment. Restlessness is an impetus. And my spirit is too easily anesthetized by a nourished libido.

Jojo's sexuality was the *attraction irresistible!* Why fool myself? … His wonderful vitality of mind and body plus the strangely conventional chivalry of his marriage offer, were much too great a temptation.

May the Lord guide me to Reason!

8/10/35

Questions:—

Am I not truly independent now of all others?

Have I not really been thus far a good influence on my children?

Am I not now mistress of myself and my soul more than at any time?

Is my acceptance of poverty (pro tem) an indication of weak complaisance?

Can I actually, by continuing proper reading and self-instruction, learn, in time to write something significant?

Am I able now to carry on my bread-winning work both ably and profitably on all sides?

Have I conquered myself at all in the last 2 ½ years?

Am I *really* free of jealousy?

Am I really properly humble in the face of the Creator's Majesty?

The King of Love has extended His goodness to me unfailingly.

God grant me patience—more and more. Less haste. Capacity for more reflection prior to action.

And do, God, bless Jojo—who is absolutely irresistibly "cute." If he's in trouble, he needs Your help, because he's fuddled and weak. Make him happy. —If it were Thy will that he come back to me, I would do a good job. Sweet nasty little liar. Yes, I love him. But *I am too perceptive:* he sees it. He's very shrewd himself. (I hate to be called 'very intelligent'! *Hate* it!)

I wrote Katharine S. a *most ridiculous* letter. Ah, me!

I have written Leslie Glenn 2–3–4 letters, pouring out my disappointment in Jojo, and my love for him, and my need for companionship.

Would I had a mirror with a God-like capacity. Am I an utter fool or just human? It would be like Bill Buckley's story of the man who glimpsed himself in the glass and cried 'It's a lie!'

—Incidentally, Bill brought on Jojo's ardour; and now he refers me back to Bill.

Ignorance has moral flaws.

Weakness. Dishonesty. Do they compensate for charm and passion? —Doesn't every tragic romance of literature emphatically warn one against being carried away by just such villainy—such delightful naughtiness?

Sic transit gloria Jo-jo.

(And I'm lamenting!—and admitting it!)

Now I must concentrate on my "career" which, in the last analysis, is undoubtedly (1) Motherhood and (2) Ability to sustain us financially—quite exclusive of wifehood. The damned old libido—! And I love it as anyone loves the devil. It's wonderfully encouraging company.

Be still, my appetite … Yet, it seems sometimes as if 6 days & nights continuously with such a man as Jo-jo, under absolutely perfect conditions, would compensate for all that has happened and all that will come. That, I know, is pure illusion!

Jon was at Lincoln Hill Camp, July 2–30, a perfect holiday. Did him worlds of good.

Sandy at Rockport June 29–July 14.

Pete at Lexington July 7–14.

The Sisters of St. Anne are wonderful friends. Yes, there is more good than bad in this world. And there is no greater fool-in-the-foolish sector than I myself.

Am I *ever* going to snap out of it?

I'm a cheap chiseler myself! [*What* a confession!] (I'm astounded I admit it.)

Aug 26

—But—Jojo's *transit* wasn't so swift; and because he is the most perfect and satisfying lover I've ever known, I find myself in that state of mind that tells me no humiliation is insufferable, if he is to be obtained through it.

Why don't I admit to myself that I'm just a Catherine of Russia—only not great.

Rockport (which Jo-jo may possibly share) still hangs fire. WCOP also (for a fortnight, at least). The latest wrinkle is a fishing crisis aboard "The Ebb" (Capt. Shea) with Jon—September 17—what a freakish, unsteady person I am!

And—POOR?—Lawsy me!

Sept 3

And while Jo is still available, I'll have no peace of mind.

—*Does* perturbation keep one young?

Oh, Jojo—you *'black Portagee!'* (I love you.)

Sept 5

Leslie Glenn wrote me a very pertinent, impressive letter anent Joe Marshall. —Any word from Leslie Glenn has great weight with me: this brings me to sobriety. Midsummer madness is over (at least *pro tem*).

Jonathan's 9th birthday, also—with an anniversary celebration of the Florida hurricane—also sobers me.

News of Henry, "stranded" in England (his native land), leaves me almost unmoved.

It would appear that there is only one way out of the present financial trouble—i.e. to "retire" from "active life"—to live on a tiny mother's pension; and to continue to keep a strong watch on these three children.

It seems best. This turbulent summer has shown me how much they need my real 24-hr supervision.

As a compensation, I can (if the 'pension' goes through) really settle down to write unhurriedly and well.

I think Leslie Glenn would approve; Mrs. Magoun advised it long ago.

Things that have happened these past months have made me infinitely more tolerant of my family. All of them have been very good. Perhaps, as the years take hold on me, my crazy, 'paranoid' imagination will be calmed to near-peace. I am sure I lived in a terrific nightmare for years—gargoylizing my family out of all possible reason. To blame someone else is reasonably human:—Jimmie Brewster, Lincoln Houghton, Rodney Long, Henry, and, as prime motivator of all, Sigmund Freud, are responsible for egging this susceptible brain [huh! one would wonder: *is* it a brain?] to such extremes.

The experience with the sick man who would be read to from the other side of a thick curtain is the most flamboyant experience of late.

Always in the back of my mind is wonder (and hope) about Jojo. What'll happen?

I look forward more to Sunday, Sept 8, and Leslie Glenn's return more than to a desolate little 9th birthday for the dearest boy in the world.

Jonathan, no question, is the finest son a mother could have. And his beautiful brain, his dear, good soul—everything about him is *perfectly* satisfactory to me! [He and the other 2 darlings vigorously objected 10 days ago when I suggested that I am only a handicap to them: they preferred a "cuckoo" mother to any other guidance. Possibly the 'mother's pension' is a sublime and Heavenly solution.]

Truly the undercurrent of Good and God sweeps on beneath the hills and hollows of a life cluttered with materialism and noxious greed. That is why one so impoverished as I is sincere in thanking

God (at table) for "these and all thy gifts." Even organized public charity is God-moved.

Sept 6

On the eve of the 9th birthday of my oldest son, I have come to a conclusion that should have reached my consciousness long ago. —The reason I am a failure is because I have a 'disintegrated personality': and the reason for that is because I have experimented too much in my search for companionship.

A few nights ago, I told Joe: "You are my last man." Now, it will be wisest to stick to that. —Devote all of that part of me to Jo, taking whatever he gives, lessening my demands. If it cannot be marriage, then at least it is a working principle for integration. [Never think of the word 'integrate' without a clear picture of Marion Zerbe; and I distinctly recall she was undertaking some such experiment herself that winter—devoting herself to the restaurant, the dance and a 'Bill,' who certainly wasn't as charming as Jo-Jo.] So now I 'have a plan': the children; the book [somehow—try on, forever, if need be!]; church (& C.L.G.) and Jo-Jo. That's certainly an all-round, full life, from any point of view. September 6, then, is a day of resolution. Let's watch it work out.

Sept 7

9 years ago tonight—oh, what agony—my first—my greatest. My dear son Jonathan.

Sept 20

Peter cracked himself up (sprained wrist) Sept 16—involving hours of endless waiting for Jon & me with him. Also x-ray. No break or fracture.

Sept 18 I was 32, without festivity, but with much love for myself from my Three.

Sept 19 Sandy's tonsillectomy. (*Much anxiety*—I *cannot* lose my daughter!)

Sept 20: all quiet, but *very poor*. And in the time between Sept 16–20 I have *wholly* lost faith in Jessie Brooks and her protestations.

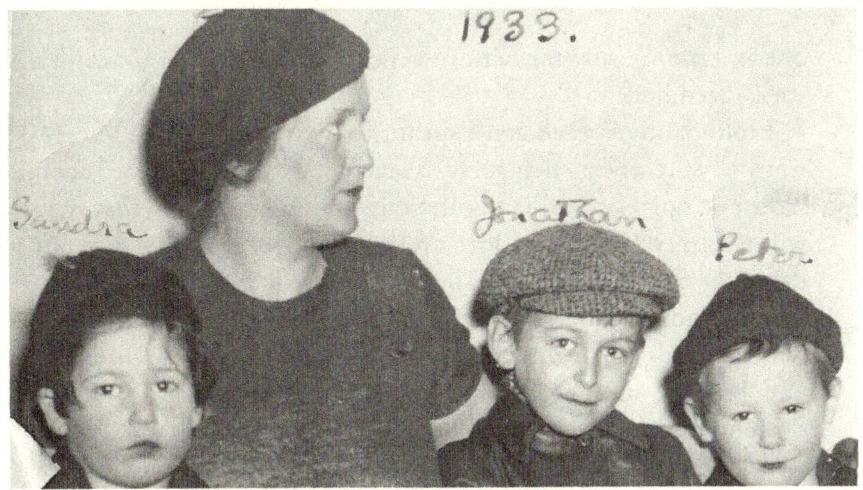

Sandra, Lois, Jonathan, Peter, 1933. "We lived at 31A Shaler Lane, Cambridge. Jon was in 3rd grade, Sandy & Pete in 1st grade (Lowell School). I was a journalist at the Boston Traveler." [LHB]

Peter, January 1936, "carrying this very album home from Craigie St." [LHB]

Jon and Sandy, Agassiz School pictures, 1935. The family was living at 57 Gorham St., Cambridge, "where we met J.A.M." [LHB]

She is *certainly after me* with merciless spite. (This is a blow—I always loved her!)

I told Sandy a week ago I meant to 'write her down.' My emotions have received such sorry shocks of late that my words come hard just now. But of Sandy there is nothing I can say that words will tell to convey how I love and pledge myself to this dear little daughter. My "fire head"—such a bundle of passionate feeling—quick to anger, quick to forgive, deeply loving. And her beauty—which could not be apparent to the insensitive eye—will deepen and become more exquisite with her maturity. God grant me strength and prudence and courage enough to keep her alive and well and happy—to fight for her, to shield her from the awful blows young women get when they are not *protected* (*I know*, oh, father of mine and spineless mother of mine, spite-cherishing parents). *My daughter shall not go alone!* And in the fight I'll wage to find her happiness, we shall be very close together. Oh, my Sandra! I cannot adequately 'write you down,' dear love!

November 18, 1935

Bless Leslie Glenn!

I have come pretty far with my new book. It makes me love him more—and it reawakens my longing—oh—gross? God forgive me!—for Andrew (Jo)! What on earth is the answer to this awful question.

"I must abjure the balm of life—I must?"

Or:

"Always watch and battle—always fast & prayer"?

(CLG keeps Omar in the church closet.)

CLG is perfect. Georgie *hates* me. No 2 ways about it. *Will* he answer my letters? Have I been pettifogging? (About Georgie?) I can't think so. Oh, Lord—here is the Prince of Light giving me so much glory; and still the Prince of Darkness is so lovely. How allegorical! I thought today maybe that peach in the Lexington orchard was the fruit of the Tree, after all—no joking. All we needed was a visible serpent.

March 25, 1936

—No poem for CLG *this* birthday (Mar 17) because I am 'growing up' (no 'insulting junk to the Rector' (see Angel Magoun)). But though I've been sulking for 3 weeks at home on Sundays, I went to hear him on "Is religion 'morality tinged with emotion'?" And he was *good*. (Poor soul is ill, though—rheumatism round his good heart, I think.) I hoped I could die in church while his voice was speaking. I have never been so much impressed with the human voice as with his. Dear soul! He says if he turns his back on me when he's shaking hands with the congregation he does it unconsciously —that Freud might explain that. What wit! But that was a bit unkind—for all the wit! Because, rather than compliment, it was *(truly)* dirty. Aren't men all awful? Poor souls, they do NOT and can NOT understand women. But thru all the oops and doons of my life since Oct 1933 (seems longer, but it's not) he has been the Kindly Light, and though he has hurt me, and often seemed to flicker, he is the light that faileth not on my present terrestrial sphere. He is an angel, dear soul! Tonight, in his sermon, he said "There's no *law* in the Comm. of Mass. that *enforces* people to be kind." Just to take it out on *someone*, I turned round and gave John Grainger a $10 dirty look. (Hope—but fear alas—that he knew why.) Harold Sedgwick is a lesser saint. John Grainger is more human. I don't like Mildred Hewitt, especially since she has so obviously fallen in love with *my* Ghostly Lover—she's so fuckingly *pious* about it—and no whit more ecstatic than I was withal.

We moved here (269 Upland Rd.) Feb 11—house is perfect for us. Lothario wants me out of his vicinity because the friendship verges on more intimacy than he feels able to sustain. But as I am thinking of going on the bandwagon for Sex in the Best Sense—if I can go thru a good lecture bureau to do it, I plan *not yet* to join the mad creative ones in the dunes of Provincetown, I think. I intend, however, to investigate those possibilities, in strong belief that Angel will advise my forsaking ambitions toward stump & soapbox till I attain further maturity.

—The affaire *(grand affaire d'amour de moi)* of Jojo the charming, is so *completely over* that I need not mention it. It's not immortalizable to anyone but me. *Magnum penis erat causa sine dubitas.* What a man! What an instrument of joy! This 'wife' (actual or mythical) may now have it *ad nauseum,* & in a way I hope she hasn't sense enough to appreciate it. I know he knew *I* did; and he said (ribald chronicle!) "I'd like to have a picture of *me* going into you! Funny idea, but I would like to!" He was sweet in his sensuousness. I shall never hope to find his peer. God love him, even if I may not longer.

"Sin Island" gets 'crusading-er and crusading-er'! It has a real *message,* besides vindicating me on the score of Chief Sullivan, Mrs. Foxy Conner, small-town ostracism; dirty politics, etc. It provides a very proper outlet for a lot of my ideas. Dick Gerould says "*too* crusading." Q.E.D. "Hokker" is in NY. Also Q.E.D.

My children are dearer and more wonderful each day. Sandra is developing so nicely. It'll be Pete's turn next. They are wonderful. Jon, my pride & joy, as I told Lothario, is my 'sine qua non.' And Sandy, my 'woman-thing' and Pete 'ma baby.' Pete has been scolded too much. He must be let alone. God give me strength for it.

Henry's plans for second marriage still progress. He returns from California in 2 mos. I feel little or nothing for him, I look back on the marriage as if it never really happened. I seem to be coming alive.

Why not go in for 'Cellini-style' autobiography? What's the use of being studied in this book. "35 Years Out" is to be the title of my autobiography when I do it. Meanwhile it's great to live in a Christian country where public institutions permit my (very bare) existence in some semblance of security with my dear three!

Jon is making a plan of a city called "The Metropolis of Mynch." Werry fanciful. I've been through a hell of menstrual upset & dental trouble. Pretty sure I'm having the menopause. I'll not—on the whole—be sorry, if only it takes away desire. Desire beats one up. I have so much of it. I suppose I should bless God for giving me enough knowledge of myself to make it so near a conscious surface. (Precluding involution psychosis, I hope.)

Poor Mrs. Brown upstairs has a speech-defective little son. God gave me 3 sound children. *Praise be!*

I look at religion so *broadly* nowadays—way back to its beginnings. I give God thanks for Christ, not caring if he were 'human or divine'; for his advent & gospels surely bound a decaying, dissolute world to better things—to unity & charity and Faith. Faith means everything! It is wholly true the Lord provides. I shall bless Leslie Glenn for his golden gift of Hope with my dying breath. I love that man.

I'm happier these days than e'en I was. God grant that my living be not too slipshod & selfish to deserve its benefits.

I am worried about Mrs. Cutter, who must be ill. I'll write Rose. She & Rose have been two of my firmest holds on life—They have real Christian charity.

Could go on writing all night tonight.

I hope Joe Joe loves me as much as he ever did.

And to bed—

Aunt Sarah Jacobs' & Tammie's diaries were different—but they embodied the same. Daddy always said they were 'in love' with Henry Anthony, and my mother never failed to be wholly incensed. To Mamma *Men* were abhorrent to the thought of 'nice' ladies. Wow!

March 8 1936

After Mrs. Magoun's recent suggestion that I extract the *lesson* from the outcome of my exorbitant passion for Joe—I have come to several conclusions.

1) That if any woman were ever equipped to talk about the sordidness of sex as practiced in the 20th Century, it is I. (That's an ironical conclusion: for, with Joe, love, by reason of its utter physical perfection, was nothing short of sublime. —But the end—his declaration of his intention to marry someone else, with all the elaborate ramifications of his explanation—that was the quintessence of sordidness. No question!)

2) That C.L.G. himself would topple under some not-too-strenuous pressure, because he bows to the artificial standard imposed upon him by Society (& Georgie). That, if C.L.G. (as perfect as a man can be) is thus impeachable, the whole structure is wrong.

Ergo Life is based on self-deception & mutual deception in a *man's world!*

It were weak & unprincipled, therefore, for me to go about 'getting a husband'—This is proof again of my robust adherence to deep ethical belief, & gives me joy—joy!—in my self-respect. —In 'getting a husband' (a la 20th Century) one must needs 'put it over'! Better the unendurable state of loneliness & longing!—better for the career of a hetaira!—than that stooping to degrading camouflage.

I pray—with what fervour! for a Walt Whitman to come my way. I know myself for the woman of his songs—fearless, understanding, natural, motherly, passionate, laughing. Oh God, I would burn these words into this book—into the dark sky of sorrow—unto the radiant Heaven of Thy perfect Radiance of Infinite Wisdom: if another male spirit such as Whitman lives today, send him to me. I am his mate, he is mine.

~

Back to practical matters: is it *possible* to arrange my Barstorming Tour? This Louis Taylor may be the man to do it. When I have discussed with Mrs. Magoun the matter of actually going ahead with it, I can know better.

~

My children—Lord! How much hast Thou given me in imperishable richness!

If ever any of my maundering journal is published, here are questions I want asked in bold back & white of the following people:

Jean Elwell:—Was marrying that a *square* thing to do for yourself? Why have you been so amiably weak all your life? (CLG offered you help you rejected.)

Virginia (Mrs. Foxy) Conner:—As you approach the inevitable grave, what hope do your little gods, Convention & the Awmy, offer you of immortality?

My mother:—Are you *still* deceiving yourself? Do you *know* what's true? Or CAN'T you see?

Laura:—How are those daughters going to grow up? Have you girt them strongly?

Dottie:—Aren't you ever going to come alive? The world is full of adventure—even for the poor.

Georgie Glenn: Will you *die* a stuffed shirt?

CLG: I love you! Meet me in Heaven later, please.

April 16—1936

Love is a topic tabu—love-affaires are shameful—love-letters are secret, awful documents—and one *denies* love-life & interests *because it's a man's world* & Love is the premise of females.

When *I* die, I ask no reticence about my love-affairs & documents amorous. I have broken my heart over unworthy men countless times, but, as it has been, all in all, good experience & lots of it lovely for memories in old age. I have no desire to have it *shushed* for my grandbabies.

I love love. I loved love. I want all my heirs & assigns to glory in it. And to do it happily & honestly & kindly & shamelessly.

As for Joe-Joe (Amen. Seven Amens) I loved him best (& worst) of all. I am never going to be sorry.

When I grow too old to dream, I'll have him to remember!

May 2 1936

Mrs. Magoun gave me such an earful today about 'playing the game according to the rules' etc. that I am all astray & distracted. I had been feeling confident. But I had a serious quarrel and a set-back late last night about "unconcern" (which I thought quite unkind—and it wasn't) that I'm upset anyway. It all started when I started further proceedings against H. for long-owed back money for the Three.

I ought to marry again. But he would have to be a wonderful man who could fill the bill.

I am awfully fed up on men who gladly come to see me & enjoy my dispensations, & then convey that under no consideration would they *marry* a woman so extra-maritally generous.

It is no matter of generosity. Sex is no barterable commodity; and I expect nothing *material* in return. But I do not countenance being looked upon by these creatures as *less* than their future wives, when, in reality, I am more. (I hope to God I am more.)

Mrs. Houston places all blame on Mamma.

May 12

Dreamed of meeting CLG as I came out of the darkness of a

barn. He was passing before I recognized him. When I called out, I came back to him & put my arms around him. I laid my head on his big bosom, & there was a moment of *deep peace!* I looked up & saw the ineffable blue of his eyes. Then he patted my fore-arm, loosening my clasp gently, & said "You're a nice old thing!" & it was a benediction!

A night before that I had an Oedipus dream, in which my Daddy came into bed with me. These two dreams seem very meaningful.

May 13

Joe came back—like a bolt from the blue, knocking all of my belief that I'd done with him into a cocked hat. Apparently there is an indestructible bond between us—we are chained to each other by it. I shall regard the future of the relationship differently from heretofore.

May 14

I'll have as much of Joe as is mutually convenient—but I will not get 'into a state' about him. I know him now for what he is. Dear to me as he is, my Three shall never live to say their mother went to pieces & led them to ruin over any man. But ever since I've known him, I've known Joe was THE man for whom there can be no substitute. When we go to the Farm in July I shall miss him—unless he cares to give me his Thursday nights each week. Oh, the delicious passion of that man!—the connoisseur's technique! And he says freely that I am his ideal (in that way—and he cares about nothing else in a woman. —After all, it *is* all the 2 sexes have in common, for except in the rare cases of true women scientists, there is no other *completely* understood meeting ground). I think I could rave on for chapters in this Book of my Thoughts about my dear Joe, my lover. I shall *never* make the mistake of trying to domesticate him now. I love my dear—but I am STRONG!

—Strong enough to have *smiled* & felt maternal when Henry went off to get married.

And, after that was over & smiled off—as if by a miracle, my dear Joe-Joe came back: "Nobody's got what you have! —I love you!" Says I: "I *knew* you loved me that way!" Says he: "And that's a LOT!" And it is, so why fuss & quibble? Nature is grand. It is Spring. (My 33rd spring.)

Maybe I can persuade Henry's Dora to stay a week with the chickabiddies, while Joe & I go off together, for a Paradise of Love-without-Interruptions.

He is my Love-Lord. My JoeJoe is my Love Lord.

—I *knew* I was his Love-*Lady!* I just *knew* it. Oh God, thanks, thanks— Bless us all, *I* can't see Sin in Beauty!

May 22

Joe didn't keep his promise to come that Sat. I *care*—so deep down that it's in every minute of my dreams. A marvellous lover—a quite impossible & unscrupulous liar, whom I *love!* (But it's not going to 'get me.' *No* sir!)

I am sending off the book about Andrew. Perhaps he has contributed something to my life—of course he has—that perfection of his, at least.

June 6

Joe *didn't* return after May 13—He probably feels that, since "Florence" has undertaken to maintain him because of his charm he must work (to be faithful) for his keep.

Henry, too, has married "well." Both "Florence" & "Dora" will find, in time to come, how purchased Love reacts—Dust in the mouth—ashes in the heart. I feel less ill-disposed to Dora, who got a worse bargain, though her purchase is better veneered. Truthfully, sometimes it *kills* me to think of a Florence who has no standards of comparison—no passion, I fear, either—taking the flaming instrument of Joe's magnificent passion into an unyielding frigid body—

Oh, Joe-Joe! *How* could you! My very dearest—!

There is no dearth of men! (Ever.) I am having a passionless & pensive alliance with Al—who fetches & carries dutifully—is well equipped sexually—& has no fire, & awakens none.

Oh, my Joseph Andrew! my very dearest! (We said "Hi!" to each other today. There is nothing between us but Love. And oh—the Love there is, & has been, & should be! —That blessed, *quite* un-purchasable love! God! God! God! I want Joe.)

June 11th

Dearest, dearest Dark Prince!
—And it's true—the baby is a fact! That means he lied *worse* by telling half-truths to me all thru these months I've tortured myself. Oh, God—do I deserve to have loved only those I can never have? Shall I give thanx for him—or bewail him? Oh, God, I love him—no one so much. No one.

Bill McF won't displace him! (No one will ever.)

June 14

Today's events—a *perfect* sermon on The Holy Ghost by CLG, and a talk with Joe-Joe—seem to show me again with even greater clarity that my Beautiful Man and my little Black Prince represent, severally, beyond a doubt the exact opposites of the two forces of human nature—the spirit and the flesh.

And, examining my heart tonight I find I have been trying to accomplish the confounding of CLG's spirit by a phantasy relating to the flesh—at the same time when I have been urging Joe Joe to come out of his benightedness & see the Holy Ghost.

—Who do I imagine myself to *be,* anyway? A god of Limbo?—or what?

I wonder what my position is, really? Am I better than my flesh or weaker than my spirit?

If I proceed with "Murder Mrs. Grundy" shall the venture be blessed with success & good fruitfulness, or doomed to an unregenerate failure because, in my vaunting for Personal Aggrandizement—Power—Notoriety, et al (as in the case of the RAG) I forget the real purpose behind it?

I pray that God give me an answer: is it good?—a proper thing to do? Would Christ have sanctioned it?

~

How am I to talk with CLG this week. So much I want to say

has been made impossible by my realization of my own stupendous folly.

My children are the only things I have ever accomplished.

God give me grace!

God bless my children.

God purge my body of its avid hunger!—or, though I do not deserve it—send a man I can love who can love me—can marry me & give me the right to appease this inordinate lust—or appetite.

(I seem to grow more & more sex-hungry. Is it explainable that I am at the fullness of my body's development and at a critical time lacking a man to appease me?)

God forgive me if I do not put Joe-Joe out of my thoughts & my life forever. After today, how can I be so wanting in pride?

But bless him & open his eyes—open them. And bless my Beautiful CLG.

Note: A *most* convincing Christian argument—I have never felt so firm in my faith!—is in the old book "Life of Christ" by Fleetwood. It is a book I've long wanted to find, because besides its theological exposition, it contains historical data. I wish it were mine so that I might read from it often—and to the children.

Note: I thought today in church how much I have gained through CLG—& how little right I had to criticize or attack him, in the face of all his invaluable gifts to me? His loveliness is much stronger & more enduring than the saturnine charm of Joe-Joe. These two present such a strong contrast. I love CLG—*beautifully.*

And yet I would lie if I denied that since I first saw him the greatest & most hopeless & most vaunting dream has been that he—the Ineffable!—might be *mine body & soul!* How little I would deserve it!

6/14/36

Dear Jonathan—"The nicest man I ever knew"—"Gift of God"—my "Unbelievable Cuss," my "Constiblety," my "Darleen," my blue flame of the holy spirit—may your Heavenly Father watch over you, dear little boy!—& so guard you against evil that from my poor frail heart He extract the evil while you, dear love, are in my care. Dear son, How many errors I must have made in rearing you!—and yet I have been truly dedicated to motherhood. You have been a miracle, & you, too, were conceived by the Holy Ghost, inasmuch as God could trust you to my care in answer to my prayers.

When I'm dead, dear, read this again—& again.

June 15

Sandy is 7 ½ today. Time *I* grew up! "Take life as it comes"—Joe says. So I will. I am "going places" with Al Wright tonight. Bill McF writes he's coming to visit us. Bill B pretends to be enamoured. None of it means a thing. How fatal it was to have let myself go as I did with J.A.M. (The perfect one!)

Okay, darling! I know you don't mean to be cruel, for, for all your rascality, you're tender-hearted. It's done, but I'll not be forgetting you.

~

I seriously mean to Exterminate Mrs. Grundy, beginning this summer. Hell, I've got to have a livelihood for you three children, haven't I? Well—it's Provincetown in August, then. No trip to the Banks that 2 weeks.

Note:—

Last night I dreamed of riding a rhinoceros through a pasture. He lifted me up in the air—for a few moments' ecstasy—and then set me down in a pool of barnyard filth. I *had* been petting him (as one does an animal) and, left in the mud, I *hated* him.

I suppose he represents JoeJoe. (I had called him a 'beast of the field' yesterday.)

Men can't *stand* not being believed in—even though JoeJoe *sneers* at me because I believed him. "You who are *supposed* to be an intelligent woman—"

—I've heard that so god damned often I could fall upon the next utterer of it—"*Supposed* to be—"etc. Supposed by whom? *I* always knew I was a God Damned Fucking Fool, & no trimmings added.—

—But I do love my children. They are surely a sanction for my life. —

Tues. June 16

I was drunk. I had bought a ½ pint deliberately to get drunk because in my mind it was profaning the Holy Ghost. (Tomorrow—at 1 Garden St—And now what can *I say?*)—and into my drunkenness came—Unexpected—Joe Joe. I was so tight I didn't know him at first. "Why," I remember saying, waking from sleep, "you *look* like Joe Joe! You have a *mouth* like Joe Joe!" —At first he thought I was kidding.

When I prayed to God to grant the solution that was best, back in Feb or March, I had my prayer answered. His contact with Florence has made a better man of him. And he loves his baby—Joseph Allen Marshall. (—It leaves me *very* lonely!)

But he comes to me for love (body-love—but understanding, too). And he will return. He expects to—at an indefinite time. And he says "This will peter out when we are older." —But in not so many words, he admits I *bind* him to me. Oh, God, thank you!

But what about CLG—& the Holy Ghost?

And what of my resolutions? I know now that for love it will be Joe Joe—always. Forever. I am not sorry. It is a secret, inner elation. There for once is Love—honoring me however unwillingly.

And dear God how glad I am to learn that he & Florence & the baby et al. are true! —And that he *is* a good, decent, honorable man. I was not, then, so very wrong! —Not so wrong.

God bless them.

And give me some advice, God, for tomorrow. Tomorrow with CLG! —Oh Lord, I am unworthy so much as to kiss the hem of his garment!

It has been Joe in July, Aug, Sept, Nov, Dec, Feb, March, May, June—it'll be Joe as long as I live, for I love him. Oh, God! I prayed for this, & you sent it!

June 17

All morning I still vibrated to the rhythm of Joe. Joe's body. And we went to Revere Beach to enjoy swim & sun.

At the Rectory, I met the quintessence of hypocrisy—a frightened soul in a great body. He was white with wrath, and I wholly disgusted.

"You have *got* to cut it out!" he says. "You will NEVER be happy. —And (jokingly) "I wish you the happiest of unhappiness."

He considers me in the light of Mrs. ("Buddy") Brown because I say what I believe as the result of personal experience with his Georgie, with his Charme School charmers & charmees.

I send him this letter tonight:—

Mr. Glenn

All my family & their friends have used the same way of shunting off the effects of the sterling or the alloyed Truth: — "Why, pay no attention to HER! She's cuckoo!" That may be Mme Grundy's ideal of decorum; but it's not mine of either courage or ethics.

Don't imagine I am in the least 'mad' because you were not interested in any suggestions I made, for I made none. I merely told you how my unconscious mind had worked about your physique until now. It was a statement of fact—not an invitation. I made no attempt to play Cleopatra, as I pointed out. And the reason why was that you had seemed the personification of Goodness. It would have been too unspeakable of me to do it. [For MY sake.] You could of course have defended yourself … There is always an inkwell at hand in a Rectory.

Decorum be dammed! It's all hypocrisy from start to finish. You say you're a 'hard guy,' and so you are! Tough as hell when it comes to defending your own impeccable reputation. You'd take any method rather than lose the repute of Perfection which the 'mashed' women (including my former self) have created for you.

Run right off: call Mrs. Musgrave long distance. Tell her never to do me any kindness any more—Nor my children— because I told YOU back what she said to me. (Told *you*. —Not anyone else!) Does my tongue wag on both ends? That's what I was telling you about yours.

I was telling YOU—don't forget!

As for my sin, I acknowledge that I shall go right on committing it, & am willing to pay the penalty of ostracism from a world that has a false foundation—a house built on the sands of self-deception erected for the safety of weak man. Your kindest wishes for the "happiest of unhappiness" are tabulated. I will stick to my guns. It is my finding, as it was last October, that my cabby is a more honest man (with himself) than my rector.

I'll call it quits, as I told you! No more parish priest. Make sure you do the same. And if you go into the house of Musgrave, I will defend myself with equal vigor and the Power of an Ex Press woman.

Oh, verily! Murder Mrs. Grundy. She obscureth Truth.

L.H.B.

—Then I wrote to Mrs. Musgrave, confessing how I had quoted her.

—Then I wrote a note to Mrs. Spencer saying "disregard my effusive slander as such, & as coming from one of unsound mind."

—Then I wrote to My Love Lord (JoJo) telling him please to forget my reason for getting drunk & my dirty thoughts about CLG—

And then—to CLG—a second letter—

II

"On further thought I see very clearly that I have been guilty of Mrs. Buddy Brown's sin—slander, which is WRONG. I haven't meant it that way. I am so stupid! Anything that makes a good tale—a way of getting attention. I apologize to you & Mrs. Glenn.

However I am not recanting out of *fear;* and all the accusations I made about you & your 'sex appeal' I am not taking back. But I've no right to Gabble, any more than you have.

It's about 6 of me and ½ doz of you, because when I say things out of my personal pique because Georgie doesn't treat me like a Duchess, I am just as guilty as you of slander when you say 'Mrs B is crazy.'

So we're quits.

I shall bear no witness against my neighbors hereafter. Inasmuch as I am not a self-acknowledged gossip, & am not interested in my neighbors enough to stay up nights over 'em, it is a surprising revelation to me to find I'm a wicked gossip, even as Biddy Brown. I will not be so silly as to think that any stuff I put in my novel about you will affect you one way or another, but you may be very sure, my dear sir, that it was all very kind stuff; because you have been very kind to me, & for all my back-fire I am grateful.

I'm grateful to my mother for what she does for me, even though I back fire on her for her Grundyisms. Grateful to my Uncle for making my mother's last day happen even though he has accepted what she says as fact about 'Lois is crazy.'

Lois *is* crazy. But why rub it in? Isn't it hard enough to BE it without being TOLD it?

I will send around a note, if you like, to my neighbor Mrs. Spencer, telling her I am crazy—that, in fact, I have at one time been sent by other neighbors to a psychopathic hospital for observation; and that you know it, and are therefore justified in telling her not to take me seriously. Shall I do that?

You see, I am Very Sensitive about the Dippy stuff. I've heard it rubbed in since I was 15. It is a dirty below-the-belt attack. You could think of nothing neater or more apparently true (ask Angel Magoun). But still I hope you will believe that I have not been consciously intent upon slander. I called it by some other name—jealousy or something. But I owe your Georgia an apology. Crazy as I am, I hope she will accept it as sincerely offered.

I shall be all the more fervid about killing off Mrs. Grundy now that I have perforce busted into tears in recognition of my own sin. Will you believe I am sorry? Repentant? Ashamed?

I am not presumptuous enough to draw a comparison—not quite—but didn't 'they' say the King of the Jews was crazy, too? Lots of people have been maligned that way, when it was the only resort others had to defame them.

Please say next time: "Lois Bayliss is a slanderer." I think I prefer a sin I can correct to a psychosis that is incurable. And I think you are rather like all the rest of the Grundys when you resort to that.

Oh, I shall MURDER Mrs. Grundy—and slit her throat to ribbons when I can.

I bawl
LHB

p.s. Van Gogh cut off his ear & sent it to his mistress. May I ship you my tongue express prepaid?

About Al—as I told Joe, without mentioning names—Al is good, thoughtful, generous—unlike my Love Lord in any way. I convinced Al (& was that night myself convinced) that I would be not only faithful but truthful to him—as regarded my Distinguished Guest—Bill McFee. *Now I cannot,* because of Florence, tell him of my Love Lord's impetuous, ardent, unexpected visit of love.

So I shall begin now to "play off" Al against Joe Joe, and vice versa. I shall be disgusted: it is a thing I have never done, & is done in deference to my Arch Enemy, Mrs. Grundy!

Helas! Has she conquered me?

Oh, my Love God, you frighten me—little Black Prince. Lover—lover, whom God sent when I prayed.

"You will *never* be happy," saith CLG. "I wish you the happiest of unhappiness."

June 19

CLG is pigeonholed forever—a wonderfully gifted and pitifully mistaken man. I have had need of my illusions about him: they have served me well.

—But my soul and body still vibrate with Joe's pulses. And it will be Joe till I die. (Maybe Al—or someone, too; but only Joe has ever reached the sanctum sanctorum of my being.) Oh Lord bless my Love Lord. How could I call it wrong, when Joe came in direct answer to prayer sincerely made?

June 20

In the effulgence of tenderness which always fills my heart while Joe's seed is still absorbing in my body, I *believed* him *implicitly* (I always do when he is here, or has just left). Les. Glenn says that the Romance of our Triangle is like a cheap movie—without doubt he doesn't believe it. Why is it that when my Love Lord is in my arms, I trust him utterly? The answer is that he is one of the few men I could ever trust (as he likes to declare) to satisfy my body— And so, in all this belief, I started a little knit suit for his baby. (Now— *does* that child exist?) And it's very cute—designed to become an olive complexion like Joe's own. But now that it is 3 nights since our delightful frenzy of love, I am not so sure I believe him. Is that *my* failing—credulousness perhaps is really impossible, after all my bitternesses.

CLG says: "You've GOT to cut it out!" I am not supposed even to *talk* socially with one of his parishioners lest I be parading under false colors. Now I might see sense to that if it could possibly be anyone else's pertinent concern with whom I spent my lovely hours. But as I can't see how Mrs A, Miss B, or Grandma G can possibly be injured by talking on the street with me because last night I was *happy,* then I can only laugh. HAW.

It is obviously necessary, once the children are gone, to get started on "Murder Mrs. Grundy"—because F.W.S. and Ch. Ch. have both excommunicated me from any charity list. (Loving Joe is a costly thing—! What?) I *can* make money on the slaughter of the old Dowager. And I *must* have something to rely on apart from chance & charity.

It has been a bitter blow to have CLG go POOF—like a burst balloon. But well did I know he would, after last October. And he is still a rarely beautiful creature to look upon & hear.

June 26

Children Promoted Today.
Jon—to Grade VI
Sandy & Pete, Grade III (Pete could have 'skipped')

The more I feel of this *deep* secret passion for Jojo—*knowing* (so *gloriously!)* that it is fully returned in kind! [Oh God, you sent him when I prayed, & he is all & more than I knew how to ask for—& it is just as I said I knew I'd no right to ask more than: just a lover who *knows* Love]—the more ashamed I feel of myself for deceiving Al about him. Al is so good & kind & thoughtful & sweet & generous. How can *I*—who am so honest?—not tell him that it's Joe Joe *always* that way? Joe Joe says: "Take life as it comes!" It has to be so in a modern world. But it is a shock to me. It sums up the code I have been trying to chrystallize & accept for myself—"Departmentalization" of which CLG disapproves. "You CAN'T!" he cries. "If you *must* wear thorns, wear them for a Crown" he quotes.

He is *so* good. Is *he* ever distressed by the same kind of keep passion J. & I suffer with? (I've a sudden understanding that Georgie & he are perfectly mated sexually. What a blessing! He is a fair-haired boy—the world falls into his hand!) (That's why he cannot understand my unsuccessfulness.) ("You will *never* be happy." —What a *wise* from the parson! Like a blight. I'm going to write him.) Katharine Sturgis says to leave him out of my inner life. That's good advice. But his shining face intrudes because a thing of beauty is a joy forever.

Dr. Harding says it's part & parcel of a woman's nature to deceive. Suppose then I *do* continue not to spoil my friendship with Al by talking of Joe's visits—& be a woman! For it would be within compatibility—I really never quite knew what adult passion meant till Joe demonstrated. He has made a woman of me emotionally. I *must* deceive Al, because I'm afraid he wouldn't care any more for me if I told him, & I couldn't sacrifice even one visit of Joe's a month for all Al's sweetness. "Oh, *I* am rotten!" And by that Joe means Florence; & I mean Al—& *oh how we understand each other!* It's the deepest (most selfish) feeling in my heart—except the Three!

I'm *going* to *Murder Mrs. Grundy!* I'm all set.

My children are prodigiously lovely. Eliz. Peaslee Davies' Nancy comes today. The world is full of kindness.

June 27:—

I woke with Joe Joe in my heart. This is the only real *passion* I've ever known. Somehow after that last night we had together brought us *much* closer together. I feel I *know* him now; and he *knows* me. Oh, God—who sent him to me in answer to prayer—send him back! If I can, let me have him for long and for a chance to make him deeply happy (as he admits he isn't with F.)—send him *without hurt* to anyone else. God only can do it—& whatever Thy Will for us, I still thank you for your sending him.

Dear JoeJoe—I wish this moment your black head lay close to my white breast— And Joe, darling, my Love Lord, I somehow *know* and *love* you better now.

God send you here!

June 28

Oh Joe—I am so *deep*—you are so *long!*

July 3

Spent my "anniversary" (Jojo) with Al & my family—Laura (who's neurasthenic), Mother & Dottie (who's stupidly thin & nervous—Perfect example of an unawakened woman) & life grows constantly more exhilarating—because I *know* Jojoe & Love now.

I am a mature human. Left so much of the world behind. It's the perfect lover, plus the analysis, plus the revival of Faith, plus financial security—however slight. Oh *I'm* on top of the world. Nothing—nothing fazes me. I *know*—Oh God be thanked!

July 6

Joe came.

July 16

Joe came—I left my "Book of Jojo" lying on the desk! *Al came & read it!* I am glad, & said so to Al by mail.

Dottie due Tuesday! I am in a frenzy. (Did not come.)

July 21

Al came.

July 29

I think today ends a little over a year of the most tremendous love, the most unbounded passion, the most soul-shaking devotion to any man I have ever known.

God bless him. It must be—*if* it must be.

Aug 2

Sent Henry an "outlawed anniversary" letter. He will probably not answer.

Aug 4

We met Mrs. Claff, who took us out to Lynn—Most important part of the drive was past #25 Falmouth St. Belmont, & the distinct picture that gave me of Joe's motivations in his descriptions to me. [He *loves* me!]

Aug 5

I'm going to write in this book hereafter in a different vein.

Aug 7–'36

Symbolically, a new leaf:—
Too long I've drifted aimlessly in my confused emotional sea. It's time to take my bearings and steer my ship intelligently, like a navigator and not a helpless sailor in the fo'c'stle.

At present I am hoping to have Al aboard my ship.

It is useless to record that the glory and misery of my love for Joe have made this year fly by like mad. It's been beautiful & terrible, but now has come the time for the end of it. Regarded as an entity, it was one of the Great Episodes of my highly-episodic existence.

I have found in myself a great strain of puritanism, at war with the strongly-opposed forces I have unleashed for 17 years. Time to investigate.

Aug 29

Well, again I was wrong. For a month, for the sake of his "wife" [and again I find myself doubting the whole tale], I *gave* him up. But two nights ago, such a hunger overtook me for his pure, strong, animal manhood, that I went to find him. He came home with me. He "takes life as it comes." He wanted me & had me. The truth was, the story Al had told me of beating & robbing a pervert, had absolutely turned me against Al (with whose (temporary) attentions I was trying to cure myself of Joe); also Al kicked our Fitch-y kitten; and I see clearly I don't like Al at all. So I went back. Joe Joe is a dear, bright, handsome, strong, manly animal. But, dear God, forgive him for his *lies*. Oh, terrific.

Nothing on earth is worthy of a woman's whole devotion except her children. Her love for them, & care for them, is unselfish. Any love for a man is selfish. No woman should make a 'profession' of a man. That way mania lies. No man is worth it. Deep in my heart I do not want any man—unless that man were Joe; and if I had him, it would spoil the allusion of his power. God, life is lonely, after all, except for my Three, for whom I thank Thee, & beg thee to make me every day, every way, a good & faithful mother. They come from camp today.

Sept 1—'36

I am now *anxious* to free myself of torment (about Joe), although my love is the most radiant emotion I have known, for it tears and terrifies me with its insistent demand for him. Oh Lord have mercy! Have mercy!

Sept 4

Burned my bridges by deliberately smacking Joe's delectable face 3 times on Garden St. I had to.

Florence is *not* married to him; there *is* no baby. All that was *rot!* Joe was playing an ornate game.

But thru him I've learned:—

1) The hollow mockery of promiscuousness. [(!) Fancy that—from *him!]*

2) My own emotional capacity for LOVE.

3) That I'm no 'lady,' nor want to be.

4) That I am, *absolutely,* a Lone Wolf.

5) That I need now an *intellectual affaire* (without conventional trappings).

6) That I am never likely to forsake my 3 dearest—even in a gale like this has been!

7) That I pray for a social revolution.

God, thanks for this year. Bless Joe & make his mouth clean of his lies now.

Sept 13 Sunday, 4:40 AM

I woke up just now from a terrific dream. I was (in the dream) standing at the top of a perilously sloping rock by the shore at Hoof-hole Cove. It was half tide. I was clinging to my perch, safely enough, waiting for Sandra to bring me a paper bag full of—I suppose candy [my gluttony!]. Out in the water the launch of a Coast Guard cutter had just delivered to the rocky, sea-weedy shore, a hunchbacked man, whose difficult passage along the small rocks at the foot of the bluffs I was watching intently. I called to Sandra, something about this man, & looked around to see her struggling towards me with the paper-bag. Just as she reached out the candy towards me, I cautioned: "*Careful,* darling." "Oh, *I'm* all right," she said— She started bravely across the rock but had on sandals, not sneakers— And suddenly, she plunged—head first into deep water. I was paralyzed—couldn't move—tried to scream—and woke.

It comes over me that they are surely not empty words I use when I say the children were better off without me. I am conscious of deep sin—but it is the reason why I am poor, lonely, unsuccessful.

I find myself a bearer of seriously false witness against my neighbor—for have I not again & again repeated the story of the "bayberry bushes" and the "hat in the widow's yard" as personal experiences of my own, when both tales are based on someone else's experience? How can I be so much the willful liar—in a case where such a serious charge against G.S. is involved—and still feel "superior" to Joe because of his lying about Florence? This is a serious flaw in me—that I could lie so baldly in such a matter. Finding: Joe, hearing me tell these tales, was sharp enough to suspect the untruth: he has yarned for me, yarn for yarn, and I have been very deeply hurt, because in the matters concerning love, I have never lied. Therefore, I condemn him. But a lie is a lie, in any department; and *I am a stark & despicable sinner.*

I have been trying to examine my motives in my mixing myself with Mrs. Brown's personal concerns. [The wider awake I grow, as I write now, the stronger becomes the temptation to deal kindly with myself, out of pride.] Women surely *ought* to know what men things are— They ought not to have to be victims of a dupe like that, nor have to swallow whole the pomposity of a hypocrite like him. But, though I am sure my deeper motives in telling her of my discovery were robust enough, a little consideration beyond the weeks of time I took to make up my mind, would have shown me another side: He has been her whole life for 13 years. She has, consciously or unconsciously, swallowed him as being righteous, upright and strong. By my revelation about his mania—and that is all true, alas! for both of them—I have shattered for them all the superstructure that these 13 years have built. Because I myself have been a shatterer in my own life, & have seen illusion after illusion crumble away—& oh these things have left me lonely!—have I, even though I know that outer, artificial values are vain and overrated—the right to shatter hers? Surely I deserve the contempt in which she holds me, of which I complained to her. It takes little effort to wreck another woman's happiness that is falsely constructed. My happinesses have all been shattered for me (all except the *real, deep,* unutterable privilege of motherhood, which I so little deserve, but value so passionately! *Oh, God, I thank thee for my Three!)* because of my intrepid courage for putting everything to the test. Is it my business to show Mrs. Brown the untenability of her devotion to that unlovely, cowardly pervert? Why did I do it? Do I not know that few women of her class and her mentality are robust enough to be able to watch their castles crumbling to the foundations, without utter personal degradation? True, the substantialities of their lives remain the same. He a hypocrite, she a self-deceiver, & the children all being reared to a belief in a non-existent condition of family security.

I ask myself, seeing her determined (long before *I* contributed this blow) to return to Scotland, I ask myself if, if truth were admitted by silly little things like her, she were not just *looking* for some excuse to break up a home ill-balanced on a misconception of robust husbandry.

No doubt! For she is not stupid; and though she complains I have taught her more "dirt" than she ever knew about, I know that is merely a catty rejoinder, for she is well-schooled (at her "Girls'" Club) in the lowest & most vulgar kind of pornography; but to her this world of sexual fact has until now seemed remote, unreal. It is my real *knowledge* of morbid psychology that proves to her unequivocally the fact that her husband is no man at all—a mealy mouthed, utterly ridiculous delayed adolescent, parading as a man of authority

& culture, he has suddenly taken the tumble his pretensions really deserved him to take. —But, be that as it may, & the untamability of such a domestic structure being unquestioned, I ask myself—boldly!—who was *I* to precipitate this crash of the House of Brown? Even though messianic impulses to share with a fellow-woman my hard-bought realization that modern marriage is a mockery, that for a woman to wrap herself up in a man's life, coddle his vanity, humor his whims, is philosophically unsound, as well as feministically unethical, merely to wheedle out of him the worldly goods needed to maintain her children—Granted my basic principles in telling her how *her* George Brown, ex-minister, high-sounding moralist, begged *me* (a sinner? Yea, Lord, a sinner, but not a hypocrite, I *hope*) to "punish him as a child" with a wicked belt-strap—*granted* they were right & robust enough, still, has anyone profited by the bomb I hurled? Will she one day *admit* she is *grateful* for this "last straw"? Was she not only waiting for someone else to destroy her last illusion? But, Lord, well do I know her kind: she will blame me for her shattered world, as if *I* were the pervert, the hypocrite. *I* will bear in her thoughts the onus for a wrecked home. Never will she grow philosophically honest enough to admit the structure of her life had been shakey and threatening long ago.

—And when she has left him—despite my sincere warnings that she *ought* to stay by him till he has been cured of his mania by a psychologist, with her (connubial) help—when she has left him, & he is lonely and oppressed by his weakness & his loneliness, will he come here & murder me in my bed?

Note: Is there not a psychological relationship between his case & that of Warren Olsen, whom I believe to be psychologically incapable of those two murders in Rockport, because he is notoriously sexually babyish? Yet, it is possible that men of that stamp, like the "fairies" one hears of, can, upon provocation, wield merciless strength and ruthless punishment? Perhaps I shall, then, be murdered in my bed? —Well, except for the next few years while the kids need me, the world will sustain no great loss. But if I die before I wake—

—Another department:

I continue to bring up my children according to my deep-seated beliefs in utter candor. I know my theories are backed up by the ultra-modern child psychologists, but I have NEVER met another woman who practised their theories with *complete* wholeheartedness; and I cannot but ask myself in fairness to them if possibly I am wrong. I want their minds to probe, & probe. I want them to test & question *everything*. And still I would have them preserve the exuberance & spontaneity that not the worst (Taunton) of all my experiences has ever killed in me. Shall I *really*, as I aim to do, "condition" them for every psychological dilemma, prepare them *invulnerably* for *every conflict* it is within my scope to foresee?—or, instead, as the croaking, sloppy-thinking majority—huge majority—warn, shall I succeed only in spoiling their lives? Am I too "crazy," too "eccentric" for their good? The pudding may have its proof, but God strike me dead if I warp their spirits & my real motives in this kind of motherhood prove themselves to be utterly base, & founded entirely on my predisposition for being rather grossly animal & ribald.

Note: No wonder people cannot understand me! Do I not combine with a natural animal vitality and animated mentality, a strange, utterly inconsistent, & very strong—really ineradicable—strain of puritanism? It has been hard for me to sort *myself* out into any kind of order. How, then, can I expect an outsider to do it, or, more than that, to care to do it.

Like the Miller of Dee

> I care for nobody, no not I
> And nobody cares for me!

That is literally true, except for the children (who, Henry used to say, loved me because they *knew no better)!* And [more especially since my strong reaction to the utterly foundationless passion—foundationless in every way, except the utter beauty of physical matedness with him—I have lavished upon Joe (till he groaned with its weight, poor soul!)] really I care less & less for human regard, except for the children's. Because I have dug down & discovered that 99% of marriages are as falsely robust as the Browns'. And to me the very nature of love, being, especially when it is MOST passionate, transitory, makes marriage less & less desirable in these modern days.

My thoughts of marriage now are only for the children, when they are of age. I wonder what conditions will prevail when Sandy wants to have babies? Anyway, I will stick by. Oh, Lord, you can trust me there: *I will be loyal to my children.* It is only for them that I have lived, or have an excuse for living.

Note. Waking, it takes not long to argue myself back to a fairly secure self-satisfaction. Deep down, whence dreams come, I am ashamed of my pusillanimous soul—& no wonder!

Bless Joe-Joe, Lord!

Sept 25

Joe *sent* back "The Beachcomber"—without comment. My knees began to shake because "J. A. Marshall" was lettered on the parcel.

I have *loved* that wicked man.

I haven't *loved* Al, who came in the evening. I like him a great deal, and find him sympathetic. But—marriage? NO! no man cares to marry.

However, I shall never (see pages to follow) LOVE again—my spirit's resources are depleted.

The children show need of tremendous discipline.

They have no shoes.

We must live (if we can) on $16 a week—all of us. Ye Wolf!

Oct 7

Saw Joe again. I know now he knows how mistaken he was to forfeit me to play his silly "skin-game"; and, for this reason, though I love him more than anyone, I am going to drop all thought of him for my future happiness.

Oct 8

Had gas for dental extractions. Same sensation, minus elation, but of a very resigned & philosophical kind—as if, even under anaesthetic, my logical mind works.

Oct 9

We sit around the table while we write letters to editors & chambers of commerce "out West"—for, if God be kind, we are moving on, following the trend. —Amen.

Oct 10

I think this is true. I had no very strong desire for Joe when he pleaded so with me three nights ago. I hope all this adolescent profligacy is overcome. Maybe, in time, real love (and so-much-to-be-desired *companionship*) will come to me.

Aside from my teeth & new plates, my whole mind is focused on Futures in the West. For the Three! The *Three!* God bless them & forgive their mother her sins—so much of imprudence! of impetuosity!

Oct 13

Had Joe tonight.

Oct 14

If God answers my prayers, something to save these children's lives will happen—eg—I'll get started on a paper of my own—I'll get my 2 bks. published ["Hokker"– "Sin Island"] or I'll land the job on the AMERICAN. It's too bad not to have outgrown commercial promotional writing—but Mrs. Magoun charged me with: "You were *determined* to have the luxury of children; but you'll do nothing to support them." That put a damper on all my selfish impulses to settle down to pure literature [for MY sake, for Art's sake] and let them suffer for it. Surely a *father* of a family would have felt he had a right to, were his urge as strong, his flair as good. Let me take a little credit to myself. But what MUST be MUST. Back I'll go to the 4th estate, saving my 'literature' for the sunset years of a lonely old age. One thing is this! tho' I would with all my heart be good & God-approved, I have lost so much from my religious fervour since CLG blew himself up. And the way these things are done in the name of Christian charity—all are so crudely commercial. Mrs. Magoun is surely a dear, but heavens above! She's NO IDEA what we are going thru. Joe Fine's unpiteous offers to either get money from Henry for us or 'take him to court'—and I know *Courts* are mockeries, too! —My hopes about my novels—And then my need (only semi-occasional now) of Joe [I had him last night—first time for a long time. I *had* to. And it wasn't what it was when I was "in love" with him. Funny what illusions have done for me!] I wonder if I'm *thoroughly disillusioned now?* Any more slaps in the face, God?—for being a dreamer, a lover, a joyous soul in this Vale of Tears.

Life is a "grim-death" affair. Anyway, now I shall buckle down & get these kids a living. *Motherhood* is no illusion: it's a hard fact and a beautiful burden.

Jonathan is dear, bright [saucy] and fine.

Peter is quick, gentle, loving, shrewd and fine.

Sandra is generous, fiery, good and fine.

My 3!

God bless me for The Task! Even in youngest youth I knew my motherhood was to be an *enormous* responsibility, but I'd no idea it would call upon a kind of horse-sense so ill-developed in my otherwise fine mind. God forgive me all my sins: lead me to wisdom for the children's sakes! My Three! My Three.

Oct 23

I do love Joe. Why must it be so painfully fruitless. Why must the facts of poverty and different environments stand in the way? I am not at all sure he loves me. I wish he did. Knowledge of that fact would beautify my existence. But I doubt if he does. Oh, God, could I *please* have Joe for a husband?

Oct 25

A sudden *frenzy* of love & passion sent me to get Joe; and when he came I was so wild with my love, & he so beautiful in his surprised reception of my eloquence that those last sublime—nearly unconscious!—moments were beyond description.

There was never such a lover! Nor will I want any other—ever. Dear, dark Joe-boy-man!

Oct 30

Face swelled to a moon. My jaw won't open. The children are being blessed little helpers!

I wonder why Christian religion & sex-nature paganism can't decently be made comfortable? In me, I hope they are—yet I can see both arguments, depending upon my moon-cycle & my fortunes.

"My brother, Robert Patrick," is *GOOD!* (Later: a *hypocritical goodness.)*

~

My children have been great comforts, as house-keepers and nurses, during my awful battle of the molars. May they live (when I am gone) to comfort others as they comfort me! And God bless me to the task of keeping them well & healthy—AND happy and *Good.*

(God bless my Joe-Joe. I could never give up loving him if I could be sure of the rightness of it. He is hard to manage, yet, I surmise, he is habitually clay in a woman's hands. Having no artfulness, I fail. But shall I try to succeed? Is it what God wants of me? —Or is it only that I want his wonderful love-making? Oh, questions without answer—!

A prayer:—

For work, O God, to support these three. For strength, for patience. For selflessness! Oh Lord, hear me now!

I can't get Dr. Tom Cody out of my mind. —This is the moony time. *What* would *he* think of such a thing? He looks so wonderful & has such unbounded energy!

Nov. 6

Last night the ("Rev") uncle, "my brother Robert Patrick" came over here for supper—later for highballs, & we sat before a baking fire & drank & talked (very happily) till 2 am. But—after declaring his celibacy, he became inclined, at the last moment, to be amorous—wherefore I—though his protestations had a distinct pleasantness of baby-to-mother flavor, something like Henry (which reminded me also of 'Berlap' in "Point CounterPoint"—) I hustled him off. Even so, "Lothario" B. Simpson had called himself 'a man of iron' & then got gooey—why do they? No will? Is my "lure"—

or my "evil"?—of Circean strength against their conviction & philosophy? I hustled him off—& still I enjoyed his peculiar frail snuggling—I can't make the thing out.

Today—at 33!—my last but 4 teeth came out. I hate novocaine (specially taken digestively) & put on a disgraceful crying act in the chair. Later, I had the inflamed temper of a b_t_h—to the poor children. This done, I'll be joyful.

What's going to happen? Money? Marshfield Ore—I have a hunch yes—Why 'exist' here. All is lost in Mass. And *we seek fortunes!*

Nov 13

Tried to get Joe at the Sq. by phoning Druggists'. No reply. *Impelled* by my desire, hastened to Sq. (no teeth—but hair newly waved & cut!). Found him at the Georgian. His dear face lit up. He hurried up home at once. *Perfect* sublimity in his arms. I have no need of anyone but him. Lord, since Love between men & women simplifies itself in the last analysis to what *we* share together, is it not *utterly* true to say I love him—& he, me? Take him not away from me, God of Wisdom!

Nov. 16

My teeth are delayed, are delaying me to distraction. Practically I am promised the Fish Pier job; and now if I can nab Meyer at the AMERICAN in a right mood—all set.

Blessings on those who, thru Ch. Ch. and FWS, are paying rent for me now. [Also shoes.] Also the merciful dollar good Miss Mitchell gave me this am. Also Jos. Fine.

Henry's Naturalization comes up on Nov 23rd at 9:30. Jos Fine & I will be present. Also Miss Mitchell.

Despite tooth-delay & my fuss to get my hair into shape before it's grown out again! my heart is very full of happy thankfulness. I am very tenderly in love with my JoeJoe, too. Oh, God, let me have what little he may spare of himself for me—for he is all I want of Love. He has already said I have had more of him than he has ever given any woman. Lord, how I love his masculinity—& his *simple, courteous* code of honor. Complete happiness involves him—what little I can get of him, *dear dear Joseph Andrew!*

Nov. 26—Thanksgiving Day

The Lord wants me to attend His church, I think. I shall hereafter be more faithful. Now I have my teeth. Everyone has been very kind. We had *3* Thanksgiving baskets. Much to be thankful for. At the service the Baptist minister preached for the 7 Hvd. Sq. churches assembled. A very fine, strong sermon.

In church I *prayed* that Jos. would come, as I wrote, & phoned, him to do. He did, too! *The most excellent darling! Never* has he been so sweet, so tender. Called me *dear* (unprecedented). Said, embarrassed, he must not give my mind *too* much to feed upon. Said maybe someday we'd marry (forgiving me for all my trespasses!). And loved me so exquisitely—praised my beauty—held me to him. I love him. I adore him. I want no one but him. I pledged him my fidelity, and he returned the pledge.

We *all* have *much,* much to be thankful for. Much much. Thank you, Lord!

1937

Since my last entry, because this book has been put away, I've recorded all my Love Outpourings in the "Book of Joe Joe" and, since the New Year, begun a diary for *bare facts* (including Joe's visits).

After Thanksgiving, he came home in December on the 6 & 20 [staying all night on the 20th—a delectable, unforgettable night & morning!].

In January, he was here on the 7th and the 12th. And came again on the 25th when I was out [Curses].

227 Concord Ave

Jan 26–'37

My Peter is 7 years old today. 7 years ago today on a Sunday I was in terrific pain and great danger of both our lives at Knickerbocker Hospital in New York. [I can never forget the bitterness of

Jon, Sandy, and Peter, July 1937.

Lois and her Three, 286 Concord Ave., Cambridge, October 31, 1937.

my experience as I fainted in the last few moments when Henry was so brutal!] I often think today how queer it is that 7 years has obliterated so much of that suffering. Peter was a child conceived in misunderstanding. I carried him thru great sorrow, great joy, and great sacrifice [of Philip] and now, seven years later, it is so fated (or am I so frail?) that aside from my love for and duty to the children, I am all absorbed with Joe.

Yesterday, because I missed his visit by a hair's breadth, and was in a frenzy, I dashed to the Sq. He was *annoyed:* said he had MADE NO SPECIAL EFFORT to see me—just "dropped in, because I was up that way." —*I* thought it rather apt that I could slip under his arm the "Book of Joe Joe."

It begins:

> Heart that lights this heart of mine
> Dimly lit so long a time
> Voice that tunes a hidden lute
> So a songless soul can flute,
> Piping "Love!" and *"Love!"* and *"Love!"*

—carries him, if (as I am sure he will) he reads it, thru everything from Feb '36 to Jan '37, and ends:

> Wisdom of an age-old kind
> Shrinking from a winsome mind
> Beauty, grace, & honor—wit
> Kindness—and the best of it
> He has tought me Love and Love!

And I leave this space blank, so that I can record his reaction to it. [*His feelings* will be kind: his words gruff—But he can no longer *doubt!*] He thinks he understands women: if he has read that record, he certainly does now!

~

Joe's reaction to the "Book of Joe-Joe"— He *is* reading it, as I thought he would! And he is pleased by it, though he is utterly nonplussed to think I love him as I do (though I can only feebly put it into words).

He *promises* to *tell me* if *ever* he chooses another girl. He declares [sincerely] that he has been *utterly faithful* to me since July 3 '35. And I *do believe* he is good & true & loyal, loving me more & more than even I can know. And my heart is *bursting* with joy and delight and gratitude to Joe & God. Oh, praise, praise. And today when I go to Fisk's for my $ I shall stop in at church to thank my good God for this!

~

And my day was utterly fizzled because of that frustration! I had been nursing an ungrateful & ungracious Dot Kleila & thus missed him. I was so outraged that I went to bed about 6. And could not sleep.

Love like this [and it never hit me so hard before, & I have scoffed at French novels whose heroines 'take on' so—!] is surely an illness. Oh, God send Joe tonight. I *pray, pray, pray.* I *must* have a long, long *talk* with him tonight, if you can grant me this necessity in Omniscient Kindness. God, I love this *man* & but for the children would give up *every* thing of pride or position or riches for him. It is a *good* love, because it is true—has weathered storms!

When I was about to sleep, Jon, fresh from a bath & setting up exercises wouldn't let me drowse because he had so much to tell me about his boat & dog. Sandra & I "picked out" our 'favorite houses' in a magazine. Peter, exhausted, had gone to sleep. We had quite a lot of fun. I have always, when my children needed talk of this kind, put away even my dearest dreams, to give my 'ear.' And so they never withhold confidences.

[I have been working on "Murder Mrs. Grundy" for the H.M. Fellowship Award. Mrs. Magoun & Jessie Knowlton refuse to 'sponsor' me [on conscientious & selfish grounds respectively, for which I cannot blame either of them] but Uncle has written a highly laudatory letter, which may help. Mrs. Magoun thinks not, on 2 counts. —"Stuffed Shirtish" policy of H.M; and my uncle's kinship. Sponsors: Mrs. Wright, Ruth Kimbard, Uncle, Margaret Sutton.]

I slept, at last. Terrible dreams—in one of which I lived in a beautiful villa in So. Europe, where the sea came to my terrace, but terror came, too—I don't remember what—Terror of Loneliness, it was, for I was cut off by the sea wherein young, lovely girls were swimming. Also I dreamed that I and an insane & naked old woman, apparently my alter ego, were huddled in a ruined shelter in cold mountains. The old lady rose from the dead leaves in the moonlight, a toothless hag, insane, wanting to find something she had lost. I think I was that old lady, having a desire to find my lost love [Joe]. It is the fear of my lonely old age that makes me cling so desperately to this Last Man of mine. He wants bachelordom. I must wait to induce him. Meanwhile I age—I hope not towards any mental deterioration. For there among the dead leaves was the mental I, still, trying to restrain the insane old woman from her hopeless search. I was patient & tolerant of her.

It has been a major fear of mine that I may actually "go mad for love" because this latter-day passion of mine has unnerved me & unloosed terrific forces of love that I had never known I possessed. I cling to my Three (very wisely!) for ballast. Therefore, I am safe until—And Peter, my baby, is already 7. What a dream to dream on such an anniversary of pain & worry as that day in 1930, 7 years ago.

It is well for me that the man I love so *wildly* is a man who, for all his innocence of "cul*chaw*" (Damn culture!) can & does (albeit soundlessly) understand something of what I feel. I love Joe. I beg God, abjectly, to sanctify this love. For I love God and His Son. I had never known how, perfectly, to love God until this time.

Jan 26

This morning we have cleaned & polished, and as usual, had our daily struggle of temperaments—a healthy, perpetual battle, in our family, to get ready for Pete's guest, little Hastings Wright whose Aunt Anne was my girlhood friend (in my elated, youthful confusion). I hope I am arming my children well to meet the struggles of the world. I hope I may justify my kindly old Uncle's praise (to H.M.–editors) "an exemplary mother." *That* I must be—however the world may quarrel with my deep-seated theories in so doing.

—Joe is half-convinced that I am as good a mother as I hope I am.

Dear, delightful black Joe. Thank you, God! One of many many blessings.

NEWS-FLASH! —[JAN 26/37] Dottie is to have a baby in August—after 12 years of waiting.

God bless & save her life & health. I am SO GLAD!

SET-BACK. This pm about 5.00 the bell rang and "Potato," Joe's erstwhile fellow-cabby came *hunting for a room.* It was obviously a stall, and obviously he expected an invitation to supper. I pretended to take it at its face value. But of course he knew what I knew he wanted. I didn't ask him in at all—though he is pleasant enough as I remember him. But the thought struck me, when he used the Happy Home Baker as a reference, that this might be Joe Joe's answer to my loan of the pitiful record of my love for him. I don't *think* it is—but if it is, he is *contemptible!*

I have *prayed* all day that he would come today. I need *him,* & a chance to *talk to him!*

If I get a lucky no. on the "Sweeps" I'll *know* God approved, for Joe & I *must* marry.

Jan 27

What a wild, crazy, suspicious fool I am! I got up at 6.00 by the light of a beautiful full moon. Took a good hot bath. Went down by st. car to the Square. Waited till 7:15 in the Waldorf for my darling. He came & had his breakfast with me, paid for my coffee, and told me he did NOT send "Potato," but that he had had several questions from Potato as to how & where I was.

It *must* have been that Happy Home baker after all. Today I shall ask *him.*

Joe drove me home, & came in. He has utterly convinced me & made me *sure* of him and his love. We shall, ultimately, be married. And this is such a joy—such an unutterable, perfect joy that the sun shines to some purpose on a clear winter morning. My soul is clear & clean. Joe is perfect. Strong, handsome, truthful, beautiful—and *such* a lover!

He says (by manly circumlocutions) that I have been stupid not to have *known* how much he cares for me, and that he has been faithful, thru "strength of will," ever since we met. [That explains

Florence's hauteur.] He again said, very grand and authoritative, in his gruff way: "If I ever decide to *make a change*" (new girl) "I'm going to tell you first." He says he will be back, "sooner than I expect" with my Book of JoeJoe. I want him to remain overnight.

7 PM (same day). And again all the old suspicions are setting in! Why is that. After we sleep I woke up doubting him again. I am no doubt a fool: but I learned to *know* Henry was a *filthy liar.* Experience teaches—I hope I am *utterly wrong!*

(Happy Home man denied knowing "Potato.") [I wrote Mother asking her to speak to Aunt J. who might induce Gov Hurley to give Joe an appointment. Would he marry me then?] He said (Joe) "I won't have ANYTHING till I can support it!"

Jan 30 Sat

My teeth remained all night at Tufts' last night. To look like a walrus gives me an execrable temper, and I went to bed early (to sulk). I felt serene this morning—loving Joe terrifically. I have prayed all day that he might come tonight. [His Saturday nights are gala ones for him, so that *if* he comes, it means he is *eager* to come.] He has half-promised to remain overnight when he brings back the Love book. I love him more calmly, more deeply—and more admiringly now than ever. What if he *does* prevaricate? [Very possibly this is undeserved.] He is *Joe,* a MAN. I love him.

Feb. 2ⁿᵈ 1937 Tues

He came this morning. Oh, Lord, I know he is beginning to know how much he loves me. I saw him in the Sq. early in the AM, just as he arrived for work. Said he MIGHT come up tonight; but instead of that, he came at 10:00 AM, between 'jobs.' I don't like this sneaking call affair between jobs; and I told him. This time his excuse was that my children, seeing him come at night, will regard me in later years with doubt. He is a child in point of culture; so he cannot understand that my children understand completely my problem, and why he (Joe!) is the beautiful solution of it. He *would* not say "I love you"—and his excuse for that was that it isn't 'decent' to say he loves me, unless he intends to 'follow it thru' with marriage. He continues to stick to the idea of bachelordom. "I've had 2 opportunities to marry—and passed them both up," he says, *proudly*. I wonder if cab-drivers take an 'oath'? He says he may someday see someone else on the street—etc …Whooo! He is like a baby in some ways. These revelations of his infantilism make me *glad* I *haven't* married him yet; because he must come fully to the realization that a good home, loving 'folks' and cleanly comfort in an atmosphere of happiness is what he wants. I would have no un-willing, unconvinced bridegroom. But I see from his talk and his reactions that slowly he is waking to the realization that he *can* and *does feel* Love. (He used to say he was incapable of it.) His dashing up here at 10 AM *proves* to me that the sight of me (and I looked pretty in red scarf & cap & my pretty complexion, when I saw him in the Sq.) stirs him, just as the merest glimpse of him stirs me. I am glad to feel the *power* I have. He intimates that 6 months ago (about the time I was wasting myself on trying to regard Al with affection) he had another girl. If he did, I think it was that divorcee from Maine whom he told me of. And I am sure enough of myself, and of the innate aestheticism in *him,* to know that I am queen of his heart. He would miss my wit, my beauty, my enthusiastic love of his sexual power, and my delicacy in any woman he is in a po-sition to meet. I have *studiously* avoided ever casting any reflection upon the limitations of his social position as a Grundy-despised cabby. He isn't yet aware that marriage to me would open to him a kind of social latitude he has never even glimpsed. For, like all would-be geniuses, I take for myself the authority to make my own social laws. Lesser, fumbling souls can't, daren't, do this. Like Henry, he would be *raised* by marriage to me. But inasmuch I do not *sanction* the class-barriers, how can I tell him this? And could he understand? If we could go together to some broader, far-away City where such restrictions as rule-bound Cambridge imposes were not known, he could rate as an accepted citizen. As for his capacity, & qualifications, why, Joe could hold his own as wit and life of any circle. Why can't he see this? But God seems to have given Joe into my hands to mould and fashion to a new beauty. God gave me a strong man, a willful man, a beautiful, witty, kind, tolerant man. *Perfect* material! And if I can work my woman's magic upon him, I can make him happy and better-adjusted to his world. God will know that I accepted the task he set gratefully.

I am sending him Emil Ludwig's "Son of Man" to read; for his acquaintance with Our Lord has been only of the incomprehensible, highly ritualistic Roman representation—which surrounds the Lonely Figure with a confusion of mixed symbols that conceal the pristine simplicity of His significance. If Joe will *read* the book, he *can* & *will* comprehend it. Far be it from me to go in for tract-distribution! Ludwig's intellectual approach to the subject, utterly reverent, will appeal to Joe who despises hypocrisy and cranks. I love my darling. This is a long & tortuous process of making him happy … But I *must* win. And God, I know, is with me.

Joe's pride in his sexual power delights me. It is the kind of simple and meritorious thankfulness to God for a priceless gift, that a MAN ought to feel. My sexual prowess delights me no less. And Joe's exposition about his 'vivid imagination,' with his dear face all lighted up with eagerness, was one of the loveliest things I ever witnessed.

Feb 3

I have just returned from an amusing interlude at Harvard Sq. Lud & I walked down for exercise, and to take my letters, the kids' letters, and the "Son of Man" into Church for God's blessing before I gave it to him. I saw his cab drive away, just as I reached the Sq—as I waited a while, and at last spoke to his boss who runs the company. The boss told me to go and wait in Joe's cab. As I crossed the Sq. (with the book, the letters, & a pack of cigs. as a gift—because I love him) he came out. He *refused* to let me get into the cab. He said all the cabbies nearby will chaff & twit him, being "Biddies" at heart. He said the boss was trying to get Joe in the wrong. Then he said he spent the night sitting in the company office because "the fishermen at my place put on a brawl last night, & I couldn't get any peace." [—What a place that must be for reading my "Book of Joe Joe." What a darling he is!]

After my time talking seemed to expire, I went back, in leisurely fashion, to his boss's cab. I said "Don't blame Joe for my coming after him. It's MY fault. I have strict orders not to bother him at his work." The poor soul was bewildered. [He looked like a haddock, anyway.] He said: "Whaasa matter? Trouble between youse or sump'n?" And when I explained I only wanted to look at Joe, & came to do so, he was flabbergasted. The Yellow cabby nearby was laughing, too.

Well, I can't get Joe unhappy; and I won't lose him his job, so I will stay away. For I can see that Joe is the only man of the world among them. He is a jewel. Only *he* can't see it himself!

At the store I had an interesting revelation. The meat-salesman (Squires) was telling Joe Golman that a glass of thin cream helped put "lead in one's pencil." And Joe had told me that he'd been drinking thin cream every bedtime.

Now I think I see the whole thing! Poor Joe is unable to get an erection for anyone but me. Simple little darling he is, he doesn't realize that he is impotent with others because he's [for the *first time in his life!*] in love—with ME! So he feverishly drinks cream. I'm his *Queen,* okay! And the reason he doesn't want me round in working hours is because it gets him *all steamed up merely to see* me! Oh, I'm *glad!*

Feb 4

Going to get my Welfare money every week makes Thursdays black enough. But today Joe, in his cab, was very cross and gruff. "I'm sick of the whole thing! What's the idea of having your children write those letters? What's the idea of sending me a letter thru the mail? What's the idea of giving me *that* book? —No, it *won't* do me any good. I think too much as it is! No, I don't need anyone to take care of me: I'm feeling fine. Stop sending me mail. Yes, I've had my shirt kidded off me. I won't say *when* I'll come to your house! I am NOT 'bursting': I've got self-control when I want it. I'm sick of the whole thing! You always spot me when you come thru the square." Etc. And I—because my moon-goddess is waning, and Power swings now into the male cycle—*I* am flat, forlorn, almost suicidal. I shall *never* love anyone else. God alone can move Joe Joe's good heart. I must marry him. I love him.

Oh, today is *very* black.

Resolve: I must NOT *chase* this beautiful, sensitive male creature whom I love.

God control my feverishness for him, and reward my control
with his *voluntary* coming. *Amen.*

Later same day: I think it's time *I* had a little self-control, too. I
have definitely learned that Joe loves me exclusively. I have definitely
learned that I return that feeling to him, full measure. But it is time
he was given a chance to *test* whether or not he really is "sick of the
whole thing." —He said, when I charged him with doing things
only to please himself, that he was going to "stop *even* that" from
now on. The children's letters were certainly medicinal: he feels
healthily like a beast for his selfishness and silly bachelordom. I love
him. I'll be true to him. But the next slice of humble pie is his to
eat. I've eaten ¾ of it now.

Still later: To express, I suppose, for my understanding, a primitive Portuguese philosophy, God sent old "Pa" Ring to visit. He says,
in his way, that *work* is man's greatest blessing. He is a dear, sweet
old thing!

Friday AM–*Feb. 5, 1937*

Yes, it's up to me to be demure. He loves me; I love him. —Well,
Joe—*so what?*

—Be demure? I *can't;* it wouldn't be ME, any more than it would
be Joe if he "made any statements." Yesterday, after terrific house-
cleaning, and getting off the children to the Church with Rosemary
Musgrave, I *meant* to stay still at home, and rest. I surely needed it.
But I got up, dressed, went out with Lud. I meant to go towards
Fresh Pond, but *found myself walking* toward the Square. I turned
in thru Radcliffe Yard, started along towards Farwell Place to the
back of the Church. The kids were already gone. I started back. Oh,
of course I *wanted* Joe to come overnight, to stay all day today. And,
after borrowing 5¢ from Cop #13, to ride home & provide an excuse for looking for Joe—ostensibly (deceiving even *myself!*) because
I wore not heavy enough clothes and was cold—at the subway entrance, I missed a bus (on purpose, really, tho I hate to admit it) because I saw his cab.

He was sweet—but he was cross, too, and he would not come to
us—Going to a *party,* he said! [Oh, *is he looking for another woman*
because I have pestered him so?] And all the evening I kept visual-

izing him attacking the heart of some other girl, as he did my heart 2 years ago. He re-iterated that he would NEVER marry. Oh, the poor darling. What a life he'll lead if he keeps this up. I *need* to comfort & warm and wait on him, and he needs me to do it. But he is stubborn. And, whatever happens, I *must* be faithful to him *because* I MUST, for *my* sake alone. I adore him. I came home in *black* despair! The kids had got home first. Somebody told Jon I had gone to the church, thence to the Sq. and he went down to look for me. He saw Joe, who (Jon reported) was in "very good humor"; and was told I had just left.

Oh, I was cast down. I came home in a cloud. I went down cellar and tried to make up my mind the world, including the kids and Joe, would be better off without me. But I *can't* do that. And I don't want to. Because *dead,* I can't *ever* have Joe; but alive, I may have him a little—as much as he can spare. This makes me frantic—to think that *I,* who have always held the aces in love, should be so much at Joe's mercy. "He's got me in the palm of his hand!" He says the days are over when he'll put himself out for *anyone.* That's a wicked philosophy, and I know he doesn't mean it. But he surely knows how to punish and torture me. I can only *pray* to God that he *didn't* find another woman.

Oh, Lord, this passion tears me to pieces.

It's another sign of Joe's strength. Tuck and Ford and Henry and Philip, the other most important ones—yes, even *Larry!*—were always at my beck and call. I could order them. I made Henry go thru the tortures of the damned—so that even now that he's married again, I am still his goddess (Heaven forgive me for knowing it); I disrupted Phil's whole brilliant career for 2 years by the power I had over him. Those men in New York were slavish to me—and now Joe—*Joe!* (my darling!)—is making me dance to his fiddle—and every so often he stops playing for long weeks together. I suppose, God, I deserve it. I've tossed people around for my own pleasure most of my life—and I'm paying the piper. Oh, Joe, dear, I don't mind paying a piper who's so exquisite. But my Bill of Human Rights doesn't include any stipulation that I *must* go on paying when you stop fiddling.

—Honey, don't stop! Don't stop.

Arlene came & found me trying to relieve my stinging eyes by forcing tears to wet them (for I *can't* cry anymore). She cheered me up a lot. Gave me a complete massage treatment. We talked of going into an establishment for physical culture at Hyannis together this summer. It would be nice. Money's in it.

The only refuge I can have from this wild love of mine is my writing, or some physical activity. I want to send the boys away to camp for the whole summer, & Sandra, too, if possible. Then I'll write & do promotion for Arlene, and try to live without Joe except when he may condescend to come.

My humble pie is a very big pasty. Yes?

Monday Feb 8/37

I feel *happy* and *good* & *well-disposed* today. Although I *hope* Joe didn't feel badly at his party. I am sure that my wild jealousies, which run an eccentric course indeed, were unfounded. He is a grown man, a dear man, an essentially good man. I wish I could show myself to him in my true light, when I am good as I am *good* today.

There is no excuse for my NOT getting the H.M. Fellowship. To work I go, seriously.

Tues. Feb 9

I love Joe. I trust him and honor him. I believe he is taking a course of some kind—for he is always busy with books & papers in his cab. I wonder if it's Civil Service exams he's getting ready for. Perhaps Aunt J & my mother— But I have little hope of Mother's having done that.

And oh God I love my darling feline, strong, graceful, beautiful, kind, passionate, stubborn, honorable, self-contained, gorgeous lovely man. I want to write him a letter. I may not. I must pour it out in this book, which is designed to provide an outlet for my passion, that I may refrain from 'pestering' him.

Oh God, give him to me by some miracle! I want to marry him. Oh, felicity—!

Will he drop in this morning? Will he? I am hoping—hoping—praying—praying. God thank Thee for Joseph Andrew!

Wed 2|10|37

Here is one of my lucid days. [The moon being all but dark.] And I see everything so clearly, with no emotional coloring. Apart from the fact that Joe has been more to me than anyone on earth, I feel very free and clear of him today. I have written this whole bookful of gush. Many of the impassioned periods of my life since I began it, as a poetry journal, 17 years ago *(17!)* are not in the book. But even the few partly recorded show me up as a tempestuously emotional woman. One after another, my loves have come and gone, waxed and waned. Death has seemed near at hand and very welcome with each amorous catastrophe. The men who've loved me best I've loved least. The ones I have loved best have treated me worst. And it's all a silly pattern of extravagance of the spirit. I am just like the women of all ages and civilizations—yet I seem to learn nothing from experience. I try, trained by Mrs. Magoun, to look at the *meaning* of things now. *What* is the meaning of my love for Joe? I'll be damned if I know the answer, unless it be that all my life I have really deeply yearned to be able to be faithful. [To Henry I was, for the years of our marriage: but it was only a forced faith: I didn't enjoy it. I was true to *vows,* not to him.] And now I take a glorious pride in *wanting* to be true to Joe, even tho' at one time he tried to make me think he didn't give a hoot for fidelity. [When he was preaching 'take life as it comes.'] At this time, I believe *he* is trying to find out what he really wants. I think he's experimenting with the same idea. Possibly I flatter myself. But in his chance remarks he had made it perfectly clear he now *wants* me to be faithful to him. Poor darling. He's so stern and gruff in trying to cover up his almost feminine emotionalism. I think *maybe* I'll win out. Maybe, if I'm patient enough, he will see the folly & threadbareness of a single life …Yet today, somehow, I am unable to visualize marriage to him. The moon is black indeed! I have no passion for anything, not even for him. But, though I suppose this lack of *passion* is responsible, and that I really do care for him steadily … Certainly there was never anyone else I loved like this! … I am bereft of all fire, even the fire of loyalty. Women are moon-mad. Unfortunate creatures, we are—but *powerful.* And when my February moon begins to acquire her power, my consuming passion will return. It is a great satisfaction to know that when it does, it will direct its full force to Joe. What I have needed all along was the proper direction for all this feminine bombast. Joe provides it, having all the qualities I admire, and being sufficiently tantalizing because of his wit and grace and beauty and volatility of temperament. Poor soul! if my devotions make him feel like a brute—and my gifts to him embarrass his real sense of honor—so much the better. If he, *sun*-empowered, but blind, is trying his experiment now, so much the better: for the women or woman herself on whom he bends his attention will be as lacking of moon-magic as I, and he will have tired of her (or them) before my power returns and I weave it round him. [The March moon will favor my designs if the Virgin and the Child are to bring me Luck in the Aintree Races.] And there is this much glory even today: marriage or no, and even if I can never convert him to any sort of emotional domesticity—even to being 'family friend' or perpetual lover—I have found my *man*. And I must harness myself, to his uncooperative gait, and somehow jog along.

… At least for now. And if ever any other man begins to be significant to me, I think I will have some really advanced methods of technique … Funny how my soul rebels, even in this temporary coolness of the day, at the mere *thought* of any other lover for any other time! Well, it's *love* all right, and the real thing.

But can ANY love really endure? The preceding parts of this crazy emotional chronicle seem to answer NO. But, after all, I didn't have Joe ever before the 3rd of July, '35 and how could I be expected to know what love was?

Ah, me, my Love Lord, verily you have bewitched this fool. (Fool. Idiot. Ass.) I will be slow to wean from my hope, my imperishable hope and spark of faith in futures with you.

Feb 11 / My mother's birthday

Saw Joe for a few moments. I have kept carefully away from the Sq since last Sat. And he was glad. He is ill again, poor darling—shivering with the cold and husky. I wish I might care for him in his illness. I wish I had $1000 to give him as a present.

~

Later: He refused to come to my house to have his cold cured. Spoke of 'being foolish,' because seriousness gets one a 'lapful of trouble.'

Feb. 15th

The whims of an unreasonable, unlettered, and busybody landlady (A. Martin, god damn her) may yet cause no serious inconvenience. She sprang a registered letter upon me at the crack of dawn. Jos. Fine (my generous savior!) pronounced her 'month's notice' illegal. Also, legally, we may keep our dog.

Saw Joe in the Sq. He came up, by way of keeping his promise.

We had a perfectly *lovely* talk. He is soothing to female hysteria. I love him, and I trust him, and he satisfies me. I am really not loathe to his being a bachelor. I don't think he'd be a good husband, except in the case of real wealth and leisure. Everything going easily, I think he would be completely charming. I think the Lord intended me for constant struggle: Any sudden wealth, coming, as all things do, from God, would be the only sign I could believe in as an indication to the contrary.

I discussed the idea of going to get a job with Joe. He is beautifully dispassionate—leaves it wholly to me. —He is really both indifferent and courteously assured of my competence to make decisions. (I'll never be a clinging vine, either, shall I, God?)

Feb 16

I resolved to put in one good day job hunting, and did so. Along those lines, it is clear I must stick to my own line—publicity. Made some good contacts.

Also resolved, upon finding the children unreliable, and not obedient to intelligent orders, tho' Jon remained home with a cold, that I am wholly prepared for 6 or 8 more years of poverty, till they are old enough to get together on a small town newspaper to earn their way through school.

Before Apr 1st I shall (without hope) submit my MSS-plans—

name to be changed from "Murder Mrs. Grundy" to "These Two Laws" to Houghton Mifflin.

I shall endeavor to go with Arlene for her phys. ed. lab.'s establishment on the Cape—perhaps to run a summer sheet.

Feb. 19

I *know* my aims now. The children need money, so I'll go to work. I won't rebel against it nor feel dismayed nor martyred now. I'm glad I have Joe to stabilize things. A job first, my book, submitted before Apr. to H.M. My plans: to be with Arlene & start a summer sheet (Cape Cod) if I can secure the children at Camp. Plenty to work for.

Mrs. Wright's *right*: I am now ready for a come-back! Watch me, God!

Feb. 24*th*

Joe came up on Monday, Feb 22nd. He had coffee with us. And we had but a few brief moments, because I was feeling very ill (with flu & "Lydia") and he drove the kids to the University.

I have done some very good writing for the Fellowship Award.

Mrs. (Biddy) Martin has been making our lives excessively uncomfortable in a very ½-assed spitefulness.

I have been disappointed again in my job at the AMERICAN. They won't pay decent wages; and I literally cannot afford to work for 'nothing' (commissions), because I have the children to care for, and, unless I can properly pay a pinch-hitter to care for them it is not worth while to leave them to run wild. They are good advertisements of this deeply-believed theory of mine. But all popular opinion is to the contrary. Most people think the Almighty Dollar more important to a child than a Loving Mother's Personal Care. *I* know better. On all sides I am confronted with: "A woman of your brains oughtn't to be staying at home on nothing-a-week." This Old Girl (me) is pretty wise. Pretty sound in her stand.

Margaret Sutton wrote a peach of a letter to the H.–M. Fellowship Editors. I wonder if my chances are utterly *nil?*

Later (still Feb 24):

After I wrote to thank Margaret Sutton for her kind words, wrote to Wilfred Dube, & his sister, and gathered my wits about me, I went down to Hvd. Sq. to pay the man who shined the kids' shoes 'on tick' yesterday. So, of course, I made a point of seeing Joe. Joe was in a wonderful mood for love (& so was I). He came up (brought me home). He and I had a *very* peaceful (undisturbed) ¾ hour. We had a *wonderful* talk. He is so sweet, intelligent, understanding, and good!

I asked him to come on Thursday (tomorrow) night, & take the day off Friday. I doubt if he will; but today he really *seemed* to love me more than ever he has loved me!

Feb. 26

He didn't come last night— Says he has made up his mind definitely not to spend any more evenings here with the children present. He said "I have some *moral* convictions—"! And when we spoke of my (faint) prospects for money, he advised me to send the Three to Boarding School! I was amazed—very evidently he wants me to himself, & thinks of that as a way to have me. He really does seriously think of me as a part of his permanent scheme, tho' he shies away from admitting it. He was beautifully wroth (sympathetic to my own stand) about my mother's last snooty letter regarding my marrying him— If anything I think his anger against her will increase the likelihood of his consenting to marry at last, though he declares (rather over-emphatically!) that bachelordom is 'his way.' —And I have only hope. He certainly *loves love* with me! And triumphs in our wholly mutual enjoyments. I love him for his fullbloodedness.

I enjoy his company terrifically!

Slowly I am 'taming' him. Long ago he admitted ours had been the paramount intimacy of *his* life.

I could go on & on about my Love Lord! —I pray—I pray! I *pray!!* Oh, God—

(He had 'business to attend to' yesterday.)

(He says he 'has to come 'round to things' by himself—I pointed out he had always been *nagged* into doing things. Says he realizes that—appreciates my not nagging.

I am his woman! He is my man!

May get a job writing pub. publicity (DC Heath) under Bessie Steuber! (Farwell Chambers—of the 20 yrs ago-period. —*Fancy!*)

Hear one way or t'other in the AM.

He came again this AM.

Feb 27

Saw Joe in the Sq en route from DC Heath's with MS. He is *puffect!*

Sun Feb 28

Saw Jos. in Sq. after church. I love that little old darling SO much!

My first experience with Lesbia. —Thwarting and hauntingly 'wrong.'

Mar 1

Joe came, providentially, assuaging the after-frustration. I shall see Lesbia no more. I earned $10 writing an extract from "Civil War & Reconstruction."

Mar 5

Joe came, in answer to my call. We talked of his starting a cab co, independently. I believe he would be very successful—but I cannot make up my mind whether money of mine should be invested, unless he is willing to marry & take a father's interest in my children. He *expects* he says NEVER to marry. I trust *him* a great deal; but *what a sap* I'd be if, with my money for capital, he got it into his head to marry someone else, after he had made enough.

Mar 7

When I asked Jos. yesterday to come today, I had very feeble expectations. But he came, after lunching at his Mother's. We discussed his cab-co-to-be (if I win my Hollidge suit) though he 'made no promises' (as per custom) he practically assented to marriage, if our 'Dream Boat Comes Home.' He was extraordinarily sweet, kissed me very chivalrously at parting. No better investment of my suit-money than to get a husband and, for the Three, a father.

I am *certain* of that!

Mar 11

Peter and I have scarlet fever; and Sandra seems to be getting it. Our house is a stronghold of quarantine, 'ruled' by me, with a Family Welfare supplied practical nurse as lieutenant. Wot a life!

I hope Jos. won't get it.

Mar 30

Mar. 1–5–7–13–17–19–23–26–29
Nine visits in one month from Joseph. He has been *wonderful* all thru our illness.

The Three have been in the hospital. I have been at home being waited on by Mrs Long (a minor saint) provided by Mrs Musgrave's generosity.

Everyone has been grand to us. Althea & Mrs Long & Sister Mary went to see the kids at the Isolation Hospital. Joe has been often to see me, was very helpful with errands, etc. Now on Mar 30, I am about to be out of quarantine. Katharine Sturgis's plants brighten everything for me. And now, with Joe's sweetness as the crowning jewel [for he LOVES me!] what a happy world! *How wonderful!*

April 12

Joe's wonderfulness to me last month came to an abrupt halt. He announces that his secret 'plans' involve a long contract-job with a rubber-company, for which he will act as supervisor of Portuguese & Spanish laborers working to make clearances out of jungle-land north of the Amazon, for the planting of rubber. He will be gone a long time—maybe *years*. Oh, God, I *almost* believe he will go! —Perhaps this is a test. I'd be lost, desolate without him. But he is *my Man;* and I'll wait. —Uselessly, I suppose. It was an awful blow. I knew something was in his mind. His mysterious 'studying' is languages … But MUST he go, God? Can't he live here and live with me? May I not be the wife of the only man I know of whom I would be proud to say 'He is my husband'! Oh, dear God, I'll be true to this love. It has been wonderful. I daren't believe (as I want to) that he is going in order to make money enough to marry me. Let me keep him, somehow.

Lord, it was good of You to send him. —No doubt I deserve your taking him away.

Sandra & I are well again; but my 2 sons are going thru *so* much with their Scarlet Fever. Send them back whole & strong, God! I'll NEVER desert them. Let Joe be their father, please God, please!

May 14

All my moods, which rule me mercilessly in a wide range, from realizations that, for my personal, private life, Joe is utterly essential to existence, if it be tolerable—to high resolutions to live the aesthetic life and renounce all human contact, have been unusually vivid and exacting since my last entry. Now that we are moved (286 Concord Ave) and all my children are gathered together, now that the Hollidge suit cannot be much longer delayed, and there is ever so faint a possibility of H-M accepting my book about Franz, and I have had a whirl of very lovely champagne night-life with Uncle Bob, and Joe and I have come to a 'working agreement' about our life together, and he has, yesterday, paid me very lovely tribute, life seems really fine and exhilarating. And prospects for a change of habitat, to some *far* place, with Doris Nelson to keep me company, and friends who have *always* stuck by manifesting signs of continued sticking, I feel happy as a lark!

But in about 3 weeks' time, with 'Lydia' looming before me, I shall no doubt again descend to cruel lonely depths of desolation— This is all in the life of any temperamental woman. God bless us all, and *thank* you, God!

May 20 '37

Today, because Jos. didn't come, when—for *no* reason—I expected him, I have been MAD again! Mad for Love—sex—whatever you call it. In such a mood, I see clearly that all his lovely silken evasions are nothing more than what Mrs. Grundy's daughters would call 'insults' to myself. —And there continues this war within me, of standards taught and ideals self-propounded. I *wish* I could teach my lover the philosophical way of thought. Yet without his funny charming innocence, he wouldn't be Joe—just Joe. Collins (oil driver) calls him 'shiftless.' What if he is? I don't love him less for that. But when I think of how people of his social level think—

unless I am sure (and sometimes I am not!) that *he* differs from all his stratum—then I know I am being dragged 'down & down, to poverty—etc' as my Angelina says. And Jos. himself tried to show me there was truth in what she said. He is without a shadow of doubt the most winsome combination of facets—my dear, dark diamond. Oh, I love him. I honor him for himself—maintaining himself, aloof, separate, in a different world—from all the rest of mankind.

But he is stubborn, cruel (in a gentle way), lazy. Says all his brains are in his penis—and that may be true, for I never knew a penis so intelligent. Oh, I daren't *leave* him (*if* money comes to me) knowing myself and how I shall go mad away from him. And yet, conversely, what kind of degradation will be the result of my remaining near him.

Boiled down, isn't it a choice between him and my Three. And it MUST, as I told Joe, be my Three. They *can* stay here; so can I. But how will all the years deal with me, a figure growing more ridiculous with age? I have asked God, in Whom I *must* believe, and to whom I have given thanks for my lover with his intellectual genitals, "what shall I do?" And no answer is given. None!

I must go! —At least it seems so just now. Still, reading back in this book for one year, I see it is perfectly hopeless to cure myself of him—the more so, even though I *know* we'll never marry, no matter *what* happens—because he had held me so long and now, on Thursday last has reached the virgin 'Secret Place'—and that will make life barren always, unless I have him.

What the deuce do I, a grown woman with false teeth and hair beginning to whiten, go on making resolutions for? Resolutions are things made by children confessionally. I am neither good nor bad. Life is happy and miserable. My character is only average. I know I can't escape Joe—or my desolation for him if I left him! I do believe I must stay.

Today was offered $25 for a contribution to the American Mercury! Watta break! and they *wanted* my article, too—were bound to have it. Being somewhat in line with "Murder Mrs Grundy" I am the more hopeful of that.

Monday my Hollidge suit comes up before a jury. All this excitement—! Dottie says to stay calm *inside*. If only I could follow advice.

Anyway, God be thanked for Joe. For the children. For this acceptance by the American Mercury.

I might as well accept Joe's recipe for peace and take life as it comes—not holler for a moon that's dead and empty to the hand!

What a crazy, careening world I have! What a nut I am—yet shudder to be called one!

Note: "Uncle Bob" Walsh is a second Burlap—no a third, for Henry is #2 Burlap—as of Huxley's "Point Counter Point." What's the use of putting up with him.

I *adore* Joe. That's enough.

Does Joe mean it when he calls me 'perfect.' I feel he does. But how can a woman of my vanity trust her credulity, especially when the compliment comes from a many-times-proved liar. Oh, happy deception! I am PERFECT. Whew! I wonder if Joe came "to pick up Mrs Jones's cook at #29 Brewster St"—and saw Collins's oil cart standing outside? Oh, bosh. He was too lazy—too irritable—has a cold—exhausted himself with other pleasures— No, he's the carefree, the illiterate!, the nonchalant, the Don Juan. And I *still* thank God for meeting him. And if I will be so foolishly glad to accept so much turmoil, what more do I deserve?

Reconcile yourself, woman, to your own hopeless folly. And submit yourself to it. What else can you do? And don't leave Joe—don't be an idiot. He'd only laugh. While you were sobbing your heart out in some tank town out west.

Les Glenn is the hero—*hero!*—of "Heaven's My Destination."

Just got a note from Wm McFee announcing his arrival at short notice soon. *Pfui!*

*May 21*ˢᵗ

I must confess to more uneasiness about the approaching court-session [Hollidge] than I care to feel guilty of. —Guilty, because of my usual high courage. There is enough 'purple' in the pages of this book alone to make a wonderful case against what Mrs. Grundy calls 'character.' I repudiate Mrs. Grundy's standards wholesale, even though, in planning the story of Franz, I see the urgent need of her authority as mentor—for such people, that is, as perpetrated the crimes resulting from the Boston Police Strike, years ago! Still *I* cannot live if *I* must live within *her* jurisdiction! I woke up this morning cold-sweating to think of the kind of muck-raking a low-life like Hollidge is capable of instituting, but for the acceptance of the truism about pots calling kettles black.

—And somehow I felt rather frightened lest one day even dear Joe be capable of trying to market the long, impassioned love-letters I have written him! *Wh-ew!* Even then, I should never deny the truth of them, nor pay a cent to suppress their publication. I *believe* in my code of honor!

Must be getting old & settled. Looking at Joe's part in my life without any illusions at all, doesn't take away its beauty, or change my mind about the need for continuance with him.

"Shiftless"? Yes. But honorable to me in this matter. We know where we stand. *I* call it *love*. What does it matter what either of us calls it?

The landlady's daughter is in much the same situation—but with a married man, & with continued fear of horrible impregnation. Thank God for my own safe situation with JAM. Hope I can never need another man. I shall certainly accept none, while Joe is available. It is as calm—if only I will realize it, & not get het-up—as a marriage 2 years old. His elusiveness, however, creates proper suspense—saves it from stagnation. Does he do it deliberately?

May 23

For some reason, I have been having *horrible* nightmares every night. That big house—sometimes an hotel, sometimes a museum, sometimes my own mansion—was last night (as it has been before) a House of Pleasure, from which I, and my boy Peter, could not escape. What is this: the 'little house of flesh' that is the body? Lord— and I cannot endure life without a God to supplicate—to explain to—to reason with—to confide in (as if He needed my confidence to *know*—!)—I think Piers Sparkenbroke's dream of death has always been mine. I have been a noted sleeper all my life. There has always been a love of oblivion—my sleeping sickness in '18, my quick and eager submission to anesthesia, my daily need for a nap, my contentment to keep a child's sleeping hours—! I must be a quitter—or a weakling. Joe, even, has remarked my love of sleep. I think he has the same love for himself. Freud would say we, two very sex-loving humans, could sleep for its fantasy-freedom. It's true that almost all my dreams are, according to Freud-propounded symbolism, very desirous. And my mother says I slept the first 8 months of my life. Perhaps I was a child who oughtn't to have lived. I think so—and that I oughtn't to have given birth to 3 more. We are a group of strongly-marked temperaments. All more or less square pegs. —Proof of my love of oblivion has been my deep inner contentment with Joe's love—a love no other woman would accept; while *I* am *profoundly,* ecstatically, humbly grateful for it. Life is queer. Where is Joe?

May 24

Because I told him my trial was scheduled for today, and haven't seen him to say it's been held over again, Joe has studiously stayed away. Why? Lest I think he wants to horn in on any money I may get—and, in pride, he wishes me to KNOW he would not take it? Or (perish the thought!) to *starve* me into chasing after him and laying it all at his feet? This much I KNOW—while he lives in Cambridge, so must we! I *love the man.*

May 25

Still no Joseph: what *are* his reasons, I wonder? This time I must prepare myself to find out from him all the things my own chatter drowns out. Another girl? But he *promised* to let me know. 3 weeks ago he spoke of our 'going on for years'—2 weeks ago I was *'perfect'!* What's amiss—Just lazy man's indolence?

May 26

In a *passion* today I went down on my knees and *urged* God to send Jos. The Lord is very obliging (at times): He sent him. There was an auto-accident outside in the early afternoon. I went to the window—and saw a crowd. Looking down on their heads I said to my soul: "Oh, if only Joe would appear there!" And lo! up drove a 'bus, and off got he! And came with very peaceful, loving mood—though by profession noncommittal. We had *lovely* talk. He had some very queer, thoughtful things to say. Said (of Henry) "He may be married to another woman, but—don't fool yourself!—when he's with her, he's thinking of you." I asked him if he spoke out of personal experience—and he rejected that. Probably within these 10 days he has been with another girl—and found himself thinking of me. What is wrong with me that I have never felt much jealousy in any affaire? Am I as conceited as Jerry the Pharmacist declares and consider my own 'lure' so powerful that I have no need for jealousy? —Joe also advised me ("testing," I think) to humor Wm McF if he asks it. "He's no ordinary person," Joe said. "So why not?" I can't think whether he means to be throwing things back in my face after Wm's fizzled plans for last year. Joe is *deep,* and *thoughtful;* I believe he could be very vengeful, tho he has been very forgiving in little ways to me. He was much pleased with the sun-glasses I had bought him. I saw him put them on as he went up the street. I love him. It seems very weird to me that he can suspect me of guile—for I am much too stupid for any subtlety.

June 1ˢᵗ 1937

We returned very sunburnt and exhausted with suddenly hot weather from dear old Pigeon Cove, the children and I yesterday. It was in a sense a revelation to me to return to that land of my dreams—because I have changed so much. I am able to regard it all quite dispassionately—and tho' everyone rave & roar, it's because of Joe! Joe, dear, delightful lover! he has made my world quite a different place. Let Theology & Mrs. Grundy do their best, the Freudian principle is proven for me for all time. I am a woman, mature, unassailable now. Of course there was a shadow—the great paunch-shaped shadow of Chief Sullivan—cast over it all, because of my days spent (1932) in a madhouse, partly thru his machinations. And maybe the sorrow it caused, and the disruption, is all to the good, despite its lasting effects; for there is nothing more now—unless it be the loss of The Three or Joe that can be too great a shock for me to bear.

The place itself is beautiful—becoming, alas! rather too civilized, with even dear old Hokker's house made 'artistic' and ready for rent to some worldly fool! So life changes with the years!

Today was to be the day the Fellowship Award is announced. I have heard nothing—perhaps shall call up the publisher this afternoon.

Another cloud: Wm McFee sent in a check for $10—which of course, not without dismayed disappointment, I shall return to him when he comes.

And another: Thornton Wilder wrote a silly note in response to my query whether Geo. Brush, lead in "Heaven's My Destination," were Leslie Glenn, erstwhile 'ghostly-lover' of my dreams. I wrote to both Wilder & Glenn my opinion of the painted lilies of the academic life—IMPOTENTS all! (Uncle Bob, for example.) I shall never again be taken in by their high-sounding tommyrot! I am wot I am—and I'll stay so. [Dear, dear Joe!]

Mrs. Magoun wants to see me. No doubt for another "well-bred" lecture. It won't sow oats here! I love her gratefully; and C.L.G., too. But no one buys me out even with kindness.

High-ho! I love life—but I'm so close to the very quick of it I have no time for superficials!

June 2

Well, Joe certainly *has* been the cause of my fine new peace! And I'm grateful to him. He said once: "When you have change of life, you won't care for men any more"—as if I were slightly *different!* He is a clever student of human nature.

—More of a student than Wm McFee, who writes such plausible explanations of the exotic women of his books. They *sound* reasonably, though rare. He came at the end of the most terrifically hot day—brought a box of melted chocolates and gave my Three a pint of ice cream. Then he took me to supper at Lynn Beach. He is so stone deaf, and the weather so terribly hot (scarcely a breath, even from the dark night sea!) that it was far from being a successful evening. He accepted the $10 back without demur, his only comment (a specious one!) "That was for the children." Later when he gets back to Westport, I'll write to him and say how keenly he misjudges people. But I suppose all romantic writers, like my own aspiring self, do garble people for the sake of their profession.

I love Joe very much. Very calmly. I was glad McFee was as casual as I could have hoped. Maybe the menopause set in already—I wouldn't be sorry. Only that I don't want to cool off about *Joseph*—

Later: Joe came this afternoon—looking very tired and unkempt. He needed sleep. I suspect he has been chasing about after some new flame—was repulsed—came to me, because of it, & because I asked him to … And I am hurt. He practically refused our Aug. fortnight. Spoke of one-day a week. Wonder if he'll come to me on any of those days. He was much more than usually considerate—I am wondering, wondering. He's a complex person, my Joseph. Told him all about Wm and my week-end.

Sometimes, after getting a letter like the *snarl* rec'd this pm from 'Uncle Bob,' I wonder if I am actually *bughouse,* for NO ONE likes me much. The behavior of Arlene & Doris, after my hospitality last winter, saddened me—and the gossip Arlene had imparted to Mrs Reed—the general distrust of my sanity in Rockport—all this, and the approach of Lydia, the attitude of Joseph today, my failure as a hostess to Wm McFee—oh, well, I have the Three! But H. always said they'd love me only as long as they knew no better. I will *not* go to Mrs. Magoun in this mood. —Joe, darling, darling— Why did you encourage my going away to live? Are you coming with me? Or are you trying to get rid of me? Was your visit, in such dishevelment today, intended as a slight?

Sunday June 6 – 37 (copy)

"Dear Jos: It would seem that about the time Lydia calls, I am usually suffering from an urge to write you a letter. I know from long experience"—Oh well, I won't copy it—It's merely a letter to reassure him that I won't pass up a real opportunity to comfortable, happy marriage because of him—"dear old thing."

What a truly new woman was I today at the kids' commencement from Sunday School! What a blessing Ch. Ch. has been. God forgive me for many lapses into bitter shortsightedness!

June 10ᵗʰ

Sad Fact (?) for Summer Consumption—
I shan't see much of Jos, alas! he's got something he likes better—a possible 'summer place in Wilmington'— Well, let him have it. He & his mysteries make me ill. (I suppose because I have no mysteries, & can't keep 'em, I am green with jealousy.) But I'm terribly hard up! I need him. He said he'd *try* to come tonight—which means he WILL NOT come tonight. And he's coming 'soon,' which means about the same. If his family *have* a summer place, then I needn't, at least, worry about a rival. I doubt if I have one. He finds the perfection of my love, & the freedom from *any* demands, too joyous & great a gift. I suit him to a 'T.' But, though I simply adore the man, it's time I gave him a run for his money. —Just wait till I get hold of some *dough!* We'll get a car—and oh, boy! we'll go places. And I'll MEET people. Oh, Jos—this is *so* insincere: there'll NEVER be anyone but you for me. And God wanted it so for all our sakes.

June 15

From the 2ⁿᵈ to the 14ᵗʰ I didn't receive one call from Joseph. I was absolutely desolated. I began getting worked up and terribly dismayed. Yesterday morning, when I was expecting to hear a possible 'yes' from the H. M. prize—(and then I heard No) I prayed to God—begged him at all costs not to take Joe from me. (Money is not my province, anyway, I guess) and I asked for yet another of his miracles—that he 'send Joe today!' —I certainly did not expect Joe—but at 11 he came and stayed 2 hours. He declares he has been completely true to me for "ages"—that it doesn't take a sledgehammer to make him see (our love is) "something very special." That he'll spend (at least one of) his days off entirely with me. Oh, Lord, I *love my man*—so much that nothing (except the Three) else is of any real importance— Not even the apparently inevitable collapse of the Hollidge suit, which was predicted by my lawyers yesterday. But, God, I can stand a great deal if only I have Joe & the Three—and mere sustenance. I love them all 4. Oh God thank you for Joseph! Thank you! Thank you! and for the Three.

Of July 6th

Joe was, I think, *really* touched when I told him how we hurried back from N.H. on the 3rd, in my *hopes* that he would spend our anniversary with me. And so on Tuesday, July 6th, after, I will admit, a terrific battle of wills, he consented to come to supper & spend the evening. We had the very loveliest of all our visits together, beginning with a bath together. [Weather very hot.] We talked very freely—admitted his 'yarns' were not vicious—admitted they were "wish-fancy" stories, rather than lies. Told me he *never "2-timed" anyone.* Reasserted his fidelity to me for 2 yrs. Spoke of Florence with candor— [Note: I wept when he said he had *liked her better*—but—well, I have him now, & he doesn't see her (he declares)]. He was *very sweet* all the evening. I am not sure I am right about him, but when he spoke of God, religion, sex—he seemed *utterly* sincere. He was lovely with the children. His silken personality, however, is not unlike Willy Idala's, and I know definitely, that *Willy* cannot be taken for his own value. Oh, Les Glenn was right when he said "You'll NEVER be happy"— But the exquisite happiness of the happy moments—why, they give me courage enough to want to risk marriage—if he will. IF!—for at the moment, though we have grown closer—he still doesn't want to marry.

Still he said he'd never been loyal to one woman so long before. Said heretofore he'd always liked 'quiet ones.' —Always makes a protest too sincere to be mere civility when I suggest a break with him. Oh, Lord God, he is a puzzle to me. But he is your child, as I am; and if we were to be better people, it might well come about by sanctified marriage, rather than this awful doubt & anxiety 2 years long now! Bless Joseph. I shall NEVER regret this. And I do feel sure that he is closer to me than he was. Shall I win—in the end? When? May I have him, & make him happier, kinder, better, while he does the same for me? I am such a FOOL!

July 12

What a day—Full of Joe, & our struggle—"*My* battle"—he called it. Mrs. Marshall saw us confabulating in the Sq. and called him names. All day he was in a fury. In his fury, he also found passion for me—and came here for supper. He LOVES me. Won't admit it. But I *know* it— Lately he has shown all the signs—Possessiveness, Confidences, and a lovely turning to me (which makes my heart glow) in discouragement, or anger, or weariness, or exuberance. I am beginning to *mean* something profoundly *real* to him. He left in fine fettle for *his battle,* against my advice. But I KNOW he won out, & now sleeps, happy, rested, self-satisfied. There is nothing I would not do for this good sweet man.

~

The Entry of July 12 is one of the most important records of my life—a MAN—good, loyal, strong, vigorous, ethical, reflective (and charming) begins to love me with all the depth of his nature. —It must be a sign that I'm on my way to being more than half a woman, now!

July 13

Joe's talk last night, wrought up as he was, may have been unduly vehement—but I woke this morning, after his words had been running over in my mind, thinking that perhaps he will, after all, carry out his threats to 'Leave this part of the country.' In Jan '36 he left his Mother's house because of me—now, considering all things, he may leave town altogether. He promises to return 'on a Thursday.' It is always outrageous in this life to take oaths— But I feel prepared to make my statement that however long away that Thursday may be, I shall save my sex-life for it—*as long as I can possibly hold out.* He has meant so much to my whole life; has made out of a wildly hysterical and foolishly delayed adolescent (as I was) a woman. I can have no rancour against him, for apart from lies (which he admittedly tells in the interests of peace) he has never let me down. It will be hard if he has gone far away for long. But my deepest love, my blessing and my prayers go with him. I cannot but feel I have meant more to him (especially of late) than any of the many women he has had, for he has shown a tendency to turn to me in times of stress of all kinds. That, then, is a sign that I am now no mere shell of Egotism—I mean something to someone else! Progress. —Oh, but it will be lonely without him! He repeatedly declared he would NEVER marry—that his 'style' is that of a bachelor—that he has never said (nor *felt*) "I love you" to any woman. Be that as it may, I have sensed strongly since March that he has loved me, whether or not he acknowledges it. Even if he were never to return—which God will surely not allow—for God approves and sanctions our love, I know—I can not feel I would do foolishly in never taking another lover. Joseph has been my *miracle*. I bless him, and I love him. And if God is gracious, that Thursday will not be long away. "You can almost *count* on it," Joe said himself. It is now my cue (and my test) to wait for that Thursday in as great a calm & clarity as I can muster. There might be this virtue in his leaving town: that an absence at a distance from me might show him he does really wish at last to change his "style," and *marry*. For that I shall always pray. And I shall always love him. God has been good. I want this never to end!

July 17

I think it has ended. Probably the last few tender episodes were manifestations of his 'style' in closing an affaire. Today—all this week—things have gone badly. *Very* badly indeed. He said today that my worry about the pretty round-limbed girl I saw him with in the Sq. was 'legitimate'—and that he had a date with her—'and her husband' (Billy) next week. I resolve today to put an end to my feeling & foolishness.

July 23ʳᵈ

Joe swore if he didn't "leave town" yesterday, he would NEVER leave. If I see him in the Sq this pm (when I go to FWS) I shall know that, with time & patience, I may win him back to the old state again. Marriage, as he says, would be foolish. Living together, out of the question. I'd like love, tenderness & protection. I will never have either from him—but HE SATISFIES ME—that's para-mount. I am sworn to go to N.Y. for one week on $16—in the mid-dle of August. I must snap out of both Poverty & Idleness, for the whole family's sake, & Joe's. And I am *ready*, as Mrs. Magoun says, for this change.

July 28th

At last—after days of horrible, black emptiness, Joe has vouch-safed to talk with me. I did not realize fully how much he has grown to mean to me until the last break. I was *so sure* it would never re-sume. I couldn't even pray to God, because I was so empty and so much at sea. Dear Joe—funny, mysterious dear fellow—I'll make you no more fuss—cause no more scenes—ask no more ques-tions—pester you no more. The hope, prayer, joy and one delight of my life is Joseph.

And again, it sweeps over me how much I have misjudged this man. If only I—poor, crazy fool! could get him for my husband [as I wrongly told him today I did not want him] he would be as dog-loyal, as fine & staunch as he is stubborn now. Oh Lord, only the few kisses of today made life much sweeter! I mustn't write much—this book is nearly full. Before it is full, pray God, I may have better news than that "some day" (or night) he will come again. I must await his coming and conceal & stifle my impatience. *How I love him!*

July 31st

Jonathan off for Camp. Joe consented to come for a 'filling-station' call, declaring it can be nothing else ever, (1) because of the children, (2) because of the Welfare—[Both specious]. I was so hurt over trying to be intimate without any love that the depression lasted all day. 'Relief' is not enough for me. Joe says he LOVES 'it,' but not *me* ("not honourable to say 'I love you' if I don't intend to marry. —And I shall NEVER marry, for it's not my style"—All the time looking *beautiful!* And I love him— Today I was absolutely desolate about life. [The moon is almost gone!] I can never have an-other man—and because I love him, I must sorrow always. But I know I am a fool—*a tool.* Why can't men love & still be *independent?* Talked to Jerry. He was comforting, though, being young, he is callow. At least I knew I'm *'purfect' physically* for a man who knows women thoroughly!

August 16th '37

Emmy Ward is the girl Joe is fascinated with. She's rich, single, a good egg. I couldn't compete there. I wonder how it will turn out? I wrote him to say "Bless you, my children" and that I'm here if he needs me later. Emmy's poker-faced enough to please him.

Oct 1st '37

We had a reunion, a complete understanding. I trust him now. But I have made a fool of myself by *considering* marriage to someone else. But if he comes to see me voluntarily, I shall be completely miserable.

Jan 28/38

In January '38 I ran into the Oxford Group again, God-guided to them without a doubt when I was needing women-friends and a better life apart from my hours with Joe. I have with difficulty told Miss Margareta Williamson what stands between Group belief and my life. She leaves it to me whether or no my conscience guides me to go to the meetings with women who would feel that every time I appeared among them I represent evil, stubborn sin—wantonness! It is not so! God sent Joe in answer to my urgent prayer before I ever saw him. Again & again God has sent him. I know Joe is good, thoughtful, conscientious: I know I am better for him than any woman could be who gave herself for love. And though Miss Williamson shook me terribly by suggesting: "What if he were to marry a young Catholic girl—how would you feel?" There is a deep, dark sympathetic rapport between us. I cannot & will not sacrifice Love as I have been sent it for superimposed standards to which life and loneliness have proved are not *my* guides. I love God. I love the spirit and leaven of the Group. But I love Joe, too. What am I to do? This is the same vexing question underlying all our unrest since

July 1935. And I cannot solve it by Group methods except to surrender to God this question: Can Joe find a way to marry me? I love him. And I trust him deeply. He is not sure himself what he should do: but he is no callow, light-minded tough guy. He is a man whose body, heart & soul are as precious to me as my own and my children's.

May 15th 1938

Last night I read over this book, & was astounded, & glad at the peace and inner calm that now persists, after the years' record of wild dreams, fears, fancies. I am calm, and I thank for it *God,* Mr. Glenn, Mrs. Magoun, and *Joe* and the *children.* I feel so still and sure inside that the little inferiority rubs that still come & go at times are but ripples on the sea. At the present writing, with several vistas backward, when closed or very dim & un-terrifying (e.g.— my family, my headlong, seeking 'Past') I must find more now in my literary-work. (People are 'disappointed' in it!) (Though no one ever tried to encourage me when a little hopefulness might have changed all my life.) Joe is important—but more *psychically* now than physically, & with him it is my office to urge his soul's growth along with mine, now both of us have experienced the "utter surrender to Instinct" the psychologists advocate. I am serene enough—even about him, the Vital Outer Force, to feel confident of my ability to issue ultimata. (I'll be weak, if I don't.) The last outburst of my former childishness occurred when C.L.G. preached on "adultery," & was unblushingly hypocritical in his pulpit. The children are well, praise God, and when, yesterday, I saw Mrs. Cooper and all that kind of life that, due to Circumstance and my peculiar Need (Joe—), I have forever foresworn, I felt no envy or regret. Joe is a MAN—Gregory a refinement. In a pinch, Joe would be the *hero,* I *think* (may be wrong). Greg. is a peach, & I was unreasoningly glad to see him. It gave me a healing sensation. Mrs. Cooper remarked that I looked "assembled." But Peace is a strange state for me. It makes me wonder. Is life about to begin? Or is it over? Q.E.D.

May 17ᵗʰ

Joe came, later in the day than usual—in one of his rare, demonstrative, *really loving* moods. And it has taken me up and out of one of the dullest fits of depression I have ever had! It was remarkable, because, without crowing, he acknowledged, of his own volition, the fact that he has mastered me, the most delightful secret joy I have ever indulged. He was conceding a little in everything, because he knew I wasn't faking. He has grown to put real trust in my sincerity. He thanked me for sewing on 2 buttons, and said, of his own accord, that I had been a blessing to him (sexually) because we are "2 nuts, crazy for it (sex)"—And his man's way of reassuring me of his regard has made me terribly thankful to God for one Great Blessing. —How I have changed. Joe is shrewd: terribly wise. Wonderful. Heroic man!

May 22ⁿᵈ 1938

Yesterday I was horrified at myself. I was utterly rude to a kind woman who offered my boys a quarter "for ice cream." She meant her offer kindly, and, no doubt, in self-denial; and though I thanked her in my refusal, it was with a spirit of angered pride. I am ashamed. I prayed last night to be forgiven; and pray that she be blessed for her kindness. Am I becoming "hard of heart"? I am aware of other signs of dulled spiritual sensibility. I am settling into a rut. God forgive me, & give me grace to come back to Awareness.

August 22ⁿᵈ 1938

Joe is being *wonderful:* I am being *happy:* everything (though decidedly pauperized) is the Most Wonderful Happiness. Oh, Lord, but I am a calm, new, happy woman these days. Thank God for my Joseph Marshall!

Sept 13, 1938

There was an 8-day hiatus in my feeling for Joe—partly because of my own unworthy suspicions of him, based on what remains of the former wantonness that I was guilty of, and partly due to several days' neglect. Scottie got him for me last night, thereby changing the whole complexion of my outlook! He was delightfully peacock-like in the resplendence of his newly-redeemed chauffeur's suit. I love him in a way that tolerates all his peculiar flaws as well as the general ridiculousness of men as a sex. Surely this kind of tolerance in *me* is *significant*.

Dec. 24, 1938

This empty page seems just the place for a summing-up-to-date of the psychological events. For 3 ½ years Joe Marshall, whom I bless with all my heart, has been the center of my life. I do not think I exaggerate or speak harshly when I say that thanks to his (characteristically inchoate) devotion, I have become again a whole personality. Poverty, consistent failure as a writer, and loneliness are now all surmounted. It seems obvious to me that the Lord willed me to be a woman—a mother, and a man's woman—first of all. For the year 1939 I hereby resolve to put aside as secondary all things extraneous to that end. This book, crazy as it is, covers a long period of my emotional chaos. The fact that all the wrinkles are so nearly ironed out, & that my daily diary contains little of the tempestuous (which used to be me!) is encouraging. If only I can convince Joe that I am worthy, willing, & work-hungry enough to be his Mrs Mash—!

Christmas Eve 1938

Along with a newly-whole soul, and a certainty & peace in my heart, comes the consciousness that I *completely* comprehend my religion. No longer do the "mysteries" of it trouble me. I believe in God the Father, God the son, and God the Holy Ghost. This credo is now unequivocal. I also begin to believe in myself. I believe in Jon, Sandra, Peter and Joe. I am free and happy. I thank God for all our blessings. And I ask God to give me the opportunity to bring about blessings for some other person or people. Since 1932 all the world has been good to *us:* it is now my turn to reestablish Faith, Peace and Confidence in someone else thru God and Jesus, *L'Avocat Sanctissimus.* I ask for that opportunity. Whoever the recipient of my work's fruits may be—and I hope it will be my dear Joseph, to whom I owe so much of my own new peace—send him or her in good time.

Oh Father, Son, & Spirit, we thank Thee! Let us do our part now we are healed & whole at last!

Jan 13, 1939

Joe & I came to Vt. & bought the Little House (courtesy of Mrs. [?]).

Feb 20, 1939

We moved to Arlington, Vt. Promises to come with us meant nothing: Joe just "disappeared." We came here alone. I felt very woe-begone, foolish & lost, & tried at first to be conventional in a village full of reactionaries. But it was useless. Before I had done a single improper thing, I got "talked about," so decided to act as I like; & began to "be myself."

June 29, 1939

Joe came. Got a job in Arlington after weeks of terrible grouching, stayed here till Sept 26— Peeved because he was "laid off," he disappeared again— Trying to avoid a scene like the coward he is. The summer was a hell of jealousy for me because Joe cannot recover from the street-corner bum's idea that any available woman must be tried out. Elsie Salter was the worst snake in the grass. Then Joe disappeared. Thinking himself smart, making an ass of me. I desperately tried to forget him all winter. Nearly succeeded. But forgetting him is forgetting I am a woman! I suffered. Thought I was drying up, because no man tempted me.

July 15, 1940

Joe came back. He is making every effort to be pleasant—so far. But he is not trustworthy. He lies— Honor is nothing to him. I love him and really despise myself for it. He is not much of a man.

Joe Marshall, dog Jack, Jon, and Lois (with cat-in-arms Alleluyah), August 31, 1939, at the Little House, Arlington, Vermont.

Peter, dog Jack, Sandra, January 26, 1940 (Peter's birthday).

Lois at the Little House, 1940.

A man without honor is no man at all, even if he has the greatest capacity for sex. Joe is the least honorable man I know. Found (today—July 15) jotted on his Drivers' Record, the name (misspelled!) "Elsie Salter." He is *raw!*

June 12 1941

Since July 3, 1935, I've loved Joe Marshall, wisely, foolishly, inanely, grandly; but it has done me so *much good!* And inasmuch as I prayed candidly to God to send me a lover to *satisfy my hungry body* (at that time, for nearly a year before he came), I can quarrel with neither God nor Joe if Joe still refuses to supply *both* spiritual and bodily needs of love. The nearest to *real* feeling Joe ever showed was on the back porch at Seabury St., Rutland, on Hallowe'en, 1940. Then he was tender. Maybe it was a Swan Song!

March 18, 1946

I am 42 years & 6 months old today—& I BELIEVE in *future happiness with Joe,* at last & TRUST *him so utterly* that the crazy passion I have always felt for him has distilled a wonderful love for us.

At 15 I wrote,

> The blossoms of my love have blown
> And on the pale green branches grown
> Two Roses, whiter than a cloud.

Sincerely: *God, watch over us & give us happiness together.* Amen.

June 14, 1953

…This book is the crazy-quilt that covered my intense life from 1920-'46 … Since then, I have learned SO MUCH. *The Bible* is THE Book. No use writing others. I believe the End of the World is coming very, very soon. I love God.

Dottie and Lois with baby Laura, Pigeon Cove, Rockport, 1910.

Lois pulling Laura's chair (Dottie on left), Pigeon Cove, about 1916.

Journal 1957–1958

While at the Convent of St. Anne
Kingston, N.Y.

January 31, 1957

GROPING
An Autobiography

My life's first memory:

On the morning of my little sister's birth, I woke and found my-SELF neglected. They had moved me, sleeping in my crib, during the night. Waking, I was no longer in my Mama's bedroom! (I *belonged* to Mama! Mama, to *me*.) I struggled up to my feet, hanging to the side-bars of the big crib, placed now in the alcove of the upstairs sitting room. Now I could see a clear reflection of my SELF in the glass doors of the bookcase at the other end of the long room—image of a *displaced child,* square-built, with long golden hair, already pouting for her Mama.

The pouting became a wail. The wail brought Aunt Jessie.

Aunt Jessie told me Mama had a "surprise" for me. The "surprise" was that *baby sister,* Laura (who displaced me!).

After Laura was born, I had to make a life of my own. I was no longer Mama's "Baby." (After 30 years, I was still to resent it!) All I have had to cling to was Mama's promise (which I had extracted from her long before I ever saw that red-faced baby who monopolized her) that we should live together, and die together, Mama and I, & (as I had suggested in my love for Mama) "our bones shall be together in the earth, and our souls shall be together in Heaven."

~

I told a lie, perpetrated a shabby deception, trying to get back my place as Mama's baby. On a hot summer's night, at the seashore cottage, when Laura ("the Baby" now!) was being fussed-over, and "changed" with much twittering and cooing by both Mama and Watsie—(Watsie, who never gave up trying to comfort me, the rejected (former) baby!)—I *deliberately wet my bed*—fresh linen and all, & cried for attention from Mama. Mama didn't even answer my call! Watsie came. She scolded me gently. She preferred to *believe* my LIE. (I said I was *asleep* when I made that big puddle in the clean bed.) She deftly changed the linen, and went back to tell Mama it was a "mistake." Mama knew better than to believe her. I could hear the scorn of my lie, of my feeble deception, in Mama's low voice.

After that, I gave up making any *conscious* attempts to recapture my babyhood place. Watsie became my substitute-refuge:—in times of cut fingers, barked knees, snarled hair, I could count on Watsie's tenderness and understanding. She gladly forgave me everything I ever did. Watsie had no children of her own. She was *glad* to accept the rejected baby of Mama, her friend.

The LIE, the attempted DECEPTION concerning that wet bed on that hot summer night remains in my memory as a reproach to my innocent childhood. No one had told me of the Tempter, God's Enemy, who will prey even upon the weaknesses of five-year-old children, to bring Sin upon their souls, to taunt God the Father with the innate frailty of man, His creature.

(How I wish that every soul born on earth could be made to understand that *every* lie, every *deception*, every "*cheap*" or *spiteful deed*, or *thought*, of which we are capable is an "act of worship" to the *Enemy of God!* I do believe that even a moron would not want to sin, if he realized his sin was Satan's triumph over the *gentle Son of God* who *commanded us only* that we *love one another!*)

It was not considered "wise," in those days of my first sorrow, to "frighten" innocent children with thoughts of the Evil One. (My Mama had been so frightened in that way by her nursemaid, Jane, that she *never* recovered from it!)

—And in the stormy years of my growing-up, because of my Ignorance in this matter, I was such an easy prey to the Devil, that he —ever he, Arch fiend & violator of a small child's clean soul!— must have become bored indeed with my stupidity and easy assent to his promptings. *Accursèd* Satan! You, too, lost your place with God the Father, who had made you a bright angel of the morning before man's Time began.

For a long while, my baby-sister was of no use to me. She lay in her crib or carriage all day, and cried half the night. The more of a

Dottie, Lois, and Arthur Henderson at 78 Phillips Avenue, Pigeon Cove, Rockport, about 1905.

Aunt Jessie B. with Lois, Dottie, Gretchen Simpson, Watsie, and Isabel, 1905 or 1906.

nuisance she was, the more Mama loved *her*. Her food didn't "agree" with her. She was called a "delicate" child.

I turned to my older sister for companionship. Dottie was 10 years old—a "big" girl, pride of my parents, for her astonishing beauty and her unusual intelligence. She was treated, even then, with "respect" (which *I never attained!*) (—I was the middle child, neither youngest, nor oldest, an ignominious position in a family.) Dottie had been taught to *read* at the age of *three!* When, at 10, she lay on her stomach on the floor, poring over the Waverley novels, I walked around her in jealous mystification. How could *she* have that secret refuge from reality, when *no one bothered* to *suggest teaching me* to read? I was not spurred to learn myself. I was dolefully jealous of Dottie's attainment, without ambition to achieve it for myself.

It must have been *reading* that gave Dottie such fertile ideas of imaginative play. She picked me as the butt of her experimental fantasies, often scaring me badly, & threatening more tortures, if I "*told on her.*" Once, enacting the part of some vividly-"lived" tyrant, she forced me to lie on the chopping-block, by our cellar wood-pile, & brandished a heavy axe over my throbbing throat, crying *"Off with her head! Off with her head!"* like the Red Queen in *Alice*. The janitor, Albert Sanford, "rescued" me (if, indeed, I was in danger of anything worse than her accidentally *dropping* the heavy axe!)—but Dottie *denied* the whole episode categorically, when Daddy scolded us for such "dangerous games."

I was deeply disappointed in Dottie's "cheap" lie! She should have been 'above' lying—in her unassailable security as oldest child of doting parents. Nobody listened to *my* testimony. They *believed* their *firstborn!*

I was always punished for wrongdoing—hers, as well as my own, because she *"lied out"* of her part, & *someone* had to bear the brunt! I suppose that is why I learned very early to regard lying as rotten cowardice (& have never yet forgiven myself for my own jealous lie about that wet bed, that summer night). Christ Himself called Satan the "Father of Lies." —How could I know that even my beautiful big sister (whom I followed slavishly and adoringly) could be prey to Satan's promptings?—could take a lie upon her own pretty pink tongue, and be defiled by the *Enemy of God*—as I had been, was, & was to be defiled my life long!

I felt very *safe* when Daddy held my hand, and took me walking beside him at his steady pace (trained as an officer in the State Militia, as a younger man) through the enchanted world on a bright summer morning at the shore! Daddy's hand held mine warmly, firmly, securely, as I capered along beside him. His hand restrained me.

(A good father restrains his children.) In the years following, during sorrow and bleak loneliness, in fantasy I was often to reach out to hold my Daddy's hand again; to long for protection and restraint.)

We passed, going up the big hill under leafy tunnels, a fearsome spot Dottie called "The Snake Pond." —Daddy said not to be afraid: there were probably no snakes there today! —(Snakes always terrified me, as they have terrified all the daughters of Eve since her traffic with the Tempter-Serpent in Eden!) I was not afraid even of the Snake Pond, when I held Daddy's strong, warm, restraining hand. I stepped beside him all the way up that lovely wood-girt road, to the little waiting-station, where the old trolley used to stop. Daddy bought us Salem Gibraltars—(creamy & delicious sugar candies, made according to a pre-Colonial recipe, by the Pepper Candy Company) (still obtainable in the "Witch City" of Salem, Massachusetts). We wrapped the paper around the base of the candy, & (stickily) "licked" the sweet stuff all the way home— Daddy kept the Sunday paper tucked under his arm, & held our hands, going home again. Dottie was eager for the "funnies," because *she could read*. I couldn't read, and didn't care about reading, and was jealous of whatever took people's attention. I *resented* "funnies" that kept Dottie from playing games with me.

I went out to the "playhouse"—which was not a house at all, but a circular clearing Daddy had cut for us at the base of a beautiful oak-tree, in the woods next to our summer-home. He had hung our big swing from a safe limb on the oak. Till I had finished my candy, I sat on a low, supple limb of that familiar, motherly tree, bouncing gently up & down, looking up into the branches that obscured the sea-clean blue sky.

I dreaded to climb up that tree. (Dottie often did it.) I would do it *alone*, while nobody was looking, to test how high I dared to go, from branch to branch. I spent a long time, clinging to the smooth-barked strong trunk, creeping higher and higher, from branch to branch, till I was on a level with the bedroom windows of our house across the wide lawn. I could see Mama and Watsie up there, bending over the big bed, where they were dressing Laura, the Baby. (She was getting bigger now, almost ready to walk.) How they cooed and gurgled to *her*, oblivious of the whole world! Mary Healy, the maid, was singing a lilting song in the kitchen. Daddy was pushing the lawn mower. Far out on the water, a busy granite-laden barge, bearing huge blocks of stone, was being towed around the rocky point by a strong-hearted red tug-boat. Churchbells began to ring in the village, 2 miles away. A sea-breeze blew between the oak-branches, & my long yellow hair got in my eyes. Carelessly, I let go my hold on the branch, to push the hair away—felt myself slipping, & frantically clutched out—

Ugh! My hand came in contact with a furry carpet of young caterpillars, nested in the tree-bole. Their soft bodies oozed slimy yellow-green custard under my frantic fingers. With a shrill scream, I *fell out of the tree-top*, to the hard ground below, striking my head on a root under the swing.

It was Watsie who heard me, above the household sounds: Watsie, who rushed downstairs and out across the lawn, to gather me up, & comfort me—as she did for many, many years to come, in every kind of sorrow I was to have. Dear, gentle, loving Watsie! Her deft fingers parted my hair, & caressed my bruised temple. Her spinster's bosom was firm and soft. Watsie was a trained nurse, most skillful at her profession, infinitely gentle, inexhaustibly compassionate! Bless her dear, tortured soul! When she died, at 83, in Arlington Hts, Mass, she was completely *insane*. The Devil of Oedipus had "possessed" her all her life—and who could ever have *suspected* it? Certainly, not the child whom she comforted and "understood" (whom all the rest of the world "rejected"). Watsie, *my refuge!* God forgive her, and God be compassionate to her, as she was to *me*. Bless dear Watsie!

Mama *scolded* me! (When Mama was upset—as she was, about my fall—her "nerves" always caused her to *scold me!* (How could *I* know it was an expression of loving concern?) She *scolded* me for my hurt. All her life, all my life, she *scolded* me! But Watsie soothed me. Daddy, when his lawn-mower was quiet, & he heard the subsiding sobs I stifled on Watsie's shoulder, came out to inspect the damage done to me, to test the sturdy ropes of the swing, & to climb up the tree himself to burn-out the caterpillars' nest. Mary Healy banged about the kitchen still singing lustily. Mama stood in the window upstairs, holding the Baby, Laura. Dottie never rose from the porch floor, where she lay, poring over "Mutt 'n' Jeff," the "funnies." Only Watsie and Daddy cared enough for me to come to me … In years to come, I always turned to Watsie, in deep troubles.

~

The years and concentration I have spent WRITING—! Yet, even if there has been a wealth of personal experience and sharply-remembered beauty to draw upon for "material," there is nothing *worth* writing about! Prophecy is being fulfilled with alarming accuracy today: it is clear to everyone that the end of the world is not far … Could one's sympathy be better invested than upon the Early Christians who, so long ago, waited for the return of their Christ to rule this world in peace and justice? They were told *by Him* that *He would come* —! Warned that His coming would be "sudden and swift"—They who had known Him as a man upon earth among them, lived and died, still awaiting his preciously-cherished promise to return. He is not yet here!

The Serpent rules us still, and every day more slyly, more triumphantly. We know about the parable of the fig-tree in the Spring;—we have heard the Promise; reason tells us that *eventually* it must be fulfilled; & all current history confirms the expectation. We know all the warnings against being caught by it, unawares, our "lamps untrimmed." —Yet blindly, we go on with our stupid sinning, in league with the Tempter whose triumphant glee is all but audible to us.

"Generation of vipers," indeed we are! Hosts of "vipers" have lived and died … The world still is waiting for its own destruction. Picture the mass of humanity alive today—and the silly moron's smirk upon its collective face, as it idles the "little time" away, beguiling itself with all that was 10 centuries ago forbidden by Him who is to be the Judge!

We know; and we care not! We "pooh-pooh" the warnings He gave when they are repeated to us.

~

"Each man for himself" is the spirit of our time. This week I saw seven old ladies, in a "home" where they are being sheltered in spendthrift "creature comfort" until Death overtakes them. They sat at the dining table, eating succulent food, expressions of in-dwelling discontent and jealousy contorting their wrinkled faces. One, seventy-six, stared off into space as, with costly dentures, she masticated her food, thinking about her unhappiness and small de-bilities, a plate of muffins, napkin-covered, before her. She was asked: "Will you have a muffin?" She replied, "No, thank you." Never glanced to left or right to see if others near her *would* "have a muffin";—went on chewing and pouting, sorry for herself because her petty desires are not *all* fulfilled. To her left, a bitter old woman cursed with the weight of wealth she means to dispose of, somehow, before she dies without *giving "one cent of it"* to *expectant heirs,* lunged across the decorous table, grabbing the muffin-plate for her-self. *"Oh, for God's sake,"* she said hoarsely, choking over the morsel between her teeth, *"loosen up on those muffins!"* She put two on her own plate, replaced the napkin cover, & went on staring into space at visions she sees of lurid and lewd occurrences that are ever before her deranged mind's eye. A third old woman, this one a British lady, reached for the muffin-plate and passed it to her next neighbor, a devout Churchwoman of 90. "I don't eat hot bread," she remarked. "But, I say, wouldn't *you* like one?" The ancient Churchwoman, shaking her head, replied: "I don't hear what you say. I'm getting very deaf, you know." The British lady, angry, muttered: *"Idjot!"* and made no further attempt to pass the muffins.

After the meal, the muffin-plate returned to the kitchen untouched, except for the two on the plate of the wealthy one. These, she carried out to the garden to feed to the birds.

The cook had labored one hour to make & serve hot muffins to the "dear old ladies" at the Guest House.

~

New York City has a widely-accepted slogan: "Mind your own business." If at any time there was virtue in the idea, none remains in it now, for it is today only a formula in defense of selfishness.

I have seen dreadful occurrences on the public streets of New York, to which the citizenry, hastening on its individual, greedy way, paid not the slightest attention. If prodded into noticing them at all, the public evoked its sacred formula: "I mind my own business."—

On Third Avenue are many bars & taverns. One day—in a grey, cold winter, two angry men, very drunk indeed, were catapulted through the swing-door of the tavern by its "bouncer." They continued their altercation fiercely, loudly & drunkenly, on the sidewalk. People passing merely separated into a double stream around them, frowning at the annoyance, but not interested in the incident.

One of the two was a great brute of a man, with hands like hams, clenched in fury. The other, a slight, weak-chested figure, had strength in his tongue, & "spoke up," in drunken fearlessness to the other, who bore down on him fiercely. At last the huge one sprang upon the small one, grasping him by his skinny throat. In a short tussle, the weaker man was flat on his back, the giant sitting on his body, squeezing his throat with both hands—while passers-by continued on their way, averting their heads.

When the great clenched hands had all but squeezed life itself from the smaller man, I cast about me for help to prevent murder being done right there on the public street. "Will *you* stop that fight?" I asked a smug little Irish lawyer in cheap new clothes, who carried his briefcase like a standard. *"They're killing each other!"*

"Not *my* business, ma'am" said the lawyer, pushing by me. *"I'm due in court in ten minutes!"*

I caught a glimpse of a face in the window of the bar-room; opened the door and called inside:

"Somebody come! Hurry!"

A half-hearted growl of protest rose from the dim interior.

"They ain't on my property, lady!" called the bar-tender. "We just t'run 'em out here."

In desperation, I acted on my own. I rushed over to the great hulking figure whose brutal strength by now had all but squeezed the last breath from his recumbent victim.

"So, Mister!" I hissed into his red, hairy ear *"Your wife wants you!"*

Instantly the great hands relaxed, the bleary eyes of the giant took on a glint of terror.

"Where's *she* at?" he muttered, managing to stagger to his feet. (I could see blood returning to the cheeks of the beaten one on the bricks below.)

I pointed to the nearest corner.

"There!" I lied to him. "She's standing behind the building. She's after you!"

"Je's" said the brute.

Without another word, he hastened away.

I had saved a life in the City that "minds its own business."

~

On Avenue A, there were children, and dogs and cats who were hungry. They were so hungry they had to steal off pushcarts passing by, propelled by angry peddlers at a loss to defend their wares.

But in Central Park an overfed Pekinese with a flannel band around its belly minced along the walk, self-consciously deliberate in his leisurely self-interest.

At the other end of the leash was a wispy, faded old lady, beaming pridefully at the fat little dog, casting timid glances at passersby, to elicit admiration for her pet.

In compassion for her deluded weakness, I obliged her.

"Nice pup." I said, conquering my aversion for the unnatural-looking little beast, which permitted me the liberty of scratching its ugly head. "*Gentle*, isn't she?" I said to the gratified owner.

"Gentle, yes!" She said. "Her name is Genevieve." She blushed.

"Intelligent, too," I hazarded. "*Nice* Genevieve!"

"*And* ever so discriminating!" boasted the proud little human woman whose life centered round the odious dog. "My cousin brought in a pint of Sherry's chocolate ice-cream, last week; & since then Genevieve just won't eat any other brand! —She's a *fussy* little thing!"

We parted. I had done my "kind act" for that day.

~

One beautiful Spring morning outside the Art Museum on Fifth Avenue, a great green bus charged up to the curb, to let off a passenger. She was a heavy-set, middle-aged woman, with a seeking look on her lonely face. Obviously she intended to visit the Museum. After the bus departed, she had crossed the street, and started up the broad steps, in the wake of other visitors. Then I saw her look back over her shoulder. An eager look lit her weary face.

Following her glance, I saw its object—a baby in a handsome English buggy, pushed by a uniformed nurse, had appeared from a mansion's doorway on the side street, across the Avenue.

Impulsively the woman on the Museum steps hurried back down to the curb, hastened across the street, approaching the baby carriage.

She spoke to the infant in a pleading tone.

"Hello, darling!"

It may have impressed her that the nursemaid suspected her sanity and her motive, and tried to get by the barrier of her thick-set body planted in the path of the baby-buggy. But I think she did not notice at all! Her eyes were full of tears, and her mouth trembled.

She said to the baby, with a half-sob:

"All *my* children *went and grew up*—*!"*

Then she swung about on her heel, and recrossed the Avenue, to climb the steps into a Museum full of paint-and-plaster representations of Humanity & Love.

~

When I learned to read—at last! a big girl seven years old!—I spelled out the mysterious letters painted high on the facade of the big steam laundry we could see from the window of Daddy's room—a smart-alecky sloganeers' perpetration that read:

This achievement in decoding cuneiform set my puzzled mind at rest, and made me glad I had finally mastered the art of reading!

Our back windows looked out across our own clothes-yard over a number of other yards, lots and gardens to the shabby street on which the laundry-building stood. I did not venture to walk on that street: only colored people lived there, the families of waiters and bus-boys and porters at the University. I had seen their shiny-eyed, white-toothed babies and children. But Daddy forbade that little street for us. (He had been raised for ten years of his childhood in Georgia, and was what today would be called a "segregationist." His use of the opprobrious term "nigger" always paled my Yankee mother's cheeks, and set her lips in silent protest—for she was the daughter of crusading Abolitionists.) My father made no secret of his unChristian sentiments: indeed, he rather prided himself upon them—so that, one year, when he "ran for mayor," he was defeated because he lost the large block of colored votes.

A couple of years later, I learned that, as his child, *I* was hated by the *children of the colored voters*. They "ganged-up" on me, as I walked down the sidewalk, pouncing-out upon me from behind a tall board fence near the livery-stable. They fell upon me, and yanked out great fistfuls of my long yellow hair. One big girl of twelve slapped my face so hard, it raised great welts of red. They told me I'd "better not tell," or they'd "git" me again.

I *did* tell—but only Mama; and Mama, comforting me as best she could, attributed it to *me*. She said I had somehow "offended" the colored children in the public school. She warned me *never* to "tell Daddy," lest to get some colored man into trouble over it. I

Arthur Richard Henderson.

was very scared of colored children after that—until I met Bessie Merriman. She was a very black and beautiful negress, star of our class, who later trained for teaching. She was a sweet girl, and I loved her so much, I forgave the others who had attacked me.

I still do not remember ever having offended any of them—certainly not intentionally. I think my beating was a visitation of "the sins of the fathers."

If he lived today, I am sure, my Daddy would be neither a "segregationist" nor a Republican. He was a reasonable man, with a kindly heart. —Today's history would not have found him wanting.

~

In one of the gardens over a high board-fence I could see from the window-seat in Daddy's bedroom, there was a neat and weedless vegetable-garden, grown in straight rows, each marked with its seed-packet-on-a-stick. The garden was scrupulously tended by a very old man named Mr. Phillips, who was said to be nearly a hundred years old.

He was too old to work under a hot sun. He came out of his little brown house, with its two slate-roofed gables, just about the time I came, every evening, before dinner, to watch the sun set behind the row of poplar trees and the chimney-stacks of the laundry. I learned to love that old man because he so diligently loved his lettuces and parsley. He had a long, white beard that touched the earth, as he bent over his weeding.

In my mind, I always called him "Father Time."

When I was fifteen, the neighbors told us that old man had "taken cold," and was very ill with pneumonia. I had never spoken to him in all my life; but I loved him dearly. He lay ill a long time; and I often prayed for him in my bed at night.

At Sunday School, we were practicing Christmas carols. It came to me that "Father Time" would be pleased to hear children's voices singing under his window at Christmas.

Almost stealthily, I organized a group of little girls. We practiced, secretly, "Silent Night," "Noel," "A Little Town"—and when Christmas Eve came, four of us stole into his snow-filled garden through the ancient picket-fence, and sang to him.

It is one of my most deeply-cherished joys still that he sent us a message of thanks, by the old women who nursed him through his illness.

But I was very much embarrassed when Mama mentioned it aloud at dinner: it seemed an invasion of my inmost secret life to have such a thing spoken-of by grown people.

~

When I was seventeen, I was very lonely. Mama had withdrawn from life (menopausally) at that period. My older sister was a College girl, in a world apart from mine. My younger sister had a friend named Lucy. It was a summer of loneliness I spent that year, at the seashore. I was *exquisitely sad*—(some of the time).

One morning we woke to a bright day following a northeast gale that had lashed our rocky shores during the past week. The high waves from mid-ocean had reached our tawny granite cliffs. Thunder of crashing surf shook the ground near the shore.

I went away for a long walk, with my little spaniel, Friday. We threaded our way along the shore-top, on a winding path through the low underbrush to a little grove of wild-apple trees and locusts, where soft, shiny grass lay very green, dappled by sunlight moving behind scudding white clouds in the rain-washed blue sky. We stopped in that quiet grove five minutes to hear the joyous birds singing to the sun. Even there, the thunder of the sea could be heard as background music to the *arias* of the joyous robins!

The path led along a granite-rubbed ridge covered with bayberry and blueberry and catbriar-growth, before it came to the cliffs and open ledges of granite above the wildly surging flood-tide. I stopped to see the rosy-&-white baby-faced fruits of the wild cranberries in a little bog, as we mounted the slope to the top of the bluff, against whose unmovable fortress the angry ocean was flinging tons of foam and spray, & spatterings of seaweed and broken shell, high into the air, and over the top of the bluff, into the bushes.

Such sea-fury exhilarates me! My little dog was somewhat doubtful. I picked him up, & carried him to a spot behind a safe boulder, where we could sit comparatively dry, with only occasional spatters of heavy salt water drops breaking overhead.

And I sang an extemporaneous song as loudly as I could shout it into the north wind and the din of the water:

> The sea is *my* father!
> My own blue-eyed mother
> Alone knows this secret—
> Nor told any other.

Such a morning I will never forget in all my life! It was an orgy of self-expression hurled into the teeth of a storm God wrought.

Mar 21, 1957 Libbett would be 51 today

Libbett

Libbett was my friend. We played together constantly, every day, every summer, for ten years. I was five when I first met her. Mama and I went to "call" upon her mother, pushing my baby-sister in her carriage (because it was the maid's "day-out").

Libbett was sitting on the steps of her low front porch. When she saw me in a new pair of brown sneakers, walking beside the baby-carriage, she opened her mouth and, in her characteristically loud, plaintive voice, wailed—to her mother, darning socks in her rocker on the porch.

"Moth-er," why can't *I* have a pair of brown shoes like *that* girl?"

And that began years of a lovely childhood association. It was a devastating blow to me when—*and how*—it ended!

Libbett was easily dominated, because, by parental conditioning, she had no experience in making up her own mind—or even of making a simple choice of alternatives. (Such things had always been done *for* her. She stood by, waiting for "orders.") Thus, when, running through the forest-paths behind our summer home, we came to a fork—if I said "Which way—Libbett? This—or that!" she would stare plaintively, with tears coming into her lovely grey green

"The Inseparables," August 29, 1916, Pigeon Cove, Rockport (Lois on right).

eyes, and answer—"*I don't know*, Lo-is!" *I* had to choose. After many such instances, I *gave up asking her preference, & chose for us both.* —I was the leader; she the unquestioning follower, until some choice involved a matter of parental training. "Father won't *allow* me to do that," she would say then; & there was no shaking her.

We played together for ten happy summers—"The Inseparables" we were called. We wrote letters to each other at least once a week all winter. "Best friends," we called ourselves. And then came *Boys* into my life. To Libbett *Boys were forbidden*—with the exception of her two brothers. "Father doesn't allow me to play with boys," she stated.

Our ways began to diverge at that juncture.

Libbett, when I was sixteen, sent a message to me at the beginning of the summer, by her brother Steve, the day our family arrived at the shore.

"Libbett tells me to tell you she doesn't want to see you this summer," Steve said. He touched his baseball cap, and peddled away on his bike, leaving me speechless. He gave me no explanation. My heart was close to breaking …

That summer Libbett-and-I were "done for."

It was perhaps three or four years later that people began to say Libbett was acting "queer." Her condition grew worse and worse. From time to time I heard news of her, & her series of ailments, doctorings & treatments.

In 1925, when I married, I invited her to my wedding. She refused to come. Steve planned to come, but something "prevented." After my son was born, I MUST show *my baby* to Libbett. I was in New York then, and she did consent to visit me. But the visit was a dismal failure, because my husband brought home a friend to have dinner with us. Without words, Libbett told me with her eyes "Father doesn't allow me to have men-friends."

When Libbett died a violent death at the age of 43, by jumping out of a 7th story hotel window, Steve told me: "Libbett said *you* ruined her life, because you bossed her all her life!" Bless Libbett's soul, Father in Heaven. *Was it* I who "ruined" Libbett's life?

June 1, 1957   Aboard the *Danish Motor Ship "Brigitte Torm"*

To A New Life—The Journey to Primavera.
Aboard the M/S "Brigitte Torm,"
bound for Buenos Aires, May 31, 1957

At last it has begun! It has taken all but six weeks of this past year to earn the money for my trip—OUT OF THE WORLD. I, who've never saved a dollar in my life, have banked most of my earnings since July 1, 1956, for this exit from my former way of life! I could not possibly have done it without the loyal, loving, prayerful backing of the Woodcrest Community of the *Society of Brothers*.

In 1955, at this same time of year, I sailed the seas before. Then I was a tired, disillusioned middle-aged woman, still clinging (unbecomingly) to the hope of "Travel-&-See-the world" adventuresomeness (that was stifled in youth, and seemingly *impossible*, thereafter). But I had found I—a grandmother!—*could* earn my way, serving as stewardess, on Norwegian ships. I worked hard; and I saw "foreign ports"; but, of course, I was *not* happy. How *could* I be happy when my life was *self*-centered?

Aboard my last ship, God sent me the key to the "open door" that stands ready for *"seeking" people* to enter into the *new life:* life in true Brotherhood. On that ship, I met Will and Kathleen Marchant, an English couple of middle age, who were traveling back to Asunción, Paraguay, to rejoin their family of 8 children at Primavera, the Society's longest-established Community, in the Paraguayan jungle. These kind people told me of the "open door"— (which, they reiterated emphatically—"swings *both* ways" to admit interested guests who wish to participate in the true *sharing* of "church-based intentional community").

(ALWAYS I had sought (hopelessly) for a chance to work *for God!* ... No Order would admit me—a worldling; a divorcée; usually a "mis-fit" in any organizational set-up ... No world-Church satisfied my critical demands for all-out *living* of the faith ... And I was never a "joiner." —But I longed deeply, and ever more needfully, as I emerged from the turmoil of youth and motherhood, and saw— aghast!—that when children are grown-up, and launched upon their

At Sea,
June 7, 1957
Dear Jonathan
& Catherine.

You asked for a picture of this ship. She is just about the same size as Mickey Mouse's *Hoegh Claire*. But she is much cleaner, better kept, & more convenient. Each cabin has a private tiled bathroom, with fine green porcelain fixtures, & a glassed-in shower, with *HOT*, *COLD* & *SALT* water. My room-mate is a little girl, 11 years old. She is the daughter of missionaries, returning to Brazil from Alberta, Canada, with 4 of their 7 children. [(3, left in Canada, for high schooling) The others are Jimmie 9, Joey, 8, & Dotty, 4. They are very well-behaved aboard ship. They've all had an adventurous life, as missionary people. The father is a (polio-victim) hunchback — yet he *drove* them all (2 adults; 7 children) a year ago, by *JEEP*, over *LAND*, (across the Panama isthmus) from eastern Brazil to northern Canada — 12,000 *miles*! The mother wrote (& *PUBLISHED*) a book about it. All of them have made TV "guest" appearances in the USA & Canada.]

The Capt., officers, & crew are all Danish & quite extraordinarily "high class." The Capt. takes evening dinner with us, each night. He is a youngish man (42), very "*ge-mütlich*" (or "easy-going") — to passengers, anyway (but he has excellent shipboard discipline over the crew.)

own way, there remains nothing in life for their loving mother to work for! … I was a lonely, unlovely woman of 52, when I shipped aboard the M/S "Bow Santos," as stewardess, bound for Buenos Aires—working my way, to "travel-&-see-the-world" (belatedly) … And what *is* there in "the world" to see, except more of the futility of living—in other ways; in other places? Restlessness drove me. — The only books I carried with me were the Bible and the Episcopal Book of Common Prayer.)

Will and Kathleen impressed me at once. I had heard from the steward that a pair of "Brothers" were on our passenger-list. They were "good people," he said. The Line had carried many of them, up and down, for years.

What I saw first was the tip of Will's long brown beard, up-tilted as he leapt up the gangway, followed by Kathleen, his wife (the other "Brother"). He had a cheery greeting for me, as I peeped down the steps, waiting to show passengers the cabins assigned to them. His first words were:

"I say, *we're* here now! You can shove off, anytime!"

Kathleen, beaming kindly, followed more sedately.

They were model passengers, from a stewardess's point of view—considerate, cooperative, compassionate. (Going over the Line, in the degrading heat, they understood why I sometimes wept into my mop-pail as I scrubbed. —They forbade my *'slaving' for them*: they looked after their *own* cabin.)

I made their acquaintance as soon as I could after the "All-Ashore" call broke up the cabin-party in their quarters. Several members of the Woodcrest Community had come aboard with them, bringing trunks, boxes, suitcases, & barrels full of gifts and goods for Primavera. (Dick and Lois Anne Domer were there, & perhaps their first child, Henry—I am not sure.) The love and joy they all felt in each other's company, and the gales of laughter to be heard from them, showed me clearly these were no long-faced pietists! Whatever their religion, it was a *happy* faith. —And there were *children* in it … (Where is there happiness without children?)

As soon as I could corner them, and tell them I was *seeking*—for something—something better to live for, to live by, to make each day an event-in-time—Will said to me:

"Visit Woodcrest, when you get back to the States. You can't find out about Community until you have *lived* it. Just write, at least, two weeks in advance, to see if they have a room for you."

"But I haven't much money—!" I began—the years'-long plaint of the wage-slave rising automatically to my lips.

"You can *work*," said Will. "We see you work aboard ship. —If one works, one eats, & has clothing & shelter."

—And so, all that south-bound trip I haunted Will & Kathleen whenever I was free. I discovered that they were "good sports," who could join in the shipboard festivities without prim disapproval, nor gloomy wet-blanketing antics even of the most mawkish sort, at cocktail parties. Will drank beer, smoked a pipe, & even sipped a cocktail, or two. When things passed the sedate stage of social intercourse, & officers and passengers became riotous & ribald, Will & Kathleen didn't shed a pall of gloom over the ridiculous capers of uninhibited adults at sea. After a while, they quietly withdrew. Never a word of disapproval—no matter what they felt about the degeneration of dignity on the part of others!

Kathleen & I played many and many a game of Scrabble. The first & most frequent topic of our conversation was always *children*. I marveled at her placid assurance that the 8 children she had left behind in Primavera, a year and a half ago, would still be as safe, as happy, as well-cared-for by the community as if she were "on location" with them herself.

That is one very salient factor in the life-of-community. All children belong to all mothers. All mothers care for all children. —Yet the family unit is preserved in its individuality with zealous respect for God's plan for personal parental responsibility.

Kathleen was excited by the possibility of her oldest child's thinking of marriage for himself. —I, already a grandmother-of-four, could readily sympathize with her on that score. But I knew nothing then of what a truly Christian marriage implies, in "church-based intentional community"! I had only the weary world's dismal outlook about 'adjustments' to children-in-law, and the difficulties of withdrawing dutifully from motherhood, to let young marriage flow freely. —And Kathleen must have been shocked at some of the plaintive tales I told her of my experiences as a "displaced person" in the family scheme of the world.—

Will always beat us unmercifully at Scrabble. We were willing that he should reject our offers of the game, and bury himself in "East of Eden" (John Steinbeck)—a current book I'd found, and lent him. (What reading-material for *a Brother!*)

Kathleen told me about Primavera, & the way of life there. She also told me about their part in the founding of the first North American community at Woodcrest, in Rifton, New York, 90 miles up the Hudson from Manhattan. She, too, urged me to visit Woodcrest. Only as a guest, *living* the life of community, could I see for myself how it worked, she said.

I got through my tour of duty on the "Bow Santos" very thankfully. We had seen Will and Kathleen welcomed by the Brothers from El Arado (Montevideo), and heart-warmed ourselves vicariously by the demonstration of genuine human love of Christian people. I firmly resolved to visit Woodcrest as a guest at the first possible opportunity.

I was amazed to find myself welcomed-by-mail in Duffy's inimitable way. Already they had heard about me in letters from Will, who predicted that I'd "turn up" at Woodcrest. —(Even Mac, the Rifton Postmaster, had heard of me from Will, I was to discover!)

Everybody who was at Woodcrest on July 5, 1955, will remember what a miserable specimen of humanity I was, that torrid night when Hans Uli came down to meet my bus at New Palz. It had been a long, *hot* trip on a bus that broke down en route. I was laden with luggage (packed for the next ship that should offer me another stewardess's job) and no less encumbered by my self-defensive exhibitionism. (My behavior must have appalled Will & Kathleen aboard ship, I realize now. They could see how much I needed the -healing love that Woodcrest has given me.) —How *can* I thank God enough for leading me, by circuitous circumstance, & over thousands of miles of sea & land, & "happenstance," to my meeting with Will & Kathleen Marchant!

> Let (me) with a thoughtful mind
> Praise the Lord, for He is kind!
> "And His mercies they endure,
> Ever faithful, ever sure!"

Now for the two subsequent years since I paid-off the Bow Santos, Woodcrest has been my heart's true home. I spent all that first summer—from July 5 to September 3—as part of the life there. When, regretfully, I went back to "the world," to continue the dreary necessity of working for a boss, for pay, Woodcrest kept in frequent touch with me by mail. (Doug Moody was the correspondent.) By April 1956, I was invited to come again for two weeks. And I spent all of a month from June to July 1956 before the Brotherhood decided to send me to Primavera in Paraguay—as soon as I had proved my seriousness-of-intention by saving money enough for a round-trip fare.

I did so with two jobs—the first, as counselor at a wealthy Jewish camp for (over-indulged) children, at Ulster Park on the Hudson. [That was a fun experience for me, setting at rest many uneasy "prejudices" I had once, concerning Jews. No one could have been more kindly and fairly treated than I was by them!] The second job also opened my eyes to the tawdry shallowness of "world religion." —I served six months as cook at the Guest House of the Convent of St. Anne, in Kingston. My deepest impression remains that the observances of Worship, assiduously carried-on, in themselves are of no avail to hearts that "have not love." I will not dwell upon the details of this revelation. I am always grateful to the good Sisters for giving me the job that made this trip to Paraguay a possibility—an ACTUALITY, rather: for I write on board the good ship "Brigitte Torm," bound for Buenos Aires, over cerulean seas of Promise to a NEW life!

June 22, 1957

Buenos Aires, Argentina

What a trip it has been!

The ship carried 12 passengers (as well as cargo). We were a strange assortment! There was a missionary-family of Irish Baptists, returning to Brazil from Canada, after a year's "furlough." The father, a patient, gentle man is a piteously-crippled hunchback. The mother is a rather loud-voiced, opinionated, clever & sanctimonious hypocrite, with fine blue Irish eyes, flossy dark hair, fresh complexion. Her most salient characteristic: (Irish) "FIGHT," on which she professes to pride herself. Her four younger children, 11, 9, 8 & 5 came along on the journey. (The eldest, a girl, shared my cabin.) Confined, as they were, during the 3-weeks they were aboard, they were not unusually unruly. They were loud, and ubiquitous, and "active" 'little dears'; but they were rather docile in their mother's hands. Father, obviously, had relinquished claims to the family "pants." He was a patient nursemaid to the flock, while Mother talked, talked, talked, ebulliently and persistently, to any and all listeners. Her chief topic was their trip northward, the previous year, when, with 7 children—(the 3 older ones were left in Canada for schooling)—they and all their baggage had driven overland, 12,000 miles, in *a jeep*, to Edmonton, Alberta. Mother was fluent and literate enough to have written a book about it (sold in "religious" bookstores). Before the family quit the ship in Santos, all of us felt *we* had driven 100,000 miles in that jeep—having been regaled with anecdotes, 'stills' & movies recording it, all during our passage.

They were the "drum-thumper" style of salvationists; who had never relinquished the error of confusing Baptist "morals" with theology. They presented God's message to (polite) fellow-passengers, Sunday mornings in the lounge of the ship, with luridly colored "chalk-talkies," mainly featuring SIN—followed by shouted hymns, accompanied by an accordion.

Mother singled me out for "conversion," because perhaps she saw I am not perfect and I was alone and known to be traveling to join a religious group. She hoped to "save" me by her exhortations, before we parted. She informed me I was "not one of us, because of sin": the sin she referred to was that I smoked cigarettes, drank whiskey, wine & beer, and danced when there was occasion for it. She consigned me to Darkness until such time as I should repent of this wickedness. Her manner was aggressive and combative, in the self-assurance of the completely blind Pharisee! I did not like her, but I refrained from quarreling with her, even when she threw down the gauntlet repeatedly. I was glad when she was gone ashore—but I missed the children. (Their departure left an emptiness we used to feel at Sandra's house, when Stevie & Susie spent a weekend with the elder Bowditches.)

The other fine passengers were Edith Morgan of Denver, a lady-pharmacist of 65, whose birthday we celebrated at sea; her traveling-companion, Alice Brooks, 40, a school teacher from Loveland, Colorado; Sergio Cadoso, 29, a Brazilian Doctor who had been Interning in New York City, with his Massachusetts-born wife, Ann; and "Don" Luis Sangronis, a 60-year-old portrait painter, who had "done" the Infanta of Spain, and many wealthy, proud aristocrats. (His albums proved his "fame.") He was a perplexing figure to us all, at first; but we learned to love and trust him, once his "off-beat" artistic clothing ceased to be a novelty.

We sunned ourselves, ate, slept, drank cocktails, played canasta, & IDLED away the 21 days of the trip very happily together, despite our un-alikeness. It was a very pleasant trip. —Even crossing the Equator was not unbearably hot, because of a good brisk wind for several days.

With every turn of screws in the ship's engine-room, my inner mind was turning upon what awaits me at the end of this trip: A NEW LIFE!

How utterly kind the Brotherhood has been in arranging for my long, complicated passage to Primavera! They have taken scrupulously good care of me (& my luggage), never failing me, nor giving me a chance for apprehension—though I am a stranger, passing through strange lands.

June 14
Rio

At Rio de Janeiro, our first port, the passengers were all greatly excited (I, an "experienced traveler," was not *quite* so "bit up" (because it was not my destination). Alice Brooks, the jolly school-teacher from Loveland, & her friend Edith Morgan, the pharmacist from Denver, were paying a month's visit to Alice's sister's home in Belo Horizonte, Brazil. (She & Edith left *after* I had gone to phone Myriam Archer. So I don't know whether or not she was met by her sister.) We also left Dr. Sergio y Ann Cadoso, who were to stay a few days at beautiful Copacabana Beach, with relatives, before they, too, went on to Belo Horizonte, where (good, jolly, kind) Sergio is to take up an internship & research for an indefinite time. (His father is an agronomist, attached to the Brazilian government.) We really missed those 4 nice people, after they debarked.

What a wonderful visit I had with the Archers, that day! Papa Raymond Archer welcomed me so kindly, over a very sputtering, dim phone-connection from the dockside, & asked me to come (by cab) to his house at once, where I would find his whole family to welcome me. My friend, Myriam, his beautiful artist-daughter, was married 10 months ago to a young chemist (since I had met her in Rio's beautiful Botanical Gardens, in 1955). However, when he drove over to Copacabana to get her—while I was en route to his house by taxi—he found poor Myriam in the throes of ptomaine-poisoning! (He acts as Doctor in case of family-ills, himself. He was born & reared in Amazon wilds, & has knowledge of emergency treatments.) So he had sent to a pharmacy for a "shot" a Negro clerk administered to the poor girl, while we all looked on! He & his wife had had a new baby, too—17 years younger than his other son, Mario.

It was a lovely, courteous reception I had from a beautifully-civilized Brazilian family. (Myriam told me her father was a descendent of the "Proper Bostonian" Archers.) (Papa) Raymond was the most *chivalrous* modern man I have ever met. He put his car & chauffeur at my disposal [after we left Myriam's 'honeymoon suite' at Copacabana], & assigned handsome young Mario to escort me—though Mario knew very little English! He managed to tell me I "looked like his Mama." She is a blue-eyed darkish-blonde German woman of very sweet nature—*Motherly*, above all things! —She proudly showed me Myriam's wedding-photos, & told me about Myriam's husband, Herbert, with proper satisfaction. She has 2 other married daughters—Mary & Marie; and now that Myriam has married has at home only son Mario, 19, & baby Max (about 2). There are also two great dogs—a Dane and a Boxer, at Casa del Archer, on the beautiful Lake Shore.

After Señor Archer was "spiffed-up," the car returned to pick him up. Mario went over to help his mother nurse poor (ptomaine-poisoned) Myriam, & we picked up Don Luis, on the Promenade at the Beach. Señor Archer bought me papaya, cherimoya, avocado and pears to take back to the missionary-children for a "treat." (They were to debark next morning, at Santos. We all enjoyed the fruit very much, at supper and breakfast.) Because we had Don Luis with us, Señor Archer invited his pretty young private secretary Hilda to lunch with us, after we had visited at his magnificent suite of offices (opposite the British consulate) in downtown Rio. Then we had a fine luncheon in a luxurious hotel (Sheraton(?) (I'm not sure)) before he drove us to the port, & came aboard ship for a chat with Hilda, Don Luis & me—till sailing-time. Such charming, perfect hospitality I have never seen anywhere!

So my 7 hours at Rio were most enjoyably-spent, & cost me— (out of the $30 I had been allotted for entertainment en route) only $1-!

June 5

Next morning, when we put in at Santos, Don Luis & I went up to the center of town to the post-office on the crazy, careening little #29 tram, from dock-side. We prowled around a bit, & mailed letters at the *Correo*, & I remembered the *very courteous young bank clerk* who had helped me 2 years ago, on a similar sortie in Santos. I found the location of his bank—but couldn't remember his name: *José Luis Martin,* & went into the place asking for a "Señor *Fernandez.*" The Bank had moved out, & an airline's office in—so we "shopped" up & down the local Bourse asking for Señor "Fernandez" from one bank to another. *Finally* we found him—at the Banca de Economica de Bahia! *He* spotted *me* first, across the lobby, & called out. (Our greetings were so effusive Don Luis asked me if he had been my 'boy-friend'! —Don Luis invited him to lunch with us, aboard ship. No one else was there—so Kit, the good, proficient dining-room steward—served us alone, & it was a very pleasant meal. We learned a bit about the poor chap's very limited life. His father died—or de-camped (?)—before his birth. He has a mother & unmarried sister to support out of his very slender bank-clerk's pay. He is *ambitious,* but almost thoroughly *defeatist.* He is taking night courses in radio, & longs to be "shards" on an airline—but his home-ties are too pressing. He is *very* honest; very *loyal*; & as handsome as an Egyptian. (His hair looks Negroid—& Don Luis & I believe he has a 'touch of color' at least.) I gave him a card Raymond Archer had given me, & wrote on it an introduction he could make very good use of if he were not *probably* too pessimistic even to *try* to present to good Señor Archer.

June 18

Montevideo, El Arado

After Santos, my *real* fulfillment was to begin, when the Brothers from *El Arado* came early to meet the ship (on a *cold* winter morning) in their "lorry," to gather the shipment of clothes Anne Marie had packed for them, & toys from Community Playthings, & take me for a few hours to the suburban farm, *El Arado* ("The Plough"), where the community lives.

It was gentle, smiling English Harry McGee and bearded Belgian Stan Erlich, with a beret & a European manner, who came aboard, & took me to the Aduano, to go through the tedious red-tape of Customs. Things were fairly easy and quick, & then Klaus (the young driver) snorted off (first to mail letters for me at the Post Office) & then to do a couple of Community errands. (My impressions of Montevideo *2 years previously* were of a *more prosperous, well-fed, well-dressed City population.* Perhaps because of the route followed by the buses I rode at that time(?).) This time, things were more down-at-heel & sordid.

The 25 acre farm at El Arado is very pretty & peaceful—& thriftily managed to the top of its (insufficient) productivity. But Charles Hedlund and Stan Erlich both hold down outside-jobs to bring in necessary cash for its support. Allen's check for my trip from B.A. to Primavera hadn't arrived yet—& I'm terribly afraid they had to "scrape bottom" to get enough together for it. I feel badly about this.

The country was very picturesque in the early-winter green. Sunlight was golden & warm. The entire community turned out to welcome me. (There was no *singing*, as at Woodcrest. Winifred has a fine voice, but perhaps they never have adopted the custom of "singing-in" arrivals, & "singing-out" departers (?).) I met Winifred Dyroff, Norah Allain, Ivy Carroll, & Lotte McGee for 2nd breakfast at the shack-converted-into-a schoolhouse. We had good, strong, hot English tea, bread & butter & jam, gathered around an oil-burner. (There is NO heating in *any* homes, restaurants or shops. —It takes adjustment to stand it.) Then Norah Allain, a 42 yr old, golden-haired English mother of 8 children, showed me all around the community. There has been a new community-building lately completed—which is now in daily use—a plain, pretty, practical building, whitewashed, with red tiled roof, & nice red-tile floors, many pretty (MATCHING!) tables & chairs with linoleum tops & wrought-iron legs & frames. The Allains also have a new second-story added to their house, & a *fine clean*, sanitary bath-&-toilet room (quite large). There are 2 or 3 (?) dwelling-units, & an outside stair to them, in the upstairs-addition. The Allains' rooms are very artistic & scrupulously neat and tidy. Norah showed me, also, the new kindergarten-room (formerly used for dining-room, I think) in the big original farmhouse. There was a very pretty tiled floor, & French doors, opening on the central patio, around which all the buildings stand. The kindergarten class was lunching at a sunny table out-of-doors, after we had made our "tour" of the farm. The sun was warm. The children were very happy, under the supervision of Irene Fros (the *Fros* girl), who is Vera Stevenson's cousin, & childhood playmate at Primavera of the young Pottses, Arnolds, Stevensons, etc. She asked eager questions about them all. I did not manage to "sort out" *all* of the children. But *all* of them *were ineffably sweet, happy, natural and polite—(as well as beautiful).* Norah's *Clara*, aged 19 months, speaks well already in English, German & Spanish—a golden-haired toddler! I was interested in the "reservoir"—a wide, shallow, galvanized iron-tank for watering the gardens which is also used, during hot weather, for a "swimming-pool" for the happy children. There are apples, strawberries, beet-root, eggs, milk (?) sold locally. But best is the strawberry-crop, of which the volume was in "tons." (An *everbearing* variety provides the fresh strawberry market long after the season for other varieties is over.) One of Norah Allain's older boys bakes dark bread to sell. There are cows, & dogs, & chickens. A little eucalyptus wood, on the farther boundary, creates a cool shade in summer. The farm is thrifty—but (alas!) far too small to produce a living for 50 people.

Their "hard times," however, didn't stint their cordiality! Stan Erlich was "ausrater" at midday meal. Harry McGee introduced me, welcomed me, & asked for "a few words" which, paragraph by paragraph, he translated for the dining-room. Many of the community were away—at work, or school—so that it seemed—compared to a mid-day gathering *at Woodcrest*, a very *small* group.

Siesta-hour was spent in the sun in the patio, with Winifred Dyroff & Ivy. (Ivy asked me to give special greetings to Hazel Brownson—which I *must* remember to do. —To tell her, especially, of the pleasant new quarters Ivy has on the new 2nd-story addition to the Allains' house.) [Roger tells me he has been "architect" for most of the new buildings. He is also Servant of the Word for the Community. Seems to be purchaser, too, for major items. —A very *practical* man for a "genius" (which he certainly is as well).]

My most vivid & lasting impression was the sweet, trusting, smiling ("adjusted") *children* of the Community. They are the SALIENT PROOF of Life in Community.

Ivy & I were guests at tea of Harry & Lotte & one of their older little girls, Kathleen.

We had to rush, then, to make the sailing-hour of the ship. We brought into town Stan Erlich, "Pauli" (Winifred's stepson), Harry & Kathleen (8) and Georg. I sat by Klaus (?) the driver, who drove with great élan through the whizzing downtown traffic over cobbled (*&* paved) streets to the Port. We were in plenty of time! —As I remember it, 4.00 "Avgang" (departure) turned out to be about *8.30 pm,* long after all my guests had departed. Young man Pauli, eager to go to get a berth on a ship, was disappointed not to have succeeded in a brief interview with Vedel (the 2nd Styrman). The Captain wasn't aboard. Young Kathleen enjoyed her visit (and Coca-Cola) which Mrs. Muller served us in my cabin. (With beer for Stan & Harry.)

Adios, people of El Arado! —Roger Allain was already preparing for my arrival in Buenos Aires, next morning. The help he gave me in the interminable transactions at the Aduano has been incalculable.

June 19 '57

It was a COLD *(frío)* drizzly dark morning on the dock at B.A. —
And there, at *6.30* a.m., under the insufficient shelter of a dockside
railway-crane, stood Roger Allain, who had come in from the suburbs by an early train, to meet the ship, patiently pacing the cobbles,
from 6.00–9.00, before he could even come aboard! I had met him
in '55, at Montevideo (when he & Norah came aboard to take Will
& Kathleen Marchant to El Arado) so I spotted him at once, & we
talked over the rail for a time, before I had to go in for "preliminar-
ies" with Immigration & Customs, prior to his being allowed to
cross the gangplank!

I think the glass of whiskey I 'scrounged' from Stewardess (Mrs)
Muller for Roger & me in the dining room was what sustained us
through the long-drawn-out red-tape that followed. *At last*, we and
the baggage & the Primavera shipment were taken to the Aduano,
where, with great procrastination & pomp, the Customs-people ex-
amined us & fellow-passenger Don Luis & the 3 Costas (who
joined the ship at Santos for a round-trip to B.A.—a nice gentle
Mama & her two grown children, Edith & Toni, Santos people taking a holiday in the "big city." VERY pleasant people).

We got away from the port at about 11.30, & with small hand-
baggage, took a cab to the Phoenix Hotel (cor San Martin-Cordoba)
to be met first with FLAT refusal. (The clerk at the desk hadn't noticed my baggage.) But after Roger's fluent diplomacy, he finally assigned me to a 3rd floor room on a gallery over a central court where
masons & brick layers were busy with repairs and renovations. There
was a nice Argentina chambermaid, named *Rosa*, who cared for our
floor.) We were *very* hungry. We got washed & combed & went to
the famous restaurant at 775 Saviliges called (en Español) the
"Palace of Steak & Fried Potatoes." It was a wonderful lunch! (I had
eaten there alone, on my day off in 1955. It is a well-patronized and
extensively advertised place and always jammed-FULL of people
waiting for places.) I was still feeling pretty giddy on *terra firma*
after 20 days at sea. After lunch, while Roger went down to the port
to complete some details of transfer of shipment & baggage to the
River boat (leaving Saturday—because we missed the 9^{00} am sailing

that same day). While Roger toiled, I *slept* hard (on a very hard *bed*, too!) till 5.00. At 6.00 Roger came to get me & take me to the office of Jere Brantt (an Insurance executive). We waited (soggily) for him to finish up his last details, & had a pleasant conversation with his tall, pretty secretary. Then we took a long subway-ride (to Bel Grano, I *think*), were met by Jere's blue-eyed wife Ruth (a very polite—pretty young hostess) & taken to their charming "semi-detached villa" for a *delicious* dinner. (Preceded by highballs;—again, very welcome to both of us.) Ruth & Jere are old friends of Roger's, & of Klaus and Renata Hilb, who came in for dessert & discussion. It was a *very* pleasant evening! (Jere mended the broken wooden handles of my knitting-bag that Lila Stanley gave me. The bag is *very* useful, & frightfully *dirty* from service rendered.) After 10.15, Jere & Klaus drove me back to the Hotel.

June 20

Next day was "Flag Day" in Argentina. It began with heavy-laden grey skies; and soon looked more promising. Roger came for me before lunch-time, & took me (by cab) to the _______ (R. R. station for many suburban electric trains), & we went out to _______ to visit a charming, gentle young couple (from Córdoba) Lucy & Jorg Bondoni (who are intending to visit El Arado for a long time, beginning next month). Jorg works in an office somewhere; Lucy is a commercial artist in an advertising agency. (She is going to have a niño in 5 more months.) They were living (as caretakers & chaperones to a young son of 24) at the home of well-to-do, artistic, religious people named PLAUT, friends of the Brotherhood. Roger also was living there (so that his many trips in & out on the train for my sake were certainly labors of Brotherly Love. (I appreciate them.) I had $11^{00} of my 'expenses-for-trip' Allen sent me left over, after good tips to the steward and stewardess, & a bill of $7.50 for cigarettes & drinks en route, so I wanted to use it in hospitality. It paid for a wonderfully good Italian dinner at an (wonderfully dirty) Italian restaurant we all walked to—under bright sun & cloudless skies, & nice warm air! (We had a LONG walk because, due to Holiday, most restaurants were closed.) The walk home after was pleasant &

leisurely—(&, once we shed heavy clothes) very nice indeed. We found 2 visitors awaiting us—who had brought themselves out from the City on a motorcycle. Lucy—a dear, gentle, loving little bride!—led me to a comfortable bed for siesta. She woke me at 6.00 o'clock, when tea was served. A number of guests (friends & family) had arrived. There were 12 of us for supper! During & after supper, there was a "Guest Meeting"—which taxed Roger's patience & translating-powers. I couldn't keep awake after 10.00—& the discussion was still under way when I left about 10.15, & lasted (I was later told) till well after midnight. I KNOW the patience of the "listening ear of Brotherhood" is always terribly exploited by just such people as the young (smart-aleck) 'thinker' who monopolized the time all evening & overtaxed Roger—(probably) futile-ly. (I keep thinking there should be some way of correcting this—Guest meetings & "smart-alecks" who visited Woodcrest used to outrage me, again & again—till I was requested to stay away from them, because I made a nuisance of myself trying to "out-smart" the smart-alecks!—) (So I shut up & listened. I couldn't understand the Castellano (Spanish), anyway. —Since Roger felt it his (Brotherly) duty to listen patiently to the endless, egotistic outpourings of the one young man (who, out of 12 people, was willing to do all the talking), & since I could do nothing but listen without comprehension, I went home.)

I was escorted to the train by a 21-yr-old advertising lay-out man everyone was calling "Mephistophe"—because of his Satanic eyebrows and goat's beard. He eagerly volunteered to see me safely to the Hotel Phoenix, all the way in from the pretty suburb (from whose heights one could see vistas of the broad waters of the La Platte—as one sees the ocean, at a seaside resort). We couldn't talk together; but we enjoyed each other's company, in the smoking compartment of the crowded little train. —(Wonderful frequency of service (every 6 minutes!); & many eager, bustling travellers, till all hours of the night! —Everyone stays up very late at night. Dinner is served about 8.30, just to BEGIN the evening!)

At the City depot, we waited in a long queue for our turn to commandeer a taxi. And at the Hotel, my *21*-yr-old (!) escort bowed, kissed my hand, & declared (in stilted text-book English—) "You are very *sympatica*, Señora. *And I am a connoisseur of women!*"—So much for the vanity of an old grandmother too sleepy to stay up after 11.00 at night!

June 21

In the morning, I finished a letter to Sandra, and one for Max Rucker (who *may* meet us at Asunción, *if* airmail from B.A. can possibly reach Missiones in time); & a long letter to "Digger," Doris, & "Sagar Heart" at the Guest House; and a postcard to my #1 grandchild, Cathy, with a picture of the *"Brigitte Torm,"* (& a foreign stamp, for her "collection" (if she starts one)—and I had all morning to "kill" while Roger went to see about putting our baggage aboard the S. S. "Berna" to Corrientes. So I walked—a long way, at first, in the wrong direction (because I used Roger's careful street map *upside down*)—down to the Port, where the Correo Centrale is, where I had mailed many letters in '55. I crossed the parking-lot & the park on the way to the docks, to look for ships I might know, & see if there was a Norwegian vessel I might go aboard. At the dock where the Bow Santos lay for 8 or 9 days in May '55 there was only a London ship—but, since I felt well & the sun was shining (murkily), I was happy & light of foot. And lo, alongside the pier across the ship-canal, I saw the "Brigitte Torm" (which had been moved since she discharged us at a pier further from town)!

So I hot-footed it up the gangplank, as if I were going *"home"* for a visit. I found Mrs. Muller, the wiry, red-headed stewardess, in the act of scrubbing the bathroom of (my own) Cabin 3. She stopped for a while—long enough to give me a whiskey-soda, & to promise to have a "dinner-date" with me that night (Friday) at 8.00, after her day's (HARD) work was done. I looked for Capt. Jenssen, just to say "Hi," but his door was locked. So I stopped in on the dignified (sweet) blonde radio operator (bride of the 2nd Styrmann). She eagerly accepted my invitation to come along with Mrs. Muller at 8.00 pm. I wanted to know her better. I *knew* she is a lovely person.

Roger came at 12.15 noon to the hotel where we were to meet Lucy & Jorg, who were to have lunch with us downtown. There is a very swank-(looking) restaurant-bar off the lobby of the (old) Hotel; & we were in a hurry, so we all ate there. We had nice food,

nice atmosphere—(& and a NICE BILL!) —Max Rucker had sent me
the name of a Christian-Science friend of Mrs. Rucker's, who lived
at 551 San Martin (3 blocks from the Hotel). Lucy, Jorg, & I went
to say 'hello' to her—she is a blonde, jolly (in a COOL way) English
woman (newly widowed) in a LARGE and beautiful Apt. on the 8th
floor, over a garden-court of a downtown building. Max's wife's step-
father's daughter (or niece) Katrinka (about 12) lives with her. She
received us very kindly, introduced us to the (lonely) little girl; &
then had to return to her office. She *entreated* me to come for dinner, to meet some American friends who would dine there for a rehearsal of a Christian Science play they were to put on.—(The
METALLIC manner of a Christian Scientist *repelled* me, after basking
in the SINCERE WARMTH of real Christian Brotherhood.) I didn't go;
didn't *want* to—and anyway, I had a date with the girls from the
ship.

I slept & read & did (Sandra's gift) crossword puzzles, then, until
7.30, when I met Jorg & Lucy & Roger down in the lobby, where
we all talked till the 2 shipmates arrived. Lucy was *very, very* tired.
(She will give up her commercial-art job in a month, because of
her "condition.") She had agreed to go *with* us to dinner, but had
to excuse herself, to go home (a long trip, by train) to *rest*. Roger &
Jorg were going somewhere together. I had to say goodbye to Lucy,
because I won't see her again—(until such time as I see her after she
& Jorg & *I* are all MEMBERS of the Brotherhood!). She really wept a
little, & clung to me. I well remember how much a pregnant girl
longs for a comforting Mama.

Mrs. Muller & Synnøva (or Sønnyva (sp?)) Vedel [the sweet, soft
lipped, golden-haired Radio Officer of the "Brigitte Torm") had
WALKED (on high heels, too!) all the (cobbly) way up from the Park
to the Hotel. Mrs. Muller is very money-mad, I discovered. She let
me pay for EVERYTHING, & hung tightly onto everything, refusing
to let me tip the waiters (though she *greedily* accepted all I tipped
her, aboard ship, & a hat, & two pair of *good* shoes, & an evening-
bag, too!). Sønnyva, however, contributed 50 pesos (about a dollar-
ten) to our expenses, which cleaned me completely out. We did
have a good time, however, & it *was my* invitation.

We walked over the dimly-lit, crowded streets to Lavalges, #775, to the "Palace of Steaks & Fried Potatoes." That is the most popular restaurant in town (the same one we had lunch in, that first day). It was very crowded. Mrs. Muller knew how to order, so we left it to her—we had red wine, green salad, rolls-&-butter, steaks & potatoes, ice cream, & anisette & coffee—All *3* of us for *1273* (pesos) which amounts to approximately *$3.25,* American! ... Then before we parted, we decided on one more drink, & Synnøve had "gin-tonic" (which makes me sick) & I, whiskey-&-soda. The 2 girls wanted to come upstairs to see the hotel-room, before we parted. Up there, we talked till about 12.30. —And I discovered, from her tremulous, tearful tenderness—that dear little Synnøve is *probably* pregnant, herself—& *very lonely* for *her* own good mother, back in Copenhagen! She clung to me so longingly! I loved that good girl the very first time I saw her! She has married a boy she went to school with, well knowing what a lonely life a seaman's wife must have. By training as a radio-"telegraphist," she has managed to spend 2 years at sea with him. But *children* can't go to sea, & now, if she is to be a mother, she must soon go home to live, & wait—(the kind of waiting MM's wife did for *32 years!*)—until he can come home—bringing up her children alone! (Poor old LHB did that, & knows well what it costs!) (*She* will have financial security, however, which LHB did *not!*) [Though this last evening in Buenos Aires was *not* a step toward the New Life I am entering upon, I valued the experience of talking to those two Danish girls. —I explained to them where I was going, & what it meant to me. I wish Synnøve could have the sheltering love of Community while her nice young husband roves the 7 seas! —I mean to write a letter to her, telling her how much I loved her, just that *one* evening!]

June 22, 23, 24, 25

Klaus Hilb & Jorg Branet came early (8.00) in the morning to drive Roger & me & our luggage to the dock of the SS *Berna,* the large ("excursion"-type) River Boat that took us to Corrientes. It was COLD, & murky & damp, on the dockside. Half the population stood on the pier waving at the passengers, as we sailed, promptly at 9.00—for the first 'leg' of the trip by water to Rosario, Paraguay.

I can't even now (aboard the *2nd* ship, the SS *Parana*) remember all the details of that part of the journey. But I was greatly impressed with the shy friendliness of my fellow-passengers. I was quartered with 2 other women in a small (2nd class) cabin on a lower deck. They were Frau Oestmann, from Hamburg Germany, whose son, Klaus, a businessman "in leather tanning" was aboard, bringing her to visit his wife & 3 children for a few months. (She came direct from Germany to Buenos Aires, by boat.) She is a *tall*, white-haired, heavy woman. (Very FRUGAL with money, I discovered! She lent me 2 pesos 60 centavos for coffee, one morning; and "stood over me" until I had 'borrowed' it back from Roger to repay her.) The other woman was a small, charming Viennese-Argentina dress-maker, on a business-trip. She was very selfish—preempted the *best* bed (though she was smaller, & younger than either of us). But she was very *pretty*, *very* sweet-mannered. We talked (?) together—in English, German, & Spanish, translating each recognizable word into each language, like a class of 3 girls in school.

I think it was the next morning, when I was writing in this book at the desk the ship's officers used, at each port, outside the Purser's office, that the "Paper Clip Club" came (spontaneously) into being. I had been peacefully alone, writing, for an hour or so, when my fellow-cabin dweller, the petite "modista," sat down opposite me with a book to read. After a few quiet minutes, we were joined by the Head "Mose" (waiter) who used the typewriter to write out menus. Then, gradually, a small cluster of other people, passengers & ship's officers, gathered. Any further writing was impossible. People asked me many (incomprehensible) *friendly* questions, which I used my hands & my 2 words of Castellano to reply to. I started to pack up my writing materials, & was just putting away a small box of paper-clips, when I caught the sparkling blue eye of a small, blonde (Jewish) bride, who was having a hard time to contain her high spirits in a crowd of rather sad-eyed, quiet, elders. So, on inspiration, I opened my box of paperclips, & announced that we had organized a club, & each member was to wear a paper-clip, for a badge. Everyone "caught on" with great enthusiasm—especially, *Fannie Goldstein*, the blue-eyed (vivacious) bride. Her husband was made *Treasurer*, & instructed to collect 2 pesos from each new member. Each of us had 2 extra clips, & had to enroll 2 new members. Señora la Modista was "La Presidente"; & other officers were nominated. (I was "Charter Member.") —The result was a beer-party —*dansant* in the dining room, just before dinner that night— a "howling success," said everyone. (But we must have dismayed the hard-working waiters (who 'double' as cabin-stewards, & work MUCH too hard, for too-long hours.) We danced to the records Fannie Goldstein found for the 'phonografo.' But not everyone knew *how*—so we formed a "Conga Line," & 'snake-danced,' clapping, around the long tables, to the music—with much enjoyable hilarity, for both young & old. It was a very successful party.—

On board was a celebrated young lady Harpist, who entertained, afternoon & evening, in the big, comfortable lounge, playing (Roger said) Paraguayan folk-music. She played very well; got much applause. She seemed 'celebrated' by a "concert tour" in B.A., of which she showed me (with gentle pride) night club photo-"shots." The Captain showed her great courtesy.

All the people were very friendly, asking many shy (but inquisitive) questions. The *moso* (steward) was a very nice smiling young fellow, who worked hard, & was in despair because he knew *I* had no money, & half-hoped El Señor (Roger) was *mi esposo*, so *he'd* TIP. —Roger finally did so, at the last moment—which relieved the *moso*'s worried tension "considerable"!

There were 3 honeymooning young couples aboard; all of them very happy (obviously); & all bound for Iguassu (the "Niagara" of Argentina. —Marvelously *wildly-rushing* waterfalls, in a State Park). Many other passengers, young & old, were also bound there. We met a very nice middle-aged couple, English-&-Italian Argentinos, the husband an executive in the Argentine subsidiary of Swift. His wife (a grandmother) was extremely cordial & pleasant; spoke good English. Another *elderly* couple, Mr. & Mrs. Smith, were having an anniversary "honeymoon," too. He was about 70, born in Lincolnshire; she, Czecho-slovakian. They have 2 sons, & live on an apple ranch, in Rio Negro. They were *very* cordial, & gave Roger their address, & got his (& mine), in hopes of our meeting again. One of the honeymoon couples (who went with us as far as Formosa) Susanah & Mario ____ (?) were *very* cordial, too. He is in an Argentine "Atoms-for-Peace" project, a chemical-researcher. Hopes to go to the USA, & will then write me, so I may put him in touch with my sons & daughter.

At Corrientes, about 3.00 (Tues.) June 25, we changed to a smaller (much newer, cleaner, more comfortable) Riverboat, the SS Parana. The passengers for Iguana took a similar boat, following us a few miles up-River to where *we* entered the Paraguay River—& they continued on toward the mighty falls. There was really great efficiency demonstrated during the Transfer:

Our large ship sidled up to the dock for moorings, & the two smaller ones, standing out in the stream, with passengers to board the south-bound BERNA, on her return to B.A., sidled up to us. First, the passengers on-coming were discharged on an upper deck, & our list, dividing, filed aboard the upper decks of the two small (Glasgow-built) ships. All this time, on lower decks, Hold baggage was being transferred. Busy *moso*s (doubling as stewards & waiters) took on *new* work, very strenuous, of cabin-baggage porters! In the glaring-HOT sun of a (winter) afternoon, the whole thing was accomplished with great dispatch.

Coming aboard the cozy little "Parana," we were delighted to find freshly-made, *clean,* comfortable beds in cabins well screened, ventilated, & lighted. The first thing most of us thought of was BAÑO (BATH)! The *moso* provided Turkish towels (the size of *bed* spreads). Alas, there was no *cabente aqua*— But cold water baths & shampoos did very well. —The hours on the open deck sailing up the clear, still River (with its *huge* width, many tributaries, well-marked channels) was the beginning of the IDYLL I had been told it would be. It was beautiful, balmy, friendly.

At dinner, we sat with Susannah and Mario ___, and the two American *medicos,* Clyde Cox (from Selma, Alabama), & Scott Wilkinson, Decatur, Illinois (a "Ha'va'd" man, whom I had spotted at once, somehow, aboard the *Berna*)—in a dainty, cosy little dining-room, with spotless table linen, shining silver-ware, & a tremendous, full-course dinner everyone liked. It was our nicest meal, so far, on the whole trip! [Scott—a "mother's child," & I, had been sarcastic to each other from the first—he, in defense against an "overwhelming" woman; & I in memory of H.H.B. & all the years afterward.]

The beds were *so nice* I didn't waste time, after dinner, which is not over till nearly 9, but went right to bed & slept well. Got up early enough in the morning to enjoy a late sunrise (no Daylight Saving Time here). And we had a nice breakfast, as usual: coffee thick & strong, & rolls. Roger had finished his accounting-work, & was in a mood to be sociable all morning. So we sat at unused tables by the screened wide windows in the dining salon—I, writing this; & he, getting his journal up to date. When the ship, about 11 a.m., put into Formosa, Clyde & Scott & Roger & I all went ashore for a little trip up the main plaza. Scott bought cigarettes, & Roger bought me a candy bar. At the fruit-market on the dock, Roger also bought me about 20 bananas (for 3 pesos) (—about 7 ½ ¢). Formosa is a nice little town. We have stopped at other nice little towns. The ship carries mail. At the end of this part of the trip, we come to Asunción. There, when we part with Clyde & Scott, we go on to Rosario by a *very* small boat.

Bruderhof Guest House, Asunción, Paraguay

June 27 30

Oho! I didn't realize *we'd stop over at the Guest House Bruderhof in Asunción! What a treat!* What a lovely group, in a lovely house. About 10 are young people "training" for some profession or industry—*very* nice children, & the lorry driver, Michael—the oldest boy of the Marchants!—And all this whole thing *began* when I first saw the tip of Will Marchant's brown beard, coming up the steps, aboard the Bow Santos, in May 1955! And *here* is staying Michael Marchant, Will's oldest son! (still a *bachelor,* though Kathleen thought he might be soon getting married, in '55). It is sheer LUCK for me to be here, where I can see for myself how the Brotherhood manages its City-office, salesroom, & this house for a group of Youth-in-Training, & guests, or Brothers *in transito,* from Primavera to "the outer world."

It was Herman Arnold (Heini's cousin) and Johnny Robinson who were on the dock here. We had only a slight delay, going through customs, & then all of us climbed into a rickety, archaic truck, & jolted over rough pavements (whose like I saw, in '51, in Peru) to this wonderful jolly house.

I still can't get *all* the names straight, but there are Betty & John Robinson (houseparents) & Veronica, 15, their only child; Cain, sales manager for the Turnery-ware), Doris Chatterton & Reg, her husband, an accountant (who lived a little way off, over the salesroom-&-office-&-shop, but eat here). Temporarily, Willi Kluver, and his (dear, *darling*) daughter, Chrystal (21)—& Greti Freideman and Fida Mathis & several others—a very happy, jolly, normal group of youngsters WITH SERIOUS PURPOSE, & a *fine* educational background in *3* languages. These children have never known what it is to be lied-to; nor cruelly, nor unjustly treated; nor in any way deprived of Love, nor of basic necessities. They are, consequently, ALL "emotionally secure" to a degree that sets them off (as the Woodcrest children are set off, in contrast to the others at Kingston High School). They are the "*proof* of the pudding" of Community!

Roger & I had to report to Police Hqrs for our passports (taken up on the SS Berna), & we had a stroll downtown (& a "beer" in a little café-bar), prowling around book-shops, etc. I got *glimpses* of Asunción that first afternoon. But when Greti Freidemann and Dorion Caine took me for a long walk, I saw more—saw how the *terribly* poor, beggars & cripples, & "lost" people live on a river mud-flat, watered by the City's sewage, with their families, chickens & hogs—each with a *radio,* & naked light-bulb—cooking over campfires, living *so* poorly (God's Created, victims of Satan's triumph over man!) —The Army & Police & Embassies & consulates live WELL, & occupy *many large* buildings, on the bluffs, overlooking the flat, whose grandeur is exceeded only by *huge* Bank-buildings & the tomb of Lopez—a patriot—(very much like Grant's Tomb on Riverside Drive, except for additional religious touches, altars & icons, etc.—for Church & State, here are one. —Thus *dis*proving the "budding" of 'World' churches)—in a city where such dreadful poverty exists & such terrible disease abounds. ("*Everyone* in Paraguay has syphilis," I was told.) (This morning we saw a beggar woman crawling on 'all-fours,' like a monkey—a dreadful sight! Willi says these terribly unfortunate creatures EXPLOIT their misery,

for beggar's *gold*. But still I pity them, & I pray to God: "Thy Kingdom Come—*quickly!*") The children here have tangerines, bananas,
grapefruit & oranges in plenty—so they crave APPLES—(as Teen
Agers at home crave hot-dogs; as *we* of the '20s crave lolly-pops—
as Duffy craves Ice Cream). Dorion is very reserved & shy, a beautiful, delicately featured child, with gold hair in very neat tight
braids. Greti is quite poised & 'mature'—*Chrystal* has been a great
pal to me! She is *21*, & through her secretarial training. She & her
father, Willi, have been on a 5-week tramping tour to the
"colonies"—German, Belgian, Japanese, etc.—of immigrant settlers—an "outreach" excursion, about which both of them have
been telling, at meals. (I am not quick at German or Spanish, except
for a word or two. But—as Florrie says—now that I really WANT to
learn, I shall.)

It has been a *very wonderful* visit here! Tomorrow, Roger, Willi, 4
'youth' (Chrystal among them, & pretty, charming Fida) & I all set
off by river-boat for Rosario, at 3.00 pm, for an overnight trip.
There is a Brotherhood house there, kept by an old German caretaker. We stop there, to await the 3 horse-drawn carts that are to
take us to Primavera. —I am *nearing* the end of this long, long journey—which was planned for me so carefully & kindly by my new
family, the Brotherhood. Thank you, God, for everything!

Loma Hoby, Primavera

July 2, 1957

I am here *at last!* (It took from May 31–July 2!)
The last part of the trip was the real experience!
At 3.00 pm on Sunday, June 30, we got off to the River-boat
going up to Rosario. We wore our warmest clothes, & kept them
on for 2 solid days! (My costume: ordinary "underpinnings," plus
'snuggies' & wool socks over nylon stockings; heavy shoes, over-
shoes; a nylon-wool jersey dress, a sweater, winter coat, raincoat &
poncho; hat tied on with neckerchief; & a rain-hat on top, &
gloves— If I am big myself, I was at least twice as big!) The travelers
were Willi Kluver, Roger Allain, Michael Marchant, Kurt Zimmerman; Fida Mathis, Chrystal Kluver, and I—Most of the household
at Asunción walked down to the 'dock' to see us off, & to help get

our bags aboard. It was a grey, cold afternoon, with mist blowing and gusts off the marshes along the River. The boat was indescribably dirty, fairly small, dirty, & most uncomfortable! One cabin, for us 3 women, was all we had. The men slept on settees in the "dining-salon,"—a cramped & dirty place, where the food served as "dinner" to us (1st class) passengers was something I didn't care to eat. (I had a touch of diarrhea—so ate just some white hard biscuits.) We all went to bed at once, to keep warm, we women; & as we didn't remove our clothes at all, & had the only good light-bulb available, & all of us wanted to read, the men opened our door on the 3-foot wide deck, & drawing up a bench, sat down to read, their books thrust through the door, to get the light. We were extremely cramped. But, after all, despite vibration of the engines, which shook our bunks all night, we slept well. (At least, I did.)

We arrived at Rosario (Paraguay) about 6.00 am. Again, a slender plank, unrailed from deck to steep-banked muddy shore, served as our "gangplank." Somehow, despite cramped limbs & stiff joints, we scrambled up slippery slopes. A wagon awaited us, to carry the baggage to the Guest House of the Brotherhood. We were very glad to walk. At the corner of Rosario's "Broadway & 42nd St.," there was mud about 6–8 inches deep. We were picking our way, as best we could, across it, when the baggage-wagon passed us, & just then, my swankest piece of luggage, a fragile light-green leather hat-box, tumbled off the pile on the cart, & was partly run-over by a rear wheel. I uttered a cry—which warned the cart drivers to hurry—& get to the house, & wipe off the mud before I got there to give vent—! (No great harm was done, & none of the things inside were damaged.)

Pearl & Fran Hall were there. From Margit and Hazel I had heard a great deal about them. (They were Asunción-bound, for a hospital check-up for Pearl.) They had come down the day & night previous through torrential rains! It must have been much worse for them than for us, on our up-trip. We had a nice hearty breakfast there, before starting out. I was too confused to remember the names of all persons present.

There was no rain for us all the way home—to Loma Hoby— but it was cold, windy, & cloudy & the roads were inundated!

They put me, & Otto, his wife, & his niece, into the one covered wagon, surrounded by bags, bales, boxes, & blankets. I was very thankful to Doris & Reg Chatterton for the loan of a nice grey-wool poncho. I sat in front with Franzhard Arnold, who drove the team. He & his horses were in great mutual sympathy. He is a very nice young lad. Ahead, in the second wagon, Michael Marchant, Fida Mathis, & Chrystal Kluver (with no cover over their heads) were driven by a small boy, 8 yrs old (Pablo's nephew), with bare feet, shorts, & a thin cotton blouse. Pearl Hall gave him her brown wool sweater to wear (for which, I hope, he was properly grateful). The lead wagon, driven by picturesque Guaraní Pablo, in faded crimson poncho & straw sombrero, contained Kurt Zimmerman, Roger Allain, & Willi Kluver (Chrystal's father). We had a jolly time, all the way—notwithstanding discomforts (even the strap & buckle of the big sash I was sitting on!). We slobbered through mire, sloshed through great pools of muddy water, tilted perilously up and over steep, slippery banks, rumbled over board bridges, teetered & clattered over what we (in NE) call "corduroy roads," & finally, about 4.30 pm, stopped for a picnic meal of maté, boiled eggs, bread & cheese—Willi Kluver directing the "camp," on the front "lawn" of a native house.

We were very hilarious over that meal. Gave the horses a 2-hour rest. It got dark, soon after we resumed our trek. Once there was nothing to be seen from my perch on the big sack except the faint white glimmer of water & white patches on the horses, & dim outlines ahead, the discomforts were magnified for me. And still, through black night, the clever horses wearily plodding, found the right, safe footing, & the proper turns in the road. —(*They* knew they were heading home!) Franzhard was alert to every move of his team, & went on gently swooshing & chuckling encouragement & reproof. I was so glad when through the darkness, came Roger's shout to STOP—we had just passed a goodsized sleeping village, & were drawn-up on a roadside. It was at the home of Pablo's father. He welcomed us *all* into his house!—herding his family (a daughter with 4 or 5 children) into one room; offering the other to us, women; & the warm (smoky) kitchen-place to the men. He built up a good (smoky) blaze and Willi had a "buffet supper" ready in no time!

How glad we all were to lie down! —I (whom they called "Die

Alte"), *most of all.* I was given a real mattress & pillow! Otto's wife & niece had a bedspring, with blankets spread over it; and Chrystal & Fida slept on the brick floor, on their bedding.

I slept quite soundly (though they said afterwards that I *snored*).

In the grey of morning, we ate a quick breakfast at Willi's "coffee-stand" in the kitchen, & set out again, learning that the menfolk had been less quick to get to sleep than we, & had been "pulling Willi's leg" with great hilarity, for a long time after we were asleep.

As day came, I could see what kind of country this is to be which is my home—for God knows how long! It was beautiful—no sun-shine yet, but great stretches of *"camp"* (pampas) & patches of primeval forest, & small native villages, &, here & there, little coun-try shops called ________, at very rare intervals along the road.

"We're nearly home!" Franzhard told me, as I was marveling at the deep forest. Just then, a spring wagon from Isla, with Hans Meier's wife, Fida's aunt, & Wilfred ________, appeared around a corner. We all got out & shook hands, & congratulated each other on the nearly-ended journey—through a night that took me the last miles over the road *out of the world!*

"There's *Loma Hoby!*" Fida called back. "HOME!"

The winding way *at last* took us to the estancia yard, where a gate was opened for us, & we trotted in through the beautiful eucalyp-tus-shaded road past the house I am now sharing with Marjorie Parker-Gray.—

The welcome gong was banging as we creaked to a stop before the dining-room. People were running from all directions to wel-come us. —They had "sung me out" at Woodcrest, on May 31, & were now welcoming me "home" here, on July 2. —*Journey's End!*

After a nice egg-&-sausage breakfast for us travelers, I went to bed with a hot water bottle, & slept through the afternoon. A hot bath before supper & the kindness of a "welcome-committee" headed, I think by Marjorie & Kathleen, who left a fresh-baked cake on my table, with a pretty welcome-card from "us all," & the ultimate abatement of the confused, 'whirly'-feeling (after so many days & weeks in motion, *en route*) brought me round to a state ap-proaching clarity.

No one wanted to *hurry* me to work. I was given the whole of the next day to write letters home, & the following day to write Woodcrest of my arrival. The sun came out! It is *beautiful* here. The clear sky (innocent of "smog," completely) & the wonderful sunsets & sunrises, & *vast* firmament, & vistas of "camp" with dark forest beyond; the *happy, courteous, sweet-faced, genuine children;* the friendly, sincere, hospitable adults who REALLY *are* GLAD I am here— (without the faintest trace of the "polite insincerity" prevalent in the world)—& the goodness of God are making me *new*.

I have made fine friends already, especially with my own middle-aged group of Sisters—& have had family-supper with the Marchants—teas & breakfasts with Marjorie and (Dr.) Margaret; a wonderful "free afternoon" with Maureen; evenings with jolly Belinda (Doris Greaves's special friend here, & friends of hers 3 years ago). [Those Friendly Crossways Hallowe'en parties are called to mind by a road-marker the young-people put up, near the Marchants' house—"Friendly Crossways."] It makes me realize that even in Oct. 1953, when I was "Madame Maltasmystic" at the Barretts' farm, with good Ruthie Miles Frost—when I first met Doris Greaves & Paul & Mary Pappas—this *all* was preparing for *me!*— for surely God's hand is at the wheel, when one begins *really* to seek His Guidance. It was He who led me here after March 6, 1953 from that Fall, 1953, & the spring of '55, when I served as stewardess on the "Bow Santos." —It *began* LONG before! Actually, I *know* it began *20 years* before, in October, 1933, when I "went home" to Cambridge with my dear little Jonathan, Sandra, & Peter, & *began* blindly to fumble for the Way, in Pew #17 at Christ Church on Cambridge Common.

~

—If *only* I could write as I feel about all this, to M.M., Leslie Glenn, Mrs. Magoun, Myra Mitchell, my dear Mama,—most of all to my dear 3, *especially my □-Girl!* —But this is *impossible!* I feel I shall be writing fewer letters, the longer I stay here—because there is a deep & awesome solemnity to my being here at all which I am unable to convey in words.

Summing it up, it is the black, lost sheep's return to the fold where the Good Shepherd has brought her, back to the other 99. —And each of my dear children (& all my friends & family) must *individually* find This Way alone, from the contrite fullness of his own heart. There is nothing *I* can do. *God* must do it. Pray God, *do* so: Bring them in, too—for thine is the Kingdom, & the power, & the glory forever.

~

There are NO CROSS PEOPLE in Community! Thank God!

Loma Hoby, Primavera, Paraguay

Thurs. July 11, 1957

I have been here 9 days—gradually accustoming myself to the *modus vivendi*, & to my job—hanging & folding clothes in the communal laundry. (This is a pleasant job here—out-of-doors, or in-doors in a thatched roofed, slat-walled building, working with *always pleasant* people, in a very useful, serviceable capacity.)

It is hard to put into words the delight I feel in being here, because the delight surely cometh from God, the Unknowable—by the wind of His Spirit. That transforms simple (not to say "primitive") living, and coarse, plain (even flavorless) food, & the plainest possible clothing—with *none* of the vanities of cosmetics, nor jewelry, nor superfluous adornment)—transforms it all into *living for Him*, by means of living in love with one's true brothers & sisters— with those who "believe on Him," as I do.

The children, & their clear-eyed, laughing friendliness—without one trace of self-conscious, distorted behavior, due to *lack of love!*— & their happiness together, & in their family & school-groups— *they* indeed are the Positive *Proof* of the Life! The well-adjusted, quiet-mannered, happy, "secure" young people—isolated from the world, but more alive by far to its needs and its sickness than those over-emphasized "Teen Agers" in the "best" worldly environments! —*They*, who have grown-up in Community &, for the most part, will elect to return to it voluntarily, when time comes for their decision—what more salient proof could there be?

As for Primavera's beauty—its flaming winter sunsets with long, bright afterglow; its pristine, innocent sunrises with pink clouds across the lucid blue-green skies and silver stars; its silver-white moonlight nights, & dense dark shadows dappling sandy roads; as for its profusion of wildflowers—bright red, blue, yellow, orange, white; its flowering shrubs, trees, & vines, in exotic (winter) bloom; its trees bent down with golden loads of oranges, yellow lemons, sweet limes, green limes, grapefruit; its banana plantations; its clustered *mamones* (papayas) under delicate-leaved trees—! How could I describe it, while I am still so joyously absorbing the wonder of it?

First and best: the fellowship! What *friends* I have here, already! EVERYONE is my *true*, trustworthy, forgiving, tolerant friend—a man (or woman) of his word—his quiet, gentle, BOND-word, which will never be broken. Merriment of the kind that is here is never found in "the world"—except in rare, outstanding persons (like Sarah Cleghorn, for example) whom one meets and considers "a little too good to be *true!*" Here, there is ready laughter, no primness, no piety, no *prating*. Nothing idle & silly is heard. Words have *meaning*. The words of songs are sung in the spirit of the writer (who could be more 'flattered' than the creative mind that wrote the songs we sing for their *meaning?*) at table, in the community dining-room, or in our own "family" meals!

Community-living attracts only *Thinking* people—people who have always asked the meaning of life, and have *found the answer*, now—& so are now OF ONE MIND, each with the other—though some are (former) "intellectuals," some clerks; some "peasants," etc. It is all one spirit that brought them—*(us!)*—together. I am truly INCLUDED here—(yet, by contrast, more radically "different" from all others than I have ever been, elsewhere).

Marjorie ("Old Humbug") Parker-Gray

Marjorie is my room-mate in the little cottage at Loma. "You are to live with a very 'aristocratic' Englishwoman," I was told, on my journey from Rosario.—I had not expected life with her to be quite so *fine* and *deep* and *beautiful* as it *is*, essentially (though we have little "spats," occasionally). She is a deeply devout and devoted Sister, painstakingly "showing me the way"; carefully thinking of and for me (just as *Florrie* did—more comprehensively, as a fellow American). Marjorie is making it quite clear to me that we can & shall always be true Sisters, despite the vast differences between us of 'background,' diversity of 'interests,' divergence of temperament, and disparity of experience. (She can hardly *believe* a great deal of what, in honest feeling & trust I have told her about my life! It is, to her, *incredible!*) Our very differences are making our friendship a *real* adventure! Thank God for Marjorie!

M.M.

All my life I have longed for love—more love—more people to love; more people to love me! For the years of motherhood—even with no husband to love & be loved by—I could *manage* on the quota of love I had. But then they (my 3) all grew up! Between March '48 and Sept '49 I had 'lost' all three of my children! —There would have been *nothing, no one* to love, *if I had not found M.M.!*

It was on July 5, 1951 that I found M.M. He was chief engineer of my first ship. The ship met with an accident at sea, just outside the port of San Pedro, California. It was a severe accident; &, of course, in the required investigation that followed, a check was made of MM's domain—the engine room—to make sure no engine-failure had caused it.

MM, when I first saw him, had hardly recovered from the shock of being thrown across the Captain's salon by the impact of the collision, and his anguish on behalf of the Captain's 8-yr-old daughter whose fear brought on hysteria—when the Insurance Investigators & Maritime Commissioners pulled his beloved engines all to bits, & kept the ship completely de-commissioned for 9 weeks, while we lay in dry dock. During that time, while he was free, we "fell in love." It was *real* love, of the human kind, deep in mutual trust, and deeper still in shared Belief! I think, because M.M. is very gentle & sensitive, he really needed love at that time as much as I did! I shall always thank God for our meeting & our long and beautiful intimacy, & the fact that (but for legal technicalities) MM was the only "husband" I ever had. Our (unauthorized) "marriage" lasted from July 1951 till March 6, 1953—& then it had reached such a *depth*, such a complete, beautiful fulfillment that I could not *stand* it any longer! (I would not have dreamed for a moment of suggesting to MM that he disrupt his home in Norway, & marry me *legally*. It was understood at the beginning that we would have to part. Each week made the prospect of parting more dreadfully unthinkable!) It was at the very topmost point of happiness—that I suddenly realized THIS *was not what God wanted of us!* Our love *wasn't* right; could *never* be right. So on the next day as I walked down to the dock to see him aboard, I told him: "I am going home (to the East Coast) tomorrow." I did go home. Then & there! I "kept the faith" with him (& Marie). I never even looked back over my shoulder to watch him go! *I loved him.* But, as I tell him whenever I wind my watch: "I love God—*more*, & more, more—And" (now that I've come to join Community) "—and God loves me!"

In the early days of our relationship, we often talked of the *need* of the world for Christ's second coming. We used to lean side by side, on the rail, looking out at the sea, & talk of Christ's promise (in which we *both* believe implicitly!): "Lo, I shall come again, with clouds & great glory, & every eye shall see!"—and "—And then the sign of the Son of Man shall appear in the Heavens; and then will the End come." —And in the deep, loving trust we felt for each other, we said we would plan to meet, again, somehow, in time to watch the End of the World together. I used to *pray* for that! Now I do not pray: it is for God to create whether our (worldly) human love *could* be right in His sight (?) & whether or not it *may* come to pass that M.M. & and I *shall* meet again, &, in the Kingdom of Heaven, where there is "no marrying, nor giving in marriage" we may resume our love, on a spiritual basis. Thank you God, for the gentle, generous, understanding love of that *very Good*, devoted, devout man, whom I shall always remember & love as my (unauthorized) "husband"—the only *true* husband I have had! [And may God forgive us both!] Bless MM forever. Amen.

The *Hoegh Clair,* after being crashed into by a tanker on the south California coast, July 8, 1951.

Lois aboard ship in San Francisco Bay, August 14, 1952.

M.M., chief engineer of the *Hoegh Clair.*

July 26, 1957 Stevie's 8th birthday is the 31st!

No presents from his Gran this year, nor hereafter. —It is so long since I got a letter from home! (I must get used to that, Will tells me.)

August 2, 1957. I have been in Primavera one month today

It was 32 years ago today that I first met Henry, when Rodney Long introduced us as "kindred spirits" across the goldfish-tank in the lobby of the Hotel Vanderbilt, in New York City. It was a hot, grey, lifeless day—that began my venture into matrimony, maternity—and, very belatedly, maturity! We were married at Park Ave Community Church, N.Y. on December 30, 1925. —I never need to wail over my marriage as a "mistake" (although *it* failed); because it was the means of my motherhood, and no other marriage to any other man than Henry could have resulted in *my Jonathan, my Sandra, my Peter!* —So this date is not an occasion for a dirge, but for a madrigal—a mother's merry madrigal. God bless my three dear, good, loving, loyal children & their children.

God has led me here—where each day slips by like a jewel on a golden chain—yes, even cold, wet days! I have been *happy* all the time! I am here, & I am "coming along" (Fran Hall told me today)—towards ultimate *membership* in the Society of Brothers! Already I have attended Gemeinde—for which purpose I made a journey of thousands of miles, en route for more than a month. — It seems *unreal;* it seems almost like suspended existence! —To be *told* that *all the others here believe* (as I dared not let myself believe) that *I* am "called by God" to live with them—to be among those chosen to *help prepare for the coming* Kingdom! When I check back, & back, over incidents & developments & crises in my life I can no longer doubt the Call—for *me!* for *me! Incredible!* The first indication was on that night in July 1932—my life's very worst moment!—when I lay in a hospital bed, locked in, with 4000 mad people, not knowing How or When I could get out, & get back to care for my dear 3. The awful events of the preceding day, & the anguish of fear that I, too, *perhaps,* was mad (like those groaning, writhing, shrieking souls-in-torment whose suffering kept the night hideously awake)——(the fear secretly cherished since 1918, when I had encephalitis lethargica, and '*might* never be the same again,' the Doctor said!). They gave me a sedative. I lay and looked at a green wall at the foot of my bed. On that wall, suddenly a light shone, & it told me that God wanted me to bring my children and come to Him, & never waver again in steadfast Faith in Him. He——that Light! The Spirit!——promised to get me safely out of that terrible place, & to protect my children for me. I went to sleep *quite certain.*

After 9 days "observation"-period, they said I had a "clean bill of health." Dr. Osterheld said it was no wonder at all I was hysterical & "collapsed." He told me——(about *Henry*, whom I had loved, & trusted, & longed to be faithful to in enduring marriage): ——"Just forget all about your marriage! Forget that man! Pretend you never knew him. Don't waste the emotional energy on hating him: just FORGET him! Write him off your books! ——You have your children. They'll always be yours."

And, though my departure was delayed for 24 more days, for which time I legally committed *myself,* in order to have a long-needed surgical operation——such a BOON to me (in *money*, which I had none of——worth over $1000 fee to the surgeon who performed it!)——God *did* get me out of there! And His hand kept my children safe & fed, through the Sisters of St. Anne——while I worked out a lonely path toward getting them back to me again. That whole year, till at last, on August 16, 1933, I reestablished our family at 31A Shaler Lane, in Cambridge, was a year to be *forgotten* ——if possible! (But I know I shall never forget it, nonetheless.)

On Sept 18, 1932, my 29th birthday, Jonathan, Sandra & Peter were baptized by Father Francis J. Powell at the Chapel of St. Anne's School, Arlington Heights. It was my birthday. I was 29 years old. Father Powell took the children to the font in turn——first Jonathan, then Sandra——& little irrepressible Peter, 2 years old, blurted out loudly: *"Now it's my turn!"*——not to be left out! (I believe Henry was not there that Sunday. He had refused to allow his children to be baptized while we were married.)

Peter, Jon, Sandy, and Lois. "One memorable day at Brant Rock, Mass.—just before my worst troubles began, July 1932." [LHB]

Jon and Peter, garden of St. Anne's School, Arlington Heights, Mass., July 24, 1932. "When good Fr. Powell came to our rescue." [LHB]

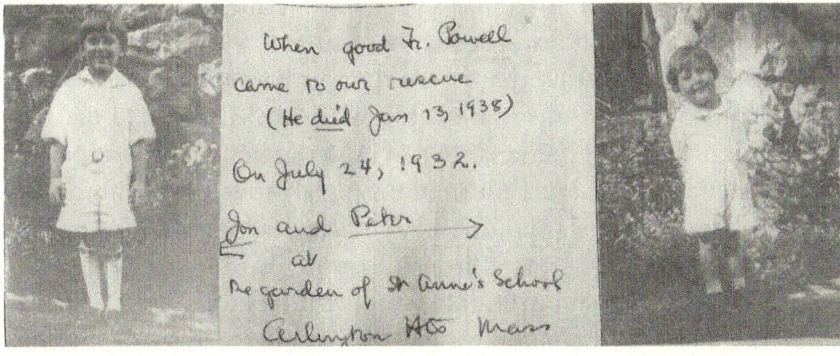

Our divorce was final not until May 1933. (It was granted—*decree nisi*—on November 30, 1932, just one month short of 7 years after our marriage.)

On Oct 3, 1933, we attended Christ Church (& Sunday School). C. Leslie Glenn's help as an inspiration to my new desire to live with my children closer to God, was immeasurable! He also helped by putting me in touch with the Oxford Group, & with Mrs. Magoun. Despite the irreligious aspects of psycho-analysis, the Jungian method Mrs. Magoun followed surely taught me— over 4 years of conferences, to "sort myself out," emotionally. (Her assurance & reiterated re-assurance, however, that I could never, never find a second husband—although I had no desire to do so!— had a certain bad effect: it made me the easier prey of "the Dragon" in his familiar form called: Rationalization. The "humanistic" code of my own generation plus her authoritative dictum that I'd *never* find anyone willing to marry me (-&-my-3-children) were what decided me in the matter of J.A.M. —He blithely called himself "not the marrying kind," thinking such a state enhanced his value—when he discovered I really did not want him for a husband, & (because he was no fit model of a man for my children to copy) that I really "had no use for him at all," it offended him! What was the use of his "playing 'hard-to-get'" when I never chased him? I know certainly that I would never have wasted 13 years of my life's prime on my relationship with J.A.M., if I had had the remotest notion of re-marriage! —(JAM was not an important part of my life at all;—but I must admit my attitude towards him was not—from a proper standpoint of Christianity—a *loving* one: it was UTILITARIAN—with a little romantic glossing-over.) Psycho-analysis helped me; but it didn't answer the questions I had asked all my life; it did not supply me with a reason for living—once my dear three were grown up & needed me no more.

August 8, 1957

It is incredible that I am here—surrounded & secured by the best love man can evince—the true love of Brotherhood & sharing. (The experience with MM helped to prepare me for this life. In a measure, his goodness, & truthfulness, & fidelity healed wounds made by H.H.B., J.A.M., & *my own self*—But it has been the love of the Brotherhood that healed up EVERY wound I ever had!—except the persistent "paranoid complex" that STILL dogs me & disrupts peace.) I wonder every day if I really AM here, setting my feet on the sandy soil of this strange out-of-the-way place? (I remember studying about Paraguay in the 7th grade in school under dear Miss Sheppard, who also read us the Psalms, unforgettably.) Whenever I can be alone, lying in bed, or walking about the *hof*, I add up all the tokens of my life's history that *prove* that GOD actually called *me* here! (*Me —!*) If I had not been so *utterly stupid*, I might have been here long ago! God has had great patience with me. —Now I *am* here! The End of the World CANNOT be far away! —Thank the Shepherd for bringing-in the sheep in time before the night of darkness comes!

~

On August 16, 1929 in New Milford, Conn. Phil Mosely came to see us in my first *great* perplexity. Phil has become a dapper little Professor of Economics in Columbia University since then. How he must have *changed* since that painful time when Henry's "*bargaining*"*-offer* half terrified him! But he was brave, & very loyal to me always. I thank him for his moral support!

~

On *August 16, 1933,* I took my dear 3 children for a long walk on the banks of the Charles River. To this day, I can recall the mood I was in: desperate determination somehow to succeed in the task of combined mother-&-fatherhood for their dear sakes! I remember how very, very (physically) tired I was, too, as we trudged along together singing 3 of our "family-songs": "When Johnny comes marching home from school" (for Jonathan); "And Sal & Sue & Sandra, too!" (for Sandra); & "Up jumps Pete & ses he 'my neck is tough,'" (for Peter) … We were all four exhausted that night! It was about that same time that I had realized WHY marriage to Henry had failed: because it was not on a true Christian-Spiritual basis. And I wrote:—

Lois's drawing about walking along the Charles River with her three children in
September 1933.

Look not for love, denying God!
That were your folly from the start
On earth, a lonely soul, forlorn,
Struggles beneath an empty heart
Without God's Love: No earthly love
Can be fulfilled, no peace be known:
And we who will not love the Lord
Must walk alone.

~

Death is EVIL. Only because of Christ's resurrection from death can we reconcile ourselves to the death of loved ones. For *his* triumph over death brought *our* triumph—so that, losing our friends to death, we are also releasing them to share in Christ's triumph over it. —Although the NATURE of "life after death" we do not, and cannot possibly know. We do know they are *"better off,"* however!

IF, when in 1932, at the depth of the World Depression, I was actually faced with imminent prospects of my 3 children's *starving*, so that I "threatened" suicide for myself, and (when asked about *them*) said, "Why, of course I will take them with me—!" (because I could *never* have left them in a world so cruel, hungry & alone, with no one who properly loved them!)—IF I *had* had the actual courage of my *conviction* that Death were better than life—would Christ's forgiveness of our sins have included forgiveness of taking my life & theirs? (Luckily, anyway, I never *did* have that "courage"!) But in "The Individual & World Need" (p. 19) there is a paragraph so descriptive of my hysteria at that time that I copy it out (in shame), never to let its import be forgotten by me:—

"We all know," wrote Eberhard Arnold, "the diseased, nervous condition in which we ... have sought, by making the most extraordinary remarks, to interest those around in us. When that did not seem likely to succeed, we tried to draw attention to ourselves by means of jokes and fun; and when that, also, did not work, we drove people by our insolent behavior to give us their attention, if only out of irritation. When that does not succeed, the hysterics of Self reach their peak, when through shivering, weeping, fainting, or even through GENUINE (or half-genuine) attempts at suicide, they succeed in making those around, however unwilling, devote themselves to the diseased, individual ego."

I ask myself: *was* it mere "hysterics," at that time; or was I really *capable* of a philosophic rationalization of the ideal of Death in preference to Life in such an evil world?

I only know that, as Dr. Osterheld told me at the time, I am very thankful for the SHOCK that brought me up short and cured me: the shock of being "taken for crazy," and committed for 9 days' observation in a mental hospital! —As for the *surgery* I got there, in addition, which was such a boon—which restored the well-being I had lost in 1926 after my first, terrible ordeal of childbirth, I am *very thankful,* too!

But now—now I am about to become a member of the Society of Brothers—I am not so sure that in asking for *sterilization* at the time of the surgery, I was not definitely guilty of pre-empting God's powers ...

How MUCH I have to *regret*—and yet now—now I am *truly* repentant, &, hence, forgiven—I cannot re-live the years, to make amends.

—I wonder if ever I can write to H.H.B. to explain things to him as I see them now. —Would that *have* to be "casting pearls before swine"? CAN'T Henry EVER understand ANYTHING? If not, *why not*? (But I do think there is a very sufficient reason: he has been SO GUILTY himself, he could never atone for what he did to me and our children! —Never, never, never—the sins of both commission & omission—the absolute abrogation of responsibilities to wife & sons & daughter! —How can he LIVE WITH *himself?* I feel sorry for him; I truly do!) (And how can Mother & Laura feel—? & Walter Whiting!)

Sept 29, 1957

My little Mama *died* (Aug 14)—and I can hardly believe it! Sandra said *she'd* always think of her ("sitting by the fire, knitting, up in Maine." I remember her in many places. —One night so perfect, so clear, at Pigeon Cove, when I must have been only 4 or 5, and we all walked down to the "Linwood rocks" to see the full moon on the broad ocean. Such a splendid night—with Northern Lights, too, in the sky towards the open Atlantic. I always think of it—in my mother's being beside me—when I sing: "The Heavens declare the glory of God." —And I think of Mama sitting wrapped up in a soft white wool shawl, sitting in the rock "chair" near Chapin's gully, a few years later, when Laura was a child of 3. Laura & I waded in the tide-pool, & Mama sat, & read her novel (her insatiably-devoured *Romances*—!), & then put her book aside, & hummed, while her soft blue eyes, like the sky over our heads, gazed wistfully out at the sea beyond Straitsmouth. I remember Mama in Cambridge, up in our cosy, red-carpeted second-floor sitting-room, reading aloud to us, as we cut out paperdolls, or painted pictures, or sewed doll's clothes—she read us (*so well*) everything—Dickens, Thackeray, Gene Stratton Porter, *Dracula*—everything, tirelessly, sometimes till she fell asleep on the French sofa, & the book slipped out of her hand! I remember her terrors at night in the City over *imagined* burglars; her fear of the sweet little field mice in our bureau-drawers at Pigeon Cove; her tolerance of our noise and energy when we rehearsed for plays we wrote; our Club-meetings in the 3rd floor rooms; our annual Baked Bean suppers; her interest & love for & by our many little playmates. I remember her happiness in Lexington, when she & Daddy "retired" (and began to get on really *well* together, after middle-age); & her jolly life in Texas with the Whitings; and her timid enjoyment of the big "family" at Nelly Clapp's in Duxbury—and *then* her last years in Maine. (She was beginning to feel lonely, as the generation of her friends died.) She used to write me brave, plaintive letters about it … And now I can't reach her *by mail* to tell her how grateful I am that her bequest left me something to "give in" to the Brotherhood!

My Confirmation

When I was to be confirmed (Spring of 1916), I said to my Daddy: "How can I be confirmed, when, though I know the words of the Apostles' Creed, I do not know the meaning of the term: 'the Holy Ghost.' What IS the Holy Ghost, Daddy?" He hemmed & hawed, made feeble attempts to define for me the essence of God's power, & at last said: "You'll understand when you're *old* enough, Lois." But I protested that it was now that I was asked to confirm my faith—not when I was "old enough." —He said: "When you stand before the Bishop to recite in unison with the others, and you say 'I believe in God the Father, God the Son, and God, the Holy Ghost' the Bishop will not notice if *you* omit the last phrase." — What a weak "out" for my own sincere, forthright Daddy to suggest to me! —"And *sneak* into the Church—?!" I cried, outraged. "Just because the Bishop 'doesn't notice'?" Now I had made my Daddy so embarrassed, he sent me to my room for "impertinence." —I *had* to use his "way out," however, because I could not comprehend the meaning of that term: "Holy Ghost." Had they taught: "Holy *Spirit*"; had they properly explained the Pentecost; & had I not been such a noisy & rebellious child, I might have understood. *Now I know*; & I am "old enough" at last to know! And God is very generous to have taken me in at last, after all my long, long sullying of the "temple" of his Holy Spirit. —Because, making so much continuous ado I have always repelled the opportunities for HEARING the "still, small voice."

Why should God have brought *me* here?! "Oh, praise Him! Alleluiah! Oh, praise Him!"

"Suicide"

I often think back to those bleak dark years of 1948-'51 (before I met *M.M.*, who helped to restore my soul!) when I sat for hours at a time, arguing with myself that I *should*, if I were only brave enough, *get off the earth* by committing suicide. I argued that since there was "no place in the world" for me; since it "cost money" to keep me alive; since I was told everywhere I was too old (at 45, et seq.) to earn a living (at my own profession); since I could no longer be useful to anyone; was "wanted" by no one—there was a vast amount of evidence to show that I *ought* to die! I used to climb up on a stool, twist a strap over a rafter, & fasten the other end about my neck, & *pull*, till I could feel my eyes begin to bulge. I never *could do* it! I would fill a bathtub with water, get into it, & try to get courage to *really* cut the veins in my wrists. (All I ever did was to *scratch* them!) I *couldn't* do it! I used to turn on all the stove-& light-outlets, & breathe in gas till I got groggy; but I always turned them off, & opened the windows again! I *couldn't* do it! *Couldn't* jump off the top of Coit's tower in San Francisco! *Couldn't* fling myself into the Bay from the deck of the Oakland ferry! COULDN'T have what I *almost* believed was the "common decency" to "remove my nuisance" from the face of the earth! —I did all these things in breathless secrecy, afraid that someone, seeing me, would (again) send me to a terrible mad-house. I *knew* I wasn't "insane"; I *thought* I was "philosophical"— What I *really* was was SELFISH, self-centered, *guilty*, & proud. —*Too proud to live* unless I could live as I thought some special quality entitled me to live—in dignity, in happiness, in the peace which my own self-love wouldn't allow!

Now, I am *killing* my *Self,* in order that I may live *quietly, without show, at the bottom,* as Gwynn says. This is a *good* "SUICIDE." *Thanks, God!*

August, 1957—Laura & I are all who are left of "The Hendersons"

My Daddy:—Born July 18, 1863; died May, 1925
My Dottie: Born Oct 27, 1899; died October 11, 1951
My Mama: Born Feb. 11, 1871; died Aug. 14, 1957—my *dear* Mama!

MRS. ISABEL HENDERSON[*]

BLUE HILL, [Maine] Aug. 15—Mrs. Isabel A Henderson, 86, the widow of the former acting ["acting" crossed out] postmaster of Boston, died Wednesday evening at a Blue Hill hospital.

Born in Cambridge, Mass., February 11, 1871, she was the daughter of Laura and Bella [Bela] Jacobs. In 1898 she married Arthur Richard Henderson then postmaster of Boston. [In 1923] They moved from Cambridge to Lexington, where Mr. Henderson died in 1925.

Since 1943 Mrs. Henderson had made her home with her daughter and son-in-law, Mr. and Mrs. Warren Partridge of Lexington, Mass. and in 1946 she came to Blue Hill with them.

Survivors are two daughters, Mrs. Laura Partridge and Mrs. Lois Bayliss, now of Paraguay, South America, seven grandchildren and five great grandchildren.

Services will be held at the family lot at Mt. Auburn Cemetery, Cambridge, Mass.

[*]Newspaper clipping with LHB edits.

When I was 4, I promised Mama to die when she died, & be buried with her. —And here I am in Paraguay, where I didn't know of her illness, nor her death-&-burial, until it was all over! My relationship with my Mama was troubled and turbulent, after I was 15; but I loved her, and she loved me, & perhaps now she has gone on—somewhere closer to God—she & I will be at peace, for always. She was such a fearful person—of perils, real & imaginary, I almost feel I *should* have gone along with her to give such protection as I could! —But that, of course, is the sort of feeling I must not indulge, for (as the Brotherhood is teaching me, slowly) I am nothing, nobody—only a "poor thing" (in God's sight) who can do nothing myself, for anyone at all—unless I am "used" by God for His purposes. Therefore, I must keep clear my spirit against the clogs & obstructions of conceited self-importance, & be an open "channel" for the Spirit that directs thought, deed, & word for the Brotherhood. —For *now*, having made my decision to forsake all the world, & *leave even my dear 3 & their 5 behind in it!*—until God calls *them*, too!—the Brotherhood is my family—my Father, Mother, Sister, Brother, Children and Grandchildren.

How very *little* I *deserve* the goodness of God in leading me to this life! —"The last of life, for which the first was made."

God, dear Father in Heaven, call Jon, & Sandy & Peter, too, I *pray!*

A Bruderhof Funeral

Last night word came to the Brotherhood, in meeting, that Gunther Homan, the librarian at Ibaté, aged 46, a bachelor "with certain infirmities," had died, in a coma, at the 'Casita' (Isolation house) at the Hospital. Only this week, two members of the Community had passed close to death, but made miraculous recovery, beyond the scope of mere medical healing. The death of this Brother, who had given just half of his whole span of life to the loving service of Brotherhood, came as a shock—because the Brotherhood regards Death as evil—one great power still held over every one of us by the Evil One. In token, the day was kept quiet, no talking at midday meal, or on the hof at all.

I had not attended Mama's burial (so far away), and I made the rites—so simple & beautiful—hers, as well as those of this Brother, in my heart.

Most of the observance was silent. The "home-made" coffin, of our good hardwood, in the shape of the Ark of the Covenant, stood on its bier in the Casita. The grey skies, shedding rain intermittently, and the rustling trees outside the place where he had died, spread over a company of perfectly silent men, women & children—all in rainwear, some with bare feet, or mere sandals. We kept a "watch" there, with white flowers & palm-tree branches gracing the simple, clean setting. Then, quietly, wagons drove up. The bearers lifted the coffin to a cart-bed, covering it with palms; and the cart drove out to the *hof* road, all the congregation following in unbroken silence. We came past the orange-groves, and found a long line of carts (horse-&ox-drawn), waiting to carry us to Isla, where in the *large* dining room, all the 3 communities could be accommodated for a funeral service. Even on the trip over, the silence was kept, with scarcely a whispered word, though some Brothers & Sisters shook hands. The coffin had been placed at the end of the room by the great brick fireplace. Two "Servants of the Word" (Georg Barth and Bruce Sumner) sat in quiet clothes beside it. —After a hymn in German, sung throughout its many stanzas, the simple funeral "sermon" was read in German by Georg, & translated, paragraph by paragraph, by Bruce, into English. Their voices could be plainly heard by all, though they spoke quietly. Two hymns followed, & then the coffin was carried to a cart, which the entire assemblage followed *on foot* for a mile & a half out to the beautiful burial-ground. Still, no words were spoken by the large company. —We stood in a circle while the coffin was lowered into a *very* deep pit (already prepared). Then (in German) we sang "Fairest Lord Jesus." Six shovels had been brought. The Brothers "spelled" each other, filling the red earth into the pit. When it was done, palm branches were heaped on the coffin, and women with flowers laid them upon the palms. We all walked back in the twilight to the hof again, boarded the lorries & carts, and returned to Loma.

After an hour's rest at home, we had a Love Meal at Loma. The dining-room was decorated simply, with palm branches. The tables were laid with white cloths. A long silence began the meal, and then a song. After all subdued bustle was subsided, Gwynn and Buddug told anecdotes about Gunther Homan in his lifetime—and lots of little human sidelights were shed on him as an individual personality by many others, who remembered him in the early Cotswold days.

I had never known the man—had only *seen* him once, from a distance, at Ibaté. But the things I heard last night—about his (6'6") great height, long legs, meticulous ways, punctuality, early theological training, love of Greek & the classics, and great awe of BOOKS— (so that he even catalogued Buddug's knitting-book!)—and his "simple, childlike nature"—made me a friend of his, even after he is buried now, deep in the soil of a country he probably never even dreamed of seeing in his youth!

~

Throughout the services I have prayed that Mama & I will be now in clearer unity. Our 'separation' was due to our sins. We forgive each other now. (I must *forget*, as well as *forgive*.)

Perhaps, when I die, I shall be buried near him.

~

It is so beautifully *quiet* here in Primavera—! That is, so free of *man-made noises!* The diesel-engine for generating electricity; the sawmill screech-&-grind; the machines in the laundry, yes—&, rarely, the sound of our lorry or our tractor, & the distant sound of Isla's steam whistle, before noon. But no "traffic-noises"! No terrible scream of brakes as a car stops suddenly; no factory-whistles; no trains, boats; no cross-sounding voices, no human quarreling! We hear Nature's noises, aplenty! *How the birds sing!* The cattle low; the horses neigh; the donkeys bray; the cocks crow; the hens cluck; the chickens peep; the frogs keep up a nightly chorus; and, before the rain, certain tree frogs 'miaw' (like cats) with exasperating continuity, in the banana-plantation behind the laundry. And on certain nights there are hideous noises of howling monkeys, across the camp. All of these are God's obedient creatures, "a joyful noise unto the Lord." No roar of the "El" train drowns their hymn.

Here, I am slowly learning—"the *hard* way"!—to do the Will of God on earth, as it is done in Heaven, that I may do my minuscule part to prepare for His Kingdom! And this is what all my life I prayed for an opportunity to do: to WORK FOR GOD! To do work well & humbly, with punctuality and goodwill was of *no avail,* out in the "world" (so thankfully left behind forever!) —For I was working *competitively,* for a "boss," for a pay-check. And in that routine I could not survive.

I am glad, & thankful, & humble in my heart for the privilege of being sent here. Surely, as all here have said, *God* directed me here. It is very late in my life to dedicate my years to Him, of which not many years are left! I could have heard His call years ago, doubtless, had I not been making so much noise myself—"showing-off," to get the center of attention, because I wished to hide from myself, my family, my fellow-men, & God Himself, too, that I was so guilty of sins that crucified His son, my Savior.

Shame on me! Thanks, God, for forgiveness of those sins. Make me *quiet & more humble!*

~

Oct 10

A year ago today, I was helping Agnes & Bill at Wappinger's Falls, N.Y. (on *my way* to Primavera)! Today I sit at the arbor-table by my little hut under the early-morning skies to write before I go to work in the laundry. I want to set down here *in writing* how thankful I am that God called me *out of the world* I shall never regret leaving! I am seeing ever more clearly how I am *really,* here, "working for God," as it has been my life-long desire to do! Humble tasks done for Brothers & Sisters to sustain them as living witnesses to the great God who made this beautiful world! —Making our part of it—or OUT of it!—ready for the time when "The sign of the Son of Man shall appear in the Heavens"... and He comes again, "with clouds and great glory" for "every eye to see."

I pray that my children & theirs will *follow* me "out of the world" where, poor young hopefuls, they are *so strained* to keep things going!

Saturday (Warren's birthday) Oct 12

—Another set-back! I am having another taste of the "pain" Tom

& Florrie predicted. It IS NOT EASY to surrender *"self."* And *all* of our 'selves' are miserable, crippled, devilish monsters of two-faced lying deceptive smugness! We have *all* "fallen short," indeed! I am now coming-up from under a *bad* time! —I had forgotten to collect my weekly-stores basket at the Lager-haus yesterday. After brewing my maté, making my toast, & collecting my daily egg, I went down to get it—in a very black mood (blaming someone else for my over-sight)—& *how wonderful* it was that I went, & saw the sun rising in the east over the wooded hill, & the mists lifting off the level vastnesses of the wide camp, pearly-grey over the blue-green "islas"! "It restoreth my soul" to see God's beauty all around me. I should be even *more grateful* to be here—and I want to go on with being "withdrawn" & QUIET—yet a while!

October 16, 1957

WRITING:—

What is happening to me here in regard to my prized "gift" for writing differs little from what many in the Brotherhood have ex-perienced—people who, in Music, Art, Drama, Literature—& even 'The Dance'!—have felt probably with equal amaze! *I can't seem to write at all anymore!* Now that is phenomenal, in itself! But what is more, I *don't care!* I, who *had* to "express myself" in order to *live* and be lived-with, am suddenly struck dumb!—even on paper, with an adequate fountain pen! I, who, years past, have written, edited & re-written 8 novels—besides bales of short stuff, & volumes of poetry!—have suddenly nothing to say, & no words to say it in! — I, who willingly worked at the "profession" of writing (journalism) for the sake of my "creative soul," & paid-out from my salaries the wages of housekeepers to do "the dirty work," am now (inchoately) living in the greatest tranquility, literally earning my (whole wheat) bread by folding (threadbare) clothes in the community laundry.

It was before I heard of the Bruderhoefe at all that I had realized the empty vanity of the life of "letters"; & long before, that I had realized what 'clanging cymbals' the 'Great' in literature are, as per-sons. —But, for *me*, the person "dedicated" (of yore) to write REAL things, eschewing the hollow pretenses of fellowship with other vain 'artists' (in all Branches of the Arts); who swore to maintain my integrity as a creative individual, & be wholly secure from taint by Bohemianism and/or Success—I am so *dumb*, now, that even writing a letter to my family is an ordeal! *The explanation:* SELF (Ego) IS dying, praise God from Whom All Blessings Flow; and I am *well out of the world,* where never was a place for me!

How I was preparing, all my years, for life in community—

I studied German in school.

I learned to love Nature at Pigeon Cove (& elsewhere).

I always "talked to God" (aloud & silently) day & night about *everything*. God was always my confidante & my Father.

I learned to enjoy singing with Dottie at the piano; & I sang in St. Cecilia's choir (Cambridge), & the church choir in Lexington.

I suffered with the misery of the people who were poor, degraded & dirty, very early in life; and ever since.

I learned about "racial problems" from the colored children on Soden St., when I was 7; & from my own husband, when I was married, at 22.

I tried to get a missionary's training (1918) from Sam'l Job. (He laughed.)

I learned the severity of "religious-&-cultural" differences in my marriage to Henry. —(Are they insurmountable *everywhere* but in Church Community?)

I learned, as a "career-girl" (from 1924 on) the horrible, cutthroat competition of life for 'professional'-workers in Worcester, Boston, New York, Whitman, Rutland, Oakland, Piedmont, etc. etc.

I learned the DIGNITY of common *labor*, & the conquest of "job-snobbery," (via the Depression & WPA) in Cambridge, Rutland; in Oakland & San Francisco & Long Beach, California.

I learned the terrible slavery of factory-workers as a woman in War-Industry, in '41–'43.

I learned the harsh lessons of WORK at sea, as a stewardess.

I learned to be "poor & humble" in my own home-City, where my family had been proud & "important"—when, in "the Bread Line" I followed the slow-moving cue for welfare-subsistence, during the Depression, into the basement of a City Hall in whose upper

Lois, summer 1942. "They dubbed me 'Droopy Drawers' when I wore this costume—working among thousands of labor slaves for Andy Mellon at Edgewater's Alcoa—my purpose was to help win the War!" [LHB]

Lois with photo of son Jon in Navy uniform, probably 1944, and Roosevelt campaign placard.

Council Chambers hung portraits of my forefathers who founded Cambridge. —And in Christ Church, where my Uncle began his life as a clergyman, I was "church mouse" (1933–39).

I learned the Gospel, at first, in Oxford Group meetings, in '33–35; & much, much more profoundly from diligent study, via "Voice of Prophecy," Lutheran, Jehovah's Witness, World Israel movement & other correspondence courses.

Oct 27, 1957

Today, Dottie would be 58 years old. I have no little Mama now, to send a letter to, about her birthday. Mama & Daddy & Dottie—the 3 "proper Victorians" of our family are now all together. Laura & I are lone survivors of the Henderson family. (Think how poor Daddy strove & struggled to keep us well & prosperous! And what did his whole life's effort come to? —A grave in Mt. Auburn!—The best thing he ever did was to entrust Mama with the little she had left of his 'fortune,' to give me ½ of to put into the Brotherhood!) —Well, the 3 Victorians are aware now that Lois, the "Black Sheep," has found her way back to the fold of the Good Shepherd now. Only valiant (foolish?) little Laura is left *in the world*. And she is protected from it by her veneer of self-preservation, & by Warren's love and generous tolerance of her self-willed whims.

I remember Dottie in her fly-away childhood, and in her radiant adolescence when her cheeks were pink, her curly golden hair, fluffy & bright, and her beautiful blue eyes, fringed with long, dark lashes, full of vigor and interest. She was a "maiden fair" in the best (Victorian) sense! —A girl, as "*Wansome*" Church used to say, of "vewwy sweet cawacter"! If Walter had not come slithering along, deceiving Dottie & our parents with his grinning *pseudo*-gentleness, Dottie might have LIVED while she was alive. As it was, neither she nor Mama ever really lived at all! —I wish I were not so sentimental as to think it makes any sort of difference that Dottie's grave is in the sandy soil of Texas, about 2000 miles from the quiet slope below Mt. Auburn tower—for of course there is no "mileage" between Daddy & Mama & their first child, Dottie now.—

Oh, God, may they all rest peacefully. For their sins forgiven, for their goodness & gentleness & long-suffering rewarded, may they yet be called for the Resurrection of the Dead, to enjoy the beauty of thy Kingdom! Amen

~

What I would (like to) say to Percy Blair (if it were advisable for guests to talk to guests):

Iconoclasm is not "smart." When one tears down every "god," there is nothing left at all! And one needs something to live by & for! Better far to heed Paul's words: "Examine all things. Hold fast that which is good." —Here in Primavera there is all the good one needs to live by. By the process of elimination, the flimsy, or unhealthy parts of living have been taken out of life-in-community, so that basically all things by which we live are good.

Scoffing is a superficial technique for 'getting a laugh' (as Broadway puts it). Everyone at the bridge-table, or the cocktail-party, or in the patio by the edge of the swimming pool laughs at the scoffing. But the scoffer himself profits nothing. Out of the emptiness of his heart, he speaketh—leaving his heart even emptier!

It is good to "face up" to the "facts of life" ("the birds & the bees") with the children one has been given to teach. But it is only a small part of parenthood. Far better to "emphasize the positive":—to demonstrate to the little ones the great power & majesty of the Creator of all things! When an adult 'dwells' on the physical functions beyond normal necessity, it is because his libido is still out of proportion to the whole of his being. After 50, it is normal for the libido to subside gradually.

Percy says he is "naturally good." He finds goodness (so he protests) a "normal" state with him. "*I* am not evil!" he declares. "*I* am not selfish!" —It is not so long ago that I felt that way about myself. —It was when Heini called me a "poor thing" that I first *began to dwindle* to my actual size in importance! When we look at the VAST skies and wide open pampas about us here, we are lost in our littleness before the vastness of Creation. "It is a fearful thing to fall into the hands of the loving God."

I pray for Percy. (Though he *denies* it, I am sure he has been & still is suffering, as I have done, from the crippling blows of life! I wish I could help him *actively*. But all I can do is pray that *he, too,* will be *healed* by LOVE-in-Brotherhood.) I hope he will not give up & go back to the fruitless wandering in the jungles of "civilization," where subsistence is the only reward; & existence is troubled by the knowledge that while one seeks only his own way, he himself is the prey of the "Great Dragon" whose insatiable appetite for the souls of men never is sated! Be kind to poor Percy & his lonely little boys, please, God!

I made a copy of the first ¾ of this letter, intending to hand it to Fran, to "censor," and pass on to Percy. But at the meeting in the morning, when I expressed myself as grateful for the *healing* of Community, after the 'casualties of the world,' it seemed *very pointed* that Pearl spoke of how Christ built his people out of sinners—*stipulating* (both genders) "adulterers & adulteresses." —I felt so antagonized (because the cap fitted too well) that, knowing Fran shares all his work with Pearl, I didn't feel like confiding that much in him. So after the Household Meeting, I invited Percy to sit on the bench in full view of the entire *hof,* to read the letter, & to talk. It was NOT obedience, & I knew it! But the Victorian attitude here towards 'morals' simply wakes old reflexes, so that I rebel almost automatically! No harm came of it—to me; but Fran spoke to me after dinner, & definitely FORBADE *any* "conversation" with Percy, because (he said) "We don't want you to form any *friendship* with him that may hinder your coming into the Brotherhood."

(I am to see Fran today, to discuss the matter further, I *hope*.)

I have no intention of allowing ANYTHING to "hinder" my coming to the Brotherhood! And the morose and bitter Percy certainly isn't going to stand in my way! —In fact, I wondered if God had sent him there (as an "element") to TEST *me* (?)

> Oh, thou, who man of baser earth didst make,
> And e'en with Paradise devise the snake
>   For all the sin wherewith the face of man is blackened
> Man's forgiveness give, and take!

But I don't feel *that* way: I am *glad* to meet challenges to the God-given power of "Free Will"! I made my *firm decision* March 6, 1953—(long before I heard of the Brotherhood). I have no intention of changing it! —It is merely *still* infuriating to me that *good people* can *read evil* into *anything!*

Later: —The above was all settled with Fran, who understood the whole matter.

Oct 28/'57

I am getting old-&-ugly now; *but I don't mind!* My "liver-spots" are changing to unsightly moles; the flesh on my arms, legs, body & bosom is sagging more & more. The "very pretty face," which I could always use as a 'mask' (to hold my guilty self-knowledge), which people (in the world) used to compliment me upon, is now *no more! I am* old-&-ugly! I only hope God can *still* "do deeds" with me, because that is what I am here for!

Nov. 4 (Monday)

Yesterday morning (Sunday), I woke up *elated* by the thought: *"I never need to take another job again, in all the rest of my life!" Such* a comforting thought (after years of work-history, so *disillusioning*, so *stormy*; so *varied!)* started my day off beautifully, befitting weather so clear, cool & perfect it might have been San Francisco in January!

First I had hot maté, to give me zest—as soon as the kitchen opened; then a nice walk through the schoolwood, down the camp to Kurt's 'Baumgarten,' & back in time to put wildflowers in water before breakfast with Bob & Hannah Peck—very *good*, in a *dainty* little house, with *hot coffee!* (2 cups), strong & black! Then 'duty' in the dining-room, with Roland K, preparing for meeting. The schedule gave me time to clean up & dress, & be on time—for an *extra* good meeting. (I am glad *Georg* has come! I feel an understanding in him that is very reassuring!) [I should like to note here that he *astutely* compared as "the same, in reverse" "Thy Kingdom Come, thy will be done" and "repent ye, for the Kingdom of Heaven is at hand"]—(*very* satisfyingly acute!)—Pearl Hall & I went rambling, to the library for books, down to the Mother House to see Ginny

Newton & little Craig Peter (strong rock) Newton, & out behind the hospital wood, after meeting. —At dinner, Ernst Plant talked to us, about Abbé Pierre's "Emmaus" movement, as adapted to conditions of poverty and poor housing in B.A. —Then siesta. After that, first a family-walk with Jan & Susi Fros & family, to the deep old Ibaté woods—& then supper with Marjorie, Vera, Rowan & Jeanie. —A *very full day!*

I don't think I shall *ever* want to *leave* Primavera. It will be lovely to me, *always!* I still feel "translated"—"unreal"—'perhaps *dead—*?' —And why *not?* For, after all, I have left the world & my old tensions, worries, struggle, & sin behind, forever! And I am here, doing Thy Will, oh, God, in order to prepare, with all my Brothers-&-Sisters-to-be for the Kingdom of Christ upon earth!— (I pray, fervently, that God will call Sandra, Peter & Jonathan, too— & that they all will have ears to hear Him!)

~

Joan & Leonard Pavitt visited Helen & Bob Mitchell in Los Gatos; and Peter & Janis in Kentfield (as per my urgent request). I do hope they will make contact, too, with Edna & Leonard Brown in Ukiah—if only they go that far! I feel *sure* that is a very RICH possibility!

~

I had a talk with Fran & Pearl today, to settle for good the question of her "hovering-over" him, & my deep-seated residual resentments that I have "transferred" from the past to the entirely unrelated present. (Isn't Pearl a little like Doris? and Fran, like Jonathan?)

Thank you, God, for bringing me here to Paraguay, to find, in Primavera, a *place of healing* for all the wounds I incurred in the cruel world!

~

In a way I kept my childhood's word to Mama, to die when *she* died; for I have *left the world* (as she has). I have left behind all the old ways—the "freedom" that was slavery! For the 'slavery' that is freedom; left the pressure of competition in work, in social life, in

Art; the vanities of dress and personality; and, very *very* slowly, the glib-tongued persiflage by which I deceived others and myself, too, into thinking I was "the life of the party" wherever I found myself—&, also even *more* slowly, the constant noise & chatter I used to make.(I am growing evermore *silent. I!* Yes, *I!*) [I shall continue on this, till I become one whose 'Yay' & 'Nay' are all others need to hear from me.]

This is a period of "training"… I am now learning to ACT "like a Brother." The irritability that has still persisted here, since I came away from the world (May 28, from So. Station, Boston) is also decreasing. I am learning how true it is that here we "do not live together" (as Fran says) "because we love each other; but because *God called us out of the world*"—to live-in-sharing of work, 'wealth' and worship. I am *learning* (SLOWLY) to tolerate more; to resent less; to give a softer answer every time.

Thank you, God, for this!

My little Mama who has left the world even farther behind than I, who now lies on that sunny, leafy slope below the Gothic tower in Mt. Auburn (where, alive & robust, she used to take us, as children, to visit the "family lot")—(*Dear* little Mama!)—*she* was *always gentle, quiet, forgiving (& forgetting), pacific!* She was *never* "quarrelsome"! —And never, never in all my years did I hear her say unkind or "witty" things about anyone! … So she is nearer ready to be called from "the place of departed spirits" when the Angel's trumpet blows; while I—though here, in Primavera, I continue to feel "*un*-real," as if *I* were '*dead*', *too!*—must work a little longer in life to destroy the evil in my spirit. But Mama and I are now (as Sandra says) better able to "talk together"; & I pray to Jesus, my "advocate & mediator" that she may understand how very, very GRATEFUL I feel to her for what she left me—to "give-in" to the Brotherhood. Here in Primavera, I keep thinking:—"Thank you for the birds that sing! Thank you, God, for *everything!*"

Nov 10.

I was bidden back to Gemeinde. What a glorious day it was—*perfect* cool, clear, tonic air; golden sun! I felt peaceful, happy, assured of God's great love for us all, even me! Tomorrow, Ernst Plant leaves us for B.A. again; and our meeting was largely concerned with his "pet-charity," the Emmaus movement in BA, which (we all pointed out) was a "good work," well-intended to help others, but far from a *permanent* solution for Poverty and Social Injustice. Also, we pointed-out to him that the *real* 'cure' is only to be found in waking all men to God's glory. (I talked too much, alas—as I usually do when I am *elated!)* I said that I knew well from personal experience that at times of direst need—with no money, no job, no hope, no expectancy—one could still Worship God for his goodness & greatness. (I've never 'blamed' Him for any of the *world's* harshness, knowing *He* did not produce it!) And when Ernst spoke (with resignation, & some bitterness (?)) of his inability to speak of spiritual matters in a Roman-Catholic movement, *because he is a Jew*, I thought of the same kind of wistfulness in Henry, & I *burst out* that *here*, with us, he has not been ('separated' as) a Jew, and would never be a Jew if he came to join us, & that I hoped his way back home from here might turn out to be his "road to Damascus." (Jorg—who translated for me—didn't grasp the allusion to Paul's conversion.) Fran warned me, after Gemeinde, that I must not *speak too much* in meetings. (I know that: & *tried hard* to hold back the flood of words that came to me.) *For in silence, is truth!* I promised to be quieter next time. — Eberhard Arnold writes: "In every conscience that has been awakened by the Spirit, the inner voice is in accord with God's objective will & purpose. This voice, therefore, is able to become *hushed* in *silent reverence*, in order to LISTEN TO GOD, and to praise him "rightly & worthily" [taking the quotation from "Martyrdom of Peter" (an old Latin ms.)]—which expounds on silence thus: "So I thank thee not with these lips, not with this word—this oratory of earthly nature; but with the voice that can only be perceived in silence, I thank thee, O King! It is not perceptibly heard. It proceedeth from no physical organ. It entereth no natural ear. It is heard not of what is transient. It belongeth not to this world. It does not sound upon this earth. With this voice, I thank thee, Jesus Christ—this voice which is the silence of the Voice—which the spirit within me (who loveth thee) speaketh with thee, and seeeth thee, doth meet. Thou art to be recognized only in spirit."

~

I BELONG *here*! [In many phases of my life I have definitely NOT "belonged"!

[I remember my bewilderment in Worcester, 1924, when I had my first newspaper-job, on the Worcester POST. I lived in a clean, newly-furnished room in a downtown Swedish hotel. I "ate out." I didn't 'belong' to the place at all, living, nor eating-out. And when I went walking, exploring the miserable city of Worcester, I was lost & lonely. Then at work, I met the unconscionable madcap, Polly Kindred, who was anxious to 'take-up' with me; & she & I & 'Bunny' Estabrook, and someone I vaguely remember as Reg, the sulky-boy son of Tait, an Ice Cream manufacturer, used to "go out" together, in cars, & to "speaks." And I wasn't happy. I never "belonged" to that life, those people.] With Monica & Dallas Graham & their boy Peter, in Worcester, I DID "belong."

I *belonged* in Pigeon Cove, & Lexington, & Cambridge; and at home with my family; & in the hearts and homes of my friends.

I remember my sensations of dismay in my first experiences with "Bohemia" on the western slope of Beacon Hill. —I didn't understand all I saw. I was mis-understood by practically every "long-haired man & short-haired woman" who lived there. My only excuse or reason for gravitating to such a place was that I was "be-reaved" for the first time—by a combination of things—Tuck's desertion; Dottie's engagement; Mama's withdrawal from any interest in me; Laura's sudden growing-up and away—and my own strivings for a "career." My job then, as publicity-writer & authors' correspondent for Little, Brown & Co made me happy at work. But it was fusty and out-of-date at Little Brown's, & the pay was ridiculous!

[So—to New York City! How DAZED I was there, at first! How terrified by Mama's dire forewarnings of the "certain fate" awaiting young-women-alone in the great city—! My first 3 days—because I was still shaken by the awful quarrel with Daddy that had precipitated my leaving home—I barricaded myself into the Hotel room, afraid even of going down to the lobby, or the café. I had heard of "Room Service," & how by lifting the phone, I could have food brought up. So, not knowing the scope of the available menu, I lived on chocolate ice cream—shivering & lonely, & longing for a good square meal.] On the 4ᵗʰ day, I ventured out for breakfast on Madison Avenue. It was 7.00 am—& the whole, jaded City was *asleep!*

It didn't take me long to re-gather my (egotistic) "forces," once I dared find my way around! Bruce Barton—the Great Publicist of the mid-Twenties—was gracious enough to see me, when (brazenly) I sent in a message by his (highly-amused) secretary that "Miss Henderson from Boston was here to see him." Bruce looked at my country-fresh face, "health" shoes, tweed coat, knitted cap—heard my "Boston accent," patted my (unmanicured) hand, & said: "Go home to Boston! Find a husband, and bring up a family!" —But I had lost hope, when my *un*true love, Tuck, with whom I had spent a lovely, dalliant summer planning domestic bliss, and even *naming* our 5 children—Lincoln, Jr., Agnes Isabel, Richard, Dorothy Mary & Ralph!—& the great living room of "the Tiad" (where we should live in affluence we would have (!) (?)) with a great stone fireplace at one end, & a builtin organ at the other, & one wall lined with our best books—the others, looking out across the country we had roamed & camped-on throughout that incredible romantic idyll— *Tuck* had gone his way! I had written (about *him):*

> My love & I would wedded be
> A family we would beget
> My love he sailed away from me
> My love, he could forget!
> Our children are but shadow-souls
> Their little hearts will know no sin
> Because they'll never see this world
> They might have bided in!
> Yet, they are mine! And every night
> I make the rounds of all their beds,
> To kiss their lovely cheeks, and ask
> God's *blessing on their unborn heads!*

> *Also:*—To My Children
> Now my youth is passing lightly

> All day long my heart is singing
> But in dreams, my fantasies nightly
> With thy future laughter ringing
> Shows this youth, its joy & graces
> Shining on *thy* lovèd faces
> All my youthful heart is yearning
> For that promisèd hereafter
> When life's ways I shall be learning
> Sweetened by thy merry laughter.

I had still not gotten a job when Rodney Long came to my rescue, Daddy's ambassador of forgiveness & goodwill, with a purse full of Daddy's "contrition"-money, to buy me smart New York clothes, "show me around" the land of Gotham, and teach me cosmopolitan ways. Rod thoroughly *enjoyed* spending that money, more of it on *himself* for "Travel & Expenses" (in a *good* Hotel) than on me, I fancy. (I didn't inquire how he divided it.) When I had been properly outfitted at good shops, & had (I well remember) a *beautiful* soft black cloth coat with a *real* leopard collar, & a pretty hat with real *chic,* & some practical business-dresses, a suit, many pairs of silk stockings & "smart" shoes, I did gather confidence. Rodney made a great fanfaron about installing me at a girls Residence-Club, under hawk-eyed chaperonage by the management. It was on my *own* that I got a fine publishing job, as Ass't to Fred Willock, & really began to be a "career-girl."

I'm afraid my confidence grew TOO fast. I had no long wait for a gay social life. I looked up Ramon Arratia, the Chilean professor of Romance languages at Columbia's International House who spent his summers at Pigeon Cove. His smart red convertible made me the "envy of other poor girls," parked outside the Club on 30th St. (E. of Lexington), with his handsome brother & his fiancée, & *he,* even handsomer, at the wheel, waiting to take me for Spring drives on Sundays out to Westchester—the association with Esther & Bill Hodgman, & their Park Avenue in-laws also "set me up" in the eyes of the Club membership. And Ozelle Mathis, when she first arrived from Texas "took me up" (till I unmasked her perversions for the horrified old-lady Directors.) And when I met the Broadway music-comedy crowd through Earl Williams, & began going to movie-& radio-studio parties on Riverside Drive, & Park Avenue, & the Carnegie Hall Studios on 57th St, I was 'gayer' than I ever bargained for! —I remember the very champagne-free party of film star Mac-Murray's, when I met the two scions of the house of Voorbees (N.Y. 'Society' boys), & Andrew singled me out. I had never had champagne before! It made me dance like an angel! We FLOATED about a golden-waxed floor, in an enchantment. When the room got over-heated, we ran, holding hands, down a long corridor where an open window admitted a draft of air, from the night. We groped inside the room, looking for a light, & smelt ROSES—beautiful roses! They were long-stemmed American Beauties, standing in inch-deep water in a *huge* bathtub.

"Oh," said I (*drunk* for the first time in my life) "*A bed of roses!*" And I climbed into the tub, & he after me, despite the water at the bottom (which *saturated* my blue velvet dress with a band of fur at the hem!)—& we lay down like kittens, and slept cool-ly, through the hot summer night, amid petals & thorns.

It was daylight when we got home. "Gorgon McMahon," the Director, saw from her window how draggled & "wrung-out" I was when I alighted in light of day before the front door of Girls Community Club Marshall! & *dared* to let myself in with my key!

Ah, that was the beginning of the end of my high-standing at the Club! I, the Boston girl of "good family," with such "careful" parents, etc. etc.—

But all the gold & glitter & flim-flam didn't do anything to stop my internal weeping for my unborn children! And all the smart New York clothes, & the worship of my little Jewish secretary at the office (who considered me a 'genius' and a 'glamour-girl') didn't help my aching empty heart. I longed for Mama & Daddy & Dottie & Laura & Friday, & Lexington, and Pigeon Cove, & Cambridge, & *honest, natural* life with dew in the morning & sweet smells from the honeysuckle vines at supper-on-the porch at home! (It's a *sad* thing when a young person starts to "conquer the world"; for there is a danger that she may, instead, *be conquered by* the world!)

Summer days on Cape Ann. Steve and Lois, off Wingaersheek Beach, Gloucester, August 1919.

"Lois, Bill, Libbett, Steve, Wingaersheek Beach in World War times, 1919." [LHB]

Thank God for preserving my inmost integrity & faith in Him, through all sorts of brash ventures into the "realistic," materialistic life of Babylon! Thank God for my early life with the beauty of sea, & sun, & wind, & sky at Pigeon Cove, where Beauty and Nature taught me to love God innocently. —And never, never let me forget the "rattle-grind" sound of the little granite-laden "dolly"-cars that I heard after the shrill 7 o'clock whistle at Halibut Pt quarry—which symbolized the wicked slavery, of the brutally-treated workers in the granite-industry. *God help Man!*

Primavera, Nov. 26

A "Sister"—(?)—told Georg Barth that I "*don't know much about Jesus*"!

This troubles me. Am I so utterly STUPID in appearance? —I simply cannot—& will not—pick up the jargon of *clichés* people here use to convey their feelings and certainties about Faith. If I cannot express my Faith in words of my own, I'll continue to be silent about it. —I told Fran Hall to remind others that Fat People are not necessarily as ridiculous as they *look!* —Why should I *be* here, if I did not "know about Jesus"?

~

I have not only asked twice, at Gemeinde, for a novitiate, but I have had long talks with Fran, Moni & Georg about it. I have been here 5 months. Am I to be a "stone rejected by the builders"? why?

Why do so many people doubt me? —I have no use for "sack-cloth-&-ashes" piety; nor any tongue for unctuous phrases. But I love God, and He knows how many, many prayers of thanks and exaltation I have offered him for the Gift of His Son—whose Death & Resurrection were for me, too—(since He "came not to save the righteous, but sinners—!")

~

Yesterday afternoon, Buddug and Belinda came up on the porch of the sewing-room (not seeing me there), and Buddug was saying with a chilly laugh "Oh, well, *they*'re ONLY *Americans*—!" When she saw me, she clapped her hand over her mouth. —She made light of it; but refused to "discuss the matter." —I wonder if I should take it up in meeting, or not? As Americans, we are expected—not to say *required!*—to bring no prejudice of any kind with us! But there is a deep, incurable contempt for Americans—mostly as "*vulgar,*" money-mad, & "loud"—by the English & Germans alike. —Still, America has 3 Bruderhoefe now, & "Americans are very generous" (with *money & goods*); & Buddug's own husband is at Woodcrest. —(I shall certainly talk to *Fran* about this, anyway. —Otherwise, "letting it go," I think, is best.)

~

Last night, at Gemeindestunde, I said: "I hope it is acceptable for me to repeat—now for the *3rd time*—my request to be accepted as a novice." Fran assured me it was; that my request was "certainly being considered." —Afterwards, Bob Peck held out his hand. "Your speeches are getting better & better, all the time," he said. "You mean, the *less* there are of them?" I asked. "*Precisely!*" he said. "And I am not speaking superficially!"

I do not quite comprehend the above. (Bob had just read the "Radiogram to the Brotherhood," which I wrote in Peabody, 1955 after my first Woodcrest summer.)

I am sure I am very THICK indeed. —But I'm "only an American," after all! What could be expected?

Radiogram to the Brotherhood:

> Send out a pilot; steer me in!
> For I have sailed seven seas of sin
> And trod the continents, and found
> The world is *all* unhallowed ground.
> My ship is foundering outside—
> Tossed by world's winds; drawn by self's tide;
> Helmed by the Enemy of Him
> In whose name, Brothers, *let me in!*
>
> This port is safe! And God above
> Is its Commandant. *Here is love.*
> And I, a fugitive from storm
> Need to be healed, and safe, & warm.
> All cargo I had stowed aboard

Is worthless here, oh God, my Lord!
I've scuttled it; & being still
Know thou art God; & will Thy will.

Years ago (1933) I wrote (concerning my dismal failure in marriage, & in subsequent seeking for love (which I never found till I met MM in *1951)):*

Look not for love, denying God
That were your folly from the start
On earth a lonely soul, forlorn,
Staggers beneath an empty heart
Without God's love! no earthly love
Can be fulfilled, no peace be known
For we who will not love the Lord
Must walk alone.

~

When I first heard CLG (in the pulpit of Christ Church, Cambridge) I began to believe in Good People again, and I wrote to him (thereby foolishly adding to the adulation with which he was smothered by a tremendously enthusiastic congregation):

The savant and the cynic pay
In tears for being over-wise.
But on your face, the light of day
Irradiates; and in your eyes
Kindles the spark of love Divine.
You've helped this sorry soul of mine
Immeasurably; and I ask
For you, when you have done your task
On earth, in Heaven a special place
Where you may watch Our Father's face.
          God shares his gentle jokes with few
          But he will tell them all to you.

—And now (1957) just the other day, he sent me a tiny card of greeting (from Ann Arbor, Michigan), an acknowledgment of my letter to him about the Brotherhood … He *never* deigns to discuss *any* question that could expose to his own mind the terrible hypocrisy of the Episcopal Church!—an organization designed for the preservation of the Clergy as a privileged class!

~

Max Rucker wants to come to Primavera for a visit after Xmas. He wrote Fran Hall about it—a terrifically "downright-honest" letter saying *he* wants "to stay right out in the open world"—but he IS "interested to see how people can live in 'community.'" (I think Fran continues to doubt his motives & my own, & the tenor of our *entirely* platonic friendship!) —It seems too bad to read evil into things! Fran can't *quite believe* that Mar 6, 1953 marked the END of what is bathetically called "love-life" for me! —And I didn't meet Max till June 1955, and then enjoyed his company only as a friend & 'escort' (ashore) and party-companion aboard ship. It was just a fact that we liked each other's personal characteristics.

I hope Fran's diligent "scrupulousness" (which I promise not to call "old-maidishness") for the "purity of the whole" will not antagonize Max, and make him think the Brotherhood is oppressive in such matters.

Dec 1 (Advent Sunday, & Susie's 5th birthday. Bless her sturdy little golden heart!)

Advent is celebrated here by the infusion of the spirit of expectation. Fran led the meetings today, with the theme: "Are you living in expectation?" It was a wonderful meeting! (I had hoped to become a novice on Advent Sunday—but because of many other more important things, the event I have long, long desired was put off for a week.) The dining room is beautiful with a great Advent wreath, slung from the rafters, & bearing 4 red candles (ingeniously dyed by clever Susi Fros). Great bunches of greens, & yellow flowers, & 2 red candles on each bracket on the pillars that support the roof. The children gave a "miracle play," with the girls in angels' robes, silver stars in their shining hair, and lighted candles in their hands.

Their clear, high, childish voices inevitably brought the tears to my eyes. We had a Love Meal at evening, & celebrated also Duffy & Susie's wedding up in Woodcrest. The square table under the Advent wreath, covered with a white cloth, had a ring of small, unlighted white tapers, surrounding a tall lit red candle. At the meeting after the meal, we were offered the opportunity to light one of the tapers, with a "reason-why," & after 3 or 4 others had done so, I lit one for Jonathan, Sandra, & Peter, & their families—(as I have done for many years, in *many places* where "votive lights" burn in token of prayers)—that the Light that brought me here would light their lives, too, & bring them into Brotherly Community. The others' prayers were largely more general—except Ed Hallowell's for his old father—until, after many were lit, Percy got up & stumbled across the brick floor, a little sheepishly, to light one for his 2 little boys & himself, in gratitude for the kindness they receive here. —It was the first visible sign he has given of being really "moved." Everyone was very glad!

It was a beautiful Advent. I wrote my children on Fran's theme: "Are *you* living in expectation?" (I think I have been too "evangelistic" in my letters home, lately. They don't write me often.)

Dec 6

I had Family Supper with the jolly Fros family. St. Nicholas came with cakes, nuts & candy, in (to me) a very new "Santa Claus" version.

Sat. Dec. 7, 1957 16th anniversary of the "Day of Infamy."
(Sandra & I were in Hartford, Conn. that Sunday afternoon in 1941)

Tomorrow I enter my novitiate. The decision is made; there is to be no turning back. I am nothing. I have nothing. I want nothing. What *good I* can do for the Brotherhood will be demonstrable only through Grace, if & when God chooses to "do deeds with" me. Meanwhile, though my intense feelings about this for the past week or 10 days have left me limp & lifeless, I am ever so *serene!* (I cannot remember ever having felt so *quiescent* in my lifetime!)

After tomorrow, Fran says I shall "attend *almost* all" of the Brotherhood meetings—more as a "silent member" than as participant. I shall then get the "gist" of the *"one-great-family"*-feeling that I have not quite yet assimilated hitherto.

I want God to know—& to let my Mama know—how thankful I am to her for leaving me what she did, to "give-in" at this time. It was, really, after all!—*worth* all the years of real struggle with "The Wolf," when she *wouldn't* give me anything at all—to have it *now!*

My one regret: *I have nothing for the dearest people in "the world," Jonathan, Sandra, & Peter!*

God, please, please send your messengers of light to my 3 dear children! *Bring them to this Life!* I ask it *in Christ's name,* in which thou hast promised to grant all requests!

Dec. 8, 1957 (Second Sunday in Advent)

Maria Weiss and I are now novice-members of the Society of Brothers—as Will Marchant said, "never to be ALONE *again"! Thanks be to God.*

Christ keeps His promises!

Once *understanding* the Bible, and the TRUTH of the Coming Kingdom, I began to pray INTELLIGENTLY: "Thy Kingdom Come"! I woke to realize (1950) that there is NO *raison d'être* at all except the promise of his Advent, his Judgment, & his Kingdom.

Said Jesus: "Seek ye first the Kingdom of Heaven, and all things shall be added unto you."

That promise, now, is fulfilled *for me!* All things HAVE been added unto me in the life of Brotherly Community!

Thank you, thank you, little child of Bethlehem!

Said He, also: "Whatsoever ye ask in my name shall be granted." And, knowing His unshakable integrity, I ask in His name that my 3 dear children, round whom my life centered for many years—as dear to me as He was to his mother, Mary!—may also find the Meaning of Life for themselves, and come, too, to live in Brotherly Community! —Amen! Amen! Amen!

(Next Sunday, Dec. 15, is Sandra's 29th birthday. My dearest, most loyal, loving little "□-girl," my "Buttersnake," my dear daughter-mother-friend-&-earthly comforter! God bless her, and keep her, & bring her to the Kingdom.)

~

The Kingdom must be near at hand. Prophecies are being fulfilled so fast now. I have prayed for 7 years that I may be still "quick" to see the overthrow of Satan, & the crowning of the Heavenly King! Amen! Amen! Amen! —The torture on the Cross was not in vain. Thank God-the-Father for his Son! Amen!

I really "lit into" Percy Blair, when he continued to scoff at the meaningfulness of my novitiate; and I think, this time, my words impressed him! I told him: "Christ Himself said that repentance freed man from *every sin*—(even the sin of blasphemy of Christ Himself!)—*except* the sin of *blasphemy against the Holy Spirit.* "It is the Holy Spirit that runs this place," I told Percy, "and all your scoffing and 'needling' are blasphemous!" For once, he seemed to *hear* with his mind's ears! —I think he IS slowly opening his heart to the life here.

Primavera. Dec 13th, '57

Notes: the daily schedule here (like everything else!) is *perfectly* designed! Now that I am eligible for attending Brotherhood meetings, I shall have to learn to keep awake late at night! But I still have my sacred privilege of getting up to watch the beautiful sunrises in this lovely land! The ineffable innocence & delicacy of the Dawn delights my soul—reminds me of happy childhood; brings me closest to God; exalts me! Pink & gold and lavender clouds in the East; mists lifting off the vast camp, to expose glistening dew on the wooded slopes. And peace & quiet unbroken by man's own noise or the hoots, shrieks, thumps and roars of his inventions! This is, indeed, the threshold of Paradise! I remember, up in Lexington, in 1923, writing a meaningless little poem to express this sort of feeling:—(only part of it remains in my memory)

> Wonder of Morn, Flower of Dawn
> Child of the music of Rhapsody born,
> Waif of a stream, soul of a dream

Thrill of the night bathed in the light
Out of the moon.

——- —— —— - —— -— (etc)

—— —— —— ——

Thou who wert given out of the Heaven
Out of the moon.

I never knew just what it *meant*, myself!—except an expression
of my own happiness & ecstasy in response to God's gifts of beauty.

Dec. 14, '57

It is wonderful to be surrounded by Love & the understanding
acceptance of love, for me—! The love I feel often wells up & runs
over! In the world, even by my family, it was often misunderstood;
& by others, quite frequently scoffed-at, and, also, rejected! *Here*, I
can love, love, love, to my heart's content—my Brothers & Sisters,
their children, the young people, the animals, poultry, song-birds,
flowers, trees, sky—the *whole world here* is willing to be loved, &
accepts my feelings!

(One day, crossing the *hof,* I was feeling so *happy,* I said to the
first person I happened to meet—Phyllis Woolston—"You know I
just LOVE *everybody* on the Bruderhof, *including you!*" She replied
matter-of-factly, "Well, I never supposed you disliked me, Lois!"
She is a dear woman, the "bringer of babies" at the Mother House.
Of course I love her—& everyone else!)

I often think of Mary's "Magnificat," & sing it from a very full
heart (Luke 1:46):

"My soul doth magnify the Lord, and my spirit hath rejoiced in
God, my Savior, for he hath regarded the lowliness of his hand-
maiden. For behold from henceforth all generations shall call me
blessed. For he that is mighty hath magnified me, & holy is his
name. His mercy is on them that fear him, from generation to generation. He hath showed strength with his arm. He hath scattered
the proud in the imagination of their hearts. He hath put down the
mighty from their seat, and hath exalted the humble & meek. He

hath filled the hungry with good things; and the rich he hath sent empty away. He hath holpen his Servant, Israel, as he spake to our fathers, Abraham & his seed, forever." "I change not; therefore ye are not consumed." —Mary knew her role in Time, little girl of nineteen centuries ago—that Baby of hers is coming again "with clouds & Great Glory, & every eye shall see!"

The Lord *keeps* his promises:—In Malachi, chiding the corrupt Priesthood who tried to cheat Him by offering *imperfect* sacrifices, He cries out: [Malachi 3:8—& 10]:

"Will a man *rob God?* Yet *ye* have robbed me!"

But for all His wrath against corruption in high places, He still begs them to repent, to turn again to Him—for Israel were his children, & He had brought them up through their stormy lives, by turns blessing and reproving & punishing them, as all good fathers do! And now, to see them trying to 'get away with' shoddy things, even in temple service, disgusted God the Father. Yet, even so, he "gives another chance"!

(*If* they will turn from their peculations, and behave), He promises: "Prove me now, if I will not open you the windows of heaven and pour you out a blessing" (so great) "that there shall not be room enough to receive it."

Oh men were wicked, and hard, & greedy even then! But God's mercy is so great, His love is so long-suffering! (To *me*—to *me*, even!)

Some remembered & kept the Faith.

"They that feared the Lord spoke often to one another: and the Lord hearkened & heard it, and a Book of Remembrance was written before him for them that feared (Him) & that thought upon His name." "And they shall be mine," said the Lord of Hosts, "in that day when I make up my jewels, and I will spare them as a man spareth his own son. Then ye shall return [to God] and discern between righteousness & wickedness, between him that serveth God & and him that serveth him not."

[Mal 4:2] "Unto you that fear my name shall the sun of Righteousness arise with healing in His wings & ye shall go forth and grow up as calves of the stall." (Ibid. 4:5) "Behold I will send you

Elijah, the prophet before the coming of the great and dreadful day of the Lord—& *he shall turn the heart of the children to the fathers, and the fathers to the children,* lest I come & smite the earth with a curse!"

[These are the last words of the Old Testament.] —*Then Christ was born.* My Xmas "text" (on homemade cards, for Primavera only) was "Consider both the kindness and the severity of God" (Romans, 11:22).

Christmas at Primavera, 1957

After the inspiring celebration of Advent Season, Christmas crowned the feasting!

I was at family supper with the Bernards (to whose family I have been assigned for the 12 days till Epiphany, for family celebrating). After supper, as we finished washing-up, we heard spirited singing coming from the direction of the cowstalls. Against the dark foliage of the orange trees, through the twilight, we saw a great star "rise," coming our way. It was a star (of transparent paper, lit inside by wax candles) carried on a pole—as a Crucifer bears the Cross, at Church. —The star-bearer wore a white robe. Following him, singing joyously, were the shepherds & the Kings. Our house was the first they came to, so that we, & the Hulectes across the road, fell in behind them, and took up the carol, & were among the first to "follow the star to Bethlehem!" At each house, mothers, fathers, children, & guests joined the procession, and added to the choral strength. When we came to the crossroads at the Hospital, a wheel-chair patient (a young Paraguayan girl) and two other young patients on litters, were carried along with us all, as we circled the *hof.* The evening skies darkened, & the afterglow faded. A tiny sliver of crescent moon, and her attendant Evening Star, went down behind the trees when we came back down the road to the cowstall. There, in a *real* stable, surrounded by His parents, a *real* ox, a *real* donkey & cow & horse, lay The Baby (Craig Peter Newton, aged 8 weeks) in a *real* manger. The scene was lit by yellow candle-glow. (Lotte Keiderling was *Maria*; Peter Mathis (Sr.), *Joseph.*) The hospital people laid their patients carefully in 'preferred' positions, and all the Community, with many visitors and neighbors (Paraguayan guests) stood (&/or sat on school-benches) to hear the Christmas Gospel, read first in German, then Spanish, then English. For 40 minutes we sang carols & anthems in all three languages, till night had deepened quite. —Then we dispersed, for small home-celebrations, the visitors being "refreshed" by a committee in the dining-room.

Next morning, all the children on the hof were up "at the crack of Dawn," fully as excited over the humble, homemade gifts they were to receive as the children at home, who have expensive modern toys!

Anita & Chrissie Bernard banged smartly at my door at daybreak, and took me to their house (as "assigned" guest). A "Xmas table," with heaps of gifts for everybody—a basketful for me, as well (from the Community) busied us until breakfast. After breakfast, we had time to clear up before an early meeting (for small children) in the dining-room began at 8.00 o'clock.

The Xmas observances were carried on after the German tradition, chiefly. (St. Nicholaus' visit had occurred in Advent.) The weather—strangely *hot,* by comparison with our snow-&-ice weather at Xmas-time—was torrid. And I, *missing my own family (with whom,* except for 1951 (when I was in Los Vilos, Chile) I have always "kept Christmas" *since they were born!)* was out of sorts, & miserably affected by extra-severe seasonal heat. I cried for my children & their children.

But, apart from the *personal* side of it, this Christmas is the most *meaningful* I have ever experienced.

As I drink in the in-all-points *acceptable* religious understanding here, I grow happier and gladder all the time that I chose to spend—to INVEST!—the remainder of my life in Brotherhood! I have NO longing whatsoever for "the world," nor for the "fleshpots," nor for the false, brittle gaiety of social life in *any* sphere. I am *completely* happy to be here. It is *really* living WITH God, & FOR Him, to live in Community at Primavera! I have made the PERFECT CHOICE! — God gave me grace to be worthy of His love in leading me to Brotherhood! *Amen.*

Dec. 31.1957

Fran says I shall probably join the class of novices ('admitted' months before me) a week from tonight (which is New Year's Eve.) —I shall be *glad* of that, as added *spiritual nourishment*. At present I feel a *need* for spiritual food. —I have been "relapsing" (a little) into "the OLD Lois," who was not nice, not happy, Self-consumed. I must *progress*, not fall into old ways.

~

Yesterday was my 32ⁿᵈ wedding anniversary—& I never even re-membered it until today. Today is Cathy's 9ᵗʰ birthday—my first grandchild—the baby with the *benevolent* smile at 6 weeks!

The Gemeinde on Sunday-after-Xmas was devoted to a review of the past year's joys & sorrows, and statements of resolve for the coming year, in very simple solemnity.

Wednesday, Jan. 1, 1958

New Year's Eve was a *fine* celebration. Hans Herman Arnold had come back from Buenos Aires, on an "outreach" trip. His recountal of his quite-successful mission work lasted through a nice evening-meal, & a meeting after it. We had one of Fran's "pauses" at about 9.00—[Percy Blair & I sat on the bench and talked—that is, *he* did, boastfully, scornfully, self-defensively, & I *think* not very truth-fully. —(I told Fran about it afterward.) Percy has been *pointedly* avoiding me ever since, which seems indicative of my feeling's being true.]—and then we "gathered" again to hear "8 Peace Street," a German-language play (translated by Leslie prior to its being given) which demonstrated very well all Eberhard Arnold said, 20 years ago, about the "Irritability" of modern man in a Christ-less world. It was well done. A "coffee break" followed it, with lots of delicious Christmas citron cake. And then a Gemeinde, which led us up to a very few minutes before midnight when our *new bell* just sent from Germany, rang out the year '57, & brought in 1958 (for better or for worse!) we were all silent and thoughtful. It has been my life's MOST SIGNIFICANT year—the year during which I spent 6 months working at St. Anne's to *prove* my *firm intention* for Community; and the second 6 here at Loma Hoby, Primavera, coming on July

2, & entering my novitiate Dec 8. (Mother's bequest made it a decent thing for me to come, at *my age*, to live in community, for such little work as I do does not actually *earn* my bread, even here where life's costs are so low.)

Fran tells me I am to join the Novice Class, when it resumes again after the coming wedding (Jan 14) of Renata Zimmerman and Georg Barth. (The *3rd* marriage in Primavera since my arrival.) It was a very *proper, fitting* way to observe a New Year's coming!

~

Now at Oak Lake is 33 yr old ex-politician & business-man Carrol King, of Denham, Minnesota, whose wife & family of 5 have all agreed, sold all their property, & prepared for complete surrender of their lives to God. —Carrol's coming to Community & the letters of his friends, fellow-politicians, & constituents created a great stir in the Press out there in Minnesota. —Excellent publicity for the Great Cause of God!

~

(I would eschew the *clichés* and *jargon* of "The Life," but nonetheless, find myself falling into it. I used to *shudder* at such unctuous phrases as "surrendering one's life to Christ," "living in the Spirit," etc. but that is, after all, the language of fact.)

This past week I had a few small troubles—and my own resolutions of them all is that the faults I manifest to get myself *into* such troubles are (as Gwynn & Buddug say) just signs that I am "the product of the world I (used to) live in"! I no longer care to bear the mark, but would prefer to wear the "seal of Christ upon my forehead." For that, I am honestly willing to "surrender" EVERYTHING!—even my "sensyuma"!—as I have already willingly given up the dubious distinction of featuring myself as "wit," "life of the party," & "eccentric." I just want to be a Christian in the SIMPLICITY of holy joy! Buddug said to me yesterday, "Look here" (her characteristic expression), "the secret of living harmoniously in community is to tolerate lovingly the characteristics of others." —This in reference to Evelyn, a "needy" girl of 27, from the lowest quarter of London's slums, who is always in trouble because she is "a product of the world she lived in"—just as *I*, too, am—and you, & he, & we

& they! Evelyn has been a thorn in my flesh in the sewing-room:—by turn she is bright & kind and friendly; then unpredictably vicious-tongued & aspish! (She reminds me of "Voices of the Mob.") She bears deep resentments towards happy folk. It is said she is beside herself whenever another woman is married. —[She is a spinster (quite unwillingly, it is plain).] She has a very obvious "complex" about dirt, immodesty, etc. that reveal her "unfulfilled desires" plainly. *Poor girl!* —But she has singled me out many times as the victim of her resentments, & it is hard not to retaliate and "put her in her place." But I must not think "analytically" (as above) because *Love* IS REALLY the only cure! Just as love has healed my wounds, *only* Love can heal Evelyn's (—or Percy's!)—*& I was created* to *love others!*

Friday Jan 5

Yesterday, the Cruelty of Nature was brought home to me! Amaryllis Cat caught, or found dropped from a nest in a high paraiso tree, a baby bird. The cat flew in at the window with the poor, fluttering fledgling in her mouth, & the angry cries of the parent-birds, flung in after her. The baby bird was still alive, so I took it out of the cat's grasp, & it flew off and out of sight. The cat seemed only *slightly* angry at the loss of her prey, & she & I settled down to *siesta* for 2 ½ hours. But the parent-birds *shrieked* without cessation outside, joined by indignant roosters & hens, and the family of a different breed of birds, in a persistent clamor till 3.00 o'clock's work bell. —It was not by any means over, even then! I don't know what went on all afternoon while I was sewing "for a living," away from home. But at 6.00 pm it was STILL going on! I found Amaryllis sitting on the arbor table, & the parent birds and their supporting neighbors swooping angrily down at her, & the screeching & screaming of all the outraged birds still continuing! Judy came in to watch from my window, & it was she who discovered that the little victim-bird was lying on the ground under the garden bench on which the cat sat while the adult-birds assailed her. The poor baby-bird was all-but-dead. Judy said (as I felt) it was best to let "Nature have her way." —So Amaryllis "got the bird," finally. What I couldn't stand was her bringing its limp, disheveled body in the house for her cruel "pitch-&-toss" Torture game. —The parent birds swooped at the windows long after dark, even when all good Birddom is nested away. Whether the cat *ate* the little bird, or not, I don't know. It wasn't in the house when I returned from dinner at 8.15.

A few days before a very lovable black dog of the Mathis's had chased Amaryllis up a tree, and gouged a great lump out of her tail-fur. Dog-eat-cat; cat-eat-bird, etc. etc. etc.

Nature is CRUEL! But *can* all the creation be satanically-ruled throughout even the Animal (& Bird) Kingdom? Does the old serpent cause all this evil even in innocent animals? —What else is the meaning of the words "and the lion shall lie down with the lamb"— When the Kingdom Comes, Love will rule, even in the lower-animal world. (In a happy human household, when dogs and cats, "natural enemies," are brought up together there is peace & even affection, & trust, between them—under a *rule* of *love!*)

(During the Advent to Epiphany season, 1957-58)

A bad period

The heat has been TERRIBLE, even on some *nights*, recently. Day-long readings of 103–04°F! I never *could endure heat!* (Cold makes cowards of people; heat *degrades* them!*) It is a poor 'out,' however, to blame heat for the discontent I have been feeling. It has been 'building-up' for quite a while (all during the heat, which has prevailed for nearly 3 weeks now). I have been prey to the Devil, I think—and have been, by turns, shooing him off, & succumbing to his insidious promptings. —It has made me rather a "lukewarm" Christian to entertain the suggestions he has put into my mind— such as: IS this place of *really*-equal 'privilege'—especially for the use of one's innate 'gifts'? DO members of the Arnold clan *really* take precedence? MUST I be 'picked-over' (sartorially) by people whose sequestration in the wilderness have made them unable to understand the trend in clothing-styles—so that *Moni* told me my (well-cut, comfortable but SLEEVELESS) cotton dress "looked like underwear"? (But for the fact that I surely do believe that 'Evil *is* in the mind of the Beholder,' I could have told her I have always thought *her* dresses looked like *nightgowns!*) —I was quite WITH dear Audrey when, at New Year's Eve Gemeindestunde, she asked that we give ourselves to the LARGER concerns! —And to tell the truth, I have tried to avoid Moni because I *know* she is concerned with 'picking me over,' & I never could TAKE that! (Buddug does the same, but with more *finesse!*) I refuse to be told that cool, sleeveless dresses, modestly cut, not at all "extreme" are *immodest.* —I think dirty bare feet with clay-clotted toes and even sores (from Athlete's Foot) at Gemeinde are in far worse "taste." I see in Moni the "K-K-K" conditioning that all German women of her generation were exposed to. I could tolerate this as understandable far more easily if she were not so "smug" about considering "Kultur" to be a mark of German superiority. —The singing in the dining-room no longer interests me. I have to *force* myself to take part in it, after the business about "O, Little town of Bethlehem" which was NOT ONCE sung, until *after* Xmas, to its proper tune—with an ugly stubbornness for clinging to a far inferior tune—*because* it is "American." (Both the Kultur-ists from Germany and the arrogant "superior" British *refused* the 8 Americans their "rights" in this matter.) Also, when I asked for "Now Thank We All Our God" at supper, the other night, Jorg just vetoed it [without apology] for "We Three Kings."—In other words, the "Sensitivity to Occasion" is supposedly given *only* to the preponderant German element. —At Gemeinde, the Sunday before the Barth-Zimmerman wedding (an All-German affair!), Georg read Eberhard Arnold's analysis about the Feminine & Masculine (spiritual) "premises." —[Dave Newton (rather stupidly) took it on a "vocational" basis, which was not meant at all. I knew better than that—*even (stupid) I!]* But when Georg spoke of using "gifts" to the fullest, he did certainly NOT intend to bestow opportunity for *me* to use my writing & propagandic gifts for the (needy) good of the Community, because Georg would just never realize (*nor believe)* that a woman's "intuition" makes her *fit* for such work: to Georg, a woman is a *wife*—(a *"k-k-k" wife!*). I have been restless ever since! Also, he divided women into 2 groups only—the married & the spinsters. —And this leaves out *very* gifted women right here—for example, Vera, Audrey, Maureen—(and myself, too)—& makes our position uncomfortably anomalous—all because, in this sequestered wilderness life, Georg has never met with women whose lives have been so full as ours! (Full of *sorrow, hurt, & valiant 'rising-to-the-occasion'*!)

I do not 'pine' for the world or the "fleshpots," or to return to life away from Community. But I have surely been unhappy in a dull, persistent way since Xmas. And I do not think that Primavera is the place for me to remain, though, in order to join the Brotherhood, I have agreed to stay here if that is the "decision." Yesterday, Buddug accused me of "wanting to live my own life," & that is not true. Because Kathleen said there was no folding in the laundry, & gave me time off to write a poem for the wedding [Question: is daring to write a poem by an American for a German wedding an intrusion on the traditions here?], the whole day went wrong! —But it does not mean that I am not willing & happy in the laundry & sewing-room work, folding & mending! I have my own (inviolate) "inner life"; I never eschewed the humble tasks. I like them! And I willingly & cheerfully rise to rising-bell, & obey the "schedules." —The damned old Devil has raised all these questions, & despite my ordering him to quit & leave me in peace, they are not yet solved! —I suppose a storm would break over my head if I showed the foregoing to Buddug.

This is a "bad" page in this book.

For the marriage of Jorg Barth & Renata Zimmerman
January 12, 1958
(To be performed by Georg Barth, the bridegroom's father, at Ibaté.)

Georg (to the marriage-pair):

> John called on all men to repent
> And humbly down to Jordan went
> Our Lord himself. The next day spent
> In calling his disciples. And
> The third, with Mary and his band
> To Cana, went to celebrate the marriage in the land
> There was no wine; but water turned to wine at his
> command.
> Thus his first miracle he wrought

> To prove the Power he had brought
> And ever after, marriage ought
> To be a sacrament.

Jorg:

> This maid I wed, whose hand I take
> To pledge our lives for Jesus' sake,
> I love; and with my heart and hand,
> I do, with God's grace, understand
> To be for me a help-mate true.
> My one word of Faith, each day a-new
> Throughout the years she'll hold me to!

Renata:

> This man as spouse whom I now wed
> By whom I will be loved and led
> Of our new life shall be the head.
> And God will give our daily bread
> While we shall work increasingly
> For Him who giveth (to Jorg) thee to me
> And me to thee. So it shall be!

Georg
Jorg
Renata

> Amen! Amen! Amen!

Jan 16

When I first came, I told Buddug & Gwynn Primavera "seemed like Paradise." Buddug reminded me of it yesterday, when I was "clearing-up" a misunderstanding with Doris Boller. She reminded me that this "paradise" has its "bad times," too. (I have been having the "collywobbles," & so have been "touch-y" over small things.) Buddug also reminded me of a prayer in the Youth's play "8 Peace

Street," in which the character, *Christian,* addressed God (in something like) these words: "Oh Lord, teach me to seek to LOVE rather than to *be loved*; to UNDERSTAND, rather than to *be understood.*" (Sandra does those things; I do not—yet.) Buddug's spiritual help to me means more and more! I am grateful for it. She sees past small matters into the real crux of problems. Thank God for her! And all the Brotherhood!

~

How *quickly* we can be *forgotten*! In the old days, I used to work hard at making by hand as many as 300 Xmas cards, sent to a long list of friends, old & new. And such *rafts* of cards as I received, in response! After 1951, when I sent my card from Peru:—

> Years ago, I told my three
> When you grow up & don't need me,
> I'll take a ship & go to sea.
> In 1951,
> That's exactly what I've done
> Good hard work; but lots of fun
> "Merry Christmas!"

About Xmas: Primavera 1957:

I made my *last* attempt to be "remembered of men." *I am sure very few people have even noticed* that *I have "dropped out of the world!"* Besides the 3 Xmas cards that came here, another 3 or 4 went to Peabody … *But I am glad, glad, glad!—to be out of the world for the rest of my life!* I had been realizing each year more vividly—especially since 1943, when I wrote "Time & ½" (about War-conditions in the USA), that it is a cruel, fickle, false, empty world. *I am* WHERE/I/BELONG now—in a place of *love* & true faithfulness. Thank you, God! Thank you endlessly! The miracle of it will never cease to rejoice my unworthy soul.

Wedding in the Wild (Jan 10: Saturday pm)

The Love Meal Eve.

If a stranger had been riding the vast Paraguayan camp, weary &

self-absorbed, last evening after a day of murky, unsettled weather, with distant thunder growling in the clouds, & heard the sound of singing, he might well have doubted his ears. And seeing through the trees on the *isla* where Loma Hoby lies, he must certainly have rubbed his eyes with disbelief ... *WHAT was going on?*

We were celebrating a Love Meal on the eve of a Christian marriage of two young people of our Brotherhood, Jorg and Renata, both teachers in Primavera. Before sunset the weather settled down, reasonably clear and much cooler than it had been for four weeks of tropical heat, unbroken even by sporadic thunder-storms. Two hundred and eighty people were assembled on a grassy level near the community dining-room at the center of the hof. They sat at white-covered trestle-tables on benches and chairs, with flowers and lighted candles, and 'groaning' platters of meat and cheese sandwiches, & great pots of hot maté! —These "crazy" Christian people, all assembled in decent, cleanly clothing, in love for the happy pair and their rejoicing families, and in thankfulness to God for blessing the Brotherhood's continuance, of which this marriage has been yet another token.

Over the heads of all these people, including children "from the 4th class up" was a pavilion-bower of green palm boughs, hung at close intervals with multi-colored ("home-made") candle-lanterns and strong-powered electric bulbs, with a low platform for the entertainers when the "evening" (after the meal) should begin.

A hush descended on the quietly conversing crowd at the tables, as the voices of a troop of children were heard. More colored candle-lanterns, carried on sticks, emerged from the darkness near the Housemother's house. Singing joyously, bearing their lights, they went across the Hof, circling round the tables on their way to "fetch the bride & groom," whom they brought back, triumphantly, and seated at the head table decorated with candles, flowers, & the *hof's* best china, silverware & glass. There followed a 'reading' about marriage by Fran, & various contributions from others. We had a Paraguayan guitarist & violinist, who gave several 'renderings.' Judy read 2 sonnets of Shakespeare. And the poem (by me) on the preceding page, & several other offerings. It was a beautiful Marriage Love Meal!

Tues., Jan 21, 1958

The Death of 2 Boys {Walter Fros, Ibaté; Jimmie Johnson, Wheathill}

Our (Ibaté) Brothers, the Fros family of Hermann & Iet, lost an 11 yr old son, Walter, in a swimming accident. The loss was not for the family alone; but for our 3 hoefe, & for all the others, too. When Wheathill's cable of condolence arrived, it brought news of 15-yr old Jimmie Johnson's death almost simultaneously—in a coasting accident, which we did not, however, receive until after our funeral for little Walter.

That was a beautifully solemn & sad occasion. I am glad that the children of the dead boy's age were allowed to attend the funeral, at which Peter Cavanna's sermon was directed to their level of understanding. The impeccable behavior of all 3 hoefe's children, on the long walk following the coffin to the burial ground was beautiful, & could not fail to inspire their proper reverence & awe in the face of the mystery of death! The mother's face & the father's, as they stood beside the yawning grave, is imprinted forever on my mind. The simple, unmasked dignity of their grief was a lovely tribute to the trust they feel in the Brothers. Again, as at Gunther's burial, the men took turns filling in the grave, as we stood in rapt silence around it. When the mound was packed down, Hermann took fresh palm-boughs, & for the last time "tucked-in" his little son for his sleep-in-death. The mother, sisters & cousins placed flowers on the palm-leaves, & the school children flowers, little notes & toys they gave to their former playmate.

Thank God for sparing others all their children in health & happiness. Thank God for his Grace to me in having still all 3 of mine, & now their spouses & their children! And, God, in the name of your Son Jesus Christ, hasten the coming of His Kingdom & the banishment of death & sin forever. Amen.

Jan 24, '58

Interhof Brudershaft. 1-23-58

Our "pan-American" conference began officially last night at Isla. The uniting *Faith* of the approximately 350 adults present was certainly impressive! It is easy to see that the (subtle) leadership of Servants, Stewards, & Housemothers is a *necessity* [though it would be anathema to cry out that the Society is actually "in the hands" of a "policymaking committee"]. —It certainly *has* to be that way! — The fact that the "problems before the Brotherhood" were first *stated* by Hans Meier—then *stipulated* by Roger and Charles Hedlund, & that the membership had not a single new idea to present, but merely reiterated over & over, at short & long length the same things, like an echo, showed that this *big group* of grown people *would be lost*, easily, & adrift in the wilds of Paraguay, without the "steering" of the "gifted" few. There is certainly no cause for discontent in this matter. It has always been said that German people flocked after *any* strong leader, like sheep—(as witness Hitler); but I must say that the Americans, English & Paraguayans here have the same need of clear-sighted people to lead them! The wonder of it is that the truly "dedicated" and modest leadership has patience and sufficient altruism to serve their great responsibility in true, Christlike humility. —So I have no "axe to grind" because of it!

~

—I have thought about my first feeling of "calling," in late May, when I visited El Arado, & saw the brave & threadbare poverty of the happy place. At that time, I felt I OUGHT to go there, and take a job, & earn money for them by day, & perhaps raise funds for them avocationally. I still KNOW I COULD! —But then I feel I'd be so loathe to leave this idyllic life of "returning & rest," where (as Cyril put it) I am being "healed" of the wounds of the world. —I have told Fran how I feel—that I OUGHT to be *doing something*: perhaps down in Asunción, raising funds from among Americans, for the Hospital & expenses of Primavera. He has definitely forbidden my making a "volunteer" suggestion of this sort. So that, in holding my peace last night, I had *two* reasons for keeping still:—(1) *Inertia* for the selfish reason of wanting to stay here in peace & quiet; and (2) Fran's stricture.

Here in the life of Brotherhood we do not say "I know *I* can DO it," we merely ask God to "use" us, and submit to the Spirit's moving the Brotherhood to select whomsoever they are "guided" to appoint to any task. Because here we are not doing things of *ourselves*, but only by the power of the Spirit, as it is given.

Rosemary (C.) Dole sent me from Rockport, last *June,* 2 lb. of coffee & a lot of tea-bags. They arrived here in *Jan* (the 21ˢᵗ!)— "ONLY 7 months!" —We are now momently expecting 29 barrels of things from Woodcrest, shipped in October. In Barrel #27 is a box for me from Sandy & Ed.

~

My Weekend (of Peter's 28th birthday): I went to Isla Sunday morning for a "change of scene," & to visit some of the people there. The milk-cart was to take me at 9.15. But, inspired, I went over with (Twin) Charles Headlund at 7.45, & rushed away so fast I left my house work undone. (Luckily, I had provided food for Amaryllis!) It was a perfect morning, the country fresh & beautiful from rain 2 days ago, and no dust on the familiar road. We arrived in time for Household Meeting, followed by Gemeinde—very good meeting! (I made a bad faux pas—but corrected it properly, in time, thank God.) The food at noon was delicious! After midday meal, siesta in the guest-room provided (at the Weave Shop). Then tea with Delf & Katie Franchom. And then a long walk, & swim, & walk back for supper in the dining room. I went to Ibaté by cart; attended the 2nd conference Brudershaft, returned, & slept at Isla. Had outdoor breakfast with Kathleen Hellenburg (sister of Maureen Burn) and 5 of her 9 children—then waited—a long time!—for the milk wagon to bring me back, not arriving at Loma until 10.00 am. By that time, I was tired; but Buddug gave me the am off—& I cleaned & tidied, washed, sponged off my winter clothes (of mildew) & aired them. Ate. Slept. Rested! Wonderful! Charles Hedlund, who came up from El Arado for our "Pan-American," conference, led the meetings at Isla on Sunday, Jan 26, 1958; and I must say (in the hackneyed Bruderhof phraseology), words were given to him of such tellingly simple eloquence that a heart of stone would have been moved!

~

In the evening, after a quick dining-room supper at Isla, we all crowded into carts, & were whisked over to Ibaté for a 2nd Conference meeting. I had swum in the beautiful orangewood spring pool with the Franchom family, & walked both ways (about 1¼ miles each way) & was tired; but I managed to keep awake through an interesting, spirited meeting, until about 11.15, when we went back to Isla. I slept overnight in the guest-room (in the weave-shop). Had breakfast with the Hasen boys, & enjoyed it SO MUCH. After considerable delay the cart (scheduled for 7.45) brought us back to Loma at 9.20, after 2nd breakfast out-of-doors with the kitchen-crew, at Isla.

I have had a perfectly wonderful rest, change of environment, & the joy of meeting intimately Hardy & Secunda Arnold, & several other people I never knew well—including the Franchoms (their 12 year old Anna, in particular), & visiting with others I did know. Hardy & Secunda drove back to Loma, along with Hans Meier's nephew—a *very nice boy* (can't remember his name) and soap, milk, mail, & lumber. Buddug mercifully gave me the remainder of the morning off—to do housework, collect laundry, hang out my winter clothing, etc. & generally re-gather my (solitary) forces. Amaryllis Cat was *delighted* when I came home. She was so lonely she killed another young bird, & brought it in under the bed. The house is now orderly & clean—my dear little, long-dreamed-of home in a shack! I shall sleep away my afternoon after midday meal and really be a "new woman."

I *am* "drawing closer into the life," & learning the new art of *gelassenheit* (which the Quakers call "sitting loose"—(in Pennsylvania) or, otherwise expressed: leaving everything to God).

Loma is to be discontinued, and people here (including *me)* "redistributed." (From Hardy, I gather it is *not impossible* that I *may*—after a "cosmic year" here—go to England, and work on the 'PLOUGH.'—PERHAPS —! Oh, joyous hope!)

Meanwhile, in "returning & rest" I shall be saved.

I have never been SO HAPPY—even *more* than ever.

The weather is clear, cool-ish, & breezy & infinitely *beautiful!*

I got 4 letters when I came back! Rosemary Brooks Goepper, Sandra, *Helen Wanchope!*

I gave Hardy the name & address of Louis Agassiz Shaw, for "Verbung" (begging-) purposes. He says *he* may himself go to Boston, & see—not only Shaw—but Sandy & Jonathan, too! Oh, I pray my 3 will join the Brotherhood!

More about the Conference—(Up to Feb 2)

Novices have not been at the last few meetings, when there were discussions about personnel for Asunción & Montevideo. But the announced results are: Gwen & John Hines for El Arado; and Olwen & Robert Rhimes for Asunción. I should think these were fine choices! (John Winter takes over the Ibaté farm, in place of Robert Rhimes.) It is impossible to express how *deeply nourished* my spirit has been by such of the meetings I have attended. I now am (as is said here) becoming 'sensitive' to the working of the Spirit in the meetings and at Gemeindesbunden. The *unity* of the Brotherhood is *real,* and undeniably the only reason why the 17-year miracle of Primavera could have been possible!

Nothing will ever shake my novice-vows. Nothing! And, when the novice-classes at last begin again, after the conference, I shall be able to learn more and more; and shall hope SOON—as soon as God wills!—to come to Baptism, and full membership—As everyone has always told me is true, the "giving-in" of possessions—even Mama's watch!—(which I have seen used first by Fran; now by Clare Walker)—has been EASY. There are lots of residual elements of 'self' to surrender before I achieve true *gelassenheit*—such as what is here called "lack of trust"—or (by Sandra) "suspiciousness" and 'reading-into' people & situations things that are products of my own diseased imagination. This I MUST WORK HARDER than ever to OVERCOME. It is a breach in my wall of resistance against the Evil One.

~

We have been *so lucky* to have Charles Hedlund and Roger Allain at Primavera! Charles especially has the gift of words—simple, forth-right, tolerant, telling words to express the spirit of Brotherhood. (Roger, too—but in a *little less* delicacy & sensitivity!) The outcome of the conference: actual giving up of Loma (the third *hof)* & an all-out effort to establish a 2nd Uruguayan Bruderhof.

All my *personal* concentration must be to complete surrender (gelassenheit). I am growing closer & closer to the inner life (for which I PINED so desolately, at Woodcrest) and the peace & inspiration I drew from our interhof Gemeindestunde on Feb 2, at Isla Margarita, has been inestimable. Also, in the afternoon, I had a long, satisfying chat with Charles Hedlund on the bench under the paraisos, outside the dining-room.

(Note:—Hardy has said the response in Oak Lake has been very gratifying, but that (alas) most American people wanted to join for "subjective" reasons, rather than "objective." This is perhaps the reason Heini used to tell me—so dismayingly: "Imposable! Imposable!" Till I began to think of him as another Miss Hartigan, who said "'tis a pity, child!"—(for not *wholly* dissimilar reasons.)) —Mine *were* "subjective" reasons; but each Sunday gives me more & more *objective* light upon the "*Cause*"; and I am really *growing!* (Sandra says my letters demonstrate a great change!) When I have grown even more, then even in this journal the first person singular pronoun will be less frequent!

Feb. 2 (evening) 7 months since I came to Primavera

I had quite a party—light-hearted & happy last night—Ruth & Charlie Hall; Dave & Ginny Newton & their Patsy, Tommy, Billy, Dorothy & even Craig Peter in his carriage; & Percy & his David & Allen, & Lora. It was a beautiful night. About ⅓ of a lb of Rosemary Dole's delicious Copley coffee helped out the whole thing, aided by a bright moonlit night. Percy brought over his photographs & snapshots to show me, when the others were leaving. (He has "*mis*spent" (as he agrees) the last 10 years in a wholly superficial atmosphere of frivolity & nightclubs. But it must be his unflagging *fidelity as a father* that has blessed him and led him here! Because his "background" as a "man-about-town" has not given him any sort of preparation or understanding of the FACT that GOD sent him to Primavera. It will still take a long time for him to realize that he has been *called* to take up his cross and follow Christ! His scoffing & sneering are over for the most part; and these questions are now timidly commencing to show that he is no longer willing to STAY "on the outside, looking in!" Charles Hedlund said yesterday that (as Buddug has told me) we really MUST "leave him to God," & let him take as long as he needs to awaken to our purpose.

Tuesday, Feb. 4—Wind-up of Conference

At the end of a *beautiful* & breezy, but nonetheless terribly HOT day—full of frustration in every work-department, because of our power-breakdown (in *both Loma & Isla!*)—we all piled into transport vehicles for the last meeting of the Conference of 1958. A *beautiful sunset* and *full-moonrise*, simultaneously were our 'treat' on the dust-choking trip over by tractor-trailer. The decisions made concerning the family-shifts to both El Arado & Asunción; the sending of part of Gerhardt Wegner's family to Sentahlof in Germany; the decision to proceed full-steam with the beginning of our lucrative-purposed RICE-growing AND modern-method citrus-bottling; the acceptance of 2 *El Arado* Youth of Brazil's McKenzie college at São Paulo of offered scholarships in Electrical Engineering (none at Primavera being qualified because of *language*-requirements); a review of a whopping BUDGET [& the amazing determination to go on when it is terribly—*impossibly!*—inadequate], & the appointment of 2 men & a youth for Outreach mission-work. It was a *sleepy* meeting. The room was packed with hot tired people. Outside, the night was brightly moonlit. (Several people crept outside, preferring to hear through the windows.) We got home after midnight, *very* tired.

Amaryllis wasn't home to greet me.

She hasn't yet appeared (8.00 a.m. on Wednesday).

—But she *did* return, a few hours later, with a happy "Meow!"

Feb. 10, 1958 [I have been here 7 months 1 week & 1 day]

"Backsliding!"

When I am STUMPED by inability to make my motives clear, I

weakly revert to my old habits of thought, & "resolve" to LEAVE! That is what I *may not ever* DO! For I have *made my vows* as a novice, to live in Brotherly Community, & stay or go, as the Brotherhood decides. I am no longer "on my own." This is, of course, sheer, unmerited *blessing!* For, though I am no longer my own mistress, I am also relieved forever of tension, pressure, necessity & loneliness. I am very happy, deeply grateful, & wholly aware of my arrant unworthiness of this blessing. God forgive my weaknesses, & fill me with thy Spirit, to the complete exclusion of self!

Tues. Feb 11 Mama's 87th birthday—her first, in Heaven (1871-1957)

    I have asked for Baptism (at a Novice Meeting).

Percy Blair, & David & Allen have been moved to Isla, for a good *job* for Percy.

I am actually *perfectly* contented here. I have *actually* had "all things added unto me"—but, when my prayer is answered—a prayer asked in Christ's name, that my 3 children and their families shall follow me into the life of Brotherhood-community—then my cup will certainly "run over." For I am now in the "green pastures, beside the still waters"—and "surely goodness and mercy shall follow me all the days of my life and I shall dwell in the House of the Lord forever." AMEN! (I cannot possibly properly describe the multitude of blessings that I now enjoy!)

Feb. 18

I have been burdened with the feeling—which is *not* a "notion," nor a paranoid fancy!—that, though *indubitably* in the best Christian sense, I—& everyone else here!—am LOVED by the entire community, still *I* am *NOT liked.* (As Fran says, our object in living together is not based on our liking each other. —We have a far *higher* purpose, indeed!) I am *quite accustomed,* as a *lifelong* state! to *emotional, mental* and *spiritual* isolation in any group, large or small, beginning in my own baby-days as the "unwanted" child. *HERE I am NOT* in *spiritual isolation! Thank God for that!* For every new revelation I have here of the Faith and the Spirit that holds the Bruderhof Communities together is PRECISELY what I have *always believed & felt* to be *God's will for men!* That is the BIGGEST thing of all. And enough, indeed, to be content forever to have! Never, oh God, allow me to lose sight of its ineffable, precious value! —Perhaps emotional isolation is my fate *only* because of my own sins-of-the-ever-less-important Past; and mental isolation—in this "Kultur" of German folk, not SO bad as to be unendurable, in *contrast* with *the joy of united Faith!* —Buddug was so sympathetic: she HUGGED me—dear soul! She is warm, too, & knows how lonely I am for Jonathan, Sandra and Peter, et al.

Feb. 27, 1958

A year ago today, I was still "in the world," BATTLING my tired, lonely way at St. Anne's Guest House— working hard, & animated always by my ONE PURPOSE—which was to be HERE, where I am now! —Thank God for his Grace & guidance which made that purpose strong enough to succeed.

How deeply contrite I should be to have "doubts," & feeble faith in the Brotherhood, after all the Love and Faith they have accorded me (and so many other new people of my own era at Woodcrest!). How ashamed I feel that only yesterday, with Fran, & Buddug & Jorg Barth I was the subject of the conference to clear away the lingering effects of my "paranoid" complex, and my lack of Trust!

God, please grant me greater humility, greater freedom from self and memories of pain and loneliness and strife and struggle in the lost, lonely years! Even my dear children, whom I pray for as Brothers-&-Sisters-to-be, are no longer *"my* children," for I am in a *new life* now, in a world of peace & love & Faith & sharing; and ALL of the past—even their babyhood, childhood, & satisfactory maturing—is ALL *past for me!* All the flaws left are like our "tropical wounds," too stubborn, too petty to heal themselves! I am NOT to consider myself "on the carpet" when we have a continuation of this conference of yesterday! I am to take the position I have seen others take of *ASKING the Brothers to help me* cure these stubborn, unhealed "sores" in my spirit. —This involves rooting out the "pride" (that I *so long failed to recognize,* at Woodcrest!) till its last traces are gone—till I, in *real, trusting* humility can be *really* a *part* of the *Circle*—not an eccentric arc, detached from the circumference by my own miserable failure to *grow & fuse myself into it!* I must utterly leave behind Lois, the "unwanted child," the "goat," the 'odd one', the "character," the "laughing-stock" & "black sheep" I have always been in the world! I must *forget how to fight*—and "make war" no more—for I am on the threshold of the Kingdom of Heaven, benignly ruled by Peace, Love, Equity and Compassion—and though I was a far-strayed, *almost* wholly LOST sheep, the Shepherd *has* led me home; and it is NO LIE that "in returning & rest we shall be saved." *All his promises are kept! I AM SAVED!* Amen. Amen.

Here, in Primavera, with no promised expectancy of my ever leaving—and WHY *should I want to? except for the awful heat?* —I must content myself—and how easy it is!—with the joy of the Life—fed on the spiritual food I love so well at Gemeinde!—nourished by peace & sufficiency of "daily bread"—CONTENTED at last never to strive again for *anything* but The CAUSE—Have I not always pined to find a cause *worth* dying for? Then *die*, you old, fat, stupid LOIS— & be born anew, and Thank God! Thank Him forever & forever! He is "working His purpose out" and one day you—the *reborn Lois* (without "trauma") may at last yourself stand "before the Great White Throne," and sing with the Angels and the Redeemed the paeans of His praise which have lain inchoate in your bursting heart since you were born, never having found the key to open the song of praise & love & adoration of God's Power, Love, Justice, Integrity.

From little girlhood on, I have felt it all deep-dwelling inside of me—wanting to free itself & come to expression in words-&-music; & my joyousness (though it often took banal, noisy form) has always come from my deep love for God, & my desire to say to him adequately: "Thank Thee! Praise Thee!"—that "Alleluyiah spirit" I used to try to defend at Single People's breakfasts at Woodcrest. — When the weather is cool & I feel well & optimistic, I can hardly contain myself for the desire to shout out God's praises, & dance before him (as David wanted to do). [David was my temperamental archetype.] (And David, though he was loved for his good heart by God himself, was very often *in trouble* with the God to whom he uttered praise and thanks in his lovely Psalms!)

I have always really LOVED my fellow man, too—like Abou Ben Adhem. But I am like a cat—suspicious that my fellow man may bite, or hurt, or sting, or turn on me. Now I am in a circle where FAITH has removed the human venom from all around me. I need NEVER "suspect," nor 'attribute motives'—nor doubt promises, nor 'see' double meanings nor look for slights from others. Even young-man Jorg Barth, a self-contained, *whole* young man, will not be saying to himself "How fat & silly she is"! He will be *praying* for God to *heal* me! Oh, thank you, Brother Jorg! It's God's Spirit that has made you strong & compassionate! As for Buddug, bless, bless, bless her for her jolly, cheerful, compassionate, generous kindness! (God's work in *her*, too!) For Fran, thank thee that he, like Peter, obeys your Voice: "*Feed my Lambs*"! He is *scrupulously careful of all of us*, his "lambs." Thank God for EVERYTHING & EVERYONE—& my 3 children & their families, always!—on this bright, cool, clear beautiful morning. —I can hear the new "First Class" (who just entered school yesterday) singing a morning song in Bob Hedlund's classroom with their innocent little voices. My cat squats trustingly beside me on the desk, in my quiet, comfortable, airy little hut. (I *always* longed to live in a hut). Why my CUP RUNNETH OVER! — Thank GOD, & forgive me.

March 1

A jewel of a day—the equivalent of a Sept 1ˢᵗ day at home—only that instead of apples being almost ripe, it's oranges. And grapefruit, lemon & limes. And bananas!

The skies are clear, vivid blue with heaps of luxurious, light-shot clouds, coming up in ranks from the far horizons over the jungles across the purple-tinted camp. *It IS paradise*—the nearest thing on earth to paradise—because of Faith and Love!

~

(I am getting worried now lest my brave, well-meant offer to go down to Asunción & take a job to earn cash for Primavera MIGHT be accepted—and I'd have to *leave* my Paradise—my cat, my hut, my life of *simplissimus,* old, plain comfortable clothes, easy work, outdoors most of the day & at night, too (with all shutters open)—

the baby sunrises in their pristine innocence! The bright hot noon-days! The golden afternoons; the magnificent sunsets—and the jeweled skies on clear moonlit nights! ... *Imagine* going to a foul & dirty city like Asunción, where misery, squalor, hunger, vice and infection abound—(a very apt setting for *Banks* and Wealth and Pride & Sin!)—after 8 months of clean, sweet Paradise here! —I *told* Fran it was an *altruistic* offer I made. (I am quite certain, even now, that I *could* get a job in some American firm or family—& do a part *much* needed for this community.) It seemed very *unlikely* that the Brotherhood would take me up on it. —Oh, I was brash indeed to offer! ... Just suppose they *did* accept—! First, my *Baptism* would have to be deferred indefinitely, I suppose & I have longed & longed for Baptism in the Brotherhood, ever since I fully realized what depth of meaning it will have! —And then, to leave these dear people, each & all of whom I have learned to love well & warmly, in these 8 months in 'paradise'—to live with CROSS *People* again in an all-too-familiar superficial, metallic, competitive 'Society'—whether as clerk or cook: it's all the same cruel, self-centered world I SO GLADLY left behind! —*If* the Brotherhood asks it, I shall of course go—but NOT GLADLY!

'Hardy remembered I needed another copy-book to continue this journal in, & sent one over to me, with a gracious note, the other day. The exquisite *little* consideration of a great-spirited, humble man. Thank you, God, for both 'Hardy & his father Eberhard, to whom I owe (posthumously) my present joy & security!

Sunday, March 2, 1958

Today I have been *8 months* in Paraguay! It is hard to believe! *Where has the time gone? —It's the shortest span of 8 months I ever experienced!*

Craig Peter Newton was "presented" to the Community this morning, at 8.30.

Today a most *awful* thing—"heavy," in Bruderhof *patois*—was announced at Germeindestunde! *Belinda Manley and Maureen Burn have left the community!* (*That* was what the Brotherhood meetings, excluding novices, were about!) I had seen a defiant restlessness in Belinda; & a sort of "closed" look about Maureen. But I never suspected such a thing. —*Breaking vows*! (The door is open to them to return, IF they learn humility by their dreadful experience! IF they can put down the *ego* that caused them both to leave!) Maureen wants to help lepers—*humble* people (like Maria and Adolph Weiss). Belinda has "ideas about teaching." Neither of them have any prospects, nor any more money than to get to Asunción. It MUST be the middle aged 'SPORT' of ambition & energy—product of the insidious endocrines! Belinda had been *very* comforting to me, at a time (months back) when I was feeling rather lost. And Maureen has always been kind. From the first they two gave me such heartwarming *welcome* to Loma's "Single People's group." [Edna & I were saying today how we've broken-up in the past months—'losing' to Isla, first Phyllis Hayes; then Marjorie; then Audrey, to Ibaté—& now at one time both Belinda & Maureen. I *wept* for those two "silly girls," right in the meeting. So *rash* of them, at their age, with their obvious "eccentricities" to set out to conquer a *"world"* they haven't seen during the last 15 years of its rapid ret-rogression! By present-day standards, they would *both* (especially Belinda, the younger of the two, who is odd-looking anyway, and in her deficient mood, really MANIC—to the outer eye of the 'nor-mal' observer!)—both be diagnosed (with glib lightness) *"Nuts!"* If they do go too far away from the encircling, merciful protection of the Brothers & Sisters they have so seriously broken the Faith with, they might even end up in a psychopathic ward! —They are not joining forces—but each going her own way. It is a pity. —"A shat-tering experience," Edna puts it, is surely in store for them. —I'd like to have *warned* them; but I knew nothing of it—they left at daybreak today!

At the meeting, when we were all so much moved by such a thing—a *new* item in the "cosmic year" I am experiencing here!—young Tabea Lachmann asked for Gemeindestund privilege. Then Ruth Hall was *really* eloquent—quite "out of herself," & inspired, & inspiring! (I had been rather worried about her, lately—knowing nothing, but seeing her unhappy.) Deborah asked for Baptism; & Charles, her husband, spoke in a very clear unstudied way. These things, the meeting concluded, were to take the place of the defec-tion of those two *rash* middle-aged women.

[*My* reaction: I shall NEVER want to leave the Brotherhood! NEVER! And I shall have learned more of "*gelassenheit*" from this vicarious experience of theirs. —They were NOT truly "surrendered," these two. Oh God watch over them.

Belinda's school-work & Maureen's laboratory-work will be MISSED!

~

A Brotherhood meeting (*including* the Novices) was held tonight, announcing two engagements for which we all deeply rejoiced: Barbara Martin & Herman Pleil; Shoneid Yates & Jack Elston. It was a joyous end to a "heavy" day.

(Dave Newton FLATLY told me NOT to *try* to take part in celebrations till I am a full member. —That has been *hinted* at before. I do not mind. I only wonder (a little) *why*.)

~

In the late afternoon, I walked down to the school wood, & found young Pablo Marchant and Montanus Mathis making candy. They had scrounged the *sugar*, & felt guilty; but they were nice & jolly, & gave me a large piece of their confection. (My relationship with the boys is improving.) I sat under the timbo tree for a half hour, & watched the clouds piling up over the jungle-tree tops, & had that lifelong "Fourth Dimension" sensation—which I have always pushed away as too metaphysical for a literalist-'realist' of my age & background & experience. I had been reading Jacob Boehme these last days, & begun to wonder if I, too, might not be entitled to religious "visions," even though I *am* "only" a Yankee, & ½-Irish-'stupid'? Perhaps, if I let myself go, & *don't* push away the '4th dimension' sensations I've had since I was a little girl, but, instead LISTEN, & *stare deeper* into the half-formed things I *see*—yet do NOT see—I will hear His voice; understand Him, and like the Child Samuel (whom Georg told the children about this very morning) I, too, can say: "*Here am I, Lord!*" (I was so *stupid*, for so long, not to have found my way, somehow, to the Bruderhof Life *long ago!* Let me not be so stupid now.) IF the Lord wants to "use" my "4th-dimension" 'visions' to tell me what he wants of me, let me be ready to believe enough that with Him, ALL things are possible—& let me open my soul, in trust, to receive Him fully. Amen.

~

The really shocking news concerning the *Apostasy* of Belinda & Maureen has been seeping down into my spirit, so that I can see the paucity of my own understanding of this *rich life!* When a young, *not* brilliant, almost inarticulate fellow novice, Elizabet Sorgius, sees so clearly that she can, in a few plain words, put my verbose superficiality to shame, then I know I *still* have a long way to come *fully* "into the Life." —It is NOT nearly as "external" a concept of Brotherly living as—up till now, even, I have believed. When it can penetrate into the young spirit of the not-at-all-Intellectual youth, and so form (as Fran puts it) a "quality of life" that makes them Brotherhood's best Witness, then I, in my own conceits of mistaken self-esteem, am put to shame for thinking *Age* makes for *wisdom!*

March 5, 1958 (Thursday a.m.)

We got up by moonlight today—a full moon (which disturbs most sleepers), to start our day on time. I have already (at 6.00) finished breakfast out-of-doors on my *laba* table, with Amaryllis-Cat chasing black velvet butterflies across the table; the morning spreading over the skies above, great scolding of parrots; concerted warning chicks of a flock of neighbors' chickens; the neighbors' breakfast-conversations dimly heard through a screen of grapefruit treelings that form our "fence" between my happy solo living and their more active family life. The sun tinges the top twigs of the young paraiso tree where last season's birdsnest hangs empty in the sky.

My mood is pensive. The long, "deep" Gemeindestunde last night which brought home to me the real seriousness of Belinda & Maureen's *disloyalty*, is still in my spirit. It is considered an act of subjection to Satan; and we were well-warned by Georg that the Devil IS here, even among us in our ideal Life, to tempt any of us to act individually and independently of our sworn unity as Brothers, by promptings too irresistible to Self-Will, Conceit, Self-Confidence

& Opinionatedness. We must continually (as Jacob Boehme wrote 350 ago) "stand in the combat, (found) to be full of heavy strivings wherein (we) are often struck down to the ground." Boehme says that the "flash" of Divine comprehension which comes to us comes only sporadically—showing "the Deity as a flash of lightning." He adds: "But the source" (Satan) "and unfolding of sin covers it suddenly again. For the Old Adam belongs to the earth; and does not, with the flesh, belong to God ... My Sun was often eclipsed, or extinguished, but did rise again; & the oftener it was eclipsed, the brighter & clearer was its rising again."

~

Instead of the 'work' *I* thought *I* could do so well in "outreach" and fund-raising & campaigning, before I reach real "retirement-age" at 60 or 65 (not long hence), I now see that this latter period of my life must take a NEW slant. This is time for deep contemplation, in Thanks to God for His Forgiveness of my sins & His leading me here; as well as a deeper penetration into the meaning of life— both here, and in the coming Kingdom. The petty self-concern & brooding over the past *must GO!* I am tired indeed of Lois Henderson Bayliss, "poor thing." Her career, stormy & sinful, was far from glorious. Leave her to Heaven! Now I must achieve "*Gelassenheit*," and "in returning & rest (I) shall be saved." *That* is why I am here. Let me, oh Lord, at last "be STILL & KNOW THAT THOU ART GOD"— & *forget—forget*—FORGIVE and FORGET everything else!

Sun. March 10, 1958

Gwynn's return, soon, will rejoice us *all*, of course! The Brotherhood is preparing for The Lord's Supper—(a solemnity here new to me)—to achieve deeper unity in the Holy Spirit before Easter. After Easter, our Novice group will be prepared for Baptism. How I long for that!

As an infant, I was baptized by Uncle Allen Jacobs in April, 1904 at Portsmouth, Rhode Island. And then, when my study of the Bible made me understand, at last, what God requires of man, and had begun to see the futile errors of humanistic, Bohemian "realism" which (like the credulous fool I used to be!) I had tried all my life to adjust to my *real, enduring* Faith in God—and *never could*, of course! I wanted so much to become a Christian in the fellowship of other simple, faithful souls, I went back to the little town of Healdsburg, California, to ask for Baptism there, in the Christian Church. Frances & Albert Beach, that devout, sincere old couple who had rented me a room in their house for 6 weeks when I was selling the Bible, were glad. A tall, gangling ex-tree-surgeon who had become their pastor—Brian Foy—baptized me there in a tank of water. If only the fussiness of wearing the great white robe, & the distractions of the people & the place had not actually taken my mind off the *real meaning* of what I was doing, it might have been an adequate Baptism. —But I fear it was not. I long to be baptized here, among my Brothers & Sisters, in token of a *far greater* understanding of *true repentance* (that will not admit ever again of Temptation by the Evil One) and a re-birth that will be far more thorough-going, now!

In reading Jacob Boehme's odd revelations of his religious experience, I feel that my whole life has been illumined by similar flashes of Understanding of God, beginning with very young days when I sat in Daddy's bedroom window-seat and stared out at the sunset over the poplar-trees past Mr. Phillips' garden, absolutely LOSING myself for hours at a time. —The greatest experience of my young maturity was the "ether dream" I had Sept 7, 1926, when Jonathan was born. Then I *ascended* height on height from earthly reality to the dazzling light of God, passing the whirling, gyrating *sun* (which smiled at me, winking, & saying: *"Woops, Bang! Bang!"*) and went on & on upward into the silence & glory, infinitely *higher* than the sun & stars, & felt wrapt and translated by God's great light. I remember His promise then, to tell me the secret of His Heart, & the meaning of life! (He has kept the promise! —That realization comes over me, again & again, here in Primavera!) Henry said, when, struggling out of anesthesia, hours later I tried to explain what God had said to me, that I must have been very near Death then, for that birth of my beloved little firstborn boy, whose survival was even more miraculous than my own, was indeed a very near end to my life on earth.

How I floundered, & foundered, & wallowed in error, *even after that!* How *could* I have continued to be a smart-alecky Bohemian wife-&-mother, when I got "back to normal" & resumed daily life in the "intellectual" circle Henry & I cultivated! How *could* I have ever lost (temporary) sight of that promise!? —For *I* have *never* considered that experience as "only an ether-dream"! I *know* it was a *real* religious experience!

And then, 6 years later, in July, 1932, the next great experience came to me, at the time of my life's greatest dilemma. I had been "railroaded" into a 'madhouse'; and led through ward after horrible ward full of wailing, howling, possessed insane women, & had door after steel door locked behind me by the nurse. I was put to bed in the "suicide ward." They gave me a sedative. But long before it took effect, I was still quite clear in my mind & memory. There was a frightfully unhappy woman in the next bed to mine—a dark-haired, hatchet-faced middle-aged woman sitting up in her bed, ringing her hand, & wailing:—"Oh, how *could* I! How *could* I—! I burned up *all my children!*" I had left my children with the Sunday School teacher in Whitman, that afternoon, & 'hitchhiked' to Brockton, to try to arrange for a free bed & operation at Brockton Hospital. They had locked me in to an examination-room there, & kept me until after dark. A parade of Drs., nurses, & internes kept coming in to "check-up" on me. One contemptible little Jewish smart-aleck Interne came again & again & subjected me repeatedly to (*quite unnecessary!*) vaginal examination, till I fought him off, & slapped him, and told him he was just a *"horrid little ball of wool."* (He was thick-lipped, freckled, & kinky-haired—and *utterly odious!*) After that, they let me alone for a while; and then they came & told me 'someone' was waiting for me downstairs. I got dressed—

I still remember the powder-blue crepe dress I wore that awful night!—& they took me down. The Chief of Police in Whitman & 2 deputies, & a smelly old woman like a gypsy grabbed me, hustled me out of the lobby, & thrust me into the tonneau of a big black limousine, driven by another country policeman. The Chief (a raw-boned Irish ignoramus) sat next to me, keeping his gun in my ribs. "Where are we going?" I demanded. *"I have to get back to my children!"* They wouldn't answer; just told me to shut up, & *"Come along quietly!"* I kept asking *where* we were going—*because I HAD to get back to my children!* And the witless old Chief of Police only butted his gun deeper into my side, and said "Where people like *you* belong!" —It couldn't be *jail,* I knew, being innocent of crime. I kept on telling them I couldn't go *anywhere! I had to get back to my children!* And then they told me the smelly old hag beside me (who was a 'special' police-matron!) was going to care for my children 'till I came back'! —My heart sank, and I kept trying to tell her what they should be fed; and about baths, naps, & bedtime. (They wouldn't say *how long* I must be gone!) I was frantic! —And then, from conversation over the back of the driver's seat, I realized we had lost our way. —The driver had missed a turn. —It was late, by now. There was a full moon shining. Whenever I spoke they told me roughly to "shut up, & things would go better (for me)!" —At last, we turned in at a high iron-grille gate, and soon a great lighted building loomed up before us on the top of the hill. The *shrieking* reverberating from the angles of its walls told me what it was: "a MAD-HOUSE!" Well, *now* I knew! Now I could not expect to be home to my children—(they were *babies*: 2 years, 3 years, and 5 years old!)—*before morning!*

I made no more resistance. The foolish old Chief of Police was the "mad" one! I followed docilely, & we waited behind others while 2 or 3 other patients were admitted. When it came to my turn, I was quite self-possessed—but *exhausted* with *anger, fear & worry!*— and I answered all their questions quietly & calmly. The admitting doctor was a small, red-haired Viennese woman, Dr. B. She looked at me narrowly, and said: "Isn't this a mistake—for *you* to be here?" "Yes, it is," I said gratefully. "The minimum is 9 days for 'observation,'" she said, implying she would look out for my interests. She made a disgusted little face behind the old Chief's back. "You need a good *rest*, child!" she said. —They undressed me, washed me, took away all my clothing, purse, & so on, & led me away behind 50 steel doors, to "rest"—while that smelly old woman was to "care for" my poor babies!

The rest of that experience—which revealed, among other things, the Pharisaical 'love' of my own mother, sisters, uncle & aunt; and the other utter despicable treachery of my husband is too bitter to record. Suffice it to say, after 9 days of observation when I was taken to a "full staff conference" and exposed to 1000 questions to test my 'sanity,' I was given by blessed Dr. Osterheld "a clean bill of health," and leave to go at once, if I chose—"unless," he said, "there is something you would like us to do for you." —I asked the staff for the much-needed, long-postponed operation I had tried to get at Brockton Hospital. And they told me I must, if I wanted surgery, *commit myself* to 24 more days in that awful asylum, and be content to convalesce in their Infirmary (full of violent senile 'cases'). I needed the job done. Having gone through so much already, I assented. —And they gave me a *$1000-⁰⁰ operation absolutely free*, treated me with the utmost kindness, & I was grateful, grateful, grateful! —The smelly old woman fed my children on canned beans, stole all Sandra's clothes for her own grandchildren, & I never saw her again.—

But the thing that saw me through that 9+24 day ordeal—(to say nothing of the post-operative shock after 5 hours' surgery!)— was what happened in that first bed I laid myself down upon in the "suicide ward" of Taunton State Hospital. —The sedative had not had time to take effect when, right before me, on a soft-green wall, a great white light shone, & God's voice spoke to me, and said "Be calm! I will be with you, and get you out of here!" It was only that I had to live by.

(Oh, how could I have been so slow to come to the Brotherhood, when He has been calling, calling me, & so patiently leading me, & forgiving me for so many, many years!)

"You must not waste your energy on hating the Chief of Police for abusing his "commitment"-authority to try to 'put you away' for political opposition of this administration," Dr. Osterheld said to me. "You must not dwell on the fact that your own family refused to come to visit you, or help you in any way. And one thing I must tell you: Forget your Henry. Write him quite off your books! He is a cad. He is a beast. You must never regret your decision to divorce him, nor ever go back to him!" —He told me how Henry had gone to the State House in Boston, & at the Commissioner of Mental Disease office had tried to have me *committed for life!* —"It is just these awful abuses that our Administration stands to oppose," he said.

God bless Dr. Osterheld, & the surgeon who patched me up & made me over. (I never saw him. He arrived at the Hospital by plane after I was 'prepared', & I was under ether before he entered the operating room.) That operation was long overdue. I had needed it since the first baby's birth, but Henry "never could afford" such things for *me*.

Sometimes, trying to get to sleep at night (when I am not admitted to a Meeting, &/or lights go out early, so I can't read) flashes of the past come to my mind. Always they make me marvel at the unfailing protection God has given me through so much poverty, loneliness, & even danger, too! People—beginning with Mama—have always said: "Lois has a good heart." (Roger said those very words, at 2nd breakfast on the sewing-room porch a month ago.) Is it for that reason that God has preserved not only my life, my health, & my "sense of humor," but my SPIRIT, too, despite its ignorant and thoughtless trafficking with Satan's temptations (to "Bohemianism")?

That old Chief of Police! His grudge against me was *hereditary!* It began when my father caught him coming (legs-first) out of the window of the Cutters' summer-home, after the resort-season ended, when the Cutters had gone back to Concord, & Daddy had gone down to close up our cottage, & board up the windows. My father confronted the old scoundrel (unarmed), & "let him go"— but the Chief never forgave Daddy for knowing he was a housebreaker. —& Then, when the Chief's own bad boy, Gene, was growing-up, & started committing the same sort of crimes, when the Chief—to save Gene—'railroaded' others, unprotected, undefended young boys—not one, but *several,* over a period of years!— into Reform Schools, & Gene, always able to *"get away with it!"* went on from 'pranks' to real crimes, & *I* was one of his victims, the Chief was 'taking it out' on my father's daughter!

I was living alone at Pigeon Cove, in the summer of 1923. The family had sold our Cambridge winter home, & moved up to Lexington, to be near Daddy's favorite 9-hole golf-course there. I had had one summer *(away from belovèd Pigeon Cove, & the ocean)* in Lexington, which had "broken my heart" over the treachery of Tuck Houghton (to whom I had become 'engaged,' until his mother returned from Europe, & put an end to our dreams so ruthlessly!);

and I couldn't bear a second one. At first, my parents refused to let me go down to spend the summer *alone* in our seashore home (though I was 20, & had my good little faithful dog Friday, to protect me). But I *went*, anyway—just took my bicycle out of the garage one early morning, & whistled to Friday to follow, & *rode* down there (45 miles) all in one day! *I* was tired on arrival; but Friday was *utterly* exhausted. I got Mr. Bailey (a local caretaker of the summer homes) to give me the keys, & went to our cottage. It was still all boarded-up for winter, & the electric lights on the Andrews Point circuits had not yet been turned-on. (I think it was in April. The summer people wouldn't arrive till June 1ˢᵗ.) But we had kerosene lamps & candles. —That first night in the shuttered house was a night of exhaustion. —Early next day, after I had opened the upstairs shutters from inside, Friday & I bicycled down to the Village for groceries, etc. and to greet my friends there, who had "known me from a baby." An out-of-season arrival in that quiet little village was a sensation—& a 20 yr old girl with her dog, who was preparing to *live alone* in an 8-room house on the edge of the shore with a half-mile wide stretch of woodland between her house & the caretaker's home made HEADLINES! *News traveled fast!*

I had a strong back, in those days! I unscrewed all the heavy board shutters Daddy always put all round the windows on the lower floor, & carried them to the attic of the big barn, & stored them in proper order in the old horse-stalls. I washed the windows, cleaned the house, aired the mattresses, etc.

My family, missing me—though at that time they were all concentrating on my sister Dorothy's engagement to Walter Whiting, M.D.!—telephoned down to Police Headquarters at Rockport, & gave orders for the old Chief to send me back home to Lexington.

How happy he was to have a real opportunity to try to intimidate me! I was the "pioneer" feminist who had *cut her hair off* (1918)!— *who rode horseback astride in riding-breeches!*—who wore the first Jansen "one-piece" bathing-suit seen in those parts!—who *smoked cigarettes!* —And old Mrs. Grundy had been "after me" (both in the resort-section & in the village among 'native' people) for the past 3 or 4 summers. The Chief now sided with these people, & had surely memorized the "Blue Laws" to read me a 'sermon'! I wasn't afraid of him—nor anyone! (I was a young 'rationalist-realist', in those days.)

But when I drove up from the village on my bicycle with my first bag of groceries & a fresh-caught haddock from Hopper's fish-shack, as I went round behind the barn to stall my bike in the rack, I found the Chief of Police examining my garbage-can (which was empty except for a few egg-shells from the lunch-box of my trip from Lexington). Daddy & his "stag-party," the Fall before, on their annual closing of the house, had left empty whiskey-&-soda-bottles on the shed shelf. The Chief held one up to me, shutting one eye under his shaggy brows, and sneering:—

"We all knowed you was a smoker! But we didn't know you'd started *drinkin*—"

I scoffed at him, & told him to drink up the ½ teaspoonful of whiskey in the 'empty.'

"My father left that swig for you there last October," I said.

He was very portentous, reading me a message taken down over the phone. My father "ordered" me to go back to Lexington.

"I'll drive you to the train," the repulsive old Chief offered magnanimously. "You can check the dog & the bike through on the baggage car."

"I'm *not* going home," I told him. "You can inspect my garbage-can for me every night. And if I ever get any whiskey, I'll leave a swig for you in the bottom of the bottle, out here, where you can find it."

I walked into the house, and started cooking my fish.

After a while, the chief drove away in his car.

I continued to live alone. My mother wrote me, saying I 'must' come back. A week or two later Mama & Daddy drove down in the car, to TAKE me home; but I refused. I talked only to Mama. Daddy didn't attempt to 'reason' with me. He knew I opposed the selling of that house, where I had lived for 20 happy summers—the house he had given Mama as a present when I was born! While Mama (weakly) urged me to "be a sensible girl, and drive back to Lexington with (them)," Daddy nailed up a red-&-white-&-black sign: "For Sale," on the post of the veranda! —I knew they didn't *really* care for my return to Lexington, because Dottie & Walter, the "engaged" couple, were the focus of their lives at the time. I wanted no part in that marriage! I had been 'against it' from the beginning! —[The death of my dear sister Dottie, in 1951, revealed even to Mama that I had been right in my instinctive distrust of the mealy-mouthed miser, Walter, from the beginning! —Too long, too sad a story of my sister's wasted life as a Doctor's wife in far-off Texas!] So, having delivered the ultimatum that if I WOULD be so "crazy" as to live alone with my dog in a big house on a dark lonely road, facing the ocean, & backing-up against the woods, then I'd have to *pay my own living-expenses*, they drove off. Mama whispered to me that there were 10 mahogany dining-room chairs up in the attic that would be salable, if I could find an antique-dealer to get rid of them.

That was a good tip she gave me! Though I sold the Queen Anne chairs for much less than their market-value, I had a small nest-egg for a start, & a plan took shape for earning money besides, running a summer-school for 'Organized Play'… It was an innovation of my own, nursery & play-schools being (1923) unheard of! It worked! I had cards printed, which I mailed out to a list of resorters in the Cape Ann Blue Book, & by June 15 had a daily class of 10 or 12 children for 3 hours every morning. *I* had more fun than any of them, & it paid me very well. Afternoons & evenings, I had for my-self—& my circle of friends among the summer people.

But there were nearly 2 whole months before my Play School was in operation, because the summer people didn't come before June 10th at earliest, & I lived a lonely, frugal life on the proceeds of the chairs, on a cash-basis at the Village grocery. —(I remember that for 5 weeks I adopted a diet of cream-of-wheat, fish & boiled onions—and LIKED it very well!)

Until about May 30, the power-company didn't turn on the An-drews Point circuit—there being no users for it, so early in the sea-son. There were plenty of kerosene lamps & candles; and I got on very well with them. Most of the time, except when spring sea-storms roared outside, I felt no alarm. But then, when the Village boys were 'alerted' by Chief Sullivan's naughty boy, Gene, that I was living all alone down there, far from protection by any neighbors, they began a series of Saturday-night "raids" from the woods behind the house. The *first* one did "give me a turn," till I realized it was just "kid-stuff." Friday & I went upstairs and buried ourselves under bed clothes, I holding his muzzle shut so he'd not bark while the gang of boys whooped out of the dark woods, clattered the full length of the lower veranda, trooped up the trellis over the old cistern to the porch roof, & stamped around it, with whistles, catcalls, & dirty jibes, banging the blinds shut, & yelling "Ooh Lois! Where are you!" —But I gave no answer. At last they went away. They repeated the 'raid' the following week, with the same results. The third week I had a plan. —Knowing what time they were likely to come (after dark), I prepared a big feast for them, & had it all set out buffet-style on the table & sideboard in the dining room. I waited in the house without light, standing just inside the front door, with the doorknob in my hand; & when they came, as soon as they ganged up at the front door, I switched on a flashlight, swung the door wide, & said: "How nice to see you! I was waiting for you! Won't you come in?" I lighted the big kerosene lamp hanging over the table, & invited them all to help themselves! It *really* took the wind out of their sails! At first they huddled sheepishly, hiding their smiles, by the door, refusing to come in. But the heaps of sandwiches, cookies, doughnuts & the hot cocoa lured them in. They all ate, acting very decent, till everything was gone. Gene Sullivan, the Chief's son, already had charming manners to use on appropriate occasions. We all talked like friends together, not mentioning past events.

The boys never raided my house again.

But many years later, in 1931, when I put on my campaign through my own little newspaper to change the Town Charter of Rockport (in order to terminate the term of office of Chief Sullivan), the old man certainly "had it in" for me! I had with my own eyes witnessed his supervision of the shipment of a huge load of contraband liquor, brought in from "Rum Row" (twelve miles out to sea) by speedboats & dories, across Cotter's Beach at 3.00 a.m. one misty August morning before daylight. I was lying in the bayberry-bushes at the top of the shore (having been 'tipped-off' by Bel Carrutt, of the Boston "American," that a load was coming in at high tide that morning) & the Chief, returning to his Police Car (to 'chaperone' the loaded truck from Thibeau's Garage over the Town Line), stepped on my elbow, as he passed me in the dark. He flashed his torch in my face, pulled me to my feet, & threatened me: "Ma'am, if you wasn't the mother of 3 young kids, I'd shoot you now! You get up & go home, & leave town within a week!"

But after that, when I *didn't leave town*, but went on & held a jam-packed meeting in the Town Hall for a hearing on "Plan E: Town Management Charter," paying a speaker from NYC's "Civic League," & entertaining him at our house, the Chief was really worried. When I was called to the platform to introduce the speaker of the evening, the Chief was alone in the upper gallery of the hall ("condemned" by the Building Laws for use by a gathering); he leaned against the wall of the movie-projector up there, in the dark, (where no one on the floor of the hall could see him) and kept his service-revolver pointed at me while I talked——(warning me not to "say nothing" about the Cotter's Beach episode, I suppose!—I knew better than *that*, having been schooled in Libel Law restrictions!). But I *was* scared. And when I told Henry about it, he was so terribly scared, he insisted on giving up our lease on the house at 127 Main St., & going back to Boston for the winter!

The Chief was by no means "through with me," even after his happy experience in getting me "committed for observation." In 1937, when a long-deferred lawsuit I had against C Crawford Hollidge came up, & Hollidge (old fox!) got in touch with Henry, & heard all about "the Rag"—& Henry (no longer my husband, & still angry at me) "told all" about that hectic Rockport summer of '31, there were a "stacked" jury & "bought" judge, & 2 questions the lawyer for the defense asked: "(1) "Were you ever ordered to leave the town of Rockport by its Chief of Police?" and (2) "Have you ever been committed to a mental hospital in Massachusetts?" that *had* to be answered "Yes" or "No," I replied truthfully 'Yes,' to both questions.

The Judge rapped with his gavel: "*Witness unreliable! Case dismissed!*" So much for "taking one's brother before the magistrate!"

The Old Chief is dead now. Gene, having successfully avoided trial for 2 murders (in which I am convinced he was involved) is still at large.

March 18, 1958 (5.00 a.m.)

I woke at 'false dawn' (when the cocks first crow) with a vivid memory of Sandra's little-girl face & trusting eyes looking up into mine as she lay on the operating-table at Cambridge (Mt. Auburn) Hospital, in the emergency-ward, with that great gash on her fair white brow, just before Dr. Dudley stitched her up. That look of hers, *deeply trusting*, I have never forgotten! It came back to me so clearly, this morning! And EVERYTHING became so clear to me that by a flash of understanding I KNOW I shall be baptized by the Holy Spirit, in the coming group-for-Preparation! And I KNOW that, in that spirit, I shall be *wholly* RE-BORN—even *virginal* again! *Thank God! Thank God! Thank God!* This has been a fulfillment of the promise God made when Jonathan was born, in my ether dream, when I rose up, & up & up, past the stars and the whirling, smiling sun (who *winked* at me, & said "*Woops, Bang! Bang!*") and God took me into his heart and promised to tell me the Secrets of His Mind, and show me all the meaning of Life.

This has been a real revelation!

March 24, 1958

> "Hokker"
> "The Lark & Cartwheels"
> "Murder Mrs. Grundy"
> "Stoopid"
> "Time & ½"
> "Drowsy Worshipper"
> "The Cellaneous Family"
> "Selma Farrington"
> "The Rockport RAG"
> "Wyndham Street"

My "Works"—! How I labored & prayed for their success! — Frustration and "near-success" crowned my efforts. Jonathan said they were "*too good.*" Editors said: "above the level of current fiction." And I said, "Then, dear God in Heaven, WHY did you give me my 'gift' for writing?" —So far, there has never been an answer. But it is not even now too late! Life is just beginning for me now— "The last of life for which the first was made." And having read carefully, over & over, & studied it, I learned (1950–et seq) that all worth being written has been written in the Bible. —I have now come to Jacob Boehme's "Confessions"—which, with David's Psalms express *exactly* all the innermost longings, hopes, aspirations & inspirations I've had from childhood. —How greatly CLUTTERED my mind (hence, my literary output!) has been by obstructions of *Self*—of bitterness, spite, hate, contempt, sneering, jeering & scorn!—and above all, of *HURT!* I have been too much hurt by the world I have known all too well and described so vividly through my 'characters'—& too much 'identified' (psychologically) with my 'heroes' & 'heroines'—!

Now, I am all-but-completely HEALED! —I still have my 'gift.' Oh, God, can *you* USE it? And use *me! Whatever* work you give— peeling onions, folding laundry, mending sheets, setting tables!— *use* my hand, my heart, my mind, my soul through YOUR HOLY SPIRIT! —I am 54—If I live for "threescore & ten" that gives me 16 more years to work in this life. —Use it all, take it all, refine & fill it all with your spirit. If it can't be done with ink & paper, use it to best advantage to serve my Brothers & Sisters, & thus serve Thee. *Amen.*

April 1st '58

Quite a day at Primavera. —The usual "April fool" jests—such as a list of assignments including MY "duty" with Christopher Mathis & Ecki Z. at the Baby House!—And Clare Walker at the cow stall; Georg with "die schweine," etc. Then Second Breakfast at the Sewing Room for Anni Mathis's 52ⁿᵈ birthday. —Bruce Sumner, just back from Brazil, brought me greetings from Ramond Archer! He talked to us in the dining-room about his difficulties in arranging for a Primavera Work Camp. —After dinner a *good* sleep. Free afternoon for me, so I was going for a walk, which turned into quite an adventure, when Bob Peck & Kurt Zimmerman, Sr. & some young boys, & Carlemon Keiderling were banana-harvesting. They took me along "for the ride." "Do you think we'll see any *snakes?*" I asked. "Maybe," they said! And WE DID! We brought home a *huge*, fat, powerful boa constrictor! (They'll sell it to a zoo, if it lives.)

Such a day!

April 4, 1958 Good Friday

(A year ago today, I was still at St. Anne's, in Kingston. —SO MUCH HAS HAPPENED to me since then! Thank God! Praise him!)

At 8.30 today, with only a small ringing of the bell to summon us, we had a Household Meeting, with the older children. Fran conducted the meeting—the only one for today, except Midday Meal, when we shall eat in silence. Fran made the great point—arresting the attention even of the wriggly boys!—that what happened in Jerusalem, on the Hill of Golgotha, was the greatest event the world has ever known—dividing Time itself, & the years of man, "BC" from "AD." Only the Son of God—obscure, meek, gentle, *quiet!*—could have brought such an impact to bear upon the ages of human life.

I thought, as he read the story of Good Friday (from JJ Phillips trans.) of the crucifix hanging on the wall over my bed at St. Anne's Guest House. Though I have a horror of pagan-Catholic symbols, that cross and its twisting figure of the Agony of Good in the throes of human death has never left my mind since the nights of 6 long, laborious months I spent in my comfortable bed beneath it. —It was the symbol not only of His sacrifice *(for me!),* but also of my repentance for my share of the sins of the world He took upon Himself to secure my forgiveness by Our Father.

Oh God, Father of us all, & of thine only Son, our Lord, Jesus Christ, in His name I pray that all 3 of my own children, & all their families, may hear the call I have heard and followed *(so belatedly),* to bring me here. Forgive me everything, and forgive me most of all for not teaching them better! Keep the Evil One away from them all! Call them to life in Church Community! Open their ears! Free them from bonds of worldly cynicism which *I*—their honestly loving mother!—so mistakenly instilled in them, in ignorance, in my years of lusty life. Forgive me, forgive me! *I love them!* Forgive me!

Sun. Apr. 20

I have spent 36 hours in absolute misery, doubt, & defiance! —
I cannot explain it away. I was deeply, bitterly hurt by being asked
to stay away from 3 or 4 meetings because I "have (?) created too
much disturbance" on the *hof* in the hearts of the dedicated Brotherhood. —Buckets of ice water, poured on my (till then) *happy*
spirit!

(It's the *old*, old story of being "unwanted"—an unwanted baby,
an unwanted child, a 'jilted' fiancée, a divorced wife, a betrayed in-
amorata!) I reacted to it by "conditioned reflexes" which have no
place on the Bruderhof!—like a patient in a psychiatric ward!

What *use* to say "I'm sorry!"? I can well be utterly sorry, because
I have been a victim of the same evil spirit of pride, ego, & ambitious vanity as that which have separated Maureen & Belinda from
us! *Sylvia* came over & asked me WHY I couldn't get on harmoniously? *Pearl* came over when, the second evening I had gone without dinner (because I didn't want to go to the dining-room), when
I had reached a *lowest* "low," & *tried* to talk with me! I flew at her,
lashed out at everything & everyone. And told her I intended to
start out *now*, & take a (20-year) "walk" back home to Massachusetts. "I'll be tired when I get home," I told her wildly. "I'll just lie
down on the Family Lot (at Mt. Auburn), & *die*."

[I really COULD do it, I think, in 20 years! And I could tell all the
people I met on the way home how OTHERS—(*not me*, the 'eccentric'!) can & do live in harmony, by obeying Christ's Laws of love! I
could send all the people to the *Bruderhof* who would listen! —
When I caught myself spinning these extravaganzas, I could understand EXACTLY what prompted Maureen & Belinda to leave & what
wild dreams, like mine, *they* must have been cherishing!]

I tried & tried to get in touch with God all night, & after I woke
before dawn—& utterly failed.

By breakfast time (I was HUNGRY!), when I went up to the
kitchen, I had regained some sanity. But it was not till the golden
light of the rising sun came up, turning everything to God's glory,
that my evil tension relaxed.

Now I must try again to reach God's ear by praying to His Son who died for us all—who, when I only *let* him, lives even in *me*, & in every thief, murderer, criminal, pervert, sinner & cynic who for one moment will open his heart & let the Spirit in.

Oh Lord, open thou my heart to receive the Spirit again! Amen. What I went through for 2 nights and a day & a half was *really* a seizure by Satan! I behaved like one of the swine in the Gadarene herd! Such a *bout!* Formerly I have called such periods "fits of depression," or of despair. Now I know I was *under assault by evil spirits* … And I pray, *pray* "Lead us not into temptation; but deliver us from evil."

I feel SPENT after this dreadful experience!

"Moral" (Bonhoeffer): "Men should *defeat* their enemies by loving them." "In the New Testament" (Covenant) our enemies are those who cherish hostility against us, NOT those against whom *we* cherish hostility, for Jesus refuses to reckon with such a possibility! The Christian must treat his enemy as a brother, and requite his hostility with love. *His behavior must be determined not by the way others treat him, but by the treatment he himself receives from Jesus*; it has only one source, and that is the will of Jesus.

"By our "enemies" Jesus means those who are quite intractable and utterly unresponsive to our love, who forgive us nothing when we forgive them all, who requite our love with hatred, and our service with derision"—

The Holy Spirit entered my heart again on Monday, April 21, at 6.30 p.m., as I sat on my favorite "park bench" on the *hof*, outside the dining-room. Thank thee, oh Christ, for thy Greatest Gift, the Paraclete!

Because I allowed myself the egotistic luxury of self-pity and unbridled vituperation, I forfeited the experience of the Lord's Supper in unity with people of the Community of Brotherly Love! —I attended the Love Meal preceding it; but now must wait a *whole year* for the experience of the communion of "saints" at the Bruderhof.

This will be a lesson never to be forgotten! *[Shame, shame, Lois, thou fool!]*

~

Buddug (at my request) came & talked to me of "being *quiet,*"

& of "harmony." WHY do I *not* —? What is there in *me* that is worth allowing to break the peace & disrupt the love at Loma Hoby, Primavera?—the City on the Hill! (as, alas, I did at Woodcrest, 1955 (Sept.) & was SENT AWAY FOR IT! *(Warning!))*

Bonhoeffer says that the fact that Christ took upon Himself the sins of all men, means that the Christian, looking into his fellow creature's face, must see the Christ in him—whether his fellow creature be 'high' or 'low,' good or bad, mighty or humble: for Christ *is* in us all, & *has* taken on Himself the weight of sin we each carry.

This past week, though I *believe* in Christ's assumption of my sins, I have felt their weight most overwhelmingly! For the dear, pure, selfless *Son of God* to bear them is *dreadful!* He, who *never* was *"separated from God"* (as I was!), *never guilty* (as I was!). This terrible reflection *stills* me, inside.

I have resolved in looking into the faces here to look *for Christ!*— for it is very clear to me that, instead, all my life I have looked for *flaws*—for signs of ill-temper, fear, greed—or even just a crooked nose, a deep wrinkle, a cast-in-the-eye! And in the same way have I analyzed character:—in 'destructive' criticism! Instead, why do I not look for the Good that is Christ, and *is* in each fellow man; & the suffering of Christ who is carrying the load of sin, sorrow, sickness—whatever the cause of wrinkle, & line, & twisted facial muscle! —*The pity of it!* The thought that Christ, our Father's son, is within the creature I stand before, *suffering, grieving!* (Just as He is in me, & bearing the terrible load *I* have heaped upon him!)

Another abhorrent thought has been weighing on me! —For years, I (who considered myself to be a "loving heart," a "happy soul," a naturally "good"-person!) have absolutely been rushing through life's dilemmas hand-in-hand with *Satan, Christ's jealous Enemy!*—In the name of "rational reason," "humanism," "Bohemianism," "free-thinking," and "adjustment to reality," I have been a fool, a swine, an abject sinner—*all the while "taking his name in vain"* by *calling myself a Christian!*

I must wait until Saturday (*at least*) to be "cleared," through a 'talk' with "several of us" (Fran says) before I can again attend either Gemeindestunde or a Brotherhood Meeting. This is PUNISHMENT for me, because these meetings are my only *real* contact with others! (Mealtimes, not quite so much.) I live *alone,* now while I wait. And my own-created lines race up in my mind to rebuke me:

> We who will not love the Lord
> Must walk alone!

> (*1933*. Shaler Lane, Cambridge, Mass.)

Fri, Apr 25

After my (temporary) term of "isolation" from the Brotherhood & the Gemeinde, Fran told me it would take more than *one* talk to "clear" all the accusations & false charges I had made in my agony-of-mind-&-spirit last weekend. I have *prayed* that I might return for Sunday's meetings! And Fran arranged a first 'conference' between Gwynn, himself, & me, this morning.

They didn't "pull their punches"—(but *I never want that!*) They set me very "wise" to my situation! Gwynn repeatedly stressed that my difficulties with human relations all stemmed from my (long-standing, abhorrent) *"overwhelming"* nature! [Oh, I *loathe* that word now, even *worse* than when Dr. Walter Whiting & his lily-livered friends at Harvard Medical School first applied it to me, in *1923!]* Gwynn says my troubles are due to a (perhaps unconscious) "power-complex"; that I want to dominate everyone—especially weak ones—(like Walter's crowd!)—& "draw them into the vortex" of my own involvements—even "stepping in where angels fear to tread" in trying to help people whom *only* GOD can help! —They cited Hanni's gentle epithet of *"Mummie,"* applied because I *"insist"* on offering her a second helping of soup! (Hanni says Lois "thinks *she* knows what's good *for everyone!"*) Fran asked me to tell Gwynn exactly what I had said to Pearl about *him* (Gwynn). It was: "Gwynn is so cold & impersonal, he doesn't care a thing about me." And at this Gwynn assented heartily! He said *he* didn't care to be "dominated" by me, either! At that I laughed, & asked how in the world I could possibly 'overwhelm' *him!* He gave a very vehement answer—a sort of hollow 'roar'! He said: *"By forcing your presence upon me!"*—To which, *stung,* I said sarcastically "Well—!" Fran broke in here, & told me: "I know you very well Lois. You are saying to yourself *right now:* 'If you don't want me, I'll get out.' —*Aren't you?*" I admitted I was. In *silence,* they both IMPLIED:—"He who has put his hand to the plough, and looks back—"! —So I *had* to "TAKE it!" Gwynn says it's TRUE people *don't like me*—especially the children & young people. (The children, he repeated, are very quick to spot the shallow, tawdry shell of 'personality' the world lays upon one, & *praises* it!) (Georg has already said I 'poison' the children with my worldly taints.) *LOVELY* CREATURE I am—!

Fran says I must not 'resent' it if Charles & Deb are baptized before I am: I must LEARN from that! And I told him truthfully I have already prepared to do so, *if necessary.* Lord, Christ, imbue me with THY GRACE—Forgive me! Command me! Accept me, I pray!

So now it is for me to live alone with Christ for my only companion. And this, with God's grace, I've set out to do. To FOLLOW HIM! ["Personal power" is a loathsome thing! Only Christ has the right to power over men.]

Sunday—April 27

"Only he who believes is obedient; & only he who is obedient believes!" (Bonhoeffer)

I believe; & I (mean to be) obedient!

Now, life here in Primavera is *again* a new life! For I see very clearly what it means that CHRIST is IN us—WITH US—"Lo, I am with you always, even to the end of the world!"

(Somehow speaking of being "filled with the Holy Spirit" is less *real* & *lively* a concept (for me) than this NEW resolve (& understanding) that Christ & I must live together.)

NOW I see why the light shines from the faces all around me here. If, at last, the Brothers & Sisters see the light on MY face, they will know that *I* have "decreased" ACTUALLY, & He in me has "increased."

Meanwhile, I must shrivel into such an inconspicuous aspect that nobody notices me at all! When I—*LOIS!*—can be invisible, the great miracle will have been worked! I, who am aware that all my adult days I "have stuck out like a sore thumb" can be, MUST be, WILL be as "mousey" & quiet as—for example, *Phyllis Hayes* (in Isla) …

Oh Lord make me forgetful of the "I," and mindful only and ever of Thee in me!

My obedience was very weak; but now, after this week-&-more of *real* misery, my faith shall make my obedience *strong*.

And I must again & again remember that I, who have "put my hand to the plough" CANnot "look back"—(even to the moribund imagery of "walking home to Massachusetts" & laying myself upon the graves of my forefathers, to die!) I am to LIVE, & He will be with me always, even to the end of the world! Amen. Amen.

~

My sleep was very disturbed last night, & the dreams I woke from, over & over, were all petty & distressing. But when the waking bell rang, I jumped up from all the noisesome-nuisance of my dreams, & said (awake) out loud: "Where is Christ? Are we not living together?" And at the very moment I heard myself speak, I FELT Him come to me again, & fill me with such Peace as I have never felt before! Such a sweetness & joy came all over me, INSTANTANEOUSLY, when I spoke the words: "Where is Christ?" Oh, He IS HERE—even in *me!*

Apr. 28

I shall live now a new life, with Christ for my Holy Husband, so that He shall be with me, even when I am (otherwise) entirely alone in my little house, with my door shut. If HE is to live with me, I must "make (my) house fair as (I) am able; trim the lamp, & set the table"—& I shall not only be never alone again; but I shall be obedient & docile to my Holy Husband, deferring to Him, asking his approval & permission in all things—& in such wise surely He will give me Grace to lay the ghost of the "old Lois," the independent "individualist" who has always considered she was a law-unto-herself!

So now, even if everyone dislikes me and refuses my presence, & assents to the children's attitude toward me, & even if I live *here in community* all alone, I shall never *really* BE alone—

For Thou art with me.

Thy rod & thy staff shall comfort me

...
> Surely goodness & mercy shall follow me all the days
> of my life
> And I shall dwell in the house of the Lord forever!

~

Fran put his finger on the *meaning* of my old *nightmare-dream!* I've tried to 'interpret' it for years—this running from house to house, sneaking in front or back doors, or windows—running over roof-tops, & through corridors, cellars, & up & down in elevators—always being *driven out!* It was not looking for houseroom, after all, nor mere "safe haven" nor shelter! (Though the chase usually started at a house on Brattle St, Cambridge, where Mama's father's people lived.) It is not even a 'homestead' my poor daft spirit has been seeking! *It was a SPIRITUAL HOME!* —Now I need *never* dream that dream again, for (even if physically & socially I am isolated even in the Brotherhood) I HAVE FOUND my spiritual *home:* Die Gemeinde!

May 2 Ten months in Primavera!

Here, as everywhere, in every situation, among any group of people, I am still "the goat"—blamed for everything that happens! This I must learn to bear patiently & quietly, because it is a part of my "cross." There is *nothing* I can do about it. If I should try to "demand justice"—even here where the Spirit rules, it would only create trouble.

There is *no justice among men,* however good & honest they are! As long as men are fettered with any unconscious prejudice that governs their actions and reactions, there will *not* be justice on earth.

Rodney Owens told me at Woodcrest, 1955: "*Shut up! It's the only thing these people understand!*" —But I would never 'shut'-up just to 'play along with' 'these people'! *My* only reason for shutting up is that I must *learn* meekly to bear this cross of mine! It is true there is no justice, *even here!* Alas! Alas! I feel much worse to *know* that such prejudice & injustice DO rule where the Brothers & Sisters truly believe *only the Spirit* rules, than that *I* should bear the brunt of it! —If I were to cite aloud the 1000 incidents of this UNintentional and UNCONSCIOUS injustice here, I would be *forever excluded* from the Brotherhood & the Gemeinde! *That I cannot bear!* I do NOT want to "be in the limelight," as everyone glibly charges, over & over & over! I can live quietly and *alone* here, as I have lived anywhere else! The loneliness here is not hard to bear. I have everything I want & need, & beauty & love & truth all around me. If I am the focal point of all the injustices that have manifest themselves since my "discipline" here began, then it must be that I *incur* all the blame that is heaped on me for everything—because, being my Irish-rebel grandfather's grandchild, I STILL *foolishly look* for & expect justice on earth!

—Yes, in 10 months I have learned that Primavera is NOT 'paradise' (as Buddug said I should). But it still LOOKS like it; & it is *nearer* to paradise than any atmosphere I've previously known.

Bear your 'cross,' Lois: *Jesus,* your Holy Husband, *who called you here* KNOWS that you are not to blame for the multitude of injustices heaped upon you.

There IS a lot of *unshakable, smug & cruel prejudice* here! And God forfend that it ever permeate my spirit! (The Americans here are *gallant* in refraining from 'organizing a bloc' to protect themselves against it! There is a great-hearted factor in the complex "American character" which will *never be seen* by the people here!) That is why I *sometimes* long to *leave* my *near*-Paradise! Bless Tom & Florrie, who endured it, & "came through" in spite of it!

May 7

Four offers of a "deeper, inner relationship" came to me today—from Dave Newton (voicing also an *apology*), from Kathleen Marchant & Janet Keiderling, & from Buddug (who also delivered plenty of *reproof*). Also I got an extremely sweet and loving letter from Judy Jory, who is studying at the Red Cross Hospital in Asunción. Though I wasn't prepared to receive these gracious advances in a *proper* way—because I thought they were MORE "admonition," *at first*—and I *fumbled,* myself, & made *ungracious* remarks!—I am *deeply, profoundly touched by all this!—all in one day!* And I pray to my Mediator-with-God, Jesus Christ, the all-compassionate, the Understanding ONE (who knows my inmost heart & thought!), that I may properly respond to these offers of Brotherly & Sisterly-ness, & not be wanting in my spirit toward Dave, Kathleen, Judy, Buddug, Janet—nor ANY of my kind, compassionate, "concerned" Brothers & Sisters here!

May 8

Fran notifies me I am NOT to be prepared for Baptism! ALAS!

—The weather has turned very warm again, & my spirits *slump* accordingly! Also, for 2 or 3 weeks now, I have not been feeling very well, having great pain in back & bowels, & a slight sniffle & very little energy.

May 11

At Isla, at the double wedding
>   Herman Pleil
>   Ruthi Martin
>   Christophe Boller
>   Marty Druyer

I had a talk with Nina. She comforted & corrected me. Käre McWhirter assured me I'll be GLAD in the end to have Baptism deferred a while.

May 18

—Since then, the weather has changed, first with much rain, then cooling, clearing, & gusty with haunting, capricious wind—I have lived through some very, very hard, black times.

But *today*, the Sunday before Whitsunday (Pentecost), I have been deeply, *richly*, & quite undeservedly rewarded at the Household Meeting with revelation of the Spirit of God, & of the Brotherhood. —The whole meeting seemed to have been designed to comfort *me*—filling me with joy, & love, & unity with the whole circle! —First, a reading from Delp (who was a Nazi victim, put to death for Faith, in 1945), who so expounded upon the meaning of

The Holy Spirit, the "Paraclete," the Comforter, that I need never, never forget again *for one minute* the Source of the strength & unity in Brotherhood; never again can "lack trust," nor forget that at meetings ("conferences") meant to put me on the right path, I am NOT being "scolded"—but, instead, am being "doctored," to be *freed from the demons* of Self, Doubt, suspicion! [HOW can I fail to be *completely* healed of my lifelong paranoia *now*, after this meeting!?] And, to heap wealth on wealth, Gwynn spoke of Loneliness—(which has been my longtime & current bugaboo)—in such a way as to show me that loneliness in Community is impossible, except insofar as I, myself, "separate" myself from the Source of Fellowship—the Holy Spirit.

[And this all recalls the Question on which I fell into *such disfavor with Daddy*, when I was 13—as to the definition of "The Holy Ghost," when I was to be confirmed in the Episcopal Church by Bishop Babcock, in 1916! —A question *never* really comprehensively answered until I came to join the Brotherhood. (I forgive Mark Kurtz for that rough rejoinder of his about it, at a Guest Meeting, at Woodcrest, when he was so embarrassed by my *trying* to clarify that doubt for many "seekers"—because there were also too many SCOFFERS present.)]

Thank God, thank His Son, thank His Spirit, & thank Gwynn & the Brotherhood for what has been revealed to me this morning!]

May 20

Last night, on the way home from dinner, with Helen Vowles and her gentle little daughter, Brenda, I was giving LOUD (and wicked!) vent to my exasperation with *Lore*, the unfortunate, unhappy, ambitious, *brilliant*, (& ever-so-COMPETITIVE!) *guest*. She had repeatedly enraged me by *interference with my work*, & the situation had been more than I could endure silently, yesterday noon. In relating the experience to Helen, who has to put up with Lore's loud-voiced, meddlesome personality *all day*, every day, at work in the laundry, I cried out: "If she doesn't leave me alone, *I'll bash her head in!*"—TERRIBLE talk on a Bruderhof!—especially in the presence of a sweet child like Brenda! —As soon as I got home, I was ashamed. And I pray for forgiveness. And I *really* repented. (I had been reading "Acts" during vespers, and I KNOW that God sent his Spirit for ALL people—"circumcised," & otherwise!)

This morning Stanley Vowles, Helen's husband, came & admonished me for it. I told him I had repented. But he very strongly called me to account for such *un-Churchly* talk! I *am* ASHAMED!

May 25, 1958

I feel *really* "identified" with the Community, at last! I no longer *pine*, at all, for my children and grandchildren. Once the phrase "Lack of Trust" clarified itself for me, so that I truly understood about not trusting the Brotherhood "in a human way"—but as the receptacles of the Holy Spirit of Christ—I began to feel *filled*—as all my life—(especially since *Aug. 16, 1929)* I have *longed & prayed* to be "filled"!—with Otherness (than self). I am a part of the Living Church! —A *part* of Christ's own "Bride"—a cell in the structure of the Kingdom of Heaven on earth!

Pearl says "the nearer (I) get to the fire, the more (I'll) *burn*." — I think now I am closer than ever to complete loss of self—I want none of the "demons" coming back into my "swept and garnished house"—EVER again! How many years, in *utter IGNORANCE*— "smart" and "alert" as I always was told I was, poor fool!—I just opened my "house" to every sort of demon—Satan, in all his forms that tempt the "thinking" *realistic* smart-alecks of the world! —But now my doors are opened wide to the sun of Christ, and the wind of the Spirit; but over the lintels of the doors I wish to smear the blood of the pascal Lamb—*to keep the devils out—for always!*—

My love for all the people in the community has grown deeper and less personal. Rancors have left altogether—and there is no feeling of "antipathy" to *anyone* (even guests, who *annoy!*). I am no longer tempted to "dominate," nor "show-off," nor display myself.

I love everyone! (I *always did;* but imperfectly, till now!)

As to the past, it recedes more and more. I can't dig up a single feeling of identification with it—except my deep regret that the real Truth of Christ was not comprehended by me *while I was a mother*, so that Jonathan, Sandra & Peter are still "left behind":—my darling children, whom I *meant* honestly to give every drop of my lifeblood to nurture and rear! God forgive me! *Send out the wind of thy spirit to Peter in California, & Jonathan & Sandra in Massachusetts, "calling to the North, 'O, come!'"* And let them *hear* with their good ears, & reply, like Samuel, "*Here am* I!"—else my motherhood's passionate devotion were all a loss, a loss I cannot *myself* ever atone for, nor correct! Amen!

June 7, 1958—Watsie's 91ˢᵗ birthday. Poor, dear, generous, loving Watsie! God bless her, & forgive her everything!

"Count it all joy" (as Paul says), to be in this beautiful world of winter in Primavera! Cool weather, but good "growing"-weather, with straight rows of tiny innocent green lettuces in Adolpho's great, square, weedless kitchen-garden, flanked by burning bushes of poinsettia, & burgeoning daisy-*trees*, & great white moon-flowers spilling dew out of their huge cups when breakfast-getters pass by on the path to the kitchen. The thick mauve & white mists lift off the lowlands on the distant camp reluctantly, as the red sun comes up, confronting a bright moon across the sky, at dawn. The silly roosters pass the word along around the hof again & again! The flock of noisome parrots in the bamboo thicket outside my window rouses each awakened bird. Thumping the air with his stubby wings as he shoots off from their mighty shelter to make his clamour elsewhere! The children are calling each other: "Mummie says 'come!'" and "Fetch the water!" The horse tethered under the grapefruit tree in the next garden munches & whiffles, & shifts his rested feet after a quiet night alone in bright moonlight with his equine reflections. Soon the babies will be brought to their day of communal living in the Baby House, where the "short-watch" girl waits now to receive them. (The babies grow so fast & "graduate" from one section to another of their Department so rapidly, leaving for kindergarten almost before one has time to realize fully that they are really born!) The drenching dew of an early-winter night lies late on the hof's 'green' when the sun's color has this northern quality of yellow—(so different from the tawny summer blaze!): You *can't* keep your shoes, or your bare feet—dry on the way to work this morning!

There's a groan of machinery audible now! —That means the laundry-man has started work, to do the Saturday "regular" Hospital

& Baby House wash. (Our modern electric laundry is really one of the substantial features at Loma!) And the children are down in the schoolwood, waiting for the whistle that calls their Circle together. (They are not *quite* as noisy as the parrots that have just vacated the bamboo-thicket!)

Today is Saturday. Lomanians will be cleaning up their yards this afternoon; & digging ditches for rain that's soon to come, & hammering at their chicken coops. —*Count it all joy* to be in Loma Hoby on Saturday, June 7, 1958!—

June 30, 1958

Sixty years ago today my parents were married, at St. Peter's Episcopal Church in Cambridge, Massachusetts. My father had been married before to a young wife with bad lungs, who, after their only child was born (a boy, Norman), died. My father, a young man, for some time managed to keep house, & care for his son alone. But when Norman needed more attention, my father sent him to his sister, Aunt Louise Hartshorn, who was married to a well-to-do transport-owner. (Hartshorn's Express Co.) That freed my father to be a dashing, marriageable widower for a few years. He was (I have been told) taking his time to find a suitable wife. His affairs were prospering (in a modest way). He had high hopes & high standards (for after all, his mother, Lady Elizabeth Hatton, had bequeathed aristocracy to her children!). My mother, Miss Isabel Jacobs, of the Intellectual Blue-stocking Jacobs family, was a fellow parishioner at St. Peter's, whom he saw every Sunday, sitting cool, diffident and demure with her two aunts, her father, & her brother Allen (a Harvard student, then) in the family pew across from the Henderson pew. I think there was some truth in the anecdotes I heard as a child about the advent of Fred Bowman, returning missionary from "darkest Africa," whose "suit" had been "pressed" in the Jacobs garden, under the tulip tree, 2 years ago before he went away. My mother, genuinely shy (because she was so *afraid*—! Afraid of life itself, poor frozen girl!), had begged him (Fred Bowman) to *"wait* for an answer." So off he had gone to the Congo (or wherever—!)

& sweated-out two years, leaving "the haughty Isabel" (my mother's sobriquet) to "think it over." If I know anything about human beings at all, it is safe for me to say that instead of "thinking over" her wooer's pleas while he was away, Isabel (ever a moral coward!) only pushed all thoughts of Fred Bowman out of her mind whenever they arose, because she was NOT "in love" with him, nor any other man; and it was her way to refuse to think at all of anything unpleasant or troubling. —So here he was, coming back to claim a bride he had envisioned night & day for two torrid years in Africa, & she was no more ready to receive him now than she was when she sent him away on the pretext of needing time to "think it over." —She was probably cold with terror, when the minister Mr. Perry, announced from the steps of the chancel, that "our beloved Fred Bowman is soon due in the port of Boston." —Perhaps, even, my father, sitting upright and decorous across the wide aisle from her, *saw* her blush—or more likely, visibly congeal!—in her seat? And then he knew that, after all his long-time playing with the fantasy of Isabel Jacobs as his wife—the obviously "pure damsel" with her golden crown of hair and soft blue eyes under demurely dropped white lids & the lips that were always *deep red* till the day of her death (10 months ago, at the age of 86)—he *had* really made up his mind to ask her hand, himself! —*[There is no stimulus like that of rivalry!]* —As children we often heard them, our parents, teasing each other about the *triangular* wooings that took place under the giant tulip tree *that* summer! Fred Bowman was a "dedicated man"; while my father was merely a very much more attractive, normal, sociable, hearty male. Both wanted the same "woman." —Fools that they were—that *all* blind men-in-love are! Neither of them saw that Isabel Jacobs was not a woman at all! She was a frozen, fearful, shy, inarticulate spinster who was never born for marriage. But for Victorian girls marriage was THE *only* "justification"! Marry she must, or confess to failure of her life! As she simply couldn't marry Fred Bowman, the alternative most easily available was marrying my father! —(So that is how my sisters & I were born!) —And even as I was growing up I saw it was *no* "marriage made in heaven."

Nonetheless, because I feel deepest compassion for both the poor darlings, I have prayed for them several times today, on the 60th anniversary of their marriage. I loved them. And—in their way, it could be said they loved me. At least, out of what Daddy bequeathed to Mama when he died, in 1925, Mama scrimped & hoarded a portion to divide between her 3 daughters—Dorothy (Whiting), Lois (Bayliss), & Laura (Partridge). —Dottie died in November, 1951—so there were but two of us, last year, to inherit the money Mama saved for us. And my part of it (*not* an *equal* share, but far more than I had expected) is now in the common purse of the Brotherhood. Thus, quite unwittingly on his part, my father's "shrewd dealing" in Massachusetts real estate has profited the Paraguayan economy! It is a very odd circumstance—Mama & Daddy, lying in Mt. Auburn Cemetery on the hillside slope just below the Gothic tower; Dottie buried in the oil-rich soil of Wichita Falls Texas—SO ALONE! poor dear girl!—Laura playing her role of efficient householder in Maine—& me, in—of all places!— *Paraguay!* So much happens in 60 years, *as a result of a marriage!*

I have been gradually getting rid of some repeating nightmares that have recurred for years & years, till now. The two latest (to go) were these:—

The Search nightmare. This always starts off in a garden on upper Brattle Street, Cambridge (near the erstwhile family-home of the Chauncy Smiths). In it, I am at first welcomed in a very gracious manner by some sweet hostess (? I don't know who she is: she changes) & then suddenly thrown out, so that I have to RUN—& rush round other houses by back, side, or front doors to get in quickly, & rest just a while before I am chased out again. Sometimes I have to climb roofs & chimneys, & cross trestles over dizzy depths:—always I'm on the run, away from an unseen, indefinable pursuer. (This has a "social" implication because of my unconventional nonconformism—*but more:)*—Fran doped *this* out that I was "seeking a spiritual home." I am sure he is right, because now I don't have the dream anymore; & now, I have found a spiritual home!

July 2, 1958 ONE YEAR IN PRIMAVERA

The House-nightmare. There is a house, painted a liverish yellow, on a corner of 2 middleclass neighborhood streets. The house is full-

to-bursting with people, jazz-music, eating, drinking, hilarity, &
light, & all the walls look as if they were to spill their contents out
into the streets! —There is a very pretty blonde woman, about 35,
highly cosmetized, wearing a navy blue bouclé suit & small navy
cloche hat, who stands on the porch by the front door of this house.
(I think she looks as I did, in 1938.) Suddenly a whistle blows. (Police?) The house suddenly is silenced, & darkened. The blinds are
closed; doors & windows, too. The trees begin to fold up. The whole
'property' recedes gradually to the farther reaches of a fine, spacious
green lawn. The house changes color—to a discrete white. It is
quiet. It is stately. Tall pillars appear in front to hold up its roof.

—I told Sylvia I connect this dream with the 'text' of an unforgettable sermon at Christ Church, Thanksgiving Day, 1933, by a
Baptist visiting pastor (at a "Union"-service): "Each of us is ALONE
in a *little house of flesh.*"

I am now changed to the sedate, dignified white "mansion," withdrawn across a vast green lawn stretching between me & "the world"
(—the corner where the noisy, "bouncy" house used to stand). And
the painted woman isn't there at all. (Perhaps she is inside, in a room
high up, reading Matthew?)

Friday, August 1. 1958

[As my SELF shrinks, I find so little need for "SELF-expression"
that it is a month-and-a-day since I wrote in this journal!] I am
about to be moved to Isla Margarita—(where, I HOPE, *novice-meet-
ings will resume!]* Eight families from Loma have been transferred
there:—Lachmanns, Wrights, Newtons, Caines, Vowles, Patricks,
Headlunds &—and my old "Headmistress" ("Humbug"—*Her-
mana)* Marjorie Parker-Gray, etc.—so I shan't by any means, be
among 'strangers' … Percy (still waiting to return to the USA) has
asked to come back here, ostensibly because one of his little boys
has got into trouble with a child there, & I am considered better-
off *not* near Percy ("the cynic-agnostic," etc.). I am awfully sorry to
leave Loma, my year-long home! *(So long since I have lived a whole
year in one place!)* (Not since Felton Hall, Cambridge! (1945–'48)).
[In Oakland, California ('48-50), I *moved* several times, before I
went to sea! And in Massachusetts again, '53–55, I moved MANY

times round Greater Boston area, *on jobs,* though "home" was at Sandra's, in Peabody! I have always been nomadic!—since 1924, when I left my parents' home for Worcester, Boston, & N.Y.C. Then, after my marriage in 1925, I lived in Florida (Winter-Haven and West Palm Beach) for one year. Then in Lexington (for 10 weeks), Tudor City (L.I.) again, Croton-on-Hudson (1927); Sunnyside; Rockport, Mass.; Brighton, Mass. 1928–29; Sunnyside, again; New Milford, Conn. 1929; Rowayton, Conn., Westport Conn. 1930; Watertown, Mass. 1931; Rockport 1931 (again), Beacon Hill, Boston 1931–32, Abington (& Whitman) 1932–33. Worcester 1933. Cambridge Mass. again (1933–1939) & then Arlington, Vermont '39-41 & Rutland, Vermont 1941. Then Hartford, Conn.; Long Island City, N.Y.; Manhattan, N.Y.; Edgewater, N.J. & then, at last, from NYC's Gramercy Park section (1942–'45) (a *series* of in-City moves here) to Rockport summer 1945 & to Felton Hall 1945–48, with a summer also at Martha's Vineyard, Mass.—BEFORE I went to California, in 1948. I lived in Piedmont, Oakland, Berkeley, Healdsburg, Ukiah, & Oakland & San Francisco, then. And then went to sea, & visited ports of Los Angeles (San Pedro & Long Beach), Powell River, British Columbia, Canada; Portland, Oregon; Jacoma, Washington; Seattle, Washington; Callao & Lima, Peru; Guayaquil, Ecuador; many small Peruvian harbors & towns besides Valparaiso, Antofagasta, Talcahuano. Then back to San Francisco. In an interval I lived in Lafayette, & Walnut Creek, & Danville, in the Walnut Creek section of greater Oakland. Then, unable to *bear* the loneliness, was persuaded by Martha Ann Mitchell to go down to Los Angeles to MM. —(I shall *never* forget that!) In Long Beach I waited for him to make port a few terrible days, during which I stayed with a sick woman, & also acted briefly as "housemother" of a Military Academy in Beacon Hill, Long Beach (an AWFUL experience!). When MM arrived, I took a "garden cottage" in Long Beach, Calif, & stayed 6 months there, seeing him every fortnight for four wonderful days, when he was in port. Then back to Oakland for another 6 or 8 months, when his ship changed its "home-port." On March 6, 1953, when I suddenly SAW that even such a *wonderful love as MM's and mine was NOT what God made us for!* I flew home to Massachusetts. In January 1955, I grew homesick for the sea again, & shipped aboard a Norwegian Oil Janka running between Portland, Maine, & Puerto La Cruz, Venezuela. I got quite weary of that run, though it was a wonderful ship, swell captain, five officers, jolly crew, & a good life altogether. Also I made friends in Venezuela's oil towns among the Americans there. In March 1955 I got another ship, the "Bow Santos" (which has *changed my* WHOLE LIFE—!) & visited, from the port of N.Y. (Brooklyn docks), Boston; Halifax, N.S.; Quebec, Montreal; & Three Rivers, Canada, before going south again. *We picked up* in NYC WILL *&* KATHLEEN *Marchant.* We visited (going So.) Philadelphia, Baltimore, Santos Brazil, Rio de Janeiro, Montevideo, Uruguay (where I met Roger & Norah Allain for the first time) & Buenos Aires. (I had 5 days of short trips there, & really *saw* BA.) Then I went back to New York, paid-off, & returned to Sandra's for a month. Then I went to *Woodcrest, July 5, 1955. Since then I lived in constant prayer, wherever I was, to become a Member of the Society of Brothers.*

By moving to Isla Margarita I am making a step very close to achieving *that* end! So I'm glad to be going there, though my cat Amaryllis isn't happy about it, & I am *loathe* to leave Loma! —It is the loveliest, quaintest spot I've ever dwelt in!

Gwynn & Buddug are going to Wheathill! (because Hans Zumpe has gone down to Bulstrode & Gwynn replaces him at Wheathill). Though Norah & Roger are here now, they are unlikely to remain very long. I would like very much to be prepared for Baptism by Roger, who certainly understands the tremendous change I am undergoing from the former worldliness to my determined pledge to live for God a Christ-based life in the Society of Brothers.—

Am I still a nomad? —Yes, but traveling no longer objectlessly— now outward & upward bound for the Kingdom of heaven! AMEN!

Note: the move to Isla was postponed *"indefinitely."* GOOD!

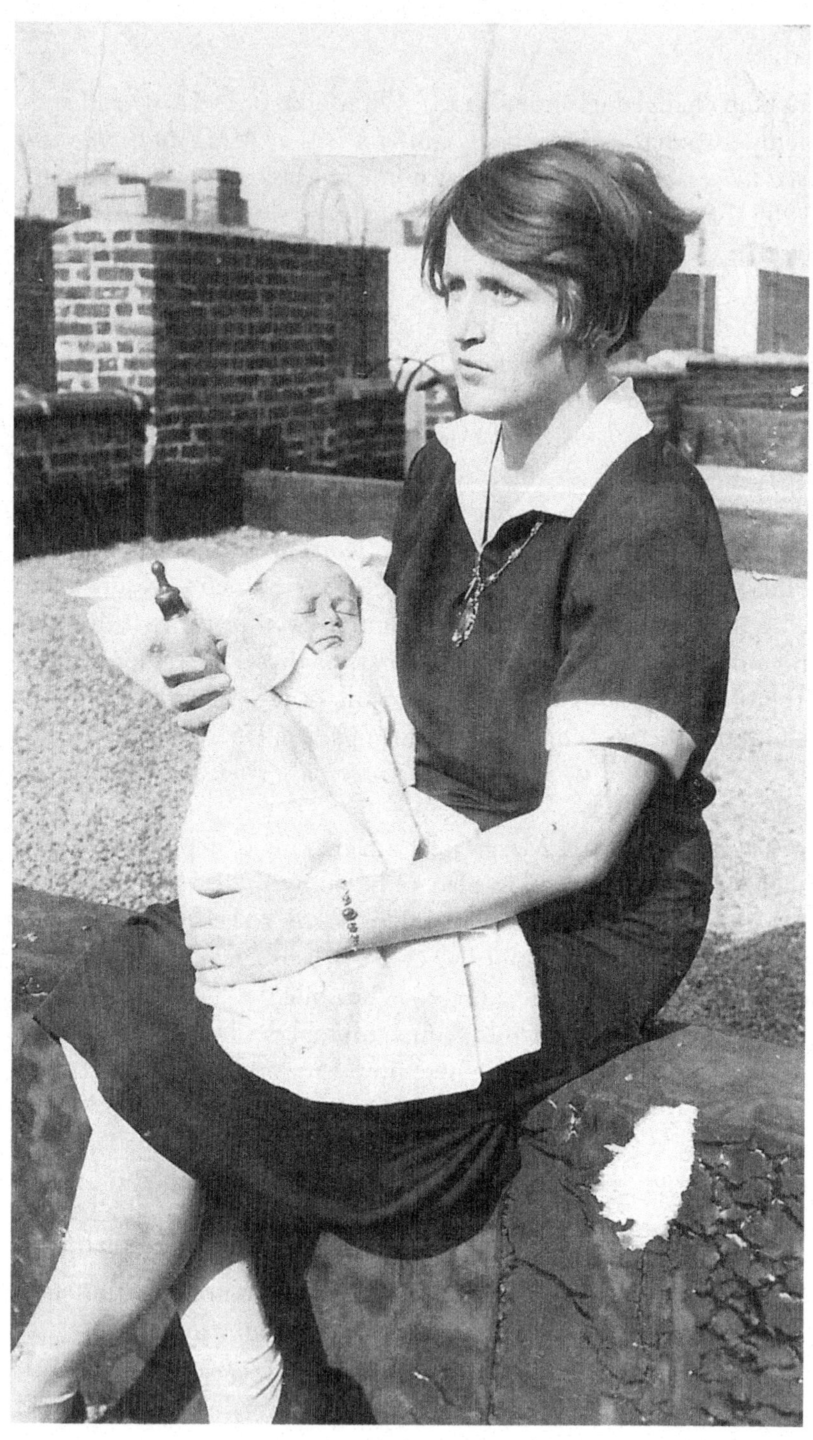

Lois and son Jonathan at 10 weeks old, New York City, November 1926.

Sept. 6, 1958

Thirty-two years ago today, I still had ONE DAY to wait for motherhood! I was at Arlington-Symmes Hospital, Arlington, Mass, in the very excruciating, protracted pangs of 3 ½ days of labor, before my Firstborn Son, Jonathan, came to me. Thirty-two years he has lived, & worked, & served, according to his best lights—my good little Oak Tree, stalwart, strong-hearted—a modest, quiet, studious GOOD young man! Bless him, God, *now*—as you blessed him then! His first 2 ½ hours in the world were spent in the hospital's *morgue*—Henry had been informed he was *dead*. And then, before I came "back" from utter, exhausted unconsciousness, they heard his feeble cry there, among the corpses!—so that when I asked for my dear baby, they could bring him to me—battered & bruised, with deep scars round his neck where the umbilical cord had twisted, *all but* strangling him!—(and giving him lifelong trouble with his larynx, so that in 1948 he had to give up teaching Freshman English classes at the University of California because he couldn't *make himself heard!*) *Oh God, thank you for my Jonathan!* Bless him. Send Him ever more of "the healthful spirit of Thy Grace," so that he may "more perfectly love thee, and worthily magnify thy Holy Name!"—Spirit of the Living God, breathe on *him* a-new—!

Sept. 9. '58

I had a "free afternoon" today. I started out from here at 2.15 when the Vespers bell rang, & walked to Ibaté through the jungle-path. It was newly-cleared-off, & just a slight hint of Spring was in the air. Some great lapacho trees were in high pink bloom against the blue sky. A great white bird—heron or egret, probably, sat in a palm-tree above a swampy patch. It was very quiet, & very beautiful. In the woods, the air was cool & damp. I love to walk *alone* in such places, missing nothing of the wood-sounds & the filtered sunlight by being taken up with conversation.

At Ibaté I saw Shoeneid & Juliana, & Iet Fros, & Jack Elston. Audrey, Edna Jorey, Katy Franchom, & Theresa and lots of familiar children. There are such wonderfully *hospitable* sisters at either Isla or Ibaté! (That's why I was so glad yesterday to share tea-&-cake

here when Norah Caine came in waiting for her Hospital-appointment.) On the way home it was even cooler in the forest, so that though I was really *lost in thought* about *how far* I must "grow" before I shall ever be *ready for Baptism*—so that I can even *begin* to *approach* the selflessness of any of the Sisters in Primavera, & *really forget Lois!*—I walked very fast & was surprised to find myself out on the road by the banana plantation. Rohan & Phlegan were there, dashing round on *one horse* (which is forbidden), scaring the cows, & really wasting time. I got home a-foot when they did "a-horse." It has been an uneventful but very re-creative afternoon I have spent.

Sat. Sept 13th

The last 3 or 4 months I have "found the Way" with practically everybody except Evelyn Bailey. She is a "weak" Sister, *hurt too much* by early days of miserable poverty in the slums of London to have been wholly healed, even after *years* of Bruderhof life. It is shameful for me to have to admit that I, who am old enough to be her mother, give way to anger at her reflex manifestations of unhappiness. But yesterday morning, when I woke about 3 o'clock, & had a very close talk with God, something seemed to happen to implement the compassion I have always felt for Evelyn, with a less-human concept of my "duty" toward her. (Sylvia has *always* told me I am inclined to view the people here from a too-*human* standpoint!) I had distressing visions of poor, terrified Evelyn trying to wave off my "overwhelming" wrath at her (for her customary, *involuntary* "insolence" to me!), & I realized I really *scared* her! I never want to "scare a *cat*," let alone a fellow human soul. I was ashamed! I had a *fine* talk with her about 9.00 o'clock. And I *do hope both* of us can overcome the "antipathy" we have felt for each other! —Yesterday was a GOOD day.

OMISSION

I quite forgot to record the birth of Amaryllis Cat's *6* kittens! — I can only *guess* now that it took place on Aug. 29th. Poor little young mother! She didn't know WHAT was a-foot when the birth-pangs overtook her! She went into a frenzy, & burrowed under my bedding to hide herself. (Made a great mess of my bed-spread before I could stop her, and, finally, when her first child was born, induce her to retire to her waiting suitcase-nest!) The first 4 were large kittens, all white-&-tiger-gray (Audrey's cat's children!)—the fifth, a little black one. When *3* had come, both Amaryllis & I thought she was done; but she *went on*, from 1. pm to 9.00 pm!—& after 5 were all cleaned & sleeping, I called on Norman Price (*compassionate* slaughter-man for this hof) to select *one boy*, & "put the rest out of their misery." He did so kindly & quickly. The first large four, being all girls, were exterminated. Amaryllis FLEW at him! (I was sent outside; but could *hear* the *c-crack!* of their little neck-bones, as, one by one, he killed them! —*Euthanasia!* How it tortures me to do this to helpless, loving-&-trusting PETS! —I have never liked to believe that *God* made *man king* over the gentle, loving, innocent beasts!) And when Norman had gone, after a couple of hours, Amaryllis bore a twin black kitten to the little male spared! —So now she is a mother! Instinct is very strong & sure in her. She is *devoted* to her job—for 3 or 4 days wouldn't leave her twins even to go outside! Now, however, the male "callers" are back (for their solstice wooings!) besieging the house! Amaryllis is restive, but embattled in defense of *Nett* & *Goldig* (the kittens' Bruderhof names)! She spent one whole night (Sept 12) literally "on the tiles," & what a caterwauling went on! Elfrieda's mama-cat (with 3 left to bring up) is in the same injudicious state of instinctual abandonment, & all over the hof were feline "romances"! Last night (Sept 13) I suffocated *myself*, keeping the shutters tightclosed against the yowling courtiers—& they literally *flung themselves* against the boards of the windows, while Amaryllis, inside, in her suitcase-nursery, growled & spat—*What a lovely night!* This morning, she is calm enough! Her ablutions performed for self & twins, the medical report should read: "Mother & twins doing nicely."

　　—But I can't *continue* to go through this every time she is fecund! She is so well & strong (thanks to the feeding I have *fought* to provide her!) she will populate Paraguay in 2 or 3 years! I can't bear to be untrue to her! And *death* for *unredeemed* beasties is *final*, with no Resurrection promise to rely on! Oh dear God, *must I be a cat-murderess again!?*—with *still* the ghost of my "little brown cat" Tassie haunting me from her watery grave on the floor of the harbor of (guano-reeking) Arico, Chile? I *MUST STEEL myself to do it!*

M.M.

Reading (again) Ibsen's plays, I learn more & more about the background that produced M.M. He never talked about Norway as it must have been in his boyhood, shortly after the period of which Ibsen was—(no *exponent*, but severe critic!)—the world's most famous literary product! But MM showed me *so* proudly, with such nostalgia, the pictures of the ancient wooden church of the 13th century that still stands as a national shrine; and the mountain-snow scenes; and the fjords, and harbors, and market-places! His love for Norway was not entirely UNcritical; but it was what *bound* him, even more inexorably, than his family! —I *know* (as Sandra says) that I *could* have induced him to leave it all, and *stay in the U.S.* —But I never even *dreamed of trying* to do so! He, like every other human soul I ever knew (including my infant children from the days of their births), belong *only to God! I never* tried (like Hedda Gabler!) to "mould human destiny!" I never *wanted* to! (Yet because of my blunt goodwill and understanding of what people *need*, I am continually being accused of overwhelming, "domineering" *will to* RULE! *And I never, never, never, may God be my witness, cared for ruler-ship at all!)* I have loved MM *more*, & more *humbly*, & more *selflessly* than anyone, *except my children*, that I ever knew! When we parted, it was a terrible wrench, but it was *my* decision—for *his* sake, to re-lease him fully & freely to fulfill the destiny of a good *Norwegian man!*—a Good man! —As I used to tell him:—"the *goodest*" man I had ever known! And I NEVER LOOKED BACK (like Lot's wife), nor ever regretted, nor amended my decision. Because I *really* loved him *better than myself!* & because he represented to me Christlike strength & humility, that no one I ever knew had—up to that time!

God bless you, MM! I often feel close to you in spirit—as if we still stood shoulder-to-shoulder at the rail of the lower deck of the little "HØEGH CLAIR," watching the exhausts from your engine-room, as we put out to sea together! We shared very deeply in my cherished sea-going experience! I think we shared EVERYTHING that life gives men & women in common … And when it all came to be TOO I*ntense*, TOO "mortal," then we HAD to *STOP* it—because *you belonged to Norway!* (in your own mind) & to God (in my mind). Bless you, you dear, dear, strong, brave, gentle, loving, generous, Christian soul! I can see your figure in the murk of the dockside on a foggy night, watching me up the lonely dark street because you couldn't leave the ship when I went home. Bless you, dear, dear, dear MM!

Oct. 1958

(Note: Gwynn & Buddug are to go to *England!* This thought brings panic to my soul. Buddug has been infinitely wise, infinitely kind, deeply understanding, & *uncompromisingly* SEVERE with me! And I love her deeply & gratefully. *Without her* I don't know what I'll do—! Loma will be so *empty!* —And Gwynn, who surely has never shown any softness of sentiment toward me, will be *sorely* missed by *me* MOST of all! for his Mosaic gift & prophecy & leadership! Alas! Alas! Alas!

Oct 6, 1958

Now I have figured-out the reason for Sanni's "breaking-up" the improved relationship I was working-out with the kids!

One day in the dining-room, before dinner began, while I rested from my labors of table-setting, the youngsters, coming early from school, as usual slammed into their chairs at my table. Then they began making many *sotto voce* snide references to BEANS, with low snickers & significant glances at me. (I, who have such terrible intestinal gas after eating beans, thought they were being low-minded!) So I told them *that* was not fit table-talk; & that they must remember the dining-room was also *die Kirche*! —They went on joking slyly about BEANS. —*Boys will be boys*; & I know *some* harmless SMUT is second-nature to them. So, on the way home from dinner I told Owen & Monty NOT to repeat to older people, nor ever in the dining-room, the following ditty coined by the Boy Scouts of America, concerning the inevitable baked-bean fodder used on hikes.

> Beans, beans, the musical fruit
> The more you eat, the more you toot!

(NOT "elevating"! And NOT very wise of me! But with all the snickering about *beans* I took it for granted they already joked in that vein.)

October 10 '58

TRIUMPH—? (My prayers answered!) (I hope so! GOD provided it!)*

About Evelyn B.—! Alas, & alas, over a year's contacts daily with her, at work in the sewing-room, have been dismally unsuccessful! Repeatedly, consistently—even after "clearances" together with Witness Brother-&-Sisters, when we became "friends" again, & agreed to "find a way together"! our antipathy would burgeon again. — She is a neurotic, product of an unkind world, & convalescent from serious illnesses. And she is only 27; & a melancholy tyke. Therefore, it has always been up to *me*—cheerfull-er, stronger, older, & presumably wiser—!

But we have been "doing better" together lately. Indeed, today, *she* even *volunteered spontaneously an (overdue) apology* for vitriolic tongue-lashings.—

*But (Oct. 13), I find when *I* am not her victim—(always the recipient of her furies "gets it" when the *Youth go off* on a trip, & *she is left behind!)*—someone *else* has to "take it." Sunday & Monday, it was *Maria Ecroyd, poor old lady* (70 ½!)! Maria, talking about it afterwards, said she "*had* to *make a face*" at Evelyn, because she had "no other way to defend herself"! —Surely, Evelyn, Member of the Brotherhood, is *really unable to help it!* I shall henceforth take NO "umbrage" at anything she ever says or does.

The Brotherhood mentions its "weaker" Sisters; but *never* says wherein nor how they are "weak." *Love* learns to *"take them as they are,"* "poor things!" But for God's grace, I might have been left like this after Sleeping Sickness.

Oct 14

Spring in (October) Primavera! What a series of *perfect days* we have been having!—(after terrible downpours that have made transportation so difficult over washed-out roads!). The trees are all in leaf, & some in blossom. The sweet smell of citrus-flowers permeates the air. The birds, so trustingly tame in our midst, are flitting about, building nests, & singing for joy. Little baby lizards are hatching in the hole in the clay-floor, under my bed—providing great sport at hunting for my two lively roly-poly kittens—black imps, named *Nett* & *Goldig*, pride of their vigilant black-&-white mother, Amaryllis—(my *young kitten* of *only a year ago!*). Work in the kitchen keeps me out-of-doors on a low bench, peeling onions in dappling sun-&-shade, facing south toward the long vista of camp stretching away & away like a blue-green sea to the "horizon" of far-distant jungle! The coolness lasts well, till I have finished my job, & then, for second-breakfast, join the sewing-room staff at 2nd breakfast on the roofless porch outside the housemother's room.

Till now, for several months, I had been setting tables every day in the community dining-room for *midtag-essen*. But, due to my inept handling of a group of unruly school-boys in the dining room, this job was taken from me—alas! (I'd learned to enjoy it, as I do all routine-tasks, for their therapeutic value!). I do *not* do enough for the community, I *know!* I am not assigned to do Watch, as other girls & women are. (The reason for this, I do not know.) This gives me much more time—besides the fact that, having no family to care for, I am not so busy at home, either. The REST I have had now for over a year has worked miracles of Peace in my soul. I feel *so tranquil* almost all the time! I am very grateful for it. But I feel I am not doing enough for God & the community.

~

"Unless a man be born again, he cannot enter the Kingdom of Heaven."

I would, I *will* be *born wholly a-new!* The "old Lois" is *slow* to die—alas, & the *half*-dead corpse of her former self should by now have ceased all breathing, twitching, & groaning—signs of the "possession" (by demonic forces) that kept her *so long* separated from God!

Oh God, give me thy power to be born wholly a-new!

November 2

I still "wear a mask." WHY? When I can see the utter trusting, un-masked, naked spirit of others bared without reservation from the others of the circle of the church, I know I STILL do "wear a mask"! Who here has ever seen my real God-made new spirit—except in short flashes of real abject repentance?!

I long for the miracle of wholeness—NEW wholeness: oneness of my spirit with that of Christ, my Savior, my Master, my TRUE & only Friend.

God grant me that miracle. Amen! Amen!

~

When I received a birthday card from Rosemary, Bessie, John & Alec Peters, sent Aug 9 from NYC with a package (not yet received out of customs, down in Asunción) reading: "Happy Birthday & Good Drinking"! I knew it was sent in real generous kindness & affection; but I felt *so sorry* for the Pigeon Cove "crowd" who still remain in fetters & deluded agnosticism, out in their well-padded, prosperous—but utterly EMPTY and MEANINGLESS—*world!* Never, never would I return to that life! And it would be right & proper if I could someday be apostle to the worldlings of the "cocktail crowd"—for I know their good-heartedness, & their emptiness, & their NEED—great as the need of the poor & sick!—the need of *starved souls!* I loved those people for their kindness & tolerance to me when I was ostracized by the sanctimonious unforgiving! —And I ask God to let some light come in to them. They have, according to their "code," been "honorable" and "neighborly." Father, forgive them! For, when they act like smutty little pubescent schoolchildren at their liquorous spring houseparties, they *surely* "know not what they do"!

Nov. 23rd

At 7.00 this morning (just as I finished writing the preceding page), Sylvia came and summoned me to a Household meeting, at which all children of the 4th Class up were, also, present. It was to announce a Quiet Day. Iet Fros's newborn baby, Hermann Walter James Fros, had died at 11 pm last night—a day-&-a-half of life, for the tiny little baby, so long-awaited by his patient mother to "replace" her son Walter, whose burial we attended last January 21ˢᵗ. The new baby was named for his father, for his lost brother, & for Jimmie Johnson who died at Wheathill in a coasting-accident at the time Walter drowned at Ibaté's swimming-place. —The double loss to the parents within 10 months is *terrible!* The shadow of the baby's death affects Doris Chatterton, too, whose newborn child was a day older. This afternoon, Sylvia and I "watched" over the tiny body in its flower-decked cradle for a little over an hour (relieving Betty Owen & Rosemary Kaiser). So many memories, *so much contrition!* passed through my mind in the clean, quiet room! [Thanks, thanks to God from my unworthy heart for my 3 strong healthy children— for my *never losing a child!* (though the ordeal of their births was terrible for me & for each of them!). Bless them now, with their families, oh Lord: Again I pray Send out the Wind of the Spirit to call them home; & thy wisdom to light their way to seeking the Kingdom!] —I can *still* see the faces of Hermann & Iet last January at their son's grave. Today, Iet will not be present: poor woman! Bless her! Comfort her! And give her peace to *believe* Thy Wisdom's perfection. This little boy of hers is now with Thee, & *happy & at rest.* Grant his parents real *gelassenheit* to bear this second sorrow.

Ibaté has had 4 deaths since I came here: Gunther Homan, Walter Fros, Rachel Marsden, & little Hermann Walter James. —Why the death of *3 innocents* here, & *2 others:* Jimme in England, & Gregor Luver, in Germany? *God knows! God* wills it for the best. These innocents will have been spared knowledge of the sins of a "generation of vipers" in the "atomic" world! Bless their ignorance of it all. *Amen.*

At 4:30, we joined the funeral procession for the tiny dead child. We waited in a group, silent and then singing, for the miniature casket to be carried out of the end-room at the mother-house, where we had "watched." Georg, carrying the tiny coffin, went first, followed by members of the baby's family. He placed the coffin, covered by lilies, palms, & flowers, into the leading wagon, which 6 other wagons followed, slowly & silently, over the road to Isla Margarita, joining the procession of the Ibaté wagons at the cross-roads. (Things were very smoothly-arranged & everything proceeded without a 'hitch.') The long ride over, & then the long walk up to the beautiful burial-ground on the hill above Isla's lovely farm-lands were times to glorify God Almighty under the extraordinary beauty of the storm-threatening heavens & their colorful majestic splendour. Thunder growled through the piled clouds, but the rain held off, the storm finally veering off without hitting Primavera. The tops of the beautiful trees on the hill were gilded against the blue-&-white sky overhead. The solemn silence of the large gathering round the grave preceded a short 'sermon' Delf gave, & his reading of a Psalm, and the passage from Matthew 18 (1-6) about the necessity for conversion to the pristine simplicity of childish innocence, as a prerequisite for membership in the Kingdom. We saw the little coffin lowered into the grave; the earth filled in & mounded over it, & the palms & flowers placed on top. Then we sang 2 German hymns, & "Brother James's" 23rd Psalm—& walked back, in silence, to the lorry, which carried us home to Loma. I had experienced so much of deep thinking and feeling, I was exhausted, & did not go to the dining-room for the Love Meal that followed.

Nov. 24 '58

Soon (in 6 days) Advent begins. It was on the 2nd Sunday of Advent last year (Dec. 8) that I became a novice. Many times since then I have asked for Baptism. A greater part of the year I have spent in semi-isolation from the Community, by way of (gentle) discipline. These past months, I have been much alone—due to my sharp-tongued "divisive" remarks about people—till the understanding at last came to me that by even the most "tolerantly"-intended comments about others, my words can and do *"divide" people from each other!* That is what Will Marchant has meant by repeatedly telling me not to "analyze" people; and, at last, after many months it came to me that in psycho-analysis—(the process of thinking by which all my writing has been influenced since girl-hood)—the object of probing & examining is *to discover the Anti-christ*—(the Devil!)—in others!—whereas here, in the life of the church—the blessèd, live, true community of those whom God has called out of the world to live a life of Witness to the validity of His teachings—the healing is done by *the search for Christ in the human spirit*—& the planting of His words in uncultivated soil; the cultivating, ploughing, weeding, pruning—&, at last the *harvest* of the fruit of His seed of truth & love! —It is good to be *sure* that the old ways were *all wrong*—though it is sad to consider the wasted years now gone! Oh Lord, if my "glib" pen can ever be used by you for your good purposes, teach me to forget *all* the *old thinking*; to begin writing *constructively* on the new, light-shedding basis of the True way—the way of *search for Christ!* For He said: "no man comes to the Father except by me. *I* am the way, the Truth and the Light." —In literature, the "good" writers of great works—like Thomas Hardy, for example—or Robert Frost—who probe the human spirits of simple, unspoiled countryfolk, like the "Wessex" gentry of Hardy's books & Frost's Vermont Yankees—are *true* workers for God! —The old WIT, vitriolic, analytical, ridiculing—of such people as Aldous Huxley, Evelyn Waugh, Dorothy Parker, etc. will not *live* as literature!—because it is the WRONG "search" into men's souls, opening-up the twisted channels of bitterness and ducts of evil! —Please God, if I may write—anything "creative" at all, now that I have left the world behind forever!—let me write about the little light of God born in each innocent child; & how that tiny flame is fanned to sacred fire to burn before men in witness to the great white light of God's truth! Amen. Amen.

Also, during this year of discipline, I have learned the terrible wickedness of my even mentioning (as I did) SUICIDE—for a year ago, on Dec. 8, I had *pledged my life to God* in *full surrender;* so that it is no longer *my* life for me to dispose of, nor my will to act upon! Never again will I even *consider* the old, despairing thought of self-destruction! The word "SUICIDE" is now a profane word! (Just as I have deliberately put out of my mind all the old smart-alec "dirty jokes" I used to think so "entertaining"; & all the musings & maunderings about sex-life. In these two things I have succeeded already. Now, suicide as a sane woman's proposition is also "out," forever!)

I am not yet back in the Gemeindestunde Circle, *because of my errors;* but I am praying for the privilege very, very soon now; & for

Baptism, to confirm my *new understanding* that *even in me God can & does dwell,* now that I believe fully the words "*all* things shall be added unto you." —EVEN, *oh my arid soul!, the Holy Spirit! Amen*

Dec 9 (Rosemary Cutter Dole's birthday; Nina Wright's birthday)

At 6.15 tonight, Renata Barth, Jorg's wife (Annemarie & Kurt Zimmerman's oldest daughter) bore a little boy baby—(after some pre-natal difficulties)—thus making Moni and Georg grandparents, & giving *another* great-grandchild to Emmy & her late husband, Eberhard Arnold (the "father" of the Bruderhoefe). —This is an historic occasion. But mostly, it is a love-feast. Jorg and Renata were married here at Loma last January 12. God bless them!

(Reading back in this Journal about the same Advent-Epiphany season last year, I see myself as very *vain, shoddy, conceited* and undisciplined! *Have* I "progressed" at all? *Have* I "come closer to the Life"? Oh, I do hope so! For when I sat down to write this just now, I had intended to write a confession of my ignominious inadequacy! — And now I am so overwhelmed with it that I find *words can't express my shame!* To be so *privileged* as to be here at Primavera at all, living in beauty & a peace that I so often break because of the evil in me!—and yet feeling anything at all beyond deepest praise and adoration of God for his goodness to me and my own terrible unworthiness of it—! *Fie,* Lois Henderson Bayliss! *Thou art a fool—and worse!* God forgive me! I can *never* be worthy of this life!

Thursday, Dec. 25 '58 Christmas Day (p.m.)

Our celebration of Christ's birth began *last* night, about dusk, when, having had family supper (at the Bernards', a second year! *Bless them!* We heard the singing at the "crossroads" (towards the Hospital). We hurried to join the procession, led by the "3 kings" (in costume). It went on to the Hospital, & between the two wings, out towards the Casita, through the gate there to the front of the main wing. Benches were arranged on the slope under the great trees. The patients (our own, & the Paraguayans and their families, as well as neighbors from nearby estancias & villages) were with us as we approached the crèche. —Bertl & his golden haired daughter, "Eso," were *Joseph* and *Mary*. Peto Keiderling, our new little boy (Janet & Peter's son) was *Jesus*. And Betsy Maas, Carol Beele, Daron Marchant, Heather Woolston were *the angels,* holding lighted candles round the manger. A magnificent, gentle ox was there, munching; and a friendly, curious donkey. The setting (of the vestibule-entrance, whitewashed brick-&-timber) was *very* good. From the window overhead, a candle-lighted paper "star"-lantern hung. The moon was full, & the night perfect—cool, clear, sweet with summer blossom-scent. It was the LOVELIEST crèche I ever saw (*putting to shame* the extensive Park-Dept. "spectaculars" that sedate old Boston has recently staged on the Common!).

We returned to the Bernards' for 2 or 3 presents each—the rest being held-over until early morning.

The children came to wake me about 4.45, & I was ready to get up & get dressed. 'Ricia & Jim were up when they conducted me home.

It was a LAVISH Xmas this year *for poor folk*. We all "did very well" with the gifts of love from each other! (Those I value the most are the "copyings-out" that meant so much careful work by people here who earnestly wish to bring me to a full realization of the meaning of this life. (Thank you, God! Thank the Child of Bethlehem for his Gift of Love to us all!)

By the time for the 9.30 Household meeting (after Family Breakfast (& washing-up) at the Bernards) I was very sleepy. But I enjoyed the meeting—& only wistfully wished I could have been at *Gemeindestunde* (which followed). I fell asleep for a short nap before *mittagessen*. Then we had a nice, festive dinner together in the big dining-room. A Paraguayan boy of 10 played the harp, accompanied by his father's guitar. I spent the afternoon sleeping very refreshingly till 4.10! (skipping Vespers) & then woke & got Maria Ecroyd to join me for cake & wine. After she left I worked on a blue sock (for Holly B.) & then dressed for the Xmas Love Meal at 7.00. The choir was very good, also a quintet of Youth and some violin-flute-&-cello music.

It has been a lovely Xmas.

I feel really new this year! Thank God! —Oh, thank Him for leading me here. Bless His Holy Name forever & ever. Amen!

~

—Renata is still at the Mother House, "not so very well." Her little son flourishes. Moni & Georg are tired, but *plainly happy!*

Journal 1959

[Written January 2, 1959]

Friday (Dec 26) was "Family Day," when, with all the Youth away on one of their excursions—[except Michael Marchant, poor lad, who drives "the M.A.N." (our red, new lorry) & the other (?), who drives the Chevvy]—all meals were "in the family." All 3 *hoefe* had the same schedule. It is a time especially arranged for *interhof* visiting. The two lorries were in action on an all-day shuttle-service, between Loma, Ibaté, & Isla, taking passengers to see friends & relatives.

I had early breakfast with the Bernards, & then we all rushed out to take the 8.00 o'clock trip to Isla. Everyone was in gala mood. Of course it was even already hot, & very, very dusty; but the "M.A.N." rides very smoothly, & holds a great many passengers, on its cross-seats. (The youngsters like to stand.) Everybody sang, & made merriment over the bumps & the brushing by trees along the jungle-roads. At Ibaté, we took Delf Franchom & some of his children aboard (leaving our own Ibaté-bound passengers there). Little Wilhelm sat in my lap, a dear little boy, cuddlesome & gentle. The Bernards arranged with the Lachmanns to use their house as a "hqrs" for our bags & trappings, while we made our own respective visits. Helen Vowles welcomed me, because Stan had gone to Loma with the young children; her older kids were off on a horseback-trip; & she was alone at home with Greta, her newest baby. We had 2nd breakfast together—*wine* & "biscuits" & Xmas cake … So that when I went to join Jim's family at "20 to 10," at Lachmanns', I was pleasantly "inebriated." We collected our gear—Salomé & Martin were both recovering from flu, so that we had *their* scheduled time for swimming at the beautiful Orangewood Pool, off in the jungle. The only other swim I had, last year, was there; & I *longed* to repeat the beautiful experience of swimming in the clean, spring-fed, sandy-bottomed, boxed in *"tajamar"* under the great forest trees. So we set off through the school-wood on the well-worn path across the sugar-plantation, to the jungle trail. 'Ricia carried her baby, *"The Mouse"* (Margery), papoose-fashion in a canvas seat strapped over her (thin) shoulder—borrowed from Judy S. We made good time, even though little Holly, with her broken collar-bone, toddled all the way! The Hasenburg family, & the Harry Barrons, with Ome Dorothy, were already there. Though we were allotted only 30 minutes' swim, the pleasure of it has lasted in memory for a whole week! —We missed the 11.00 'bus' & waited in Isla's center, while Jim & Chico went back to get Chico's forgotten hat. At 11.30 Michael came back again with the MAN, & took the last-remaining pre-*mittag* passengers back to Loma.

We separated for lunch, & for siesta. But came together at my house for family supper. (They brought the food & we ate very sumptuously, holiday-wise: I made cocoa & scrambled eggs, & we had also canned fish, tomatoes & peas; and I had made a fruit compote of watermelon & bananas & mamones.) The 2 younger children, Holly & 'The Mouse,' were at home, asleep. The other 4 behaved very well (after being (*too-vigorously*) cautioned by me against tampering with the fire I cooked by, the lamp in the windows, & clock on the sill.) Then 'Ricia took 3 home, & Chrissie & I "washed-up" & got ready for a canasta game. My beautiful little back-yard 'patio' has been a source of *deep* satisfaction to me!

It was a wonderful day—even though we had a quarrel that was patched-up later, which brought us all much closer together through the love engendered by our "seeking together" for reconciliation. —The fault was mine: it is (alas) true that I have not yet learned to resist The Tempter when he prompts me with appeals for meddling into other people's private lives, via 'psychology' & my silly over-emphasis on wanting 'justice'! The love of Jim & Sylvia, when we "cleared-up" the matter on Wednesday, before the New Year's Eve "Watch Night" meeting, for *me,* the erring daughter of the world I must *totally* PUT BEHIND MY MEMORY (*under* the "Cloud of Forgetting"! (Jim had given me "The Cloud of UnKnowing," for Xmas.)— that love would melt a granite block to repentance! [Note: The Youth presented a play on Sat. night, "All Men." It wasn't up to their usual standard.])

When we met at 10.00 p.m. for watching the New Year in, we were all washed, relaxed, & in unity with all the others there. We heard Georg's talk (translated by Nickie) & we sang. We lit candles for certain 'concerns.' (Most of the others' 'concerns' were far more objective than I have yet become in my thinking.) —I lit mine *"For Love"*—& by that, I meant to LEARN LOVE; to *live at peace!* After we were sitting in a beautiful, God-seeking SILENCE, suddenly someone in the austeiler's room struck the 12 strokes of midnight with a beautiful rich, ringing tone (a spoon-&-metal-bowl, for a gong!). And then we got up, sang once more, & all shook hands sincerely & lovingly with each other. Xmas cake & wine were served.

Celia D'Headt, Alberto & Constancia's oldest, beautiful (& courteous!) daughter was admitted to the novitiate.

New Year's Day was a second family-day which I spent chiefly in (pleasant) solitude. I was reading William Faulkner's *"Light in August,"* its main theme being very very revealing to me about myself in relation to JAM—the psychological parallels of the characters, & mine & JAM's certainly 'give me to think,' & teach me—TOO LATE—to "see myself as others saw me, during those 13 wastrel years ('35 to '48)! Thank God for His forgiveness of it all; & for his ineffable grace in bringing me (in spite of my erring & my capitulation to the Tempter—again & habitually, due to his insidious promptings of 'psychology' & my demands for non-existent, impossible *human* "Justice"!)—nonetheless, bringing me to Primavera, to find TRUE LOVE and to *learn* THE WAYS OF PEACE.

"Peace on earth: GOD'S WILL FOR MEN."
This is to be my theme for the year 1959.

~

When Constancia goes down to Asunción today, *Fran & Pearl* are coming back, *with Evelyn.* I am so happy that I shall see them again! I hope their coming will coincide with steps forward "into the Life" for me; for I truly LOVE Primavera now; am no longer lonely for my (dear) family; am quite ready & prepared—even looking forward, joyously—to ending my life here, ultimately.

Thank God, Thank Him! Danke! Gracias! In excelsis Gloria deo! Et in Terra, Pax!

It is appropriate that, just as 1958 ends, this book is filled—& gives a (shameful) record of my life in Primavera (July 2, 1957–January 2, 1959).

Much has happened here that, due to self-centeredness, I have not recorded.

As I told Jim & Sylvia, I came to Primavera to *CHANGE Lois*, with God's grace to help me. Question: how far have I succeeded in doing so? Not so, alas! God forgive me my sins.

Prayer: God bring my children & theirs to Brotherly community in Christ our Lord! *Amen*

> "Consider both the kindness and the severity of God."

[Written sometime in 1959]

Now, I am fifty-six years old.

Thank you, God, for a wonderful life! If I should die in the next hour, I could not reproach my Creator for withholding from me anything inherent in His gift of life! *I've had everything:* robust health, a sunny, abundant childhood; two intelligent, compassionate parents; two loving sisters; many loyal friends with whom I have enjoyed living for long years; the delight and disillusionment of many kinds of love; marriage; two sons and a daughter—God's *very most precious gifts!*—and a broad life-experience of exhilarating joy, sorrows a-plenty, hardships galore, and such profoundly illuminating experiences in self-revelation and humiliation that, at my age, I should be far wiser than I am. It has been a good life, a *full* life!

I ask you, God, to hear my prayer for a quick death, when death comes. Grant that I do not become a burden to my children, causing protracted worry and work. Send your Angel to call for and take me away express, so that my departure may be speedy and complete! I beseech you to hear me, O good Lord!

Thank you for everything! Sophisticates and intellectuals pooh-pooh a personal God who listens to the prayers of individual human beings, and "saves their souls." But you, God, my dear, all-wise Creator, have attended my prayers and answered them in compassionate wisdom. I know you from my own experience in this life you gave me. What greater assurance have I than that you have given me "every good and perfect gift" in life for which I asked? and have disciplined me as a wise, kind father, even while your omniscience and omnipotence have been engaged in the conduct of the great affairs of all worlds, simultaneously?

I was born Sept 18, 1903, in Cambridge, Massachusetts, the second daughter of my parents. "Dr. Mac" delivered me into the world in my mother's bedroom, with great difficulty to himself, my mother, and me. It was a large, square room, with a low brass bedstead—(so low that "Dr. Mac" complained of necessitous, back-breaking exertion); mahogany furniture; yellow-and-gold wallpaper. My bassinet stood beside my mother's bed. Later it was replaced by a large crib painted white, with brass knobs at the four corners—to be dented with infant tooth-cutting, through the years. My life was completely secure as long as I occupied that bed. I was *safe*, with my mother!

I can't be sure which was my very first conscious memory—perhaps the puzzling yellow-and-gold designs on the wallpaper. I can see them still—like little girls' bonnets blown about in an April breeze. Or was my first memory the azure blue of Mama's gentle eyes? or the comfort of Watsie's white-starched bosom, when she lifted me from my crib to wash and dress me, and comb out the tangles of my hair—without provoking a single outcry of pain. (No one else could comb me painlessly.) As soon as I learned to walk along the road beside my father, holding his strong hand, I began to regard Daddy as my stronghold.

> My old blue Journal—record of
> Transition from the world to Christ's
> Way—is now "full-up" (with motley
> thoughts & trivia)

[January 17, 1959]

I woke very early this morning, finding in the grey light of dawn that rain had cooled the parched, hot earth. We have had a long stretch of very dry weather—on the whole, very good for the rice-growing. But rain was needed now, to fill the irrigation ditches—and to cool off humanity! God is so good to those who believe; & when he promises to grant what is asked of Him in Jesus' name, for Jesus' sake, He fulfills his promises! (My life here is *proof* of it!)

In my nightgown & housecoat & slippers, I wandered down to the lovely school-wood, before full daylight. I found the new, high, strong swings, lately erected there, & swung myself in the cool Southern breeze, wafted across Antarctica's faraway frozen wastes, to bring us relief. I *cannot describe* the *joy and inspiration I feel!* Then, when I came back home, I found weeds in the backyard that Jim Bernard had so kindly hoed-out for me. (*Symbolic* of the *weeds* of *pride, anger, faultfinding in my fool's soul!*) So I pulled them up, clearing them quite out of the way of my little glade of a clothesyard! (I had never pulled weeds in gardens before!) and found that the vines I had planted last week are taking hold well at the base of the mouldy old trellis (Jacob G. didn't have time to rebuild it before he & Juliana moved, to vacate this dear little hut for *me!*) and three of the strange dried black beans in pods on the vine on another trellis, which I planted experimentally, have sprouted! So also, please God, may the seeds of thy Holy Spirit sprout in the *soil* of my soul, giving me ever more strength from Thee to learn the ways of Peace and practice them!

When full morning came, it was cool, clear & golden. And I thank God from the depths of my heart for the privilege of living here in Primavera and associating myself with these dear people who are dedicated to a life of Witness to Christ's laws of Love. Amen!

Jan 25, '59

I have made my peace with Lee Kleiss & Maria Ecroyd. Next Sunday, I shall ask to return to Gemeindestunde, if there is an occasion at the Household meeting. I hope there will be!

Sat eve. (last night), Lee came over for supper, & we ate & talked. Then Therese came, too (to bring me a prized gift of MATCHES—for this has been a *matchless hof* for 10 days! and I have had to keep a wood-consuming blaze going in my backyard fireplace, all week, to avoid pestering Brothers for 'a light'). They two went off to an interhof Brudershaft at Isla—lasting until 11.00 pm. (I haven't yet learned the subject of the conclave—something Francis referred to as "letters from No. America.") As no decision was reached by 11.00, the meeting resumes today (Sun.), instead of Household meeting. I am scheduled for "table-service" for noonday meal today. Otherwise I have a long, free morning, & can write some letters. The weather continues to be *lovely,* clear & bright, & not unbearably hot, even at midday, because of a nice breeze. My little house, *which I LOVE,* & its "annex," the backyard *laba* (*patio*—what have you?) is in order. Amaryllis Cat had a good breakfast, & is nursing her brood of 5—dear little kittens, all healthy & normal. (I shall grieve at our *inevitable* parting!) [I can't be SURE I want to lose Amaryllis herself, even though she is *so prolific!]* I am reading Conrad's *"Nostromo"* for the first time. For anyone visiting in So America it is a "must," I should say, if he is to understand the turbulent politics anywhere on the great continent.

Jan 26

My dear Baby, Peter, is only 29 today! What a tremendous (worldly) experience he has packed into a short life! And how the child has always *perceived every item* of what goes on around him, and has still withstood the impact of so many impressions! He *has accomplished a great deal,* at *a very tender age!* And now he is to be a father, in July! That may *change everything in life* for him! *I am so glad.* From his last letter which refers pointedly to psycho-analysis, I gather that either (or both) he & Janis have been undergoing a course in it, with the determination for parenthood as the outcome (?). Peter's letters to me are always cynical & never fail to grieve me—(which is exactly what I have deserved in payment for the way I always wrote to *my* mother! (*Anything,* to try to impress her with my 'importance' & virtues!)) Peter is also quite "hard boiled" about the significance of his work-for-a-living: the manufacture of plastic & light aluminum parts for war—planes & rockets. He says (of the *End,* to which all this armament race is hastening) "we hope (it) comes quickly!" My *first* reaction to his letter was the *reflex:* "What a smart aleck he still is"—but rereading his 3 pages today, I see they contain a lot of love, a lot of serious thinking, and an appeal for sympathy. I do *love* my Baby! But I have never yet been able to convince him of it!

Jan 27

My "month of testing" (self-assumed) of the newly-learned "Ways of Peace," fortified by strength from God, to supplement my feeble will-to-do-His-will, is nearly at an end, now. In another day or two, I shall ask to go back to the Gemeindestunde Circle. Pray to God, it will be granted! Amen.

Feb. 1-8, 1959

19 months ago today I arrived at Loma! Today, I am *back in Asunción, preparing* to *return to my homeland!* I have been healed, in Primavera, of the wounds of the world. Now, I have been bidden: "Set yourself a task; & DO it."

My days here at Bruderhof House, where Love & Faith achieve the miracle of peaceful, loving, useful selfless group-life in the midst of a city of turmoil, & unrest, greed, poverty, militarism, fear, & terrible human oppression—have opened my eyes to God's will. During this week I have (while living in a daze of self-condemning indecision) at last come upon the key to my plan for a task: "I am going back to Cambridge, to the neighborhood of the house where I was born, & there do what I can to "Help People" (as Georg bids me)—a sort of Bruderhof House on "the Wedge"—the old 'Locust Lot,' site of the First Baptist Manse, founded by my great-grandfather, Bela Jacobs, in 1803 (circa). I am going to invest the last years of my life in helping people there! And for my "text" I am taking Paul's epistle to *Titus*, which is to be my guide.

May God grant me strength & clearsightedness. I have, at best, only 15 years ahead—unless, before that time, the End of the world happens, & the Kingdom comes—for which all Christians pray!

Dateline January 31–Feb. 23

During which time I made safe, swift, comfortable passage, first by lumber-lorry from Loma to Rosario; thence, by steamer, to Bruderhof House, Asunción; thence by two ships from Asunción— to Corientes;—to Buenos Aires. Stopping at the San Antonio Hotel (avenida del Paraguay) overnight, where—by sheer coincidence, I met Dorothea Greeting, en route to Stuttgart, Germany! (And was able to help her by introducing her to Mrs Holland, who offered her *unstinting* hospitality, till her ship (delayed by 4 days) was to sail!) I then went next day by bus to the Buenos Aires Airport, & took off (Fri. the 13th) in a storm, for Miami Florida. I was overwhelmed with awe at the economical rates, efficiency, courtesy, service, & comfort of the whole Airline procedure! We flew from BA to Lima; & there were "guests of the company" for dinner at an expensive & beautiful upstairs airport restaurant (I was *too tired* to eat anything on the extensive menu but fruit cup & ice cream!). We sat at midnight, for 2 hours, on an airport roof garden, talking & waiting for the plane to be gassed, cleaned, & serviced. Then off to Guayaquil, Ecuador—to a little *shack* of an airport-building, where officials couldn't *even read!,* stopping for 30 minutes. Thence to Tegucigalpa, Honduras (seeing, en route, live volcanic eruptions of fire, by night; of rosy pink vapor, after dawn); &, on the *last* lap, to Miami, crossing the Island of Cuba. I called Uncle Allen from Miami bus depot; & was (as usual) "turned down cold" so that I had to go to a hotel. I took the (cheap) Airport bus to Miami Bus depot, checking-in to a hotel round the corner from Greyhound. It was the cheapest available (so I was told)—a nice room with private bath, telephone, radio & (metered) TV!— for $7 for *one night!* (Resort-"Season" price, of course.) I took a welcome bath; had a sleep; phoned the McNultys—who only recently moved back into the Miami City phone-district! (lucky for me). We arranged a picnic for Sunday noon, at Miami Beach. John ("Knee") & 2 children of theirs called for me in his yellow-painted jeep; drove me to the beach & we ate & swam (talked of old times at Felton Hall, etc.) & stayed till time to take the Boston-Express bus from Greyhound. *That was a remarkable trip!* For $37 (*tax*free, because ticket was purchased in Asunción!), over super-highways, making stops only at Jacksonville, Raleigh, Richmond, Washington, New York & Boston, I arrived in only 45 hours, not *too* tired, & not sleep*less,* at Boston's bus terminal. Sandra, Davy, & Ed met me, & drove me HOME to Peabody. —The whole thing—the removal from the uneventful peace of the Life at Loma!—the hot, jolting lorry-trip to Rosario, the life at Bruderhof House, the River-trip, the B.A. episodes, the plane trip, the Miami interlude—so MUCH has happened, over so many thousands of miles, by road, river, air, bus & road again, in such a short time!

It is COLD here! And I have caught a cold, & feel very stupid & lifeless & "congested"—but *not apprehensive,* for I trust the Lord to give me strength for whatever now comes to me.

I do not deserve at all to be readmitted to Bruderhof life; but I pray from the depths of my heart for it, with every fiber of my being! The people "of the world" are all jittery, "frustrated," & directionless. Ed & Sandra have THROWN themselves into (Episc)

Church work, & I do not know whether in it they find anything *truly* nourishing for their spirits (?). (For they are living on a salary earned by working for the *War* that we are expecting in the whole world.) They are *loving* people; their children are loved, nurtured, & brought up *well* (by 'worldly' standards). But like John McNulty's children, my own little Stevie, Susie & Davy are jittery, nervous, directionless little people, "worldlings."

Tonight (Mon. Feb 23) we are due to "dine" at Jonathan's, at Gloucester. —The sky is grey, lowering, threatening snow. —*What contrasts!* since I (regretfully) left Loma, 24 days ago!

May 25, 1959

I was in real doubt about "a task" Georg challenged me to do. At first, full of the objectivity and social consciousness learned at Primavera, I felt I really could & ought to *try* to organize a "Helpers"-project for the combined social groups at Central Sq Baptist Church ("The First Baptist," founded by my own great-grandfather, Bela Jacobs!), the parish where I was brought up—St. Peter's Episcopal; and other Protestant churches in that area. I put off for some time going to Cambridge to see about it. —I was sick, at first. Then, in sorry resignation to economic & social pressure [which I, *alone,* cannot combat!] I took a *very hard* (temporary) job, for pay, as cook at Salem's Home for Aged Women. I worked hard—futile-ly trying to do a job too big for my lack of experience—cooking 3 meals a day for 45 people, 6 days a week. The hours were 'brutal'—(from 5.00 am to 2. pm.—a 'break' till 4.30—from 2^{00}–7.00 pm!) Worse than that, the place had the usual Institution "house politics," against which the best will in the world was useless! So I gave notice before the first month was up, & quit at exactly the end of one month. After that during a 3-week interval of joblessness & being "stuck" down at Peabody, because of a bus-strike, I had a chance to take my youngest grandchild walking a lot, in beautiful early Spring weather, only to find that "our country" all charted-out by "Nana" & her "infantry" a few years past ('53 et seq.) has been so changed & spoiled by "progress" that little Davy couldn't enjoy it as much as Stevie & Susie did in their respective toddling days! However, I really got acquainted with Davy. The 'Blair Village Kids' of 1953 are now so grown-up and 'sophisticated,' I could hardly believe it! But none of them, even those now in High School, had forgotten the "good old times" we had together, when (I) Nana took them walking. [In fact, the very day I got home from Paraguay, several of them came to Sandra's door to ask: "Is Nana really home?" And that, to me, was *real* welcome!] Blair Village has changed! There are many newcomers there, with plenty of small children. But lots of the Village's "first settlers"—chiefly the Driscolls, Doucettes, Hockridges, McDonalds, Macmillans, Nelsons, Newmans (et al) have gone. And now Sandra & Ed—having sold #25 to some nice young people (*glad* to leave a Lynn apartment for *a house with a yard, near the woods!*) and having bought a new house of their own in Lynnfield, where a better "atmosphere," finer "class" of people, *better schools*— the *prime consideration* they had!—and a very active Episcopal parish offer *them* new horizons, at #42 Pillings Pond Rd. They are fortunate to be welcomed into Lynnfield by some well-established cousins of Ed's, who live there, and "know all the angles." Their house, though not much roomier, is far better-built, more attractive, & in better condition, on a very nice secluded street, with a grove of trees in its yard, front & back. (They have great plans for improving the grounds, & enlarging the building with a "wing" already a-planning!)

NOTE BENE: Peter is to be a father, in July; & now Sandra has discovered herself to be "expectant," for December! (By next Xmas, *deo volente,* I shall thus have *7* grandchildren!)

—At last, I managed to get up to Cambridge, to see about the (dubious) possibility of organizing "Helpers."—

I had an invitation to lunch with Myra Mitchell in Cambridge, at noon-time. Ed drove me to Lynn depot on his (early) way to work one morning, & after I had gone to see if I could get a job at Bennett St.'s Medical Center (formerly Boston Dispensary) & was kept waiting & coolly dismissed (probably as 'too old' or as a 'freak'—for wanting to *help mankind,* as I rashly stated in the brief interview) & had also registered at an agency (where I was similarly disposed-of) I first went to Central Square. The place is hardly recognizable as the same Square of my childhood! But the First Baptist Church is still there! And, also, Farwell Chambers, still kept-up spic & span in its run-down surroundings, on "The Wedge" (Locust Lot). #318 Franklin, where I was born, is well-preserved, too. But

Margaret Lyons' house, the Leeds's, the Castellos', the Dillinghams', the Norris's, all look pretty dilapidated. The old "block" on Western Ave, & the *Gingras'* house on Pleasant St., however, are newly-painted. Where, in my babyhood, a haymarket-loft was kept [while the Fire engines were still horse-drawn, & our St. Bernard dog "Tiny" (playfully named for his gigantic size) used to hang-out, & then run to all the fires under the very bellies of the great white horses!], which was afterward the much-advertised Olympia Theatre, whose stock-company-plays—"Alabama," etc, *soon failed,* & the new "movies" began to be shown—(Pearl White & Theda Bara, Mary Pickford, Margarite Clark) in competition with the other 5¢ [imagine that!] shows at the YMCA's Durrell Hall—now, Thespis & her dying fires have given way to a chrome-&-glass Calso gas-station! —The little triangular "park" which our family donated to the city—the point of the "wedge" of Locust Lot—is now nicely planted & kept up by the Park Dept.

Well, first I went to call on the present pastor of my great-grand-father's church. He listened without taking fire at all to my ideas about *Helpers. No comment! No welcome!* (despite the sign over the entrance of the Church on the square!) —Then I went over to see if Esther Miles was home. Her house is *very* shabby & neglected. (I learned later she has been having a 'breakdown' there, since her mother's death, & Prudy Frost, Ruth's girl, & her young husband have been living there, in loyal support. Nobody was home. Ruth told me, afterwards, they were all at *Cardie Stubbs's mother's funeral!*)

Revisiting the "old haunts" was a deep emotional experience for me, recalling the past, musing on the future, & *despairing* of the *present!* I called at St. Peter's Parish office. The rector was on a week's vacation … Then I went to Miss Mitchell's, & renewed my happy association with that dear, dear lady! (now 75, & *wobbly*-er than ever!). Such a clear brain, such an immense, loving heart! and such a treasury of memory in her long life as a TRUE social worker. (Reminds me of Marjorie Parker-Gray & her reminiscences of London's East End settlement-work!) I never *did* hear from either minister about my projected "task" for social improvement in the old neighborhood. Yesterday I attended 11.00 am Morning Prayer, & met the rector, who is not very attractive—but I think, from the look in his eyes, he is REAL and COMPASSIONATE! —Some day, I shall go to have a real talk with him. —But the project of HELPERS isn't likely to be my "task."

—That was pointed out to me by Ruth Frost, when she drove down to Peabody one evening (I had gone to bed, after waiting at the house for her since the early afternoon. She came up & sat on my bed). I told her about "the task" I was bidden to do. She—in her gift of clear-sightedness—showed me that organizational leadership of any kind was only the "show-off's" gesture of a "DO-Gooder." I should take a *HUMBLE* job!

So, now, I find myself complying! I am *hired* & being *trained as a baby-nurse* to 18 mos old Rob Roy Evans, child of a "career" mother, & a young academic father. I am living in the apt on Beacon St (facing the Charles Basin & Cambridge shore), which the parents have been living-in this winter, but have vacated as the Season at Wellesley's "Theatre-on-the-Green" now approaches. Alison Ridley Evans is its producer (& its corporation-president). Mrs. Ridley, her mother, is training me to take over full charge of the little charmer. She has an exquisitely painstaking routine worked-out for the little boy, adapted to life in her City apartment (on the next block) also on Beacon St. I am doing my best to learn from her, admiring her devotion to a task she (at 62) is too old to have undertaken, & completely "sold" on the *reasons* for her regimen. She has been wonderfully gracious to me, & very patient with my blunders! [She is the (grass-) widow of Roy Ridley, Master of Balliol College at Oxford University. As his wife, she was 'official hostess' for Oxford, entertaining V. I. P.'s of all kinds, including Princes & Prime Ministers from all over the world, & guiding star to many a Rhodes Scholar!]

When I came up for interview for this job at Mrs. Ridley's, I came again with Ed (a week later) on an early morning train, & again registered at an employment agency, etc. again job-hunted (applying for ads, including one I couldn't fulfill at the new restaurant at Hotel Ambassador, on Cambridge St., Cambridge). Walked over to Miss Mitch's, & had another nice lunch with her; then managed (in a *cold rain storm!*) to get up to Arlington Hts to pay a visit to Buba Peaslee, dear old soul, who was delighted to see me!—*before* the interview with the Ridleys.

Insert. The previous week, when I lunched with Miss Mitchell, we drove to Mt. Auburn, & saw the grave of my poor little Mama, with Daddy, under the new marker which Laura arranged for their headstone. Then we drove out to Lexington through blossoming Spring weather & golden sunshine, & saw Helen Moakley Packard, Ken, Sally, Sally's boy, & Helen's lovely daughter, Anne. It was a wonderful visit! Miss Mitchell drives slowly, but knows every street & route for avoiding traffic. Very kindly, she drove me round via Somerville's Beacon St to the rear of Helen Wanchope's parked car on Kirkland, where Helen sat waiting for me. Helen & I (who haven't seen each other for four years, I guess) drove down to Peabody. We stopped for dinner at a new & wonderful restaurant on County St. which has been built very lately on the site of "Grapevine Path" & the "2nd Catwalk" (part of the "country" we mapped-out for 'Nana's infantry')!—*one* of the "progress"-items that spoiled "our" country! Helen has an apt on Marlboro St just 4 blocks from mine here! So, with her, with Eugenia, Myra Mitchell, Ruth Frost, Cardie Stubbs (with whom I've as yet only *talked by phone*) & Rosemary Cutter AND MY DEAR FAMILY—(Sandy's & Ed's) & the "Blair Village Kids," I am "back in the bosom" of my old acquaintances, by being here!

Mrs. Ridley's own 2 daughters, at Oxford, in *her* "old days" (of social glory) were brought-up by a Scottish "nanny." She hoped to find one for her grandchild. But her 'ad' in the GLOBE got no response so she hired me. [I, diligently searching the columns for a 'task,' applied because of her wording of the 'ad'—which showed love, intellect, & a "standard"—she hired me because she couldn't find anyone else. Miss Mitchell "gave her a reference" which satisfied her. I took the job, beginning May 8.

In another week, or so, I'll be moved, with Rob Roy, to Wellesley, to join the child's parents for the busy (social) season of "Group 20." (Mrs. Ridley will probably go up to Breadloaf in Vermont for a well deserved & *needed* rest, at her father's farm near the famous Breadloaf Inn, where Writers' Conferences are held, annually.) I shall be much ALONE, & fully responsible for the child, & extremely tied-down, I know! But I'm game for it. Because another infant is expected in September, whose care, too, I am to assume (from the first day at home from the hospital!). I have ruefully laid aside all hope of returning to a Bruderhof before *Nov. 1960*—a LONG, LONG (& laborious!) "stretch"!

I love little Rob Roy already: a really fine little chap! And his mother, I admire; & his grandmother, likewise! I know the situation of a "career"-mother, because I "was there" myself—under *far* more STRINGENT—even PITILESS! circumstances. I hope I can continue to erase SELF from my consideration in fulfillment of this 'task.'

~

I have had a lovely Sunday at Rockport with Rosemary, after which we drove over to Gloucester, to be received *most graciously* by Doris & Jonathan, Cathy & Vickie at Gloucester. —Then, the evening following, Jonathan & the two dear little girls had dinner with me here in "my" apt, & we had a VERY merry, merry time together. —Last Friday evening, the eve of Davy's 3rd birthday, Sandy, Ed, Stevie, Susie, & Davy came up to pay me homage. I had a birthday-cake for Davy & orange juice. (Shrimps & wine, for the adults.) We walked on the Esplanade just at sunset. Nice evening. The following pages will reveal my fidelity or failure to this "task."

How I *long for a worship-meeting with the Brotherhood!* Church-going doesn't supply the need at all!

June 9 A NEW JOB, begun (Sun) June 7! (Watsie's birthday)

After *extracting* an honorable promise *from me* that I would stay on with little Rob Roy & his brother (or sister), to be born in September, *the Ridley family broke their part of the bargain!*—"for financial reasons," they *said;* [but it's my opinion they never intended to keep me permanently; only *promised* to do so because they needed someone urgently, & preferred me to other applicants! I had STRESSED my desire for a long-term job]. However, while I *was* there, they "did right" by me, as the saying is. And, in the month I had the lovely River-view apartment on Beacon St. all to myself, I had the joy of re-uniting with *many* dear old friends: Myra Mitchell, Theodora Keith, Helen Wanchope, Carolyn Stubbs, Eugenia (S. H.) Cox, Bob Walsh—& the privilege of "entertaining" both Sandra & her whole family at Davy's 3 Birthday-eve party, & Jonathan & his 2 bright little girls for supper a few nights later. —Also, I met a charming young couple (from California & NY State respectively)

Joyce & Jim McCarthy, who live over on Newbury St, who came over for an evening, &, the following Sunday went down to Rockport with me (by train). We took a cab up to the top of Pigeon Hill, where we ate our picnic. Then we *walked* down to Rosemary's (via the Witch House, Lucy Robertson's, 78 Phillips Ave, the "boat landing," the seawall & St Mary's Pool (where we dabbled our feet). Rosemary talked with us a while, then drove us to the depot for a 3.30 train to Salem. There, Sandra & Joan Foster picked us up by car, & took us over to Blair Terrace for supper. (Larry Foster & Ed were re-painting the house.) We came back (Ed driving us to Salem depot) by train. Had a wonderful day! —So that job has meant not only PAID-UP *bills,* & the use of a nice roomy place to myself, but *real* "social life." Also, the Charles Embankment was lovely, by *day* (pushing Rob Roy's 'pram') & by evening (with Sandy & her family, & with Bob Walsh).

But NOW, I have at last taken the kind of job I've long considered taking—as *manager of* 8 Commonwealth's (run-down-at-heel former Guy Currier mansion) *rooming-house*—for *very little pay* ($30 wk) & *lots of work*—but "managerial" enough to use my (regrettable) 'aggressiveness' to advantage. And here, already, I have "entertained" *Theodora Keith & Eugenia* (in 2 days' time); have attended an opera at the Arts Festival on the Public Gardens (last eve, *with Joyce McCarthy:* "The Scarf" & "The Devil & David Webster"). The *beauty* of both setting & weather, & the orderly audience—HUGE!— were worth the experience; & *unforgettable!* But I was dog-tired; the seats were uncomfortable; & I almost fell asleep—so I left Joyce to finish it out alone, & came home & SLEPT! (I was *exhausted.*) Tonight, *Helen Wanchope* will be over (?) at 7.15 (or so—IF she comes) & later on this week, Jim & Joyce again (on Friday), Carolyn Stubbs tomorrow (Wednesday), & I'm to be "entertained" by Eugenia & Joe, either at their house (#13—right across the parked street!) or at some nearby restaurant. My boss, Mr. Raymond Bemis, is a *very* nice man. (He is having a rug cleaned, for my room; & has lent me his brand-new TV set with remote control & indoor antenna. He is buying me a (reconditioned) Singer sewing-machine, to mend the house linen (long neglected).

—Another humanly heart-warming 'contact' I've had is with Anabelle (Leavitt) Cutting (the former incumbent at this job), whom I knew as a *very* little girl in the summer(s) at Pigeon Cove. Her father & my father were co-founders of the Rockport Country Club! She's a *darling* person. Like me, she is "reduced in circumstances," but still—to quote Mrs. Ridley when she gave me a 'reference'— "a *lady* to her finger-tips!" She has scrubbed & grubbed here at the rooming-house trade for 4 years! —(There IS a certain amount of freedom entailed, along with backache, sweat, & tired-to-the-boneness!)

I have "established credit" at the United Nat'l Store, so as to avoid expensive "eating-out" by having a full supply of comestibles on hand (for self &/or guests)!

Today I went to get stockings (Ironwear brand) at Gilchrist's, and was "lured" (by posters) into the Orpheum to see "Green Mansions"—a *good* film, with marvelous cineramic photography—but sadly "Hollywoodized," both in close-up scene-sets, & in change of "love-angle." Nonetheless Audrey Hepburn was her usual intelligent, beautiful self—AN *ACTRESS!*—Later: Helen Wanchope came over, & had dinner with me—cubed steak, mashed potatoes, Lima beans, salad, fruit & cookies—following sherry & hors d'oeuvres. We spent the evening listening to TV. I was very tired, & so was she, so we willingly parted at 10.00 pm. —At midnight, a girl called up, wanting to rent a room 'for her mother.' Mrs. Cutting had warned me NEVER to rent a room after 6.00 pm. So I—aroused from heavy sleep!—turned her down. I'm sorry, in a way: the poor girl sounded very discouraged. (I feared the mother was ill—or drunk.) The house is full of (young & old) people "going their own way." A man downstairs, proud of his 'hi-fi' equipment, which he runs full blast (in the "bridal-suite" apt.) had a long, loud party last night—doorbell ringing all evening till very late.

Wed June 10

Woke (LATE, for *me!*) at 6:15, & took a good showerbath, made my bed, & tidied my room.

My waking thought: *This* isn't *life. Life* is at the Bruderhoefe! I am *never* relinquishing my *intent, desire, & prayerful Hope* of going back to the *beautiful, devout, poverty-joyous LIFE of Community!* God bless my hope; grant my prayer; recognize my desire; affirm the sincerity of my intention! *Amen!*

June 11—(Thurs.)

I "took it *easy*" today—completing my light chores about 11 a.m. I went out, at noon, for stamps. The nearest PO is the Back Bay (16) branch on Stuart St, where I got stamps, mailing to Hollis, N.H. a bundle of personal letters & *documents*, left here in a storage-closet by a Harvard man who was "in arrears" about 4 years ago (it cost 50¢, first class). Then, being near the Bristol, where Aunt Jessie Knowlton lived for years, I made a (second) visit there to the janitrix, Mrs. Chapman (or Chatham?), & learned from her that Aunt Jessie is in a "rest home" (or nursing-home?) out in Jamaica Plain. (I did this for my little Mama, who lies up in Mt. Auburn now!—for her oldest friend, child-playmate of *1871–et seq!)* Mrs. Chapman referred me to Mr. Shattuck, ass't rector (to Mr. Ferris) at Trinity Church. I went to call on him at his ("posh"!) new office, & he gave me Aunt J's address. [I sent Aunt J a note, after I got home.] He says the fierce, fighting *'false pride'* of Aunt J remains unbroken, though she is fragile & cannot be away from an R.N. —It remains to be seen whether she regards me kindly enough to send for me to see her. (She was at Mama's funeral, Aug 14, 1957) (when I was at Primavera.) I had "lunch out"—sandwich & soda, & bought some frozen pudding for supper. I spent a very quiet afternoon, interspersed with phone-messages & doorbells, & receipt-makings-out on rentals. At 5.40 Cardie Stubbs came over. We had supper here—creamed-chicken on toast, green peas, salad, & frozen pudding for dessert. We talked, & had a fine reunion (after *5 years,* I think!), & then went over to the festival at the Gardens to prowl round. We admired Gardner Cox's 2 "impressionist" portraits (one of Robert Frost). Gardner Cox was at CHLS when we were! I put Cardie into the subway, walked home, & was overtaken on my front steps by Eugenia, who invited me to sit on a bench on the mall (or *"Bois"?)* with her & Joe, where we chatted amiably. Tonight I must stay in & receive rentals for tomorrow's Bank deposit (by Mr. Sullivan, who manages #10, next door, also for Mr. Bemis).

Mrs. Ridley (whom I phoned yesterday) told me she was forwarding a letter from Oak Lake. It should arrive this morning. —From Hazel? Or Hardy? Or Bob Greenwood? *I await it eagerly! If* it is a summons to the Bruderhof—! just as I have started this job—!?

Hazel's letter (June 6) from Oak Lake gives me *real hope!* In closing, she said: "Again, I want to say how very much we all want to carry this difficult time with you, and hope that your faith will be greatly strengthened, *and your expectation great.* (!)"

Sundays at Emanuel Church (June 7 & 14)

Harold Sedgwick, who was a young curate from ETS when we transferred to Christ Church, Cambridge, is now Rector of Newbury St's Emanuel Church (where Guerdon Worcester's father used to be). I went there, just after I brought my baggage from 336 Beacon St. I was a little early for the 11 o'clock service, & waited for the Communion Service (in the Leslie Chapel), sitting in the big, empty church, LIVING *with God,* in the cool, still, shadowy beauty of "a temple made with hands." I felt very close to the Brothers & Sisters, at their worship-meetings all over the world. —After the service, Harold was very cordial—remembering me instantly! He still has an unfortunate way of "gargling mashed potatoes" (with a hint of *lisp*); but his sermon was *good.* —He is the *John*-type, "whom Jesus loved." I do hope he will come to call on me here, because I *have SO MUCH to tell him!* Mr. Shattuck (at Trinity) says Harold is 49 or 50 years old;—but *he still looks very much like a young boy, even now!*

[Sandy, Ed, Stevie, Susie, Davy, Joyce & Jim were all here Sunday. *I was horrid!]*

Sat pm, Eugenia & Joe took me out to cocktails & dinner (by cab, because it *poured!)* at the Statler! I could have enjoyed it even more, but for the *cost* (to Joe!).

Wed June 17

Yesterday, Ruth Miles Frost came in to see me. We had a (*very light*) lunch, & drove over to Cambridge to pick up a parcel (thereby missing the carpet-cleaning delivery, by *minutes!).* Ruth is certainly a "natural" (in her spirit & her personal circumstances) for "community." She is a dear, God-loving woman! I have written her today, to suggest that she visit one of the 3 US-Hoefe as a guest this summer.

I have also written Cousin Ruthie Brown Macgregor, to ask her to visit me here.

(I've not been feeling well since last Saturday pm. (Digestive-upset, plus a sniffle.) The weather has been cold, rainy & persistently stormy (from Fri–thru Wed am!)—& has dampened the Arts Festival on the Gardens-green; but after such a seasonal storm, we are bound to have the kind of weather that inspired the poet to say: "O, what is so rare as a day in June?" Then, if ever, come perfect days.)

I went to bed at 8.00 last night & got up at 5.00 this am, the girls on the 3rd floor taking phone-calls for me (obligingly).

A Yorkshire man & his ½ Egyptian wife are coming today to look at rooms #1 & #2, with serious intent for *permanent* occupancy. He is a member of the English-speaking Union up the street, & should be a good liaison-man for more British roomers here. I have a "Room" (to rent) sign in the door which has brought *too* many responses.

Ruth Frost will send Alice's daughter here, when she comes to attend BU next Fall. The repair-crew for the burnt rooms hasn't yet shown-up, & the "crew" of "handymen" (quartered rent-free in our basements) have disappeared! They were SO GOOD for 2 days, & did a LOT of work for this house. I hope they'll show-up again soon. I've had to check the furnace myself.

June 24

I have seen a lot of Joyce McCarthy lately. She has been so bored since she gave up her nursing, because of her pregnancy—& even *I* am 'company' for her! Today, I went over to her house on the way home from the grocery-store. (I've been laying-in supplies for *Susie's* coming to visit me over the week-end, while Sandy & Ed, helped by *Stevie*, move to Lynnfield. —To save money, they are renting a truck, & have 3 friends of Ed's to do the labor with him. *Davy* will be at Melrose with the 'Big' Bowditches.) I'm much cast-down about this job, which is *definitely* wholly *of the world*—permitting me no service to Christ except to *pray* for those for whom I work. Yet I am loathe to leave the privacy, & independence, & comparative freedom of it, & I am only "marking time"—(till I go back to Community)—*whatever* work I am doing while I wait! The pay is very low, but covers my few needs, because I was well-supplied with clothing & "accessories" before I came. I had then a little in the bank, & have a *bit* (*very* little) left of it. By good management, I hope to hold on here *till Fall*—(and the *possibility*, by then, of *a return to Community!—Amen! Amen!)*! I have a chance to do *some* therapeutic "dirty work" every day, which IS a *blessing!* (mopping, "vac"-ing, dusting, making beds) and I have my (dear) sewing-machine (supplied by my boss) on which I have sewed, and *already* saved (from wasteful discard) at least *18 sheets* and *10 pillowcases* for economy's sake! (Sewing, alone (in my room), gives me a chance for *reflection & useful busy-ness*.) —The gracious architectural lines of this panelled room *do help* too, to redeem this atmosphere around me from *total squalor!* Run-down, dirty, & out of repair as it is, this house is STILL a "mansion." The difficulties are the same *every* rooming-house manager in the Back Bay has *every* summer-season, when paying tenants have moved out, & a sign "Rooms," or "Apartments," hangs in every doorway. —It is the deadly "slack" season. And the impossibility of getting chore-boys to help with rubbish & garbage, & sidewalk-sweeping etc. is well-known to everybody. As for the current tenants—the people here (except one) have all been here a long time, & plan to stay, I believe. Their way of life is "their own business," & if they are blindly led to self-destruction and opportunistic compromise with the Prince of this World, there is nothing *I* can do to prevent or help them: for (How clearly events at Loma demonstrated!) *one human individual* alone can do nothing against the *Evil One!* I can pray for them, poor fuddled worldlings, & give them leeway to lead their mistaken lives as they wish! (I had a long talk with Joyce—a Presbyterian minister's thoughtful daughter!—about this yesterday. *She understands.* And I can't "confide" nor unburden myself to Sandra *by phone*—so Joyce is the only one to understand!) I have many good old friends around me here— first & oldest of all, dear "Hoomie" (Eugenia), right across the street! (as we lived across the street, as children!). She is warmly loving & pitifully eager to keep me near her—for when her (failing) gentle husband dies, she knows she will be even MORE starkly alone in life than she has *ever been!* Good, loyal Hoomie! —But she makes the error of erecting barriers between us by trying to dissuade me from my (*ever-strengthening!*) *Intention* to leave the world behind forever, when (at last!) I become a Member of the Brotherhood! Hoomie was reared a Roman Catholic by her mother (Bless dear, departed

Alma Houston!) and she can't be *expected* to comprehend The Life! (of Bruderhof Community). Only to Joyce can I really confide. [The Brotherhood has requested that I neither talk nor write about Life in Community (for public presentation). I comply with that. I *cannot* talk even *privately* (to *anyone, but Joyce & Sandra!*) because it were a profanation of Christ's teaching to "cast pearls before swine"!—& so it means I have to talk *directly to Christ only, in prayer.*] I have never needed nor loved Him more than I do now, nor—(in this isolation from the Brotherhood!)—*felt closer, nor surer of his Power of Loving Redemption for us all,* in this wicked, nervous modern world of 1959! I told Georg before I came home that I have never been AFRAID of The World. I am still *not* AFRAID of it, even here in this job—(as I was not AFRAID at sea, at work on newspaper-staffs, & nor in various other situations in my lifetime! (especially in the old, foolish 'Bohemian' days of my youth!)—because *my Faith is,* with His Spirit's strengthening guidance!—*stronger than the powers of Mammon all around me!* But I felt *apprehensive* all day yesterday, & very sorry for my "boss," Mr. Bemis, who seems to be feeling TRAPPED by his enterprise here. (There are sinister reasons behind this, I am sure.) He obviously is *trying* to "rationalize" his situation & is torn between good instincts & a favorable "genteel" background, & the needs for 'compromise' that bind him (financially) to it. —Again, I praise God, for the decision I made, in 1941, thereafter to OWN NOTHING! For it is the ties with money & possessions that lead us to alliance with Christ's enemy, Mammon! — *I* cannot "reform the world" nor in any way "influence" worldlings! I can only PRAY for them in love. And that is what my heart is doing here. Is this a "task" (as Georg conceived of a 'task' for me, when I left Loma)? —Those 20 months of peace at Primavera have STILLED and ENDED all 'conflicts' in my soul! I can never thank God (& the Brotherhood) enough for them. Even in the midst of all this, I am HAPPY—though I am aggrieved for the lost people I keep seeing here!

I've seen Carolyn Stubbs, Ruth Frost, Helen Wanchope, Eugenia, Myra Mitchell, Helen (Moakley) Packard, Rosemary (Cutter) Dole, & Jessie Knowlton—& others of my dear old friends, of late; & it has been really HEARTWARMING! But how deeply grateful & humble it makes me feel to know that *Christ* chose ME——(a sinner among them all, good, kind friends!)——to lead me to meet Will & Kathleen aboard the SS "Bow Santos" in the Spring of 1955, & to give me His Light to live by in happiness & contentment with whatever He chooses to supply me with in life, until I die! And, as I have always felt & known, *death* will be sweet, when it comes; because He will decree its time, place, & circumstance. And I will submit, & descend into the grave physically, while my spirit will (——as He promised) goes to wait in "the place of departed spirits" for the Call to Judgment. All the sins I have committed——so many & so vile! are already forgiven——because He lived & died to deliver us from sin. *"All who believe in me shall not perish, but have everlasting life!"* God, the Father, & God the Son, & God the Holy Spirit——one, or "trinitarian"——all KNOW that from the depths of my heart & spirit I BELIEVE!——ergo, I have *everlasting life* near His throne, in timeless eternity! And have no fear of death. I fear nothing of the world. *Nothing* can hurt me, touch me, nor change my Love & Faith. *"My cup runneth over!——Surely, goodness & mercy shall follow me all my days, and I shall dwell in the House of the Lord forever!"*

June 26-28 (Susie's week-end with me)

Susie left her home (where she has ALWAYS lived, throughout her 6 ½ years of life) in Peabody *for good* when she came to visit me;——for, when she returns, "home" will be in the *new* house at Lynnfield! I am keeping *her*, & Grammy is keeping Davy, while Stevie remains with his parents "to help" *them* move. They have hired a truck, & got 3 friends——Larry Foster, Warren Prescott, & Don Greim——to help Ed with the labor of moving! (Thus they will save a considerable amount of money on moving!) Susie brought a fancy coat-hangerfull of summer fluff——which rainy, cold weather makes *useless*——and *forgot* her *suitcase*, which she was entrusted to bring. So she is in a *plight* for wardrobe! But we have been having a good time. The first evening (Fri.) after they left her here——(Sandra was *very TIRED!*)——we managed a ride on the swan-boats, and then (at *her* request) "dinner *out*" (at Child's). She was overwhelmed by the *huge*, elaborate serving of the swordfish 'platter' she ordered. She ate a big baked potato & all the fish, & then a piece of apple pie (ample size). We took a walk around the Public Garden, saw the live swans (who hissed at us!), & then came home to bed. —Up "betimes" & a good breakfast of egg, toast & marmalade, Susie had milk, & I coffee. We made our beds, washed ourselves, & went out "to ride on a STREETCAR!" (New experience for Susie!) We went via subway to Cambridge & out to Mt. Auburn. I wanted to develop her "feeling of race," so told her all about the ancestors in the Jacobs lot, & about my Daddy & Mama there. We took a high climb up to the tower—but found it LOCKED! (because of rain, I suppose). We walked a long way round *via* the rhododendron pool, & bussed back to Harvard Sq., where, waiting for the Mass. Ave bus, we met Joe Fine (going out for a "take-out coffee"). It obviously touched him to see me with my (favorite) grandchild. We had to pick up my bag of clean wash at the (Mass-Ave-at-Marlboro-St) Launderette. Then we met the Schwartz family at the grocers. We saw the beginning of the US Marines' parade, resplendent in dress uniform, with the famous band, coming down Commonwealth Ave. We went over to pick up Joyce, who is bringing 8-yr-old Denise Tibbetts (her neighbor) down here to lunch. Mr. Tibbetts (a "mortician") drove us from Joyce's back here. Denise & Susie had a wonderful time together! We had green-peas & creamed chicken on toast, strawberries & ice cream. We washed the dishes, & went out to the Gardens to (again) ride on the swan-boats, feed the pigeons, see the rest of the big parade (going by on Charles St.), & then again walk around the pond. [It is amazing how *fine* the Gardens look, even on this last day of the Festival!] When we parted with Joyce & Denise, we crossed over to drop in on Eugenia, & met her & Joe just leaving the house. Susie & I came back here & rested. Susie SLEPT hard. I had to wake her up at 4.30. We went to the movies— Danny Kaye in "The 5 Pennies" at the Paramount, starting-out well in time for the 6.30 show, & stopping for ice cream sodas (& gumdrops to eat in the movies) at Schraffts on Boylston St. Susie really LOVED the movie, which was about a cornet-playing father (Danny Kaye) married to a (Brooklyn-born) show girl (Barbara bel Geddis) whose little girl (at 6) got polio—so that the father gave up his career to help the child. It took her 10 years of diligent rehabilitation—& exercise to *walk* again before her father returned to the world of jazz. (As it was "my era"—the Roarin' Twenties!—I found it very comprehensible!) Susie *wouldn't leave* till we came back to *"where we came in!"* Then we walked home, at dusk, across the Common.

For today (Sunday) I am planning to take her to Emanuel Church to hear Harold Sedgwick at 11—(spending a couple of quiet hours here first, to do my ironing, & distribute clean linen). In the early afternoon, we shall make a quick visit to Aunt Jessie Knowlton, & at 4.00, we expect her parents to come for her again. I'm sure she's *enjoyed* her weekend at her Gran's in the "big city." She is a *fine child!*

Later: we *didn't* go to church. As Susie had forgotten her suitcase, she had no decent shoes to wear at "fashionable" Emanuel! and, besides, it rained hard all morning. We did "chores" together, washing-down 2 flights of stairs (wet with the downpour through the skylight (broken in the fire, before I came here)), & distributing the linen to tenants, etc. Then we "wrote" & painted, & kept busy till lunch time. (We had a 'Frozen Dinner' of roast beef that wasn't very good.) In the afternoon, Susie had a rest, though she didn't sleep, before we set out to see Aunt Jessie. —In the week since I saw that poor little woman, who *un*willingly nurses the spark of life!—she has *failed* a lot! But she was truly delighted to see us, & loved Susie very much. Susie longed to take the River-excursion boat, & we walked way down there; but the weather prevented its running. So she had ice cream & pie (I had just ice cream) at the Riverside Cafeteria (where, I am told, habituées love the place! Just because *everybody* "gets into the act," & there is a feeling of 'belonging'! —[Poor, lost 'moderns' of '59!]) and walked home. We "painted" & played games, & Susie was LONGING "for Mummie" before they finally came, bringing my dear *Pancho*, who was glad to see me. They had parked just outside Hoomie's. When they drove away, I rang Hoomie's bell, but got no answer. I came home & spent a lonely evening (*willingly* enough!), going to bed early.

I love my Susie! I know she enjoyed herself; but she *did* long to get home! And I was 'worn out' with her exuberance!

Monday

I have been 'fixing-up' vacant rooms, *trying* to make them rentable & attractive. It is tough going! Today, I took myself out to a 90¢ lunch (at Child's) & then went shopping. I bought some of Hoomie's (recommended) Widmer sherry (for myself) & for the house, 2 lampshades, an attractive plastic table-cover, & a plant (for Rm 2, which Mr. Bemis is advertising in Tuesday's GLOBE). I made the room look MUCH better, with these little touches! But the windows need washing, & if Ted hasn't free time to help me, I can't do it (the frames stick). The first *sun* in 22 days! shone a while late in the afternoon! A whole 3 weeks of downpour! [The Vermont farmers say a *"new moon"* (June 6) *on Sat* means 21 days of rain!—& *so it did!*] The *human* side of my job is running fairly successfully. *Thank God!*

Tuesday

A clear, hot day is just beginning! I'll have *lots of work to do!* And must stick by the telephone—replies to our 'ad'—*if any!*

Yesterday afternoon, Eugenia & I had a "celebration" of 'the passing of "Little Eva"'—(the execrable lithograph over the mantle, which covered the panel where the wall-safe was). I replaced it with a very *good* ($1.⁰⁰) reproduction of a painting of Paris, "Un Rue Montmarte," on a travel-poster I bought at the Book Clearing House on Boylston St.

~

Yesterday, I had got big, empty-looking Rm 7 into shape for renting—with the added touches (from Woolworth's) of 3 new lampshades, a sofa-pillow, & a plastic table-cover (total $6.08) and all day, though I stopped work for good nap from 2:45 to 4.15, so that, after coffee I managed to keep alert, I was busy with the task of RENTING ROOMS (which Mr. Bemis says is my #1 task—(rather than cleaning-up rooms for messy tenants)). [There was a *LOUD explosion* from Rm 15—but Mr. Bemis had foreseen that, & I was prepared to 'deal with' it.] There is a very gentle, philosophical young Irish student who is coming on Friday to take Rm 10 (until Dick Finn vacates Rm 11). *Then* the *house will be FULL!* I have such a "take" to send (via Sullivan) to the Bank, I am astonished at it! —But, as Mr. Bemis says, it is not an *"average,"* & it's the *average* that must *stay high, every week*!

I am certainly NOT "right out there in front" (in Self-importance) on this job; but I do have a certain amount of authority (under Bemis) for keeping things going here & dealing with "all sorts & conditions of men" (and women). Bearing in mind principally the Brotherhood's teaching of not "judging"—nor "analyzing," I may have now under this roof (—which leaks when it rains!)—some really "undesirable" tenants, from many viewpoints. But it's not for me to "refuse a customer" (Bemis's teaching)—& I know I have a chance to work for God here—though I didn't foresee it!—in a number of ways. Helen Wanchope was very pleasant about coming to sit & watch TV while I went on with "first things first" (room-rental!) until 11.00 pm! [It was lucky I had my nap & my coffee in the afternoon!] Helen is going to leave Boston soon, & I shall miss my good old friend "God's Little Messenger" (as we called her, 1924—*25 years ago*!)!

July 25, 1959—36 years ago, a Lexington Summer idyll!

I'm getting a wholly-new perspective about this job. To hold it successfully, according to worldly practices, I must entirely set aside ANY notion of "working for God"—because every detail practiced (or practicable!) is a compromise with Mammon! This, I have "learned the hard way" in 7 weeks' tenure. I will have to confine my impulses of outgoing love to my visits to Jessie Knowlton—or others *outside* of "business." 'Good intentions' here have all led to trouble. —Yesterday, after hours of real stress, I took a solitary River-boat ride up the Charles, to face the facts of my failures, honestly & alone, away from 'location.' —I came to the conclusion I must cease to be "friendly" or "interested" in ANY tenant; & must *expect*, if I fail to do so, to be called (as Mr. Bemis says I *have* been called) 'nosy'. —I have been accused of other things unjustly; & I have been vilified in vulgar, obscene language. And I am now thoroughly 'cold' to my tenants. —No scope for the warmhearted, loving 'Landlady' of the poem I wrote (*before* I got 'hooked' for $4.^{00} loaned in compassion to a former tenant the police came looking for, for a 'con'-game!). Also, the "madcap" girls, whom I have tried to befriend & accord 'motherly' sympathy, are no *mere 'madcaps'*—! They are *definitely worse than 'naughty.'* —While my heart goes out to them for their feckless foolishness, still I *must* be 'hard'; & I must—to hold my job here—compromise with Mammon myself;—else, I would *'shake the dust'* of this house *from my feet! For Christ's 'peace' is surely not in it! (Against* this, I am encouraged by (a) Sandra (b) Eugenia, & (c) my *cowardice.) [I* do LONG to *stay put* somewhere!—till I go back to a Bruderhof—IF I ever do!] (I am daily discouraged about it!)

Tues., July 28 The Fire

Events of this day, after my cleaning-chores & laundry-count were done: Sandi came down to my room in a white dress, saying she was going shopping & offering to bring back a loaf of bread for me. She didn't return very soon; so I went out to SS Pierce's—bought $5.86 of canned goods, frozen food & bread. After I got back she came in, practically WITH a strange man—not very prepossessing: in fact, rather like a 'bum' from the Common! who sat downstairs in the hall, while she was dressing to go out with him. She made herself *very* beautiful, in a freshly-pressed white dress—NOT the one worn earlier—and gave me back my bread-money. She said she was going out. It was her day-off from work. Usually she *irons* on her day-off. Fran Hatch had told me she has twice left her *iron heating ALL DAY!* (Question: should I have gone up to *check* on that when she left the house? —It was, I believe, about 4.30. Fran her room-mate should return from work an hour later.) Elliot Sulpiva hadn't been in to answer calls from his partners, Clark & Schultz & his mother & a girl since early morning. About 6.00 he returned, with Schultz. They were *exceptionally QUIET* as they moved out (I believe 2 or more) hi-fi sets, from Elliot's apartment! I didn't hear anything more of or for Elliot that day. I had an early supper alone. At 8.00 I met Eugenia & Joe on the bench on the Mall, where we sat talking. [Note: there was a great, fat (mulatto?) woman who sat around the Mall in various shady corners, all that afternoon & early evening. Was it *she* who, on July 29 (Wed) in a 4.30 postmarked envelope, sent me 2 cards reading 'Miss Godel: astrological palmist, 230 Boylston St.'?] Eugenia & Joe & I walked over to Charles St for a soda at Brigham's. Later, we sat until 10.15 by the 'Her-Trav' clock, on a bench in the gardens, before we returned home. I let myself into a quiet house—no warnings of trouble to come. But I had a hard time getting to sleep!

At 12.05 I was awakened by a cry "Fire! Fire!" I roused quickly, put on housecoat & slippers, put Mr. Bemis's rent-money ($125.⁰⁰) into my bag, got my flashlight. As I started out the door, I heard the shout repeated, in our house, & in Mr. Sullivan's (#10). [He rapped at my emergency exit-door by the head of my bed.] My windows were open, on the rear alley. When I opened my regularly used door, a thick draft of black smoke was sucked in. I hastily shut the windows, & tried again to get out into the hall (of #8). Just then ALL lights went out, & a great crash of glass from the (newly-repaired) skylight over the elevator dropped outside my door. By flashlight-beam, I returned to the emergency exit, & got out quite safely—in nightwear—through #10. The fire department was just about arriving. Mr. Sullivan was on the phone, trying to contact Mr. Bemis. Throngs of people were already collected. Every window of #8 was lit up—by the inside blaze! I tried to find my tenants. Dorothy Perrin (Vickers) was there, in her housecoat asking others (from #12 & #14) for use of their telephone. Firemen, policemen, reporters, & Red Cross people, discovering I was "in charge" of #8, ganged up on me. The sequences are now (a week later) somewhat confused—but I saw Kalenah, Bennett, Chambers, Laurence, Koch, Lynch, in the crowd. Maybe others. I couldn't see Elliott Sulkis, whose apt was next to the music room, where the blaze was started (according to firemen). There were screams of *Help! Help!* from above, & we saw Helene Kruger hanging out of her 4ᵗʰ floor windows, seemingly prepared to JUMP! Also, Sandi Shavin helplessly wailing on the 3ʳᵈ floor window ledge. Firemen ran up great long extension-ladders, to carry them down. [Newsmen took photos of these rescues, for morning & evening editions Wednesday.] I inquired everywhere for Dawn Vye & Elliot. Mrs. Sanderson was not in the house, I knew. Walter Vickers came for Dorothy—but I did not see them. I knew Janey & Fran had gone to Revere Beach, with "Taffy" (Cyril Lloyd) from HMS "Victorious." —Christopher O

Hanley wasn't in—& I never heard from him. Dick Finn was up at Ft. Devens (having dropped in earlier for clothing, with Ruth Angell). I supplied lists of names of all tenants, & their home- or work-addresses to Police, Fire Chief, Red Cross, & (inadvertently) to reporters. Then I went over to #13 to ask 'Hoomie' to take me in. Joe was alone (with his teeth out). He said Eugenia was down in the crowd, looking for me. I found her there. It was 4.30 am before the crowd began to thin-out & the blaze was "under control." Eugenia's neighbors provided a Roll-a-Way for me, in Eugenia's apartment. Kenneth Koch was sheltered in the flat just above, by a co-worker at the "First" (Bank). I went to sleep not knowing—nor greatly caring—whether any of my clothing or possessions would be left.

At 9.00 a.m., I crossed the street (still in a housecoat!) & found Mr. Bemis at Mr. Sullivan's. Firemen permitted me inside. My clothes in the hall-closet were intact! Also the things in my room. I packed in great haste (& disorder), & my (friendly, helpful) co-worker Ted (Dennis) Davenport got them into a cab for me. It cost $1 to get across the street to Hoomie's (round the one-way traffic circuits). Then I went over & turned in the rent-money. Mr. Bemis was "floored," but *very dapper in appearance!* He & Mrs. Bemis sat side by side, saying very little. He appeared unconcerned about the tenants' losses. I found Rachel Sanderson, & presented her to him. (I'm glad he gave her a refund on her month-in-advance rent.) *Poor woman!* How she had worked to move in there, for 2 weeks—only to be burnt out of the room she liked SO WELL! But all her things & her room were *quite* undamaged! *I don't know where she will go!* I was busy all morning. Joyce McCarthy walked all the way down, & inquiring, finally met Mr. Koch, who led her to Hoomey's. Joe was feeling INVADED—so Joyce & I went out to lunch together. After that, while Hoomey& Joe ate lunch, I fell asleep for 2 hours. Eugenia, Joe & I went out to supper together at Schraffts, sat a while in the Gardens, & then went over to the Mall, to watch for Sandra & Ed who—faithful, loyal, loving, as ever!—came in by car for me, with the kids, & took me out to Lynnfield.

I *SLEPT*. For a whole week I rested there, walked with the children, got my clothing washed & pressed, & scanned the *Help Wanted* columns.

On Saturday I found an 'ad' for a cook's job in a Watertown nursing-home. Mrs. Faye Smith & her son Bob drove down Saturday afternoon, for an interview, & hired me, to start Wednesday morning. Tuesday evening (the night before) young Mr. Smith again drove down & picked me up, bag & baggage. Today was my first day on the new job. I have an adequate, quiet 3rd floor room. The house, the help, & young Mr. Smith, & the duties on the job are all *just* right!

I am thankful God spared my life & my possessions! "*Surely goodness & mercy shall follow me all my life*"—& Oh, Christ, my Savior! May I "*dwell in the house of the Lord forever*"—!—*at the Bruderhof!* Just *before* the fire I had written to Hardy about my unease in keeping that job and 'winking-at' the evil all around me! I had no time, of course, to hear from Hardy, before I wrote them of the fire. Now, mail will be going from one address to another, so I shan't get their reply soon, anyway. Meanwhile I pray for the opportunity & the grace to continue at this job here, *until I am* CALLED by the Lord who protected me & saved me from the fire! to return to life-in-community.

(When I went up to my room to get a forgotten item or two, at dusk, on the Wednesday evening after the fire, the floor was an inch deep in water, the room dank & murky, & then—really for the *first* time—*I was shaking with fear!* (a delayed reaction).

At Sandra's I got calls from Janey & Fran Hatch & Eugenia about the fire. Poor, rash foolish Sandi lies in City Hospital so badly burnt she will be "scarred for life," breathing through a tube because of the smoke-effects on her throat. Her *hands* were badly burnt … Her *kitchen* was *entirely burnt*. I cannot help asking myself: DID she leave her IRON going? And WHY did Mr. Bemis REFUSE repeatedly to have an electrician repair the faulty wiring in that whole house? WHO was using *fuses* in the telephone-closet on the 3rd floor on the day of the fire?

Over & over, the questions repeat themselves in my mind.

Inspector Kennedy of the Arson Squad, in charge of the investigation ordered by the Chief, is off on 2 weeks' vacation.

On job at Smith's Nursing Home,
53 Spruce St., Watertown, Mass

Friday, August 14 (Steve Emery's 58ᵗʰ birthday—Poor old Steve!)

—[I am SO GLAD to be *old* myself, & to have outgrown the necessity for personal attachments!] Where is my former URGE for *creative* writing? Surely, the Life at Primavera gave me so much *inner peace* that, IF my creative flair were (after all the reams of paper I have covered) only urge for 'self-expression' and "cleverness," the *proof* is here that I am at last LOSING a great weight of SELF! *Thank God!*

The hum-drum of this simple, regular routine of cooking 3 ultra-simple meals *per diem* for patients & staff, doesn't (yet) seem to overwhelm me! Instead, *I feel very peaceful!* Thanks to the *gentle* forcefulness of my boss—young Mr. Smith, son of the founder of this nursing-home—I feel just like one cog in a wheel—neither 'important' nor 'unimportant' (as an individual);—just a member of the team keeping a job going. And, though this is a NEW feeling for me, it's high time I had the experience of it.

My room is HOT, under the eaves, & airless. And I don't sleep very well in it. (It is conspicuously a 'servant's' room, of the premodern mode, when servants were considered 'low' people! Mrs. Smith obviously hasn't caught up with the trend of people *accustomed* to servants, a la 1959! —It was also *young* Mr. Smith's room, when he was a schoolboy. It is obvious she has manipulated her son right out of any independence-of-choice, all his good life! And, whereas, this has made a very *wonderful man* of *him*, it seems to have overwhelmed him with a sense of insignificance that breaks my heart! —He is a fine father to 4 children, & a wonderful, tireless worker—smoothly self-controlled—but (I don't know WHY!) *too* humble in his own opinion of himself! Perhaps that's due to the religious training at the school he attended—Mt. Herman, in the Berkshires. He has a very charming wife, who went to Northfield.)

Being here—in a well-run, wonderfully equipped & superbly 'kept-up' nursing-home, with an ever-so-insignificant job of my own, is giving me JUST the proper chance to think over—even MORE!—the deep longing I have to return to the Life at the Bruder-hof. —I am now in communication with Bob Clement at Wood-crest—only! (for *my sins?*)—& have just sent (yesterday) a note asking if I may *again* try to become a true part of the Life! —World conditions are BLACK with gathering war-clouds, &—*everywhere!*—a sense of unavoidable DOOM! The papers, which I have been read-ing attentively—are no longer even pretending that War can be avoided. The diplomatic pow-wows "at the summit" between the "Big-Four" powers' representatives, are hardly disguisable any longer as attempts at peaceful settlements or compromise-conferences: they are ever-more-obviously mere "strategy-"planning sessions to deter-mine *not only* WHEN War will *start*, but WHICH side will be able to outsmart the other with the delivery of the *first* H-bombs! Mean-while, though editorials cry out for civilian-defense preparedness, the public seems stunned into a sense of futility: as if to say, "What's the USE of trying to devise means of survival? We know the end is coming!"—And, indeed, I believe it is! —*ever so soon!* The petty offi-cers we met from the HMS "Victorious" (British aircraft carrier, on a 'goodwill' mission, to introduce to the USA, & share the secret of its 500-mile range radar-detector device) were of the same mind as I: *this very month of August* may well see the *beginning of the end of civilization!* And because I believe in the Bible and the prophets who foresaw the whole picture-panorama of thousands of years of man's defiance of his Creator's purpose—and keep remembering the warn-ing: *"the earth will dissolve in fervent heat,"* I, too, have a strong feel-ing that *nothing can be done*; that IF it's coming so soon, we *cannot* avoid nor evade it; & *God will select the survivors*, if there are to be any! —Just as he selected Lot when Sodom & Gomorrah were de-stroyed. (Though the modern American *thinks* he has little or no religion, & claims no knowledge of the Bible or the prophets, still, there must be deep down in all of us, as a heritage from our Bible-loving Puritan founders, a *real certainty* that THIS is IT—! I think *that's* why no one shows much inclination to build bomb-shelters in family-cellars; & stock up with supplies of food for 2 weeks life-in-a-cellar, to shelter from '*fall-out*'! —No one, that is, except the Jewish people such as the wealthy ("intruders") at Swampscott & Marblehead, who began to prepare this way *several years* ago—obeying promptings of a 'sense of guilt' due to their greedy acquisition of "more than their share" of money & power!) —It's all so crystal-clear to *me* I have no desire to join a Civilian defense squad. The world has got out of hand—*can't* control itself (though now it aspires to *control* the *moon & Mars*—*before the Soviets do!*)—and the momentum of its hell-bent course to destruction can be stopped ONLY by the Hand of God! —It is a sorry, sinful world—Satan's huge toy! a big balloon, about to burst in Satan's face!

Of course, I share, with all its inhabitants, the guilt and responsibility for its condition of evil. For I, too, have given way to all the promptings & snares the Devil laid for me! —"Spare thou those, oh God, who confess their faults! Restore thou those who are penitent!" —And I *deserve* whatever judgment is passed upon me. But for my dear children—who, if they have failed to understand, have *me*, their mother, to blame for her failure in teaching & example!—& their dear little innocent children: my Cathy, Stevie, Vickie, Susie, Davy, &, (*so far* the 'last-but-not-least') little Nickie James (my Baby's baby, out in California!)—oh, how I pray *they* may be spared the Wrath of God in the coming of the Judgment! —As for my dear daughter, Sandra, the pride & joy of my whole life, that little, gentle, loving, tender, loyal, understanding compassionate WOMAN-child of mine, now pregnant again—oh, God, *spare her!* and judge her according to her GOODNESS! and bless her, again, & again! ("*Woe to women with child, & to those who give suck, in those days —!*" —It *frightens* me!) And it frightens me, too, for sweet, gentle Joyce McCarthy & her child-to-be! And for dear, good (alas, *blind!*) Eugenia, my proven first-&-fast *friend!* When I pass Mt. Auburn, where my people lie in peace beneath the green lawns of cemetery-calm, I realize that man's "importance" is non-existent! *None of us amount* to *anything!*—for all our striving, preening, lusting, yearning, and ambition! "*Dust thou art & to dust returneth!*"

Oh, Lois, what *storms* you have weathered, all of your own making!
God grant us all His Grace & His forgiveness! Amen! Amen!

Well—ANOTHER upheaval! The *"permanent"* job *promised* by Mrs.
Smith in Watertown lasted only through her vacation time, & she
fired me (for no cause) without notice, *by phone* while I was on my
day-off, at home with Sandra! Nize people in this world! —But I
did really *love & honor* her patient, quiet, gentle, generous son, Bob.
She has let him "take over" her business—so she declares; but everybody up there says she can't keep her hands off! *She* was doing the
cooking the day I came down here! And *what* did *she* give the poor,
senile patients to eat? Imagine! Canned ravioli and baker's pies!—
when they can't swallow *ground* meat nor custards, without persua-
sion! The old girl is a faker, a boaster, & an ignoramus from "'way
down East"—& how *she* ever got such a wonderful son is a mystery!

This has meant another upheaval—domestic, financial and vocational, all-together! I went up to Boston for the day to job-
hunt—was PROMISED a job at Gilchrist's, & told to find a room
in Boston—which I *did*, paying for it for a week in advance (Sept
2–9). Then *that* fell through—the former incumbent, who had
taken off to have a baby, came back & claimed her job! —That
was *after* I had been (previously) promised a job at Salem Hospital
only to be notified the woman who was to have left it (as housemother of the Nurses' Home, Highland Hall) had decided NOT
to leave! —So I came up (thanks to my dear Ed! who drove me &
my goods from Lynnfield) and the first day's hunt was *so* much of
a let-down that I *took* a very, very menial job at Radcliffe as
pantry-maid in a college hall! —And *now* I am asked for an interview with the District Mgr of Singer Sewing Machine, to be considered as floor-saleswoman-bookkeeper-demonstrator at one of
their shops! I don't know which way to jump—either choice I
make will pan out *disastrously*—! Because I don't BELONG in the
WORLD at all—but the only proper way *out* of its rotten maelstrom
is the Brotherhood, & I have not (yet—if ever!) been asked to return to a Bruderhof! I have *never* belonged *in the world*, nor

wanted to! And I LONG to re-join the Brothers & Sisters who live "in it, but are not *of* it," who LIVE their faith, & every day draw closer to Christ, the King, & to each other through Him. *Amen!*

Sept 5

Rereading 10 pages of the foregoing (at 2.00 a.m. Sat Sept 5th— a HOT "midnight dreary!") I am overwhelmed with a sense of hopelessness. I have turned-down the Singer job for the *promise* of *security* in the Radcliffe job. Oh, God, may I please be allowed to KEEP the job of pantry-maid till June?—*unless*, or *until* the Brotherhood calls me! Amen. Amen.

I simply *cannot write* these days! The creative urge is very weak in me, & the *frustration* of my years-long literary hopes, too profoundly weighty to crawl out from under! One thing is certain: *the world is mad!* with wickedness & folly & inertia!

Sunday, Sept 6, 1959 Thirty-three years ago today both my first child and I were fighting for life together! God bless my dear son, Jonathan!

In Feb, when I left Primavera, I was mystified as to the meaning of Georg Barth's instruction to me to "set myself the task, and DO it—!" I have sought for *any* task that the wretched *world* can offer— and not found it, in all these long, chaotic 7 months. But *now* I have discovered one to do: to accept & successfully *hold* the very, very humble job offered me at Radcliffe as pantry-maid—where I'll be up against the inevitable hostility of fellow workers—& *keep it* till the end of the school year in June 1960. [*Unless*, of course, I am called by the Brotherhood—or, also unless the world itself *ends* before that date! (which is obviously *not* unlikely, according to the trends of our perilous world-confusion)!] —*Can* I do such a thing? *Why not?* Only if I have God's grace in me to *keep my mouth shut* and to *keep the peace*. [That *big* lesson, learned at Primavera!] Since I was able, in 1956–57 to do the task I set myself of *working hard* at St. Anne's Guest House, to save the $1000 for the round-trip fare to Paraguay—because God gave me His Holy Spirit to strengthen me, so I may also, *only* with His help, do *this* simple task! The object, primarily: *self-immolation!* The result, *either* (a) the Brotherhood's summons, or (b) the possibility of a head-of-house job, befitting my age & my qualifications, for the year after that (*et seq anni*). *This is my task,* therefore: *and I MUST do it,* God willing. *Amen! Amen!*

What my dear friend Eugenia told me last evening about her trip down to Rockport (at 11 years of age) to visit us, & being forgotten by us, & having to return by train alone & humiliated has *shamed me for myself* and *my whole family!* In tribute to her dear mother Alma, I *can* write (yet *another*—!) "great American novel" to use my need for artistic 'outlet,' during the *proving* of my '*task*'—somehow! —Perhaps by the time it is done & ready to be read, I will have proved my indebtedness to Eugenia for her *lifelong, forgiving loyalty!* God Bless dear Eugenia & her mother, the kind, understanding friend of my (confused) girlhood!

Thurs, Sept 10

I've been REALLY scared by circumstances now. It is plain that I *must* take thought for my ADVANCING AGE!

Sunday, October 25, at 4:15 AM E.S.T.

I have "survived" the first month (Sept 18-Oct 18) at Radcliffe's job. I like the "head" housekeeper, Miss McAndrews, especially because she assigned me to work (at Briggs Hall) under Mary Mahony, who is a *grand* old Irish woman (64)! I am *happy* here, because my co-workers, with whom I am also housed at #20 Walker St. ('round the corner from my work-place!) have treated me so kindly and hospitably! The people I work with—[there has been only *one* exception; and as of this week, Miss McAndrew has *changed my schedule* to remove *her* from my picture (Bless Miss McA!)!]—are all *helpful* to me & to each other. We work cooperatively & in peace & comradeship. [I learned *a lot* about 'community' at Primavera!] I can *write,* too—and have started a new novel, to be called "*Vi*', for Violence" and have been getting on with the story, by getting up at 4.30 or 5.00 every morning, to work for 1 ½ hours before I go to work & breakfast at Briggs Hall. This job has *every comfort & convenience!* A *tiny* room, which I have contrived to fix up to my liking, in a modest way. Good food & plentiful. The privacy of my room to be alone in—or the fellowship of the other women at their T.V. shows, or day-off 'community' meals in the house. I still see *Eugenia often;* & have "looked-up" both the Machairs & Myra Mitchell. Soon Theodora will be back from Vermont. Cardie Stubbs lives right round on Avon St. I am *praying* now for a literary 'recognition,' & with God's help *only* can I get it! I am just where an old woman at my time of life ought to be—(if she can't be in a *Bruderhof!)* *Thank you God!*

I am happily *amazed* at the pleasant behavior and civility of the students who work after meals in the pantry with us. They are well-bred & dignified and not at all "snobby." [Radcliffe outlook has *changed* since dear Dottie's time!] I am happy and thankful for this job—and I mean to *keep* it! with God's grace.

God, guide my pen in my creative writing, to give the "flow" of my story the proper message to the world! And, oh dear Lord, I petition thee, work for me *a miracle!*—a most unworthy sinner and helpless soul in the maelstrom of the world!—a chance to be PUBLISHED at last! Amen! Amen! (If I could make 'Best Seller' ratings, think of how much I could help the Bruderhof communities financially!) Oh, God, I BEG thee to work this (long deferred) *miracle of publication!*

Mon, Oct 26 5.45 am 1959

I've just waked up, after a night of very very bad dreams, all connected, somehow, with that awful quarrel I had with my father on Feb. 23, 1924, when he "threw me out" and said he 'never wanted to see me again as long as he lived.' [Next time I saw him was *at his funeral,* in May, 1925!] I loved my father, & he loved me. But he knew I was misbehaving; and there were "snakes in the grass"—(mainly Rodney Long, Walter Whiting, & my little sister Laura). I thought, long ago, that all the bitterness of that time was forgotten & forgiven! In my dream everything was a chaos about being *"thrown out"* of one place after another [even from this *current job* I have!] (God forbid!) Oh, I pray that I may *live in the spirit of Christ,* in peace and amity with those around me! The story of my heroine 'Angela,' in my newly-started book *"Consider Both"* is about a girl tortured by these unforgiven violences of life. Perhaps that was why I dreamed all night of all the turmoil of past and present? *The twenty months of peace in Primavera were so healing!* (as Cyril Davies said!). And I have, since then, been more tranquil than ever since I was a child. I opened the Moffatt Bible to John 5, this morning—seeking peace & comfort, & found the story of the man at the pool who had been for 38 years a *cripple*, yet, by *Christ's spirit, "took up his bed, and walked"!* May my crippled state of soul & heart & spirit pass away. For I, too, "must worship the Father in spirit and in 're-ality'" (Moffat), else I am not after all, "called" of God! It has been a terrible night I've had! Have I become too intent lately on literary success?—which, after all, is only worldly "vanity"? Yet, IF God wishes me to succeed, I shall—but only by his grace!

N.B. The syrup-y words of the Atlantic's "author-contact" woman were *quite meaningless:* the MS came back. There is *no justice, & no integrity in mankind!*

> AFTER I took up the ONE "Task" (Writing) *in earnest for which God made me.*

51 Hereford St. Boston Mass

April 6, 1964

Peter (my 34-yr-old 'Baby') came to see me *unannounced* this afternoon (from California) bringing Jonathan's Cathy and Vickie with him in a rented car.

Peter is a *beautiful personality*, "silky," endearing, BRILLIANT, kind, and *generous!:* to the 2 pennies I had left in my battered wallet—(until next Wed!) he added a $20^{00} bill (*because* he was pleased that I had *lost 53 lb.!*). He took us all out to dinner, & a long drive (both ways). It was a VISITATION! He is a very nice MATURE, *fearless, debonair,* "finished" young man, *full of love* and OUT*going interest in others!*

Thank you, God! Thank you for all my children (3) and their children (8).

Shall I live long enough to see Peter "in 3 years" (as he said)? — I have had strong INTIMATIONS of *mortality*, of late (& consciousness of the "stigmata" I have often *"felt"*—(nail wounds in my hands)). I would *die joyously!* My baby is GOOD! My family are *SOUND & fine; all of them!* Thank you!

Journal 1966–1974

The Slums of the South End,
131 Warren Ave, Boston, Mass

(From Feb-May) 1966

I wanted to throw myself into the program of *renewal* (both
"Urban" *and* spiritual, that is) under way in the South End. I *had*
to move, anyway, from the Back Bay. My landlady—a virago of a
Frenchwoman!—wanted to remodel the top floor (of 249 Newbury) where I had lived for 8 months. The story of my departure
was STORMY! I *owed* her not a penny; for the sight of green money
always moved her to *extend* my tenancy, every rent day. But finally
her growing hostility and her *utter vulgarity* in expressing it caused
me to come over *here*, to the *upheaval* of Boston's Renewal-work (to
seek *lower* rent, for one thing) and to do what I could for *St.
Stephen's (Mission) Church* of our Diocese.

Things here are really going on! The Castle Square Housing Project
is now 3 (& more) stories above the ground (leveled long ago),
where once stood the crumbling old brick houses where William
Huntington Thompson, and Betsy, his tall & kindly "old Cam-
bridge" wife used to minister, in '61, when the *restored* Church of
the Good Shepherd had been rebuilt after a fire. I worked at Morgan
Memorial at that time, & lived in one of its houses, Eliza Henry
Home, run as a Residence for old retired "Morgy" workers and for
married BU (Methodist) theologs. (That was where I'd met *Eunice
Marden*, in her TERRIBLE pangs of misery, after she came back from
Miami.) How I *TRIED* to *befriend* her, year after year, until Dr.
Joseph Barth, of King's Chapel, put one straight about *Schizo-phren-
ics!* —Poor Eunice! She grows *away & away*, with every year! I do
not see her any more. She has barred her door (on St. Botolph St)
to *any* visitors—(except her (Imaginary (?)) *"lover,"* a "millionaire"
from New Hampshire, who *"loves her madly")* *(at 62 or so)* but is
forbidden to marry her by a *nonagenarian father.* (She's "STUCK"
with her story, dreamed-up to compensate for her jealousy of a
lovely, successful sister, Ruth, who "married well.")

Eunice disdains Established religion, & takes comfort in Unity—(an offshoot of Christian Science). For 3 or 4 years, to carry out my one-sided "friendship" I left Trinity, in Copley Sq (missing the coffee-hour and human fellowship of my own fellow Churchmen), & dashed across to the N.E. Life "hall," where her "church" meets. I don't do it anymore. It didn't affect her at all.

(At a Fair there, one evening, I had a long talk with affable (Engineer) John Jones, of Roxbury, who told me the story of Urban Renewal as it was then affecting Roxbury's Washington Park area. He and his delightful wife—(both Negroes)—were very hospitable to me! They invited me to their home for Sunday dinner.)

Freedom House, which is *Church*-Supported (interdenominationally), sent its speakers to a Parish Dinner we had (for Trinity), two or three years ago. The Renewal was *really* going!

Now the Youth of Canterbury & Phillips Brooks Clubs at Trinity have been working at St. Stephen's (our own "High Church" mission) down on Shawmut Ave at Franklin Sq.

—So, with the encouragement of dear young David Van Dusen, *I came over here* to look for a place on the edge of the Castle Sq. Project (future) "Cultural Center."

I began work by contributing to St. Stephen's "Sentinel" (a parish newsletter); mending the vicar's pants, etc. etc.

The interest on my part was a sort of tribute to my late (great) Aunt Sarah, of the Cambridge of a century ago, who worked as a writer of Abolitionist-"pamphlets" for Wm. Lloyd Garrison. She was a highly educated pioneer in women's "emancipation" and in the field of languages, she *excelled.* (She translated 40 volumes of the works of the poet, Tasso, from the Italian. We had the original parchment volumes, bound in green, in our Cambridge attic, when I was a child. The green cloth binding had been a (hoop-) skirt of the English poet, Robert Southey's wife—& the volumes were inscribed in *his* hand to Aunt Sarah Sprague Jacobs. My mother, *lost in her sorrow of my father's death* in 1925, in Lexington, threw them into a *Morgan Memorial bag,* when she sold 90 North Hancock St. Lexington to George Morey!) So we have now *no Jacobs family* mementos left except the portrait of Bela (that "eminent divine") hanging in the rooms of his Church in Central Sq. where it is honored.

Son of a New Bedford whaling Master, he rebelled against the sea; educated himself, graduated from Brown Univ. in Providence in 1799 (*I believe*) & then, about 1803, married the "gently bred" (debutante) daughter of a fashionable Newport, Rhode Island, "Society" Doctor. Her family disowned her for marrying a penniless Baptist preacher. But he brought her as a brave bride to the "manse" in Cambridgeport (19 Pleasant St, where now Farwell Chambers stands). She bore him 5 children (who *lived)*. Her two sons were Harvard-educated: one Bela Farwell Jacobs (my mother's father), a lawyer; the other Justin Allen Jacobs, a musician (first flutist in the ORIGINAL Boston Symphony Orchestra.) Aunt Sarah, the oldest girl, was "taught at home" until she joined the late great Margaret Fuller in Providence, to found her school for "young ladies of good family." —The stories of the days of 1815 *et seq* I read in scads of old diaries & in my copy of Aunt Sarah's biography of her father—! —Aunt Sarah was brilliant, a writer, & opinionated. I feel I am her natural *heir-ess,* & I want to *carry on* a century later what she did in the Abolition Movement! by doing my share in the Civil Rights of 1966.

Great-grandmother Sarah Sprague Jacobs, when her Baptist spouse was accidentally thrown from his horse & killed, quietly took her children back to her own Episcopalian church locally, St. Peter's, Cambridge. In 1898 my mother & father met & were married there. I was brought up in that Sunday School & made lifelong friends there. Time takes its toll & *changes* the face of the earth! But *I* still remember with colorful clarity my childhood there in the shadow of the tall spire of Bela Jacob's First Baptist Church. (The parishioners of his day so *loved* his wife for her gentleness & tirelessness, they even forgave her for returning to "Popish" Anglicanism.) She & her husband & five children with 3 servants lived on *his* earnings of $800 a year, & gave the 5 children excellent educations! (Talk about INFLATION! —)

~

It is true, alas, that the "white" man has "projected" upon the Negro *his* "image" of Negro-psychology. I have just had two weeks' work at SNAP—with an "integrated" staff of white & (MOSTLY) "black," Cuban, & Chinese people that convince me neither my lazy-going & (pleasant-spoken) Boss, Reginald Eaves, nor the *well-dressed*, well bred Chinese Miss Chan (called "Community Organizer" despite her most conspicuous quality of vagueness and *inability to make decisions)*, are NOT qualified to undertake the *project's aim* & that the Federal Anti-Poverty funding—no one, as yet, is *paid*— is a political "plum" Mr. Eaves *cannot* "digest."

So I quit.

I am surprised how *kindly* all the young workers were to me, despite my age (& superior education & wide "social exposure"). The *kindness* in Negro hearts passes my understanding, considering their bitter life in America.

But, like the Emergent Nations of Africa, the "emancipated" Negro of 1966 is NOT ready *yet* to administer his own (debased) destiny. MORE education & *deeper* "integration" MUST precede his Executive-ship, for *his* sake. —Right here & now, his "caste" system aims at competition with café society and acquisition of "status-symbols"—skipping blithely from the ghetto to "21"—without stopping on the way-stations of philosophic *osmosis*.

~

Odd—odd as my meeting Eunice yesterday, Peter Lawrence (son of Fred'k, our Bishop) with good Ohioan Molly Shera, Father Dwyer's secretary, is again coming to lunch here (131 Warren Ave.) in my (crowded) "housekeeping room" overlooking a *neat back yard* of a Lebanese landlord, *Abdul*—on a *garbage-littered alley* next to an antiquated public school (such as Louise Day Hicks thinks *good* enough for Negroes!).

[I am "out" to "get" Mrs. Hicks, a So. Boston "paddy" (a woman lawyer & hypocrite, aspiring to be Boston's next *mayor*(ess!). She has *wrecked* the Schools of once-educated Boston in her *hatreds*, as chairman of our infamous School Committee.]

~

Aunt Sarah S. Jacobs was *America's very first* woman School Committee woman, in Cambridge. *She* was a *lady* & a *cultivated Christian.*

History repeats itself!

May 15, 1966

My Daddy died forty-one years ago this month, at 62 years and 10 months of age. —A heart attack, very sudden (& stunningly shocking to poor Mama). He died before we had a chance at reconciliation. In February we'd had a dreadful fight (over Laura's characteristic sly trickiness). And I took a midnight train to NY with my father's fury (at *my* SAUCY and intransigent behavior) ringing in my ears: *"I never want to see you again!"* he roared … *And he didn't.* He was in his coffin when, in May, I came back for his funeral. Dottie's wedding had taken place while I was tearing around New York in TAXIS, with Lou and Ramola Martin, "showing off" & wasting money I earned as Asst Circulation Mgr to good old Fred Willock of the "*People's Home-Journal*" (80 Lafayette Street, NY) & living at the Girls Community Club Marshall on East 30th… A lot of things happened, while I still mourned & felt stunned & confused over my terrible scene in the upper hall, in Lexington (90 North Hancock St.). I was an obstreperous & opinionated girl—what's now tolerantly called "a crazy mixed-up kid," who realized MUCH TOO LATE that Daddy was *my life's most influential, positive force! —*(My story *"HONEY Cat"* began (with the horror of his wrath still haunting my dreams, making me *suicidal)* on the day I met *Dave* (Henry) over the gold fish tank in the lobby of the Hotel Vanderbilt on lower Park Ave.)

And now at just 2 months younger than Daddy was when *he* died, I have been praying to die myself—I want to *join him* in the quiet of God's heaven, & tell him how I loved him, & how much I have *learned "the hard way," as he predicted that I'd have to*—"bumping my head against stone walls" he said (&, as I am learning even now: the futility of "trying to 'fight City Hall'" or the EVIL of God's beautiful world in the hearts of the unregenerate & unrepentant!)

Now *I* am a worshipper at Trinity Church (where my dear Daddy attended services in his *youth* (before marriage) and adored Phillips Brooks, whose wisdom he passed on down to me!)

Today I am "*wasting* (?)" a $5 bill on flowers (white lilies) for the chapel where *Phillips Brooks's bust* is installed, to try to say to Daddy: *"I'm sorry, dear Daddy!* Please *take my hand, as you used to do, leading me by the terrifying "Snake Pond" on Haven Avenue* Pigeon Cove, when I was four years old. We'll get the Sunday paper at the Waiting Station, on Granite St. Buy me a lemon-flavored Salem Gibraltar; & then we'll take the road back via *upper* Phillips Avenue, & you can show the bubbling spring that comes up in the dirt-road by the Moultons' private park (after a heavy rain) under the sun & shadows of the trees in the woods where I grew up for all the 20 happy summers you gave me & Dottie & Laura by the ocean—with, as you used to say, on the broad front porch—*"nothing between us and Spain"* except the Atlantic Ocean.

The fat red "sea-going" tugs pulling a chain of barges *passed*, on their way to New York, laden with granite from the Halibut Point quarry, in those early days! to build the foundations of the *Woolworth Building*! —*We were* SAFE, *we 3 little girls of yours, because* YOU PROTECTED US! Your hand held mine so firmly when we passed the "Snake Pond" (Dottie *scared* me about). And your kind, warm, jolly, BRAVE protection was the only *real* shelter of *my soul any human being ever gave me. Bless you,* my dear Daddy! Teddy the Airedale *was always with us* on those walks. I'm sure he's with you now "up there"—where *I* long to be! to tell you I'm SORRY I hurt your heart! I know I was (secretly) *your favorite child,* though I didn't realize it then.

Everybody's gone—I want to go, too. I am afraid of *LIVING TOO LONG* (like all the agèd people I know). I am already an *eye-sore* (to Youth).

(I was in Oxford Mass the Sunday, May 22nd, my white lilies were placed in your memory in the Phillips Brooks Chapel—on a visit to Cousin Ruthie Brown Macgregor.)

Ruthie is only 19 months older than I; and she has been left "well-fixed" & secure (since Bob died, last winter). She has a beautiful & very "modern" apt—much *TOO large,* to my way of thinking (for I like a *"ship's cabin"* outfit!) in an old village house in an UN-spoiled country town. Ruth's hair is as pretty grey, as it was *brown*—soft & naturally curly. But she is badly handicapped by her crippling arthritis, chiefly in her *(always ailing)* feet. She must walk with a cane—poor darling. She was SO NICE to me; & the vacation did me a lot of good. (Though I wanted to *get back* "home" to my own slum-dwelling with all its imperfections.) Her daughter, Myra, with 5 children (from 1–15) is a great comfort to her. (Like me, Ruth no longer *can* "*take*" life with young children!) (even though they *wanted her* at each of her 4 daughters' homes—in Massachusetts, Pennsylvania, Oregon & Washington, when she "*toured*" the country. We are OLD. And we being WISE, do not TRY to DENY it. To *me*, 'OLD' is not a "BAD" word. It is a sign of "*arriving*"—& I still *do pray* that I won't have to pass through any farther stages of deterioration! (A skin fungus, & badly behaved intestines, & my *horrible* "pituitary apron" (or belly-"flap") (—Ruth has one too, & from bad obstetrics. We also have the same narrow jaw, & "double curvature" (*birth* defect)! We are related to each other thus: my mother's mother was her grandmother's sister (Laura Demmon (of Vt.)). (There were Dem-*ings* in Arlington, Vermont. *Any kin?*)

~

On the 3rd of June, Fri, I went down to visit Rosemary (at P. C.) (Cutter) Dole. *She*, poor darling, is *really senile* now, in her forgetfulness & confusion of mind. She's as nice & jolly as ever, except when she "SUSPECTS" that Buzzie is "trying to RUN her life." Buzzie or *someone* MUST, for she is NOT SAFE alone any longer. And her *car* is *not* a good thing for her to have. —Alas!

I hurried back on Saturday, after a brief visit with Roland MacCallum, who has bought a house next to Emily Story's on Edgemere Rd, Pigeon Cove! I wanted to be at Church on Father Dwyer's last Sunday before his stomach surgery.

The poor (schizo-phrenic) alcoholic woman upstairs came to Church with me, wearing a raincoat over her nightgown! She objected to Father Dwyer's *Spanish* prayers, & to "sitting with niggers"—& so left in the middle of the service.

I have *definitely*, now, made up my mind to leave Trinity and its "fashionable Rector" & "Elite" congregation, to *take part* in APPLIED Christianity by *Activist* Episcopalians at St. Stephen's. This means *finishing* my year's pledge & another $5 for the DAF pledge (next year), besides contributing to St. Stephen's—But it COSTS more than MONEY! —It means the "ignominy of being regarded by my former

Churchmates as a "slum-dweller." (Nan Hall has already *gibed* at me—! in her characteristic way!) I PROTEST against an "ELITE" caste in Christian Churchmanship. It took a *lot* of tact by (Sr.) Gardiner Shattuck, & gentle suasion from *(still-a-snob)* Connie Worcester, as well as Dave Van Dusen's "Tip" to make me SURE I was *persona non grata* with 'is Nibs, "Hector the Rector"!

["Letter": transferred by Dr. Ferris to St. Stephen's, June 7, without comment.]

I've had NO literary *urge* at all for 2 months. It worries me. I PRAY for *creative*-ness to COME BACK! (I was doing well with a sheaf of stories Ruthie *said* she would type for me. —I haven't got them back YET! & silly old fool that I am, I *lost carbon-copies.)*

June 6-20

Another visit to Rosemary—which shall be my *last*, I vow! She *ought* not to be *alone!* She is completely confused & dis-oriented; no longer a *safe* driver, because she is using her *car* emotionally— to "show" people *no one can tell HER what to do!—deliberately* parking under a "No-Park" sign, in sight of a watching policeman, *daring* him to give *her* a ticket! & *deliberately* ramming another car's fender in a parking-lot! She is *no longer safe!*

She *professes* friendship & *welcome* to *me*, & begs me to stay *another day!* But, though I missed Church & Tako's birthday-party, to stay over, she was SO *glad* when I went home—! She "asserted" herself enough to remark: "You're a DISTURBING person." That TIES it! —[I indeed have always been so accursed—(being an Irish-er! with OPINIONS)]—& now I realize Bessie, for her own ends, put *that* idea in Rosie's head, because *she* wanted that weekend there herself, & had Alec Peters phone—*(to see if I'd GONE!).* Bessie will be there next week, with Jack's daughter, Caroline; while Virginia James is here, from Denver.—

The financial pickle *I'll* be in, "entertaining" Virginia in *The New Boston,* will be severe. I *don't* want to move to change my "special interest acct" because July 1st will give it *more* interest (to leave my picayune "fortune" (of $200—*Ha! Ha!)* to my *dearest friend,* Sandra). So I am borrowing from Ed, on the security of my first-of-the-month checks, to "do the right thing" by a *wealthy* woman who was VERY good to me, for a long stay with her in Denver.

~

Fr. Dwyer is back from MGH—looking *fine;* but feeling very "pooped." Tako is keeping *away* "disturbing" people from him (like ME, primarily). *I wanted* him to read my story: "We're Only Bums: To Hell with Us"—but I can easily see WHY he doesn't *dare* "approve" it! Connie says it's *"unkind"* to *Hector-the-Rector. Too bad!* It's very much MORE "unkind" when HE refuses to help a hungry "bum" (or beggar), isn't it?

Now I have to get ready for Tako's "Unit" meeting of the So End *LWV.*

~

The Chamber of Commerce, as a body, shies away from a "low-income housing" drive because its Real Estate brother-members are OPPOSING the use of valuable land in the City for the residents of low-income people. They continue to draft plans for MORE high rise, high rent apartments, to add *more* VACANCYs to the scene—for *where* can a multitude of millionaires be found who can PAY such rates? It is utterly stupid! (We learned this at our "delegation"-meeting at the Chamber of Commerce. It's FACT!)

June 29, 1966

I'm about (a) to clean my "pad," in case Virginia (arriving tomorrow) insists on seeing my slum-quarters; and (b) getting a haircut (which I had planned NOT to do till the first of July. I MUST do it—to look presentable to my guest, when I meet her tomorrow at the Airport.

~

It is HOT-and-*humid*—a condition that reduces my morale to its lowest pitch. But I woke at 4.00 am, & *had* to *get up*—(for I'm *unable* to "luxuriate" like a sybarite, lying in bed, once I am awake). And I find myself giving thanks to God for my Blessèd *Poverty* and my isolation, too—because here in my horrid little "ship's cabin," I can BE *myself,* & be "let alone" *as I like.*

~

An interesting (ancient Oriental-religious) idea has come to my attention: that God created man-&-woman *together* in *one* body, in

His own image; and then *separated* them! *That's the way I like it!* I wish I didn't feel *wicked* with my dream-"images" of God Himself as *my* "other half"! —What presumption—for a nobody that gets nowhere (in a worldly sense) and doesn't OWN ANYTHING to regret leaving behind when she dies, and is resurrected *to meet Him!*

ONE *ambition* I have had (after the fulfillment of motherhood came—and went away again!): my WRITING. And who can *"fight"* the Literary Establishment (inexorably controlled by Zionists, in the USA today) when ALL OBSTACLES prevent so-called "success."

"So rare (as) a day in June"! Beautiful!

June 30, 1966 (my Mama's & Daddy's Wedding Day, in Cambridge, Mass (1898))

What a *wonderful* day—Besides my MATUTINAL solitary prayers for Mama and Daddy (whom—I hope—I shall soon *join*, both on earth, at Mt. Auburn, and in Heaven with God)—the whole day & evening was a *great success!*

I had got to work to CLEAN my (dismal) "pad" Wednesday. (It is NOT so much the ancient dirt on the wall-paper—so *greasy* that my map of the South End Renewal Plan, on the wall over the head of my bed, will NOT *stick*; but keeps *sliding* from the (greased) 'grip' of its (surgical-tape) fastenings, to the floor! (Often scaring me in my sleep!) and the *chipped* old paint-of-many-slapped-on coats of *once-* white & cream color, nor the bilious pieced out salmon-colored linoleum on the (creak-y) floor—that makes this place pretty seedy. It is the NOISE—*overhead,* from jets coming off the airport, heading south; the screams of children playing (&/or fighting) in the play-ground of the ancient Rice School next door; the sad cries of ped-dlers of grapes and cabbages, on old horse-drawn carts; the screech of teen-agers' wildly driven cars; the "gunning" of motor-cycle mo-tors; the sharp quarrels of the neighbors up & down Dartmouth Street; the sirens of the ubiquitous fire-apparatus(es), and the wail of City Hospital ambulances carrying the sick and dying—to say nought of the ever-so-busy "black marias" of the local police (Sta. 4, Capt. Doocey's men in blue!) collecting drunks and 'dopes' from

the alleys, where the huge rubbish collection vans are always crunch-
ing over beer-cans and bottles!—that make this location all that a
SLUM must (alas) be, for God's "Forgotten" Men, women and grand-
mothers! —It is the *hopelessness* of the populace, congregating at the
little "meal ticket" corner café, to get their charity-meals, before putting down their hard-bought (?) betting money on today's races at
the horse-or-dog track, before the day's drinking starts, to the ac-
companiment of women's shrill or vicious screeches of derision (at
the jests or 'insults' of the staggering men they "latch on" to at the
taverns!). (Or the shrill yipping of mangey puppies, often sharply
changed to terrible canine death cries, when dogs are mowed down
in traffic and expire protestingly under the wheels, while little-boy
owners sob with grief at the loss of a flea-bitten pet ... Yes, it's a
deep & dreary HOPELESSNESS for these lost souls (many sunk so low
that their likeness to "the image of God" in which they were created
has disappeared, and the "demons" have taken them over as he did
the *herd* of *Gadarene swine!*).

But while the organ plays and the scrubbed young boy sopranos
follow the crucifer into the Holy Temple at Trinity Church (just
across the bridge) and the *fashionable* congregation of the well-
heeled who *pay the bills* of the Church generously—so long as they
are not distressed by *understanding* of the 'War on Poverty!' here
(on "the other side of the tracks" (N.Y. NH & H RR-tracks AND
new (roaring) Mass Turnpike)—nor, when PUT to it (by such voices
as mine, crying in the wilderness) to AGONIZE over "the sins of the
whole world" (*abetted* by their *Republican* vote!), there is a kind of
elation for them in the scent of flowers on the altar, perfume on the
women's hair, & pomade on the men's, the spirited full-choir music,
the *beautiful beautiful* Temple of God they occupy comfortable
pews in—and their wily, mesmeristic Prophet, *TPF,* in his famous
pulpit, "showing off for the grown-ups"—those who remain of his
(late) mother's circle of friends, & making personal & pious fame
with every word spoken through his somewhat adenoidal (and su-
percilious) nose—while all this cozened "privilege" gathers together
believing itself adherents of Christ, in a lovely setting, on a glittering
"uptown" Square where Boston's intellectual center lies between the

huge library and the "elegant" Sheraton Plaza—over *here, across* the *busy bridge,* is MAN-facing-DESTITUTION that is being alleviated by (aforesaid) meal-tickets & Salvation Army coffee or soup, with the finest (old) clothing available at dirt-low prices at Morgan Memorial's Good Will Stores, or sectarian thrift-shops run by (condescending) volunteers from the suburbs (half-days, twice a week), who bring in Rogers Peet's & Brooks Brothers (cast-off) clothing in the station-wagons, on the days they do "volunteer" work that justifies (in their shallow souls) their technical nomenclature as "Christian" citizens of a Republic.

—Ah, though, my love: there *is* a difference between an American *Republic* and an American *Democracy*—even if the latter has not YET been able to *educate* the former into understanding of the phrases of *our Constitution* with its Bill of Rights guaranteeing "life, liberty & the pursuit of happiness" to us *all, "every one"* piped Tiny Tim on Xmas eve in the slums of London long ago.

The slums here, where I live & move & have my being, *differ* from London's; but the *principle* is the same; it is the *tracks* (& superhighway) under the bridge that geographically divide the *"Haves"* from the *"Have-Nots"*—the *"sheep"* (of the Back Bay) from the *"Goats"* of society … *Silly sheep!* sleeping in their air-conditioned bedrooms! The "clouds" they sit on in Heaven won't be any softer nor more sanitary than the one waiting for *me!* (whither I would go, as the "hart panteth after the water-brook")—just as soon as God orders Gabriel to toot his horn for me (—for *me,* I hope a *flute,* rather than a *saxophone!).*

Because there IS *hope over here!* The Urban Renewal map sets it forth in clear color on all the walls in every thinking-man's home in the South End.

And the money mesmerized out of the well-heeled "fashionable" congregation over at Trinity by "Hector the Rector's" *"charming"* sermons—with the Blessing of the Bishopric—if *NOT* God's own!— *pays* for the *work,* the *love,* the *sacrifice* and the *thinking*-for *one's fellow man* that are the 24-hr a day *concern*—deep, honest, REAL Christian concern, of Vicar Father William Dwyer and his assistant, (Volunteer) Peter Lawrence, who sees the *needs* and *understands* the *hearts* of the *people of the slums*—so that instead of climbing the stairs of a traditional family ascent into the pulpit, Peter is going to study *City Planning* & specialize in providing LOW INCOME HOUSING for the Poor. (*Uphill* work against the "vested interests of the members of Real Estate firms and the Powerful Chamber Of Commerce.) Because *housing* is LITERALLY "where a man LIVES"—alone, or with his family—and *that*, our dear Peter Lawrence sees as the "*POSITION*-on-earth" of *all* men made "in the image of God"— whom alas, man variously attests to both in the sonorous tones of *piety* in the pulpit and the despairing call upon Him *in profanity* and doubt in the lives of the degenerate. Above ALL OF US, on Both Sides of the (dividing) "tracks" HE IS!

(I, *really*, am glad to be *here!*)

~

Molly is very happy when the Summer Program gives her "new faces" of *young* folks. She was sweet & cheery to me yesterday, a few hours before Virginia James's arrival at the Airport, from Denver, & promised to tell Peter I'd love to have him meet the plane & help me WELCOME Virginia! (I do HOPE Virginia may *donate* to his programme).

One of the Summer Program workers, it turned out, had to go to the Airport, to "hop" to NYC to meet friends (or family) so Peter, *God bless him!* drove me also over to Logan, to meet Virginia's Denver plane. It was 30 min late.

Virginia had only *1* hr's sleep the night before, but she kept awake & alert & *always good-natured.*

Later (July 2, 1966 Sat)

What a 2-day *night-mare* this has been, playing the Hostess to Egotism and Lack-of-Taste to the "Ugly American" from Denver— because *she* was so kind & hospitable to *me* when I visited her a mile above sea level in the city! The score is even now, & I "gave my all" to make it so.

Peter Lawrence was SO kind! (*Unexpectedly!*) one of his Summer Programme-workers (Bruce Bloise) had to go to NY, to meet a plane. So Peter dropped him off at No. East and took me to United, to meet Virginia. Her plane was 30 min late. Peter said he ENJOYED a chance to talk to me "without interruption." —(I gave him A+ for Courtliness!)) (I had no time to worry about WHY *Molly* seemed to be ill at ease at the time; but I wonder, *now* (?).)

We met Virginia & her ½ ton of "matched" luggage, & dropped it off on a porter's truck. We said farewell to *Gentleman* Peter, & went upstairs, while Virginia hung up her garments in Rm 1245, & we had ICE WATER. Then we went out by B & M to Melrose, where Stevie met our train. Ed served Manhattans, & we chatted about generalities. Though the house was torn up, Sandra served us a perfectly delicious & beautiful summer dinner. *All 4 children* behaved *like Angels!* (Was I *proud* of them *all!*) Stevie was broken up because Ed & Sandra drove Virginia & me back to Boston, to see the sunset & the full moon rise over a *beautiful* Charles Basin. They dropped me *here*—so Virginia could see my "pad"—(though *no one* could be expected to realize how happily *I LIVE & AM* in this slum-sector!)

Virginia talked steadily & crudely & egotistically all through the episode. (She BOASTS and BRAGS without a *notion* of her "ugly Americanism"!) (No one really *exists* in her world but herself. She's both uneducated & schizoid.) But at the same time, she *is* GOOD-natured. —That was Thursday.

On Friday, it was WORSE! I spent $26.00 on hiring a car which she drove. She continued her monologue from Boston to Cambridge (where we lunched *(she paid* for it!) at Le Petit Gourmet), & then drove up to Concord. She likes to buy slides & keep travel-notes, & have photos of herself posed at historic shrines, to "show-off" to her Denver pals. Everywhere she went she called herself a *native Bostonian*—which is true, legally; but no great asset to Boston's repute! (I wouldn't DREAM of introducing her to Connie, or any other "Proper Bostonians" I know!) In Concord, she went to buy at the Country Store—& we finally found Bessie's house, & it was empty; & then we drove down to Rockport. —By coincidence, Rosemary & Virginia are BOTH *Sargent alumnae!* Rosemary's lack of "culture" is very *beautifully* hidden by true graciousness of soul. Virginia "PATRONIZED" poor darling Rosie, unconscious of her blunderbuss *crudity!*—& went on BOASTING & blundering—!

We got home about 5.15. We had driven 133 miles & I *paid* for

Lois with her children, Jonathan, Sandra, and Peter, at Sandra's house, early 1960s.

Smoking at her desk, Boston, 1970s.

it (out of my frugal funds)—& have settled the "debt." Virginia said she had given $1000 a year to the Church—(tax-deductible, no doubt) & was willing her mansion to St. Luke's, Denver, as a rectory. So she wouldn't help Peter's Summer Program fund. (I *asked* her to do so, rather than "go divvies" on the car-cost.) I was *exhausted* & terribly hot (in corsets & a knit-suit). Could hardly peel them off, when I lugged my bathing-bag back—a-foot from Park Sqr., while she sailed over to meet Eugenia & Joe for dinner & drinks—*and drinks*—at Pier 4.—(I wonder how they went on *showing-off* to EACH OTHER, at that get-together?) Both are *pretenders*. If I was mentioned, it was with condescension! (*Silly geese!*) That was *Friday*.

Saturday, three hours more, showing her Trinity Church—where she bragged to a REALLY fine *lady*, on the Altar Guild. (Mrs. Wise)—Then to the Copley Plaza, the Library & the Prudential—yak-yaking STILL.

She hardly noticed it when we said goodbye at the Copley Square bus-stop.

Oh, I am GLAD it's over! (I doubt if she'll *ever* feel *cheap* about it. She paid for me at the Skywalk at the Pru & 15¢ for ice-coffee.)

Tra-la-la, to Eugenia (two months ago) & now to Virginia. *Amen!*

Note from the "Ugly American" boastfully "doing Europe" in *de luxe* style.

~

Tako Dwyer, my "friend forever," & the people I have known (since I was (so *adroitly*) "eased out" of the "fashionable" Trinity Parish), make me much happier than the *un*sincere civilities of the "Right People" who worship at the "cult"-center of T. P. Ferris. I am SURE of the Agape at St. Stephen's, where the Action is! And I am SURE of the thesis of Harvey Cox's *"Secular City,"* which I am STUDYING, word-by-word.

July 8 (Friday)

We had a *fine*—all-too-brief—trip to Pigeon Cove, Father Dwyer, Tako, Nori Ko, Yo Yo San, & I, picking up, *via* Melrose, Sandra, Susie, Davy & Chrissie. (We *tried* to see Rosemary; but she went to Concord.) We ate our lunch on the rocks at St. Mary's Pool; then swam at the Front Beach in Rockport. We had to park up on Main St, & so walked through the back lanes, via the cemetery, to the Beach. (Davy shows a delightful "spirit of peace." He is ZIPPIER, too, than any of Sandra's children. His high, hopeful eagerness is often crushed by the Bowditch minor-key QUIETNESS. I love that little boy!)

July 25, 1966

I'd give *anything* to know FOR SURE *if* there really were a "conspiracy" to "ease me out of Trinity" (because I CRITICIZE(d)—& continue to do!—the Great Vanity of the pulpit)! Father Dwyer told me yesterday not to let this become an obsession, because, taking the Eucharist, one must have *nought* "against" one's neighbor! I *am glad* it happened to me to meet Father Dwyer and dear Tako, who (I *warned* Sandra!) is fast becoming a "daughter-substitute" and to meet FRIENDs who are *honestly* CORDIAL at coffee-hour after church.

131 Warren Avenue, So. End. Boston

July 29, 1966

A letter (she probably will never read) to Tako Dwyer
Dear "Friend-Forever":
    You have been a light to my dark loneliness, since Feb, when I moved here! You & Father Dwyer are real friends, tolerant of any sinful traits, but ready to "scold" vigorously, as good "parents" of your motley church-family. The intimate circle of your church-goers is a delight, after the 6 years I spent as "Church Mouse," on the outside of the closed "establishment" at Trinity—to be seated (at parish dinners) at the table reserved for Paupers and "Untouchables!" (Poor Eddy & Serape Kondyan would rather be there than to be free and self-respecting at St. Stephen's! They are too "'umble" for their health!) When I think of my 6 years in the vast gallery, listening to TPF "showing off" in his pulpit, I am sorry I "wasted my time"!! I was scorned, and laughed-at, and pitied by the Rich and Snobby and Would-Be's. —I was "snooted-at" by the (so-called)

"professional" women of the 'B&P's—because I was frankly poor, & never "put on affected airs," and did not try to "imitate the Rector"—(as they all try to do!);—while the Rector himself so brazenly asserted in his pulpit that he "imitates Christ"—! —He, who despises poverty and slums, beggars and bums, & boasts he "does not dispense money to beggars!" —Dave Van Dusen first suggested I "help out" at St. Stephen's. (Tipped-off that I should be "got rid of" Gardiner Shattuck asserted "churches never want to get rid of parishioners!) Then Connie Worcester went to work on me, urging me to leave—! I believe it was because I made vocal protest at the diocesan Venture in Faith group against the meetings in Lent being "Dr.-Ferris Cults," instead of prayer-groups! I do not accept even now Connie's statement that "There are 'all kinds' of Churches" (within the Church). The "fashionable parish" is not a church: it is not even a Christian! It is a salve to social sinners against their fellow men—a travesty of the meaning of the Crucifixion. I protest— and, as a Protestant—oddly enough—find myself happy in an Anglo-Catholic group of real loving Christians! And Tako & Father Dwyer never fail their "sheep"! —It is as if, in planning his DVF for Lent, Bishop Stokes was sorting out the people of the diocese, to separate "sheep & goats." —I grew sick indeed of "taking it" from Trinity people!—who feel so "superior & righteous" while they vote Republican against the poor, the for- gotten, & the needy! & donate huge sums for the "Temple" that is the setting for their vain and pompous Rector (who says his "well-wishers" 'protect' him against such people as I am & poor (crazy) Carlleton Thomine & Ernie (of the Coast Guard) who was badly hurt by his experience in the Phillips Brooks Club—under either Hiles or Van Dusen (?)— The snooty treat- ment of Miss Ruth Cheyne (TPF's sec'y) that I have consis- tently been exposed to, because I gave that grad-student's letter to the Rector, in which he said TPF was a "lascivious hyp- ocrite"—believing TPF would "take" my motive in doing so as I meant it:—to show him the youth's reaction against his mes- meristic sermons, which lull "moneyed" people to sleep. — [Mrs. Allen Forbes was tight at the first Parish dinner! (She is the First Nat'l Bank—! and an arrogant, cruel-mouthed wife & woman.)]

From now on, I'll take the Gospel "straight," as preached and *PRACTICED* by Father Dwyer and Tako—who have been my *"comforters."* God bless you, you who are "practical and applied" Christian advocates of social justice!

And *thank you,* "friend forever"

Lois Bayliss

To TPF: Bury your dead, you've hypnotized them into making over their estates to your church … If their money-power isn't *TOO great,* you know Gardiner Shattuck will conduct their last rites very suitably *for you*—You vied with him for the funeral of Mrs. *Daland Chaneller*—" & LOST MY (unimportant) RESPECT thereby! I don't *think* you *are* "lascivious"(as the student's letter charged)— though when you've traveled abroad, a flock of ladies (& women) you met on shipboard come to Boston to *try* to *ensnare* the BACHELOR-priest! [How will you manage to *elude* them! —WHY?] But I KNOW you *are* a *hypocrite* indeed—and the most conceited man on earth—falling down "humbly"on your (graceful!) knees to ASK GOD PUBLICLY "Oh, *why* do we have to have *beggars* & *bums*—?— & then VOTING for Wall Street to protect your investments.

I *was* DUPED by you, TPF, *for 6 long years!*

But no more! No more!

N.B. a jest I heard: "Definition of an Episcopalian: *A PRAYING Republican."* RIGHT! (at Trinity, that is).

August 10, 1966

Sandra came and visited me! (Only *one* postponement, *this* time.)

Aug 11, 1966

Tako, bless her, & I had a wonderful walk by the River. (We saw Connie on our way back, who told me (again) *she* "never spoke of me in 'that way'" (as "far-left," I think she meant). Old Mr. Pier is dying—painfully; & his son had started home by plane to be "in at the death." Connie sails along on her GUTS—!)

Aug 17

Mr. Pier's Memorial Service. *Many* there.

August 21

Sandra, Ed, Susie, Davy & Chrissie came to visit after lunch.

[Oct 3ʳᵈ 1966]

Recalling Christ Church's Picnic 1934 (with CLG)

Oh, the "Ministers in my Life—!" They have done so much to help & *strengthen me!* to "get *Nowhere*"—(to die a *pauper!*)— but a *fulfilled & happy Christian!* Amen!

We had a great time on this St. Stephen's picnic [8/15/66]. The bus-driver's 3 teeny little children were my special charge, on the road, while I "directed" the rest of the passengers —all "Elderly" people—in the (unmelodious) singing of the Good Old Songs of yesteryear! I had a really UNINHIBITED good time. —"Adonis" (Peter) Lawrence was the satyr in the pine-wood, lying, bare-shouldered in a pool of ice-water. (As I write this, Oct 3ʳᵈ 66) Peter's plans to "phase-out" of his conscientious, indefatigable WORK at St. Stephen's are announced for next Sunday. Peter is a man best described by a witticism of C.L.G's (30 +/- odd years ago):—"Than which there IS no which-or!"

~

The "ministers in my life"—even up to Anson P., the Rt. Rev. Bishop Stokes, whom I have dubbed "the APPROACHABLE Bishop"— have meant more to me than my beaux, husband and lover(s) of all my years. Right now, the ineffable SPIRITUALITY and the "*Dottie*-look" on *Fr. Dwyer's (sensitive) face at Communion* haunts my agèd musing. And his responsive and understanding (Japanese) wife, Tako, *very nearly* matches Sandra (!) in my affections! *Let* the *cynics* laugh at Church, ministers, and the alleged *"death"* of our Eternal God! I do *not* "join the chorus!" I *believe* in God the Father, God the Son, and God the Holy Spirit. I am *happy* in my (very threadbare (& often lonely) old age, in poverty & the slums—BECAUSE I *love* God and my fellow-believers *truly*. I'm so *full* of *love & thankfulness* for what I have that words fail me—right here & now. (Amen!)

Dec 4, 1970 Entering HAW (Home for Aged Women) 201 So. Huntington Ave.

After a very "up-heaved" move, because of Mrs. Sheehan's resolve to "re-hab" her whole house at 71 Montgomery St—which got me to 3 Union Park in an attic (surrounded by packed goods & appurtenances), I was saved by HAW (Home for Aged Women)—a *wonderful* SANCTUARY for the Geriatric Group of (circa) 150 elderly dames. (*100* level-four women (who are "well" enough to come & go, & "register" their whereabouts, as in a hotel) & 45-50 who are cared for *lovingly* in the Infirmary.)

Such "spoiling" (!)—cosseting, protecting, sheltering well—& safely housed & superbly *nourished* "old dames"!

The saintly devotion of (Social Worker) Margaret Griffeth, & the sponsoring by the Rev. Gardiner H. Shattuck, Assisting Rector of Trinity Church, Copley Square, saved me (!) [an undeserving victim of Poverty & Old Age] from the awfulness of such places as the (private) 'nursing-homes' & "shelters" (Morgan Memorial).

A 4-year "*sentence*" to *real* Old Age (& *impending death*)!

September 23, 1974

On Sept 22 (yesterday, as I write), 1974, I have been "*installed*" at 80 West Dedham St., at the ETC Tower, back in my *beloved* South End! (& Parcel 19 of the Boston Redevelopment Project (BRA)).

My acceptance here is an answer to long, urgent prayer and supplication to God the Father, God the Son, & God the Holy Spirit. (Father Dwyer helped me pray for this (*latest*) removal, & Tako helped us both.)

HUD, HEW, OAA, SS, BHA, BRA—From April '74 to Sept '74 I was trotting all over Boston to the above (initialed) agencies (Federal, State, & City) to "clear" my record of transient poverty.

~

This journal has *lapsed* (since, in 1966, I made many mistakes in *storing* my goods) after moving out of 71 Montgomery St, in the urgency of *houselessness*.

Laura and Arthur Henderson, Pigeon Cove, 1916.

The Youngest

Laura Henderson Partridge

- 1 -

Across Massachusetts Avenue, almost directly opposite the City Hall in Cambridge, is Pleasant Street.

If you walk down Pleasant Street, cross Green Street, you come to Franklin Street. On the opposite corner is a large apartment building, and next to it is a fairly large single house where my sisters and I were born.

These buildings are on the property which once belonged to my Mother's family. The original house in which my Mother was born was torn down after the death of her relatives. There was never a picture of that house.

I was the youngest of three girls. My older sister, Dorothy, was eleven years my senior, and my sister Lois, six. Supposedly the youngest child is spoiled, but as I look back on it, I think I was more neglected than spoiled—due to circumstances beyond any-one's control.

My Father had been married before he married my Mother. His wife died, leaving one son. Norman was twelve when my Mother and Father were married. He ran away from home when he was fif-teen and I never knew I had a half brother until I was eight years old and he made a brief visit. He must have been in his thirtys and no one had known where he was in all that time. He died of pneu-monia a few years later and my Father went to New York for the funeral. Although Norman had a wife there had been no commu-nication between them in all that time.

My Mother many, many years later, confessed that it had been her fault that Norman had run away from home. More than that I will never know.

In the early married life of my Mother and Father, things had been very prosperous. He was Assistant Post Master of Boston and later Acting Post Master when the Post Master became ill. My Father instigated the Special Delivery System. He had built our house and also the large apartment house next door. He did all the plans and is the only man I ever knew who put enough closets in a house. Some were walk-in closets with windows!

Our house had eleven rooms not including two large pantries, a storage room on the third floor, and a laundry room in the basement.

Mother had a live-in maid named Annie who had to leave when political parties changed and my Father no longer had his job with the Post Office. Daddy went into Real Estate and Insurance. This is a very Up and Down affair and sometimes we were quite poor and sometimes quite rich. I have just one memory of Annie. I don't believe I was more than four when she left. She was working in the kitchen in our summer home making gingerbread cookie men for me and I was standing on a chair watching her.

After Annie left, Mother had a woman who came twice a week and did the cleaning and the washing and ironing. Her name was Bridget and she was a rosy Irish woman with about twelve grown children. After Bridget retired, we had a Mrs. Barrows who insisted on washing the hardwood dining room floor with strong soap and very hot water. My Father would roar and holler every night when he got home from work but my Mother never tried to stop her. I think she was always trying to punish my Father by doing things she knew he didn't like or not doing things he wanted her to do. At least looking back it certainly seems that way. But it was never a direct confrontation.

They had separate bedrooms and I was made to sleep in my Mother's room. In the beginning it was because I was a sickly baby and couldn't drink milk or baby formulas. I was brought up on spaghetti and beef juice, which I am sure accounts for my good health today. In those days it was considered a miracle that a baby could survive on such a diet.

Despite the fact that my two sisters each had her own room and there was still an empty bedroom that had been Annie's, I was not allowed to sleep in it. It was too cold! Although I used this room as a play room and had all my toys there!

I think this was because my Mother was using me as a protection from my Father—either because she disliked sex or she was afraid of becoming pregnant. I guess in those days there wasn't much known about birth control. Sometimes when I was not quite asleep I was aware that my Father persuaded her into his bedroom. My situation never changed and I never had a room of my own unless one of my sisters was away for awhile and I just moved in and refused to budge. I think I was twelve before that happened.

I spent a lot of time sitting in the parlor window watching what went on outside. My Mother wouldn't let me play outside if it was damp, cold, or snowy. This was due to my supposedly delicate health which was a pack of nonsense. For the same reason I was not allowed to start school until I was seven years old. I was not allowed to play with the neighborhood children because Franklin was getting to be a run-down section of Cambridge at that time. So a lot of the time I was housebound and from my parlor window I would watch at dusk for the lamp lighter to come to light the old-fashioned gas lamps on the street. There was no electricity in that section of the city and our house was lighted by gas as long as we lived there.

So my only companion in those days (except in the summer) was the janitor—Mr. Sanford—in the apartment house next door. As Daddy owned the building he worked for my Father and I suppose he couldn't avoid me. I followed him around the basement of that apartment house. Day after day I watched him throw coal into the boilers, watched him in his carpenter's shop when he had to repair things, watched him clean the laundries and the main halls. He never complained except just once when I threw some peanut shells on a floor he had just varnished. For that I was forbidden the building for a short time but we were back together again after a short while. He never talked to me. It was a silent friendship but he would show me how to put shavings in my hair so I could pretend I had long golden curls. Or he would prop up a smooth board for me to slide down.

His name was Albert Sanford and he had a shrew for a wife who was calling him for something he had forgotten to do. She called him "Albeart." She disliked me so when I heard the call I would always run home.

Before I went to school my father would come home from work and ask me to go upstairs to get his slippers because he had a bone in his foot. I thought that must be very painful and I asked my Mother if he really did have a bone in his foot. She said he did! I worried about that a lot.

Then he would set me on his lap and open the Evening paper. The Boston Globe had the weather report on the front page. In a small square there was a picture of a little girl. If she had an umbrella it was going to rain or snow but if there was a sun in the picture and the little girl was dancing, it was going to be fair. From that we went on to words and that is how I learned to read—from the weather report in the Boston Globe. This was quite awhile before I went to school.

- 2-

In those early days before World War I and later, there were no immunizations and we always seemed to have some disease. I had scarlet fever when I was three. Then later we all had measles, regular and German, then mumps and chicken pox. My older sister had pneumonia as well. But Lois had the worst record. She had diphtheria very badly and then at sixteen she had encephalitis which was also called sleeping sickness.

We were all quarantined in those days. They put a little pink notice on the front door, and my father had to live away from home until all danger was past. Of course we never had all these diseases at the same starting time so it went from child to child and things really dragged out.

My Mother was a devoted nurse. She spent untold hours taking care of us—reading to us when we were convalescing, and making special things for us to eat. Although I think she was unkind in some ways, she should have a lot of credit for that part of her life which must have been exhausting as well as frightening when one of us was very sick and she was all alone with us as my Father couldn't be there.

Laura, friend Clara, and Lois, Cambridge, 1917.

Farwell Chambers, Pleasant St., Cambridge, the apartment house built by Arthur Henderson in 1909.

She and my sister Dorothy had the flu in the epidemic of 1918. There was a stable and a funeral parlor at the end of the street and it was frightening to watch the horse-drawn hearses go by the house all day long. My Mother and sister were both very sick and Watsie had to come.

Watsie was a private nurse who had been with my Mother when each of us were born. She became a close friend of Mother's and while she was not on a case she was with us often.

She was one of my Godmothers and took it very seriously. She was always the one who shampooed my hair, took me for a haircut, told my Mother when she thought I needed new clothes. She took me out for treats and to have my photograph taken. She remembered every Valentine's day or St. Patrick's Day or some such. She had a little toy for each event.

The most thoughtful thing she did for me was when I was sixteen. I had been invited to a dance and had a new pair of silver slippers. While I was in school she wore those slippers all day to break them in so they would be more comfortable for me the night of the dance. It must have been torture for her as her feet were larger than mine. And it worked. The slippers felt great.

- 3-

We had a summer home in Pigeon Cove which is on the North Shore between Rockport and Annisquam. Daddy belonged to the Rockport Golf Club and I still have trophies that he won there.

We made the summer trek by train as very few people had cars in those days. The trunks came down from the attic as soon as school closed and were packed and sent off. The cat travelled in a green school bag with the strings tied around his neck and just his head out.

The dog had to be on a leash and was supposed to ride in the baggage car but if there was a nice conductor, he was allowed to sit in the smoking car with my Father. If the conductor was a stickler for rules, Daddy rode in the baggage car with Teddy—our large Airedale. The cat was Dotty's responsibility and I have a dim memory of his getting out of the bag and my sister streaking down the aisle of the train until she captured it.

Pigeon Cove was a treat for us all and it had electric lights which was a real pleasure. My Father came down for weekends and we all felt we had come home for the summer.

It was a summer colony just outside the village—the same families year after year and the same friends we had grown up with. We all went to everyone's parties and played at everyone's houses. We had a big barn attached to the house and my sisters put on plays and sometimes gave lawn parties to which everyone came—grown-ups and children.

There was one elderly couple who had a granddaughter visit in the summer. They were sweet people and thought I was a good companion for Margaret. I think she was a year or so younger than I. They asked me a lot for picnics and suppers. They had a horse and a "Surrey with a fringe on top."

Sometimes we rode as far as Marblehead for beach picnics. It took practically all day for such an expedition. We all enjoyed that because there was no beach in Pigeon Cove. I really didn't like Margaret very much but being an opportunist in those days I put up with her for the treats offered. But sometimes if I saw her coming up the road I would climb up into a tree until she went home.

One of my summer friends was Lucy Robertson. She was the grandchild of an elderly couple named Mr. and Mrs. Canney. They ran a boarding house on a farm a short way from our house. Mrs. Canney was always surrounded by steam in the kitchen or stretched in a state of exhaustion on the living room couch. She was a marvelous cook and everything she served was homemade. Lucy and I were always given special treats like ice cream or angel cake.

Mr. Canney had a large herd of cows which occasionally got out of the pasture and wandered down the road to our house and beyond.

Lucy also had an aunt Marion who had married a very wealthy man. They arrived for the summer in a black limousine driven by a jolly black man. When he had to take the car for an errand we were allowed to go with him. This was as much fun as the Surrey because car rides were very rare in those days.

When the aforementioned cows took off for their brief freedom walk, Aunt Marion was delegated to retrieve them. When going after the cows she never carried a switch. She always carried a golf club. Somehow that raised the stature of her menial task.

Two houses up the street from our house there lived a Miss Moulton all alone. She had a beautiful garden surrounded by a high wall so unless we climbed over it after she left for her winter home we couldn't see it.

However across the road from her house she had a little park. It had gravel walks beautifully raked and in the center was a small area of mowed grass surrounded by trees and there was a bench there.

Every summer Miss Moulton would send down a message by one of her servants that she would like me and one of my friends to play in the park whenever we liked. She herself was not well enough to go out.

Lucy and I spent a lot of time there. It had a turnstile entrance and a much larger one for the gardener to take in his tools and mower. That entrance was chained off except when he was using it.

Lucy had a red wagon which we would fill with dolls and a picnic lunch. There was a little hill and we took turns riding down it in the wagon. It made grooves in fully raked walks but if we happened a second day those walks had been raked to perfection. We loved that little park and I don't think anyone else ever used it during the summers that we played in it. Some day I would like to see if it is still there.

Miss Moulton's house was burned to the ground as was ours later by an arsonist who was never caught. Also Mr. Canney's barn and three other houses. However there is a new house on Miss Moulton's property and perhaps they kept the park.

Warren, my husband, drove me down to Pigeon Cove some years later and I stopped at the Canneys' to see if Lucy ever came there and if the house was still in the family. Lucy was at work and Aunt Marion told me that she had been married and then divorced and was supporting a young son. It was not a happy occasion and I gathered that she and Lucy were all that was left of the family. I was sorry to have missed Lucy.

- 4 -

When we were in Pigeon Cove and school time arrived, there was often an epidemic going on in Cambridge. I don't remember what they were except that one was polio. It seems that things were very germy during my childhood. There were no vaccines and the schools were very crowded.

So my Father wouldn't let us go back to the city until things seemed to be under control. We would have to stay a month sometimes.

When a summer colony is full of people and fun, it is one thing, but when all the houses are empty, and all the people have left, it is pretty sad. We were a mile from the village and felt lost and abandoned. Except walking to the village for food and mail, and picking flowers in the gardens of the empty houses. there was not much to do.

We had never had much to do with the village children except for a young Finnish girl who helped Mother one summer. She used to make the beds by tucking them in one side and then, laughing uproariously, she would roll across the bed and then tuck in the other side. The result was less than perfect. But she was a brave girl and killed a rattlesnake that was across the path when she was taking us home from a place in the woods where we had a swing. She pushed us back, picked up a heavy rock, and dropped it on its head. We ran home and Daddy went up to see and the snake was dead.

To return to our long stay in Pigeon Cove—when my Father came down for the weekend and I would ask him when we could go home to Cambridge he always answered in the same way—

> When the September winds
> have spent their equinoxial fury
> Then we shall embark.

If this a quotation I have never been able to find it.

- 5 -

As I knew how to read when I finally got into the first grade, they only kept me a short while and then put me into the second. In the middle of the year they put me into the third! Later on I skipped the fifth! This was not because I was brilliant but because the schools were crowded.

It was a great mistake because although I finally caught up with my age group, it played hob with my conception of arithmetic.

I remember one ghastly experience in the third grade when I had practically just gotten there and they had been working on multiplication. Each person in the row had a number to multiply. I had 9 x 9. It was all a mystery to me and the teacher should have realized that I wouldn't be able to know the answer. She said I would have to stay after school until I knew the answer. We both sat there for quite a while. She finally went home and left me in charge of an eighth grader who was a great deal smarter then the teacher. She showed me that if I added nine nines, I would have the same answer as 9 x 9. To this day when I come to a 9, my brain halts for a second.

But I got even with Miss Harrington. She broke her leg shortly after that, and came to school with a cast on it and kept her leg up on a chair.

Each child was to have the honor of passing out or collecting papers or writing on the blackboard. When my turn came I simply didn't get up. I just sat there. Finally she got the message and passed me by. Revenge was sweet.

- 5 -

My Mother and Father were an odd mixture. He was the youngest of 10 children. His Father was Irish and his Mother was English. They came to this country when my Father was three years old. They came from Clonmell, Ireland. They arrived on a ship that docked in Savannah and they settled in Georgia for awhile and then moved to the Boston area. Both grandparents died ten years before I was born.

My Father was self-educated and privately tutored in classical subjects. His sisters and brothers were always having feuds and I had two aunts and two uncles that I never knew. My uncle John was the oldest and had been educated in Trinity College in Dublin where he trained for the ministry but he left Ireland before the rest of the family and went to New Zealand. Later he became a rancher.

My uncle Tom lived not far from us but I never saw him.

I knew an Uncle Fred who was a dear man——very gentle and not at all well. Then I had an Aunt Emma, an Aunt Lou, an Aunt Belle, and an Aunt Agnes.

Aunt Agnes had married a very wealthy man and we spent one Christmas there which was one of the high points of my childhood.

The two aunts I never met were Aunt Lilly and Aunt Mary. I think all but Aunt Lou and Aunt Agnes had children but any cousins that I had were all older than my older sister. My Father was 48 when I was born so there was a big age difference in the second generation.

My Mother's grandfather was the first Baptist minister in Cambridge. Her father was a lawyer and her mother came from Vermont. Her mother died when she was four years old and her brother two. They were brought up by her father's two unmarried sisters. One was a school teacher and one was a governess.

Mother never went to school but was taught well and thoroughly by those two aunts. Her brother, my Uncle Allen, went to Harvard, then Divinity School and became an Episcopalian minister.

I think my Mother felt superior because of her background but my Father was a talented man. He did some beautiful drawings but they were burned when our house in Pigeon Cove was destroyed. My half-brother Norman had considerable talent and did some lovely wood carvings which were also destroyed in that fire.

My Father was probably selfish. He belonged to the Colonial Club in Cambridge. He played bridge. He was on a bowling team. In his younger days he played baseball and was always an ardent golfer. But although Mother was good at cards, she would not learn to play bridge and refused to entertain his friends and wouldn't join him for family affairs at the Club. "I have no clothes. I can't go."

When I was very small I remember going to a dressmakers with her who gave me lovely cloth scraps to make into doll's clothes. Those trips gradually disappeared.

My Father had his suits made to order. He didn't cut down on his extravagances, and whether he was punishing her or she was punishing him, no one will ever know.

I remember once, however, when he gave her money for a new suit and she came home with six housecoats! All very pretty but hardly wearable for social occasions. This was when I began to sympathize with my Father.

Years after my Father died, a daughter of my Uncle John's came to visit from New Zealand. Before he died he had told her that the real family name was O'Brien and not Henderson, and that my grandfather had had to change his name and flee from Ireland because he was in such trouble with the I.R.A.

The older children who were still alive had never told the younger ones any of this and it was a great shock. My Father would have loved this story. None of this can be substantiated except that there was a record of John Henderson who graduated from Trinity College in Dublin.

Also I had a letter from a minister of an Episcopal Church in Clonmell. He was very old and said the records were hard to read but he thought he could read names corresponding to those of my aunts and uncles and my Father in the christening records. I went to Clonmell some years later but he had died and there were no available records. They said everything had been burned by the I.R.A.

According to this cousin from New Zealand, my grandmother was supposed to be Lady Elizabeth Hatton of England, but there could be no records of her unless there were definite dates. I never saw this cousin as she visited cousins in New Jersey and I heard it all second-hand some years later.

In this country there are no records except of my Father becoming an American citizen. Unless I had a definite date when their ship arrived in Savannah, Georgia and the name of the ship. the government could give me no records.

- 6 -

When I was about ten years old, my Mother was gradually refusing to leave the house. Probably this was caused by some psychological disorder related to menopause. As by this time my older sister was working and saving money to go to Radcliffe, and my other sister was unreliable, I was elected to do the grocery shopping every day after school.

Until this time, my Mother had taken me to the theater or to the movies whenever there was something special to see. We went to all sorts of light comedies and children's plays like Little Women, Mrs.

Wiggs of the cabbage patch, David Copperfield, and Oliver Twist. There were many more and it was a start of my love for the theater.

Every evening after supper when the dishes were done, my Mother went to bed to read, leaving my Father and me downstairs. My sisters were usually out, and after I had done my homework, my Father taught me several games and we played until my bedtime. This, of course, was only if he was at home and not bowling or at the Colonial Club. If he was out my Mother often read aloud to us in the upstairs sitting room in front of the open fire.

Then my sister Lois came down with encephalitis and things were hectic. She was in a coma for six weeks and very ill. The Doctor said there would be some brain damage if she came through and some personality changes. It was drummed into me every day that Lois would not be responsible for some of the things she might do or say, and I would just have to make allowances for her.

From a rather quiet and amenable girl she became aggressive and completely irresponsible and my life became pretty difficult at times. She was very quick and very clever and by far the smartest of the three of us. After she got her strength back it didn't take her very long to realize that she could get away with almost anything.

Her marks were excellent but she refused to stay in school because she couldn't get along with the teachers.

Her first excitement was to bring home a dirty child from a slum district. She bathed her, shampooed her, and dressed her in some of my clothes and sent her home with some of the new books I had received for Christmas.

I came home from school, found out what had happened and was told that Lois meant well and was only trying to help this child. I doubt this very much.

Then one night she decided to take me coasting. There was a hill nearby where we could go in safety. But as soon as we left the house Lois informed me that we were going to the Harvard Observatory where some of her school friends always went.

I don't remember how we got there but after one coast down the hill she went off with some boys and left me to my own devices. I waited quite a while but she didn't come back so I decided to go home. I got to Harvard Square somehow but then instead of going down Mass. Ave. I decided to go home by way of Franklin Street which runs about parallel with the Avenue but at the Harvard Square end had a pretty bad slum section.

But it was a cold night and quite late and I didn't meet a soul. When I got to the house I could hear my Father yelling and my sister crying. Her story was that I had run off and she couldn't find me, which was true as far as it went. But she managed to gloss over the fact that she had deserted me before I decided I had had enough.

My parents were relieved to see me. I got lectured for coming home via Franklin Street and my sister was forbidden to take me anywhere again. To this day I have no idea where the Harvard Observatory is located and how I managed to get to Harvard Square.

As my Mother was not doing very well at coping with life at this time, my sister Dorothy took her place. She told Daddy that I needed new clothes and they took me shopping and bought me a whole new wardrobe. I remember a coat with a fur collar and a beaver hat with a big brim.

~

The summer I was twelve was the last we spent in Pigeon Cove. Lois was causing ructions with her behavior. She was boy crazy and the parents of some of the boys were making complaints to Mother, who didn't know what to do. But some of the time things were as much fun as they had always been.

One of the cottages was rented to an opera star, her accompanyist, and her three children. When the wind was right we would be awakened in the early morning by her beautiful contralto voice nearly a quarter of a mile away. We were late getting back to school my last year in grammar school.

- 7 -

That winter my Father had been talking about selling the Cambridge house and moving to the suburbs. But we would have to give up Pigeon Cove if we moved. My Mother loved the summers there and was against the idea, but the choice was taken out of everyone's hands by an arsonist who burned down two barns and three houses on our street in Pigeon Cove. As far as I know he was never caught.

Of our place they saved only the two front rooms downstairs and the dining room furniture, which was mahogany Duncan Phyffe. Daddy stored this and later gave it to my sister Dorothy when she married. He sold the wreck of the property to a carpenter who built it into a four room cottage. It had been an eight room house with a large barn. The other buildings on the street were burned to the ground.

~

While we were still in Cambridge there was a dance at the Colonial Club for the children of the members. Of course I was too young to go but I have never forgotten how beautiful my sisters looked that night. They were very different in appearance. Dotty had light brown natural wavy hair, big dark blue eyes, and a lovely smile. She wore a dark blue chiffon dress and a dark blue velvet sash.

Lois was very blond with small regular features, light blue eyes, and a beautiful figure. She wore a taffeta dress, cream-colored with tiny green leaves. It had puffed sleeves and a full skirt. And my Father in a dress suit. It was an impressive trio. It must have been for me to remember it all these years.

I was not much to look at at that time. Straight dark brown hair, sort of hazel eyes, and pudgy. Dotty thought I was cute but Lois thought I was a pest which I probably was.

Daddy bought a car that year. Our First. And he and I toured the countrysides looking at Real Estate. My Mother wouldn't go. These were regular Sunday afternoon trips.

I think he had already made up his mind that Lexington was where he would like to live. He already belonged to the Golf Club there. He finally had two houses that he insisted my Mother look at. One was on a fairly busy street but it had five bedrooms so I was hoping that was the one they would choose.

The other was in a much nicer location and had a lot of land around it. There was a large apple orchard, well taken care of, grape vines, fruit trees, flowers, and shrubs. There was a long drive up from the street and trees around the house so it was completely private. There was a strawberry bed and an asparagus bed as well. The house was nice but it had only four bedrooms and they bought it.

That was the year that I graduated from the eighth grade at the Webster School. The girls wore white pleated skirts and white middy blouses with red ties. The boys were in dark blue suits. We looked pretty cute.

Dotty helped me to get ready. She showed me how to tie my tie and went with me. I think she probably bought my outfit as my Mother was still not leaving the house. I was hurt and embarrassed to be the only child whose Mother had not come for this great occasion. I think Daddy was there too but I am not sure.

So then we moved to Lexington. Lois and I did most of the packing as Mother was still dragging her feet about everything. Lois could work like a beaver when she wanted to and was also a lot of fun part of the time.

Lois took off on her bicycle to ride to Lexington when we thought everything was under control. Then Daddy discovered that the storage room on the third floor had not been touched. Mother was supposed to have sorted it out and gotten rid of what was just junk and had the rest ready for the movers. So I sat in the car while Daddy did a lot of Irish yelling and Mother was stubbornly silent. Somehow with Mr. Sanford to help solve the crisis, they got it settled.

I loved that house and hated to leave it but there were new adventures to look forward to and many unknowns.

A whole new school and all new friends. It was a very uneasy feeling but exciting!

- 8 -

The first summer we were in Lexington we sort of settled in. I went to visit my Cambridge friend whose family went to Concord in the summer. I was there a few weeks and then I was busy helping my Father spray trees, pick strawberries and grapes, pick cherries and paint screens.

Mother was coming out of her lethargy and was making jellies, jams, pickles, preserves, and canning vegetables. She loved the new activities and she and my Father seemed to be more in tune—helping each other with these chores.

But the dreaded day arrived and I entered High School. My Father took me down and introduced me to the Principal. I didn't know a soul. No one in any of my classes came from my section of town.

The worst blow came when they put me into an algebra class. The other students had had algebra in the eighth grade but I had not. It was all unexplainable to me so they put me in a class with some other dummies. I only passed that year because the teacher was the Principal and was partial to girls and I was the only girl in the class.

That first winter I made friends. My Father bought me a bicycle to ride to school before snow time. We lived at least a mile and a half from the school. There was a lot of snow that winter. People put away their cars and commuted to Boston and Cambridge by train. This was in 1923. There was even a midnight from Boston for theater goers.

My sister Lois joined the choir in the Episcopal Church with me, and although she left home the following year, I continued to attend even though I moved to Boston some years later.

All deliveries were made by horse drawn pungs and the streets were white as they didn't plow down to the macadam.

I got skis for Christmas and had a marvelous time learning how to ski. I played basketball although not on the team. I was never good at sports but I enjoyed the ones I could do at all. I used to run a lot. I had a friend who lived three quarters of a mile from our house and I ran that distance quite often. I think I might have been good on a track team but they didn't have one for girls.

Two High School boys lived across from us and one lived next door, so all three and I walked to school every morning, and back home again in the afternoon.

In those days no one drove children to school. They either rode bikes, walked, or took the bus. No one liked the bus. It was crowded and full of kids from the town beyond us and some of them were pretty rough and rowdy.

Watsie came from Canada and she taught me how to hop a pung. If you got on the runners and couldn't manage to get into the body of the pung, you just rode on the runners. The choir master lived beyond our house and had a two-seated sleigh for himself and his wife, but he would slow down if I were waiting on the corner and let me hop on the runners, and that was how I got to choir rehearsal.

There were all kinds of school activities. Also all the churches took turns with young people's meetings and Dramatic Club performances. I never acted in any of these except as one of a chorus group dressed as a gypsy. That was my one stage appearance. All of these meetings were in the evening. Mostly I walked downtown unless a friend gave me a ride, and usually some boy walked me home. I was supposed to take the bus if all else failed, but I was free to make my own decisions about getting home.

I was never good at group friendships and Lexington was pretty 'clickly,' but I did have two close friends who were also new in town and had not been absorbed in the "in" group. I was invited for visits in their summer places in Vermont—different locations—and my first two years of school were good years.

- 9 -

Then my sister Lois came home.

She had run away from home and gotten a job in Worcester as a fashion editor on a newspaper. Lois was very smart and could get herself any kind of a job with no training or experience. But it always ended up with not getting along with fellow workers.

She had run up all kinds of bills and sent them to my Father, and things were under quite a strain. She took off again for a little while, rented an apartment on Beacon Hill and furnished it with second-hand furniture. Then she gave that up and had the furniture sent up to Lexington.

I remember seeing that load of stuff arrive, and knowing something unpleasant was bound to happen, I took off for a friend's house and was lucky enough to be invited to supper. I got home as late as I could. There was no furniture in the driveway and everyone was very quiet. So I just went to bed. I never dared to ask what happened. I imagined it was noisy.

Then my sister Dorothy came down with rheumatic fever. When we first moved to Lexington Dotty stayed at the YWCA in Cambridge because she was working there. But after a year she came back home and got a job in a bank.

Lois and dog outside the Henderson house in Lexington, 1923.

When she became ill she was going with a young intern at the Peter Bent Brigham Hospital and he insisted that she go there by ambulance. She stayed there for a while and then came home to be under Mother's care as a complete bed patient. She was now engaged to the young doctor.

But before that great event she had had scads of boyfriends, who were always staying to dinner and Mother entertained them without protest.

One was a drama critic for one of the Boston papers and he would show up without warning and ask Dotty to go to an opening of some play or show. She would always say that she had already made plans and why didn't he take me?

I was a fifteen-year-old kid who was practically speechless because I was so shy with anyone older than myself, and he must have been close to thirty. But he took me! And then he had to drive me back to Lexington after the show. We went together time after time when Dotty turned him down, so he couldn't have suffered too much because he never learned.

It was simply great for me because I saw all manner of plays and musicals.

When Dotty got engaged all we saw was Walter. It was quite a come-down for me. He had a lot of very white teeth and he would give a big smile and show them all. This was to charm my Mother into making him some homemade ice cream. It worked on her but to me he looked like a barracuda.

After Dotty came home from the hospital Mother spent practically all her time with her as she had when Lois was so sick, and it was not a good fall or winter.

No one asked about my schoolwork and when I asked what courses I should take for my senior year no one seemed to care. So I figured I could drop Latin because I was apparently not to go further than High School. All my friends were taking college boards and talking about where they were going after graduation.

At the time I was pretty hurt by my parents' apparent lack of interest but later I realized that they had had a great deal of anxiety. Lois had run away and no one knew where she was, and of course they worried about Dotty's health for the future.

Then one day when my Father and I were out looking at Real Estate—I was still being elected for these excursions—he asked me how I would like to go to college! I replied that I couldn't because I hadn't the grades or taken a straight college course!

I was pretty mad and said that no one had been interested enough to discuss it with me. And he was upset because he hadn't realized that it was more than a matter of money to get a further education. The rest of the ride was completely silent.

I could have planned on it if I had known it was a possibility but they were inclined to think that I was just the "baby" and was going to continue in that role for life. Of course as things turned out it wouldn't have been possible anyway; my Father had a heart attack.

- 10 -

I don't think I shall ever forget the circumstances of my Father's death.

I was upstairs talking to Dotty, who was still kept in bed for her recovery from rheumatic fever. During the day she lay under some sort of a heat lamp. It had an odd sulphuric odor and was supposed to have therapeutic effects. However it was also supposed to perhaps cause cancer. I have also suspected that it may have been the reason that both my Mother and sister did later develop cancer. My Mother was in the room a good deal of the time and because of this possible danger, I was never allowed in the room—I talked to Dotty from the doorway.

Downstairs on this night, Walter and Daddy's assistant in the office, Rodney Long, were talking to Daddy and Mother was in the kitchen clearing up the dinner dishes. We could hear the men talking and laughing and then Daddy said he would get something in the dining room. So it was quiet for a few minutes while he was gone.

Then we heard a very loud and strangled cry which could have been "water" but was probably "Walter."

Dotty told me not to go downstairs but to look over the bannister in the hall to see if I could see what had happened. I saw the two young men carrying Daddy through the hall. His arms were around each of their shoulders and his head was hanging down. Mother opened the door and they went out to Rodney's car.

Mother came upstairs to tell us that they were going to take him to the hospital and would then come back and report to us. I don't think there was any ambulance service in Lexington at that time. This was 1925. When Dotty was first taken sick the ambulance came out from Boston, and she came back the same way. So it was quicker for them to take Daddy in Rodney's car.

Mother settled Dotty for the night and then she and I sat in the living room and waited for some word—a telephone call or for Rodney to come back.

We sat there until one or two in the morning. When Rodney came back he came to the glass door in the living room and I can still see his outline in the glass. It was not the usual way we came in to the house so it was startling, but he saw the lights on so he came that way.

He told us that Daddy had died before they reached the Cambridge hospital. They had had to fill out papers and sign things and see a physician. All of this had taken a lot of time and then Rodney had driven Walter into Boston as he was on duty then as an intern at the hospital.

I don't think I realized what an ordeal this must have been for Rodney until I just now wrote it out. He was about Lois's age—maybe a few years older—which would have made him under 25 at the time. It was an awful lot of responsibility to cope with and he was not family. Just a business connection.

He also made the arrangements for the funeral which was to be held at the chapel at the Mt. Auburn cemetery.

A limousine arrived at the house for just Mother and me. Dotty of course was still a bed patient and Lois was still missing. No one had heard from her since she ran away. I think it was Rodney who found out from mutual friends that she was hitchhiking to Florida with a young man named Henry Balos whom she later married.

Dotty had written an obituary for Daddy and the chapel was full of friends and business associates and some aunts and uncles of mine that I hadn't seen for a long long time. The Hendersons were not a very close family.

We heard later that the flag had been flown at half mast at the City Hall on the day of the funeral. I suppose for his previous service as a government official in the Post Office of Boston.

We all went to the family lot in the cemetery only to find that the grave had been dug in the wrong lot.

This arrangement had supposedly been taken care of by my two aunts—courtesy title as they were two friends of my Mother's. One lived in Cambridge and one in Boston and both were familiar with the family names.

They harangued each other across the grave to everyone's embarrassment. The minister finally quieted them down and arrangements were made to have the interment the following day when the mistake could be corrected.

Everyone was very kind and sympathetic with Mother—not only because of Daddy's death but because of the mix-up and the behavior of the two Jessies. They were both named Jessie.

So the limousine took us home to tell Dotty about it all. I'm not at all clear at what happened at the house that day but I think a few friends gathered there with a few neighbors and one of the Aunt Jessies served refreshments.

The next day was cold and a deluge of rain was falling. The limousine arrived and Mother and I were driven to Cambridge. There was no one else except the minister. We just stood in the pouring rain until the brief service was over.

- 11 -

All of this was just before my 16th birthday in May and Dotty had made wedding plans for June. Walter had finished his internship and gotten a job as a heart specialist in a clinic in Texas.

Everyone thought that Dotty should not leave Mother, at least for awhile. Watsie was in New York but she wrote Dotty and was very angry with her about her decision. Aunt Jessie and the neighbors also had a lot to say. But Dotty became ambulatory and stuck to her guns about leaving right after the wedding.

I didn't blame her as we both knew she might never get away if she stayed. Walter was not the type to wait for her if he left and she stayed.

Mother had never managed money. She called in her grocery order in the morning and it was delivered. At the end of the month Daddy did a lot of yelling about the size of the bill. Daddy had overextended himself on buying the house and it seemed that he had saved nothing. So she was to sell the house and live on the proceeds. Also Daddy's assistant, Rodney, was to buy the insurance side of the business.

Rodney persuaded Mother to keep the car and let me learn to drive so that we would have some transportation. Also everyone insisted that I must have some further education after High School so that I would be able to earn my living.

So Dotty took off after a small home wedding, and the following summer was not too bad. I had substituted in my Father's office when his secretary was on vacation and I did that year as well. I had other offers for the same sort of job. I didn't do much but answer the phone, take messages, and greet people who came in, but I had to be there from 9 to 5 and until 12 on Saturday. I worked for a criminal lawyer in Scollay Square and for a stock broker.

My senior year in school was a busy one and I also became enrolled in a Secretarial school in Boston for the following year.

But the winter that year was hard. We had the boy next door to run the furnace but he was not an expert and the house was always cold. He and I shoveled out the long driveway which was no mean achievement. No one seemed interested in buying the house, which was expensive to run for two of us. So we were glad when summer came.

- 12 -

Then my sister Lois and husband came home. She was very much pregnant and he thought it would be a good idea for us to take care of her while he looked for a job and a place to live! We had never met Henry and we were not overcome with enthusiasm for him.

As we hadn't been able to get in touch with them, Lois hadn't known that my Father had died until she came to Lexington. She was very indignant that Daddy hadn't left her any money, and it took some time to convince her that there was none for him to leave. She was very disagreeable about the whole situation. She was hardly overcome with grief and not at all grateful that Daddy had been bailing her out for years and had just expected that it would continue for ever.

Henry didn't show up for the whole summer and not until the baby was four weeks old. She had false labor and I was awakened in the middle of the night to drive her to the hospital with her screaming all the way that I was trying to kill her by going over all the bumps in the road.

I had to go and get her the next day and we went through the whole thing again the following week.

She had spent the time with us telling tales to my Mother about my behavior—most of it untrue. The mother of the boy I was going with found some condoms in his closet and came to the house to tell my Mother about it. Lois was the only one at home and Mrs. Fuller being unaware of Lois's love of scandal when it concerned me, thought this pregnant young woman would be a sensible person to confide in and would have my best interest at heart, told her what she had discovered.

Lois was in her element and told Mother all about it with great gusto. However when I came home and laughed about the whole story and told them I didn't know what the boy had in mind but it certainly had nothing to do with me, they had to believe me because I told them they would have to take it up with George.

Jonathan was born and Mother had to pay all the expenses and Henry refused to repay her until he could better afford it. He never did.

I never did know what Henry did for a living but he never paid for anything if he could find someone else to do it. But at least he took Lois and the baby. I guess all of us had been worried that he would never come back. They moved to Connecticut.

So I was free to enjoy life again, and I loved my new school and new friends. We spent the fall in Lexington but when winter came we closed the house and Mother rented a furnished apartment. This was cheaper than keeping the house open, specially as I would have to commute to Boston every school day.

It was a miserable little apartment but I loved being near the theaters again. In those days a student could get a seat in the second balcony for fifty cents!

Weekends I visited old friends in Lexington and still sang in the church choir. And also visited new friends in Concord, Danvers, and Jamaica Plain.

This was mostly to get away from my Mother, who had some crazy Victorian idea that the last child at home stayed and cared for the aging parent. My Mother was 53 at this time. She wouldn't entertain any of my boyfriends for meals or just visits. If they came to the apartment to pick me up, she would go in the kitchen or bathroom and close the door!

She wouldn't even speak to them! After having watched her entertain my two sisters' boyfriends, I considered this rather unfair behavior. I haven't mentioned Lois's but she had a lot of them when she was in High School and she and Dotty had all sorts of young people who came to the house and to whom she was always cordial.

I was upset by this and had no one to talk to about it. Watsie was far away in New York and had been for a couple of years. I wrote to Dotty about it and she advised me to come to Texas after I finished school and get a job there and I could live with them. When I broached this invitation to Mother she threw such a storm that I never had the nerve to try it although I did continue to give it great consideration.

It was impossible for me to talk to my Mother on what the future had in store. When I tried to discuss the selling of the house and of her complete trust in Rodney of which I was a little suspicious, she would say that I was too young to know anything about it. That had always been the whole trouble with my Mother. I was the baby and apparently the youngest never outgrows such a stigma.

She relied on Rodney to do the honorable thing. He had worked with my Father for about two years and she expected that he would buy the real estate and insurance business. I have no idea what a business like that would be worth but I know that he never gave her any lump sum. He doled out small amounts which he said was all the insurance part of the business was bringing in and nothing was said about buying the Real Estate part of the business. Daddy was a really highly respected businessman in Harvard Square and operating from his office with his name must have been worth something. She had given him exclusive rights to sell the house and when he did, it was to one of his friends, and when he arranged the price I think it was far less than what Daddy had paid for it and he had added a two car garage and a large apple storage house. He had also black topped the driveway and kept the orchard in perfect condition.

On what was one of our Real Estate trips, my Father had discussed with me what he had planned for the future when he could no longer work in the orchard.

Lexington was growing like mad and land was in great demand. He planned to divide the orchard into house lots and sell them off as needed. Because of the pines and cedars and other shrubberies, the house itself would still be completely private and probably increase in value as property became more in demand. Mother was only 53 when Daddy died and young enough to take a chance on selling some land and keeping the house. The orchard would have made at least five or six house lots without one of them being close to our own house and surrounding lawns. Also there could have been one more on the other side of the driveway.

It didn't seem possible that Daddy wouldn't have told Mother about these plans, but when I tried to talk to her about it she said it was a ridiculous idea and that I was too young to know what I was talking about. I was only a child!

Twenty-five years later I visited the owner. He was a friend of Rodney's and I had known him when I was working in the office. He was doing just what Daddy had planned. He had sold one lot for $30,000 and the next one would be going for a higher price.

Now they would be worth twice that amount. Mother would have been set for life.

- 13 -

I could do nothing with my Mother, so I concentrated on having a good time. I had one boyfriend who loved to dance. We were well matched in height, and he danced so beautifully that it was impossible not to dance as I had never danced before. We went to Norumbega and to Roseland where the big bands were playing. There were colored spotlights at Roseland which were turned on to the best dancers before the end of the evening and two or three we were rated the best. It was a real thrill.

Other boys took me to the movies or to the theater and I had a lot of good times. I remember one time when I went out to dinner at the Statler Hotel and my host ordered oysters on the half shell. They arrived on ice and whenever I tried to spear one it just slid around the dish. It was very embarrassing. I don't remember how I conquered those oysters. Perhaps I had to hold on to them with my fingers.

And then I fell in love with Warren and all the other boys fell by the wayside. We were in the same class in High School but I had never known him then except by sight and had never danced with him at any of the school dances. It was two years later that we met at a friend's house in Lexington.

~

Mother finally sold the house and all the furniture had to be removed. We got an unfurnished apartment in Boston and she was to pick out the things we needed for that.

I was working and not able to help her with the sale of household things. But she said that a young neighbor had told her how to arrange this sale. This young woman was a complete stranger to her and to me. I never saw her, but Mother trusted her completely. We had neighbors that we knew and trusted but Mother for some strange reason decided to take the advice of this complete stranger, who probably robbed her blind. I didn't know she had arranged all

The Henderson house on North Hancock St., Lexington, Mass., 1925.

Isabel Jacobs Henderson,
Lexington, about 1928.

this until it was all over. She was staying at the house and I was staying in Boston because of my job.

I had put everything I wanted to keep in one little room. That weekend I found that she had sold all my books, my tennis racket, my golf clubs that Daddy had given me the year he died when he was teaching me the game, and my skis.

When I blew up she said she was sorry about the books but as for the skis, the racket, and golf clubs, I wouldn't be able to use them anymore! Apparently she expected me to have my nose to the grindstone for eternity with no time for physical activities. They would all have kept until I was able to use them. We had storage space at the apartment house, so there was no excuse. I said I would buy the books back but she said she had no idea who bought them.

I wished Watsie had been around, as I always did when I had trouble with my Mother. But Watsie was away sometimes for a year or two at a stretch. She told my Mother exactly what she thought about everything, and my Mother would accept it, but my Mother's only reaction to me was: "You are only a child." At this time I was about 19, which seems fairly adult.

Watsie was also a lot of fun, had a lot of physical courage and a great sense of humor. When we were still living in Lexington and I was practicing my skiing down through the orchard, Watsie came out of the house. She had spent the afternoon and was on her way to the bus stop, and asked if she could try the skis as it looked like fun. She was good on skates but had never tried to ski.

Although she was probably only in her early fifties—to me at fourteen she seemed quite old and I was worried about her trying.

But she took off. She had on a hat and a racoon coat which she hadn't even buttoned. She lost her hat on a branch of an apple tree, her hair streamed out behind her as her "Pug" came undone, and she landed laughing in a heap of snow. Her coat was half off and covered with snow and she thought she needed a little more practice!

Years later I tried to teach her to drive and we ended up on the sacred Lexington Green. I was lucky enough to get the car off before we were discovered. Watsie was no help. She thought it was a big joke. I decided she needed professional help and she finally got her license.

- 14 -

Of course on the subject of my sister Lois, I am biased. I readily admit to it. I think if she had had therapy after her illness she would probably have been helped a great deal. She knew right from wrong and when she was in a mental hospital for a short time there was a psychiatrist who helped her. The few times when I gave her a piece of my mind in no uncertain terms, she backed right down from whatever needling she was doing and became quite apologetic.

The theory my parents used—that she was not responsible for anything she said or did, I think was all wrong. I was forced to treat her that way. She loved to shock people. If she couldn't find anything scandalous about someone she would make something up, and I learned very early in life that I couldn't believe a word she said.

Her first story was that Daddy had a mistress. She had no proof of this but that didn't keep people being hurt by this story. Then she decided that Mother and Watsie were Lesbians. When Dotty and Walter were engaged she came up with a story that he was carrying on with another girl who lived near by. She would have had to have quite a team of investigators to compile all her material. I was always around to bear the brunt of some of her stories when I was going to High School.

If there was something going on at school in the evening I liked to take a bath when I got home from school and get all ready before supper. We had a hot-water boiler heated by the coal cooking stove. It only heated enough hot water for one bath and then it took hours to heat enough for another.

Lois was at home all day but she would find out my plans for the evening and then take all the water for her own bath just as I got home from basketball practice. My complaints to Mother did no good at all.

So one day as she dashed into the bathroom and locked the door, I ran down cellar and turned on the hot water in the set tubs until it was all gone. There was a lot of screaming from the bathroom but she never pulled that trick again.

Before Warren and I were married, she and Henry had a cottage for the summer on Pigeon Hill by the quarries that were no longer worked and were filled with water. She asked us over and over again to come down for the weekend. I didn't really want to go. I had a premonition that things would go wrong, but I finally gave in. We found that she and Henry already had one guest. The place was very small and right near a quarry. They all went swimming except Henry and me. Warren and the guest were diving off some high rocks on the other side of the quarry and I sat down beside Henry on the edge and dangled my feet. I am afraid of deep water and am not a swimmer—a few strokes and I am exhausted. I don't think Henry could swim either.

Suddenly I was pushed into the water and I heard Lois's gleeful laugh as I plummeted down what seemed like thirty feet before I started up to the surface. The boys were too far away to help and Henry couldn't, so I finally managed to get myself into a horizontal position and to swim my few strokes to safety. I was damned if I would let Lois know how frightened I had been, so I never mentioned it.

When the sleeping arrangements were made, Sherry as guest had the extra bed, and Lois and Henry were on the other side of a short four-foot partition. Warren and I were to share a single bed right next to this partition. I told Warren I was not about to lose my virginity with Lois waiting with bated breath on the other side of that partition! So we went to sleep.

On the way home I told Warren that Lois would inform Mother that we had slept together if she had to walk a mile to get to a telephone. Of course there was a lot of sexual activity going on in the twenties even when I was in High School, but it wasn't talked about as it is today and to my Mother's generation it was considered something that "nice" girls didn't do. It was fear of pregnancy that kept a lot of us in a pure state.

We had both gone directly to work when we got back to Boston, and sure enough when I got home from work, Mother was waiting to give me a lecture about my behavior. Lois had lost no time! She loved to tell tales on me but usually she only told half the story or made the whole thing up.

When Lois and I were both married and both had kids we had times when we did enjoy each other. She could tell some tremendously funny stories and entertain the whole family for hours.

I did my best to help her when she was in trouble but I was never able to help her financially.

- 15 -

I was out of school and had a good job with an advertising agency. I had been working almost two years when Warren and I decided to get married. Of course my Mother refused to realize it, or to accept it in any way. She wouldn't agree to meet Warren's parents, so finally Warren's mother came to see her. Mother was far from cordial.

Mother's friend of long standing whom I called Aunt Jessie was also my godmother, and she realized that nothing was going to prevent the marriage. She took my Mother's wedding-dress, which had been packed away, and had her own dressmaker make it over to fit me. She got my Mother and me to her home in Cambridge where we had supper and then I got dressed in my bridal attire.

Then she and her family got Mother to Lexington for the ceremony and her son Billy drove me in a separate car. I had wanted to be married in that little Lexington church where I had sung in the choir for so many years, and of course Warren and I had many friends in Lexington.

My sister Lois, Henry, and Jon were there. Jon was all dressed in white and looked perfectly adorable. Lois was just out of the hospital after giving birth to Sandra who was asleep in a bureau drawer in Warren's family's house. They had been invited to spend the night there. Lois had made her own dress and looked lovely. She was in a very sweet mood. They were living in Brookline at the time and Jon had been staying with us while Lois was in the hospital. Actually neither of us was ready for marriage but there had been so many problems in our lives that we hoped might be solved if we left our respective homes. Instead we acquired new ones.

My Mother's lack of understanding that I had my own life to live and her constant prejudice against any boy that I tried to bring home and her outright rudeness made it impossible to have anyone come to the house.

Warren, who had hoped to go to college, was told by his father that they had a family business that he expected both he and his younger brother to carry on. He would give him no help for a college education.

All this was in 1929 when we had friends who had graduated from college and were unable to find work, and it seemed smarter to stay with a sure thing. He had had a postgraduate year at high school and had a year at Massachusetts Maritime Academy. He was back working for his father—as he had been all through and his father seldom gave him a day off or a real vacation.

I had been working for quite awhile but hadn't saved any money, and I had no conception of all the expenses we were to acquire. I had had some experiences with buying groceries and keeping to economical meals although I didn't know to cook.

I think I grew up a little faster than he did. I hated owing any bills and tried desperately to make our finances cover them all. Warren couldn't have cared less.

He used to stay up until two or three in the morning and consequently found it almost impossible to get up in time to go to work. So instead of allowing time for breakfast, he just got up and rushed off.

That went on for months and then we got a bill from the owner of the Coffee Shop which was in the same building as the Partridge Ice Cream Factory. As an occasional thing it wouldn't have amounted to much, but seven days a week for two months it was a tremendous expense for us as we didn't have two extra dimes to rub together. Warren's argument was that if he worked a twelve-hour day for seven days a week (and he did), he deserved to have a little leeway.

My answer was that I worked longer hours than he did and just as many days, but I bought and paid for my lunch.

We were both working, but I had to commute from Lexington

to Boston every day, and when at home I did housework, and washing and ironing or some such. This became a constant argument through years of marriage.

Sometimes he would rant and rave about how we could manage theoretically. He was great on theory! He would plan a complicated system of budgeting with quantities of little envelopes all marked and the amounts we should put in them. But he never took into account all the back bills still unpaid! When I brought up this fact he would go into a huff and say that I should manage better!

Then of course I got pregnant, and although I worked until the baby was due, I had complications and was advised to go to a specialist. In the end it had to be a Caesarean birth and the doctor charged all outdoors. When I tried to talk about our finances with the doctor, he said Warren's father could afford to pay. Warren's father had no such intention and finally Warren had to go to court and agree to pay so much a month. I hated not being able to pay, but it didn't bother Warren.

Our money problems went on like this for about six years until he finally agreed to keep a certain amount of his salary and give me the rest. He didn't think it would work, but I managed to keep our heads above water with no thanks from Warren. And that was the way it went from then on. I was no longer working outside the home.

We had two little girls, and I read all manner of books about child rearing and worked very hard at being a good mother. Warren's idea of child rearing was to see that they had food and clothing and then let nature take its course without any help from him. He never played with them or took them for walks or outings. When they were very little he would read to them sometimes. He would never go on a family picnic or to a movie. I enjoyed all the things that go with having children (except the worry), and although at first I was angry, I finally felt sorry for him that he missed so much. I never made a real issue of this because I was obsessed with the idea that my children should have a calm and peaceful home life.

The day that Anne graduated from grammar school she won a

Silver Medal. (Lee won one three years later but because of the War it was not silver.)

After the ceremony, my sister Dorothy, who was visiting us, and one of Warren's friends who loved children, were congratulating her and Warren pulled her on to his lap to tell her he was proud of her. Anne stiffened up like a board. It was the first sign of affection or pride that he had shown to her in years. I thought again what a sad thing it was that he had missed so much. She was about to go into Junior High before he really noticed her.

Then his friend Benny said "Let's take the girls for a treat." And off they went—Benny enjoying them every minute and Warren completely out of his depth on this very first occasion of a Father and Daughter outing. I can't remember what they did but they came home with balloons and talks of all the wonderful fun they had had.

- 16 -

Then Warren's father sold the ice cream business without consulting his wife or the boys. The Hood Company, which bought him out, agreed to give both the boys a job, and that is how he came to be working for Hood's for a few years.

However it was a bitter blow as A.W. (that is what Warren's father was called by everyone except his wife) had told them that it was a family business. This was a far cry from what they had been led to expect ever since they had left school and for which they had worked twelve hours a day. Before that it was every day after school for many years.

A.W.'s idea for compensation was to give Warren's younger brother $3,000 and to put $3,000 into a small house for us. We lived there about eleven years.

The whole thing was settled before anyone was told—not even his wife. He gave her $10,000, which she invested in Fuller Brush stock. Her brother was the owner of the Fuller Brush Company, but I don't think she was very pleased with what he had done to the boys.

Warren always thought his father was a remarkable businessman but I never went along with that opinion. After he sold the business he spent money like water. He took Nannie (the children's name for their grandmother) on a cruise to California. When they got back he bought a cabin cruiser which Warren enjoyed and took care of its anchorage and upkeep on the Charles River in Cambridge. A.W. paid the bills, but Warren did all the work.

Then A.W. decided he wanted to live in Maine on a farm. He had been married before and his wife had died. However, her mother lived on a farm and A.W. had helped her out financially at times. After she died he acquired it.

He must have spent thousands doing over the house and putting in a bathroom. It was really a lovely house after he fixed it up.

Then he repaired the barn and got two horses and a few cows, some hens, and a tractor. Then he hired a farmhand and a housekeeper to make Nannie happy. She did not want to move to Maine and she hated the housekeeper, who was always in her way. She hated all of it.

How he expected to make a living I'll never know. I don't think he ever planted anything. I don't remember any crops—just the horses and the hens. And the cows.

Then A.W. sold his Lexington house which probably gave him a little more capital and Warren's youngest sister went to college to have the education that Warren should have had. My children loved the farm and visited there every summer.

Then A.W. realized he wasn't getting very rich and he arranged to swap the farm with a man who had a house and cabins on Route #1 in Portland. The house was very comfortable and cabins were very much in vogue.

Nannie was delighted to think that some money was coming in rather than all going out She was also delighted to be back with noise and traffic! She worked very hard and enjoyed it.

But motels came in and cabins became unpopular. When they couldn't make a go of it they were finally reduced to a little place in East Blue Hill which A.W. modernized somewhat. But Nannie was miserable. It wasn't very warm. All her children were married and lived too far away and there were not many people there that she enjoyed.

Then Warren's youngest sister lost her husband and she came home and persuaded her father and mother to buy a house in Portland and she would get a job and live with them. She later married again but Warren's father and mother both lived there until they died.

- 17 -

It seemed that we almost always had someone living with us, during our married lives.

Our first paying guest was a cousin of Warren's who came from a farm in Maine to work for A.W. He was supposed to live with Uncle Gene (a brother of A.W.'s), but Uncle Gene became very ill and Aunt Jo didn't want the bother of another person. So we inherited him. I wasn't too pleased at first, but Harland was quiet and polite and never fussed about anything.

Even when we sometimes had only enough money for a dinner of toast and applesauce or potato soup. These were Depression years. We had friends who dropped in for meals or coffee and toast. They were out of work and we shared what we had.

Then one day there was a knock on the door and a dark-haired young man said, when I opened, "I am Watson." This meant nothing to me. I noticed he had a bulging suitcase beside him. Then he said "I am Harland's brother." I said Harland wasn't home. So he said "Then I'll wait," and just barged in. He was a pretty rough-looking character and I wasn't crazy about having him in the house, but it was nearly time for Warren and Harland to come home so we waited.

He stayed for supper and during the meal he rose to his feet and with his fork firmly grasped in his fist, he speared a slice of bread from the other end of the table. That was the living end for me. He had come down to look for work and had planned to share Harland's room and settle in. I told Warren that I wouldn't have him in the house. It was impossible to talk to him and he was rude beyond belief.

Then I explained very nicely to Harland that there were enough of us in the house and his room was too small to share. Harland understood and took him away. I never saw him again, and I think he went back to the farm, where probably even the cows hated him. He looked as though he would be cruel.

Harland got along with everyone and was never any bother. He sometimes took my side when there were arguments and always helped. We moved twice while he was with us, and he always helped. Once when my sister and my husband were criticizing me for something, Harland said, "The thing I like about Laura is that she is always herself." I feel that is one of the nicest things anyone ever said about me and I have never forgotten it.

Harland was with us for at least six years and it may have been more. He finally got married and moved away.

Then when A. W. moved to Maine, we inherited Warren's brother Ossie. This didn't last too long because I couldn't get him up in the morning to go to work. He left his clothes all over the place and kept bringing home his girlfriend, whom we couldn't stand. Finally his sister took him off our hands.

Then after that my Mother had no place to go, and after talking over the pros and cons, Warren said he thought we should ask her to live with us. She must have been about 70 at that time. She had been living with a friend in Duxbury for about ten years, and her friend and husband decided they were too old to have a large household. They had a divorced daughter, a grandson, an elderly cousin, and Mother. My sister in Texas had invited Mother, but after a couple of years had decided she couldn't cope with it. She had a small house, two small children, and Mother didn't offer to help at all.

So Mother lived with us for the rest of her life except for a short visit to see her brother and one last visit to Texas. It was an uphill battle much of the time. She had a good sense of humour and when the girls were at home and there were a lot of young people around, she seemed contented.

But she did not want to live with us, and although Warren was always nice to her and very polite, she never liked him, and complained to me when he was not present that he should do more for me! He should buy me a car. It mattered not that he didn't have the funds!

In the meantime things were happening to Warren and me. The war was on and Warren wanted to enlist, and save home and country. Working at Hood's he was deferred because that was considered a Dairy Industry and besides that he was 35 years old and had a family. Then they began to take the 35-year-olds, and Warren became more and more anxious to enlist. I didn't have any faith in this romantic notion but he wouldn't listen to any practical reasoning. He thought they would need his refrigeration expertise and I said they would probably make him drive trucks or some such.

Well he became so restless it seemed senseless to argue against it, and he talked his brother-in-law into the same romantic nonsense and they both enlisted.

Well Warren's sister Marguerite was luckier than I. She went home to Mummy and Daddy who rented a house in Portland, Maine, in a community of houses built for the Army wives and children.

But I was stuck with a house to manage, two teenagers, and my Mother, who was living with us.

I had $25.00 a week from the government plus $10 that my Mother gave me each week. (That amount never changed in fifteen years no matter how hard a time I was having either then or later.)

We had a coal furnace and they refused to deliver coal to the house due to lack of manpower. They dumped it in the street and a very good friend of Warren's and the two girls carried it up a steep walk in bushel baskets and dumped it through the cellar window.

Then we had an oil stove in the kitchen (a black iron stove with an oil burner) with a coil around the burner for heating the water. The men on the board who allotted the oil never heard of this arrangement. They were all rich retired men who had probably never been in a kitchen.

If I had no oil heater in the basement for heating water then I could only have enough oil to cook with which was not even adequate for that! I spent a lot of time with that dumb board before I finally got through to them.

We did pretty well with our food rationing, although we got quite tired of chicken and margarine. But it was almost impossible to keep the girls dressed properly and to have enough money for their school activities.

I had made most of the girls' clothes and my own for years and was well known in the department store where I bought cloth and sewing supplies.

One day, the owner, who knew that Warren was in the army, offered me a job in that area of the store. I would have loved to do it and could have managed it beautifully. But my Mother immediately took to her bed and said I couldn't possibly leave her alone when she was so sick.

Finally I had to get the Doctor who told me that there was nothing wrong with my Mother.

This was the first occurrence of this little trick, and the job was filled before I got things straightened out.

My Mother got in the habit of doing this, and how could I tell when it was real? When Watsie was able to make us a visit she gave Mother a talking to and when the doctor told her—on one of his visits—to get dressed and put on her corsets and she would feel a lot better—she was livid for weeks. When I thought she was actually sick she would have a tantrum if I suggested a doctor and I would just have to call him and surprise her with his appearance. Fortunately I had a sweet doctor who understood the problem.

So I was not able to work to earn extra money and we weathered through as best we could, and occasionally I would have to borrow a little money from A.W. I hated to do this because I knew he didn't have much.

I wrote my sister in Texas, whose husband could well afford to have been a little help, but she wrote back "during the war time we all have to make sacrifices!" I have never forgotten that little bit of wisdom! She did suggest to Mother that she could well afford to help but that, of course, was a lost cause.

Incidentally they put Warren in the Arms Department. He knew nothing about guns! He wanted me to go down to visit him in Maryland at the Aberdeen Proving Grounds. A.W. sent me the money to go. Mother, of course, took to her bed, but my sweet doctor told me to go and pay no attention.

My sister Lois helped out by telling Mother that it was a shame that she was so sick! And I had gotten her up after a week of trying to ignore her little trick.

Back she went to bed but the morning I left she was up at 6 A.M. and glowered at me all through breakfast.

She never said, "I hope you will have a good time"—just "Good-by" with a cold glare.

Of course Anne was 16 and Lee was 13, and both were capable of handling things, and it was summertime so there was no furnace to cope with, but she managed to make me feel guilty.

However I did have a good time and visited my sister's sister-in-law, of whom I was very fond. It was great to see Warren and we had some good times. I stayed part of the time with my sister's relatives in Delwaware and part of the time in Aberdeen, Maryland. It was my first trip out of New England.

After I came home they made Warren a cook! He knew as much about cooking as he did about guns. He learned fast and would write occasionally for some recipe he wanted to try and then would have to multiply it about in the hundreds. The only one I remember was a cranberry and orange relish which he made for Thanksgiving dinner and was a great success. He couldn't get home for the holiday so we had Lois, her younger son Peter and her daughter Sandra for dinner. Jon was in the Navy. Peter carved the chicken. At 15 he looked like Errol Flynn.

I was always fond of Lois's boys. They lived in Cambridge and would often bicycle up to Lexington in the summer for a picnic.

When the girls were away, as they usually spent their summers in Maine with their grandparents, our dog Blitzen would join their party. On one such occasion they brought a steak to cook and while they were building their fire, Blitzen ate the steak. They were so good about it. Jon said it was their own fault for leaving it in the way of Temptation.

Another time Peter did not feel too well, and I decided to keep him overnight and sent Jon home alone. The girls were home at that time and while we were eating supper, Peter started to break out in bright red spots. Warren took him home, and the next day

Lois called to tell me that he had scarlet fever. There were no immunizations in those days but the girls remained unscathed.

As Lois had always been a thorn in my flesh for many years my theory as to her behavior was finally vindicated. Although the circumstances were pretty frightening at the time.

Anne was almost three years old and I was three months pregnant when I got a telephone call from a doctor in a psychiatric ward in a hospital in Taunton, Mass. Lois was living in some surrounding town and Henry had walked out and left her with three small children and no money.

She needed an operation and there was apparently no organisation to give her any help. So she put on a suicide act. Fortunately she told someone what she was going to do; she had put all the children in bed and turned on the gas. But it was reported and she had been taken to the hospital.

The authorities had tried to reach Mother, who at that time was in Texas visiting my sister Dotty. They had gotten hold of Henry but had wanted to talk to me as the nearest relative. I was only 23 and scared to death as to what they were going to expect of me. Was I going to have Lois as my responsibility?

However Warren drove me down and I was shown into a room with one female doctor and one male doctor, and Henry. They laid Henry out in lavender and then began to question me about her behavior, so I told them about her sleeping sickness and how it had been drummed into me that she was not responsible for anything she did or said. And they said that she probably took advantage of this as she certainly was not stupid. The first time in my life that anyone had recognized that fact!

The doctors were very understanding. They said they would keep her to have her hysterectomy that she needed and could I do anything to help?

I said that financially it just wasn't possible, but when she was well again she could stay with us until she could find a job. It was probable that she and Henry were never going to make a go of it. He must have had to make some provision for the children as they never mentioned them to me.

They took me in to see her before I left and she was at her sweet-est. She could be that way at times and malicious an hour later. Al-though I probably stress the worst times, I always had this feeling of duty towards her, and we did enjoy each other at times. She could do little kindnesses. I can honestly say that I tried to help her at times and disliked her intensely at others.

Lois had the operation and after she was released she somehow got a Catholic convent in Arlington to keep the children. She stayed with us and was in the process of divorcing Henry and looking for a job. She tried two or three and was with us for four months. I had only counted on a few weeks.

When Lois came I had Harland still with us, which made four adults and one small child. I was preparing for a Caesarean around Christmas time and there wasn't enough room for her to stay after the baby came. And I was never more relieved than when she de-cided to get a job in Cambridge, and get the children out of the convent. I think there had been some pressure from there.

- 18 -

When we were still living in Lexington, Warren's Uncle Gene be-came very ill. He ran the Partridge store which was an outlet for A.W.'s ice cream business and was also a bakery and delicatessen.

Gene had an older wife of whom everyone was a little afraid. They lived a very quiet life and never entertained family members, but they always remembered the children at Christmas.

When Gene was in the Cambridge Hospital I was elected to drive Aunt Jo to see him. We didn't have a car so I had to drive Gene's very large and expensive car. It was so wide I didn't think it would go through the gates to the parking lot: I was so afraid of that car that I forgot to be afraid of Aunt Jo. I think we made three trips be-fore he died.

The day of the funeral A.W. came down from Maine. There was a big ceremony at the church and another at the grave. After we got back home and started to relax, people started to come to the house.

We were the only members of the family still living in Lexington, and Aunt Jo was not well and hadn't been able to attend the funeral.

We didn't know any of these people. They were relatives from out state and we hadn't expected that anyone would be coming to the house.

A.W. went scouting and brought home some ice cream and some rolls, and by some miracle I had made a pot roast with lots of carrots and onions.

So Warren and I tore out to the kitchen to look it over and see if it would be enough. Warren sent me back to the living room to count. I came back with 11 and with two of us it would 13.

Warren sharpened up the carving knife so he could slice the meat very thin and sent me back to count again—still 11. So I put leaves in the table and set it but we only had six knives! We had enough forks and spoons but I had to run next door and borrow seven knives.

Then when everything was ready to put on the table Warren's Uncle Chester walked in the back door. He had been out in the yard every time I counted! So we hastily divided the last plateful for ourselves and with pickles, and cranberry sauce and rolls, we made a meal with ice cream for dessert.

But everyone was pretty quiet and pretty grim. So to liven things up a little and meaning it as a joke, I said: "I hope no one will steal the silver as I had to borrow some from the neighbors." Nobody seemed to think it was funny, and when I cleared the table put their silverware carefully on their plates. But when everything was in the kitchen one knife was missing and it was one of Mrs. Dailey's!

We searched for that knife under the table and all the chairs and in the kitchen we counted and counted. Finally we took the leaves out of the table, and found that somehow that knife had dropped down into the pedestal of that oak table! It was a relief to everyone engaged in the search.

Years later I was able to warn Marguerite about having lots of food after her mother's funeral. There were probably thirty and we were all ready for them!

I kept my eye on Uncle Chester who was always running in and out.

- 19 -

When Warren got out of the Army he wanted to live in Maine. He had good prospects of becoming manager of the Refrigeration at Hood's as his former boss was retiring. But he was tired of an office job and tired of commuting 30 miles a day at this point in his life. He was 35 and both girls were in High School.

I agreed with him that if he made a change it should be at this time, but I had all manner of objections otherwise. I didn't see how he could start out in business for himself when he knew nothing about the territory. How could he support us all?

Well he had it all figured out—(his theories again). We could sell the Lexington house and have enough money to live on until he got going. He thought there would be a great deal of refrigeration because there was none in the area. That was not true, as there was a big company in Bangor. I said the schools would not be as good and he said they would be as good as Lexington—which did not prove to be true.

But he finally overcame my objections and we moved to East Blue Hill. There had been nothing to rent in Blue Hill which fit our requirements.

Well that was when I ran aground about Advertising! His Father said that word of mouth was the best Advertising!

That may be in a settled community but in a little village the size that East Blue Hill was then, who was apt to discuss commercial refrigeration?

So we spent that first winter in a cold house with a cellar full of water, and a gas refrigerator with a flame that sometimes blew out when there was too much of a draft.

But we did have some fun times. Everyone was friendly and the girls fitted in well with their new school friends.

But we were running out of money. Finally A.W. bought the house on Main Street in Blue Hill and we moved in there. Except for the kitchen it was a real wreck inside. Some of the ceilings were gone, the wallpaper was hanging in strips, and nothing had been painted in years. The rooms over the kitchen had been damaged by fire and the charred beams were still there.

We fixed my Mother's bedroom and ours was usable but the girls slept on the hall floor until we had a room for them.

There was no advertising done of course, but finally word did sift through and Warren began to get jobs. He did some big jobs for fish plants and blueberry plants—freezing plants that is, and had to hire extra help. However no one could do things well enough to please him, so he worked alone most of the time. He could have made a lot more money had he acquired a crew because one man alone takes a long time to accomplish big tasks and with a crew he could have done five times as much business. But his reputation spread further and further and he was much in demand.

Actually I think he didn't want the paperwork which would be involved with a crew. The hours worked, the insurance and Social Security etc. were too much. I made out all his bills but I had a hard time getting him to write out his time slips and cost of equipment used. That little missing section of his brain again. I have always imagined that as shaped like the state of Massachusetts with the little hook on the side (Cape Cod) to grasp New Ideas. I think his little hook was underdeveloped.

My son-in-law was a great admirer of my husband and gets very angry with me when I don't agree with him about Warren's various abilities. I haven't meant to be unfair and I readily admit he had a tremendous amount of skills, but he had no concept of what really necessary precautions are needed to live in the world today.

We fought year after year on the subject of Advertising, Insurance, and Social Security. As I understand it, if you are self-employed you put as much as you like towards your Social Security, provided you kept above the minimum. Warren never put in more than the minimum. To get him to discuss plans for the future was a dead issue.

Health insurance was unnecessary because he had never been sick. So when Blue Cross would accept non-group people, I simply applied for it. Three months later, Warren was in the hospital in Portland, where he was operated on for an aneurism of his aorta. He was pretty sick for two months and Blue Cross covered all but the doctor's bills.

He wouldn't take out life insurance and dropped his G.I. insurance before I asked him about it.

After we bought the house I asked him about fire insurance, and he said that A.W. had taken care of that and it was adequate. I looked it up and it was insured for $3,000 and the shop building was not included!

I tried to discuss this with Warren. This was one of our big communication problems. He would simply say "I don't care to discuss it." And walk into another room or out the door.

So I simply took things into my own hands and acquired a marvelous policy and a separate one for the shop. I don't know what you would call that type of policy but it simply meant that the company would restore everything as it had been. When we did have a fire in the town which destroyed four stores and damaged our house and one other, the expenses were more than $25,000. Even our clothes were included.

I think he hated me for doing these things—mostly because it turned out that I was right. Some little section of his brain was missing—the part labeled "the practical aspects of life."

- 20 -

When we were living in Blue Hill my Mother thought up a new trick!

The house had 14 rooms and I was trying to earn a little extra money by renting rooms. Lee was working to pay for her expenses at school and I was trying to help as much as I could.

One morning my Mother informed me that Miss Wadleigh and Watsie were arriving the next day for a visit. They lived together and had always been good to us. They had us for tea, took us out to dinner at times when Warren was in the Army, or for a ride in the country. They were perfect guests and helped with everything from doing dishes to binding blankets! They were shocked that Mother did so little to help. All manner of kindnesses. So I was delighted to see them although I had had very little time to prepare for company.

After I got over that crisis, Mother informed me that her brother, his wife, their daughter and husband, and their two children were due to arrive. Well obviously I couldn't put them up, so they stayed at the Inn and had their meals with us. Anne was in New York so there were four of us and six of them to feed every day. This meant an awful lot of cooking and I spent most of the time in the kitchen. Mother retired to her room and held court—so to speak! Aunt Lois helped me a lot and was horrified that Mother did nothing.

The last time Mother pulled this stunt, it was Dotty, Walter, and their two girls. Mother even had requests for roast beef and blueberry pie while they were with us, but no help was offered either physically or financially.

Walter still smiled with all those white teeth even when he was scolding the children. This was supposed to make all the females present swoon with admiration.

Mother went back to Texas with Dotty for a couple of years, but Dotty couldn't cope and she returned to us.

Needless to say I was not able to rent very many rooms that summer!

- 21 -

Warren and I had a lot of fun together. We liked the same things, the same friends and—when he was not thinking of maintaining his dignified self-image—we got along beautifully. As he got older I think he realized what he had missed when the children were little. Once when my granddaughter and I were having a hilarious time pasting colored pictures in a book, he came out of the living room to see what we were doing and said—"I wish I could have as good a time as you are having."

I had tried so hard to maintain an even and normal marriage that I was practically a door mat for years. I wanted the children to have a calm family life and not all the ups and downs to which I had been subjected. So I went too far in the opposite direction and let Warren have his way a lot of the time. I should have laid down a few ground rules. Even a good shouting match might have worked, but it is pretty hard to have a good fight with someone who says—

"I don't care to discuss it." And simply walks out of the room or out of the house.

But Warren did become more amenable as he grew older and he was always polite and nice to my Mother and she was never very nice to him.

About his treatment of the girls when they were small, Warren's mother said that A.W. had been the same with their first three children and she felt that he had been jealous of the time it had been necessary for her to spend with them. She said when Barbara was born some years later A.W. had really enjoyed her childhood, and Warren did pay the girls much more attention when they got into their teens.

We were very lucky about gifts of money during some of the hard times we had. After Warren's operation and long convalescence, his uncle Alfred Fuller (the Fuller Brush Man who was his mother's brother) gave us a large check which kept us going until Warren was working again. And after Warren's mother died he inherited enough money to remodel the apartment over the ell in our house. He made it into a beautiful little one bedroom apartment which we rented to the Callahan Mining Company for several years. They used it very seldom—just for visiting heads of the company, but the rent was paid promptly every month whether or not they had used it.

To show how little Warren was aware of business affairs: we had the following conversation. He had been working very little one winter and he said one day—"I wish I hadn't spent all that money on the apartment. I thought we would get a nice profit from it." And I replied, "What do you think has been paying the mortgage-payments, the oil bill, and the electric bill every month?" There was a look of complete amazement on his face!

My Mother left me some money when she died and Lois also had her share. But Lois had joined some religious organization which decreed that in exchange for her care and training she must give them any money she received. I had my lawyer look in to this group which had headquarters in New York. It was found reputable and legally responsible, so Lois's share went to them. She had been sent to some jungle outpost in South America. She later left them and went back to the United States. Lois considered herself a free spirit, but she was always looking for someone to take care of her. She got herself into a church-related nursing home when there was nothing the matter with her. She later left it and got herself a small apartment where she stayed until she really became ill.

When my Mother died I was able to buy my first car and to start the shop, which was my pride and joy. Warren helped me so much with that and had such great ideas for fixing it up.

Warren's Uncle Chester left me some money—the one who was always outside whenever I was trying to count the number of guests! I have written a separate chapter for him.

Then after my friend Nela died I inherited a big hunk of money from her which I used for my luxury trip to Europe as I knew I would never have such an opportunity again. I felt guilty about this as it didn't seem a very practical decision, but we did make some good contacts for the shop in Scotland and Wales.

Shortly after that Warren's Uncle Alfred died and left me another big hunk of money so I decided it hadn't been such a bad decision after all.

And Watsie also left me some money.

I wish my children had all such chances and I am trying hard to keep some for them.

About my trip to Europe and to Scotland and England—I needed a companion as it is no fun to do these things alone. I had no friends who were able to go with me, so my daughter Anne, who is capable of great deeds of unselfishness, said that if Lee would go, she would take care of her children for two months.

It meant a lot of work and responsibility and I know I will always be grateful. It was a tremendous thing for her to do and I am sure that Lee realized this as it was an opportunity she would probably never have again. It was hard for her to leave the children. Amanda was ten, Duncan was six, and Breton was two! So they both sacrificed a lot for me. I did leave Anne enough money so that she would have help whenever she needed it.

It was a great trip. We spent a week in Paris, which we loved, and made bus trips into the countryside. From there we went to Vienna and then to Salzburg, which was my favorite next to Paris. Then to Switzerland—Zurich and Lucern, then on to Amsterdam and into the country for the bulb festivals. Then on to Scotland where we hired a ear and drove down to London.

- 22 -

I have a complete journal of our trip under separate cover so to speak but I had left out this little bit.

Lee's husband Earle is the supply officer on the Maine State Academy ship. They were to dock in Glasgow, and Earl planned to take the train from there and to join us in London for a few days.

However there was a bad storm off the coast of Ireland which prevented them from getting into Glasgow on the right day at the right tide. So he only had two nights and one whole day with us.

He spent the whole first night getting to London after having been up the previous 48 hours due to the storm and its results. So he was tired and irritable when he arrived in the early afternoon and needed something to eat.

We were staying in a luxury hotel with very formal waiters. In the afternoon if you wanted tea or some such the wine steward would come to the drawing room to take your order.

Earle said he would like a peanut-butter sandwich. The wine steward, with a look of complete horror, said "We don't have any peanut butter. I am sorry." Earle, who gets very argumentative when things don't go his way, said—"I have never heard such nonsense. Haven't you ever eaten peanut butter?" And the wine steward replied, "During the war I had some but I hope never to have it again." Lee and I managed to calm Earle down and ordered him a chicken sandwich.

At dinner that night we were all sitting around the table waiting to be served when Earle looked down at his place setting. There was a dinner fork, salad fork, an oyster fork, and a dessert fork on the left and on the right a regular knife, a steak knife, a butter knife, and a fruit knife. And across the top soup spoon, a dessert spoon, and a teaspoon.

Earle said "This is ridiculous—all this silverware." And he picked up all but a knife, fork, and spoon and piled it in the middle of the table.

Just then the waiter arrived with our dinners. He took one look at the table and put down his tray on a side table. The he replaced all Earle's silverware very slowly and deliberately. Earle was completely cowed by this subtle disapproval and said absolutely nothing. I had a spell of hilarious laughter into my copious napkin at the expression on that waiter's face.

- 23 -

Our friend Frank had had an education in Art and he started a weekly series of lessons with a great bunch of us in Blue Hill and after we had had some ground work he interested us in some group shows. Some of them were juried shows. There were quite a few in Rockland, some at the university of Maine in Orono, one in Augusta at the State House, and one in Portland.

But in Blue Hill we had no outlet for our work. And my thought was to fix up a building that we had next to our house that had once been a gas station.

I wanted to make it into a combination gallery and gift shop. Warren did the building all over and I did most of the interior painting.

Our crafts were not all local as we managed to contact a Japanese importer through Frank and then by going to craft shows in Boston and New York, and making contacts overseas, we had crafts from Denmark, France, India, Sweden, Scotland, Ireland, and Wales. And we had many from Maine as well. It became a successful venture and Warren doubled the building after the first year.

We had a show of one local person every two weeks on one side of the shop and a general show on the other. We sold quite a few paintings including some of mine.

We were in business for 16 years but our craftsmen grew older.

Some of them died or were unable to do the work and we had to fill in with commercial products.

I loved that shop—THE PAINT BOX—and I hated to give it up but after Warren died I couldn't keep it going as well as my big house.

My daughter Lee, who was a one-third partner, and I stuck it out for four more years after my husband died. He had done all manner of marvelous things building shelves, gondolas, and niches to fit the many things we displayed.

But changes happen and I had to sell all the property. I feel that we had been an addition to the town and now—years later—there are some gift shops and galleries in town but none quite like the Paint Box, which was the first gallery in Blue Hill.

Lee and I both loved the buying trips we took and I even liked the bookkeeping. Warren thought I didn't know how to do it and tried several times to get someone to help me. The fact that I had been taking care of all the household bills for years and also made out his bills, meant nothing. I had even set up some books for him but he wouldn't do anything with them. He really seemed afraid of figures. Perhaps they were too definite for him.

The state had a problem one year about gift shops not sending in the actual amount of sales tax. So they sent an inspector around to go over all the books. I hadn't known about this until he arrived but I gave him 3 years of books to go over and went home to lunch. I told Warren what had happened and he said "Aren't you upset about this?" And I said "Of course not."

The inspector later complimented me on my bookkeeping and within a few weeks I received an award from the state in Augusta for my impeccable bookkeeping. "How about that?" I said to my flabbergasted husband, who was always blind to my capabilities.

And so life makes changes and I still miss the Paint Box and I dream about it very often—opening for the season, arranging the stock, and making sure to lock up at nights—even now sixteen years later!

-24 -

I have lived in Maine about half my life and I have been very happy here, but sometimes I have wished that I could go back to see my old home in Cambridge. There never seemed to be an opportunity and no one in the family was particularly interested. But this year of '91 my daughter Lee offered to take me on a trip to see the house, to see the Mt. Auburn Cemetery family lot, and to visit my nephew Jon in Gloucester and on around Cape Ann to Pigeon Cove where I had spent many summers.

There was an awful hassle of one-way streets trying to get to Franklin. We finally approached from the Harvard Square end. The slums were gone as were the blacksmith's shop, the stable, the old laundry, and some of the poorer houses. There was one large new apartment house where we parked illegally and walked. I almost missed the house because nothing looked the same with so many of the big old houses gone.

And then I saw the house and Farwell Chambers—the apartment house that Daddy had built—and that corner looked just the same. There was no name sign on the apartment house however.

Then I walked up the cement walk along the side of the building where I had walked so many times so many, many years ago. At the end it branched to a wooden walk to the back porch of my old home.

There was a lovely lady there who was watering her plants, and when I explained why we were there, she invited us to come in. She said she had always been interested in the history of the house. Her name was Anne McCloud and she claimed to be 94 years old, but mentally and physically she seemed much, much younger.

She said she had bought the house in 1950 and between our leaving in 1922 and 1950 it had been a boarding house and it was dirty and in very bad condition when she acquired it. She had put it all back in good shape. There wasn't a warp, a crack, or a squeak anywhere.

She told me I could go upstairs if I wanted to and I certainly did! She said she rented the sitting room on the second floor to a social worker and that room was locked. I was disappointed because it was the room where Mother used to read to us in front of the fireplace and it was where we always had the Christmas tree. I had wanted to see it. But I went on up to the third floor. Dotty's old room was bright and cheery as was my old playroom. The storage room had been made into a kitchenette with a door through to the room beside it (Lois's Club room). I guess it had been rented as an apartment. The wood of the stairways and bannisters seemed to be in perfect condition. They were polished and dusted.

She and Lee had a good talk while I was upstairs and when I joined them, she told me that when she first lived there Mr. Sanford was still the janitor of the apartment house next door. All my lifetime in that house he worked for Daddy and was my only winter playmate before I went to school! And I thought he was an old man when we left in 1922! She spoke of the wooden walks he used to put under the clothes lines in the winter. The clothes yard is now gone and the back yard divided between two owners.

I always loved that house. The house in Lexington never seemed like home even before things went so wrong. The house in Pigeon Cove, although I loved that too, was just a part-time house.

I hated to leave Mrs. McCloud but I didn't want to tire her out and she had a man fixing the roof who wanted to talk to her. I would love to visit her again but I doubt if I will ever have another chance. All the pictures I thought I was taking did not develop as I had not put the film in properly. That was a big disappointment.

We went on to the Mt. Auburn Cemetery, which is a beautiful park-like place, and a very nice man opened up the chapel where my father's funeral had been held. The stained glass windows were beautiful. I hadn't remembered that. We also visited the family lot to see the stone that Jon and Peter had put in for Lois.

Then we went on to Gloucester to see Jon and his son Geoff. Geoffrey has done so well with his therapy since his terrible automobile accident many years ago. He has a nice young man with him all the time. He had learned to walk, to speak and has an indoor swimming pool for exercise and is taking painting lessons.

They live in a large and beautiful house high on a hill. Jon has an apartment on the third floor and a study on the second floor. Decks and fire escapes throughout. We had tea with Jon and then went on to Pigeon Cove. The village looks the same but the tool factory has shut down. I used to love to watch the men turning the metal in the red hot furnaces as the front of the factory was always open to the street when they were working.

I showed Lee where our house used to be. What was left after the fire was just the two front rooms downstairs and they had been made into a small cottage. It seemed to be occupied so we didn't poke around. The little park where Lucy and I used to play had a house in the middle of it. And after spending the night in a lovely place in Rockport we ended our trip to Massachusetts.

But next spring I shall again get homesick for Boston and Cambridge. My mother and I lived in Boston for about two years before I was married. There is a springtime there! The swan boats were out in the Public Garden and all along Commonwealth Avenue there are Magnolias in bloom, and there are sculls on the Charles River. There are soft rains in Massachusetts.

That is a season Maine doesn't have. Maine has cold, and cold rain, lots of mud, and dirty wet snow. All of that until well into the month of May!

Beside the climate I do miss sidewalks, umbrellas, public transportation, theaters, individual stores, and window shopping. I loathe malls. They are like open caves with piles of garments. There is so much of everything that nothing is attractively displayed and if you do find someone to wait on you they know nothing about what they are selling.

I think my nephews will be interested in what I have written even though I haven't been too kind to their mother in this record, but in order to explain some of my own experiences, I have had to show the difficult times that occurred to all of us.

My two daughters will have to write their own histories. It would take volumes to include all family-members. I am sorry that I wasn't able to give them some of the wonderful advantages that I had from time to time but at least they escaped some of the traumas.

I loved them when they were little. I loved them when they became older. I loved them when they began to think as adolescents

I wasn't very bright, and I loved them as teenagers when they were sure that I wasn't very bright. Now they are grown and married and I have no idea what they think but I still love them—but I don't always understand them.

To relate a few excerpts from their childhood—Anne was about four years old when her grandfather came to Lexington to pick her up and take her back to Maine to spend the summer with her grandparents. She was very shy with him as she hadn't seen him for some time and refused to talk.

He tried to put her at ease and kept up a one-sided conversation hoping to get her to relax. But miles and miles went by and then suddenly she had this to offer—

> A wise old owl sat in an oak
> The more he heard, the less he spoke
> The less he spoke, the more he heard
> Why not be like that wise old bird?

A.W. said he had never been so thoroughly snubbed before or since, and it was one of his favorite stories.

And a short tale about Lee that I have always loved—We were on our way to Maine with our friend Emmet Zink with Warren and myself in the front seat and the children sleeping in the back. We always went at night when they were little because we could bed them down and it made the trip from Lexington easier for them, and Warren liked driving at night when there was less traffic.

It was about three A.M. and we were travelling through a very heavily wooded section when this little sepulchral voice whispered in our ears—"There are Lions, and Tigers, and Gooses in those woods."

And another little bit about my granddaughter, who presented me with a picture she had drawn of a row of flowers and above them hovered a row of angels with watering pots. When asked why the angels were watering the flowers, she replied—"Why those are the gardening angels."

Because I didn't know how to fit them in, I have separate happenings, character sketches, and little stories as part of this history. They are all related but they seem to stand alone.

Index

Page numbers in *italics* refer to illustrations

CPSIA information can be obtained
at www.ICGtesting.com
Printed in the USA
BVOW09s0449190218
508424BV00001B/29/P